HARRIS COUNTY PUBLIC LIBRARY

3 4028 06692 6933

W9-DJB-814

Twentieth-Century Science | **Earth Science**

Decade by Decade

Twentieth-Century Science | **Earth Science**

Decade by Decade

Christina Reed

Set Editor: William J. Cannon

Facts On File
An imprint of Infobase Publishing

To my parents:
Thank you for your love and support.
—Christy

EARTH SCIENCE: Decade by Decade

Facts On File, Inc.
An imprint of Infobase Publishing
132 West 31st Street
New York NY 10001

Library of Congress Cataloging-in-Publication Data
Reed, Christina.
Earth science : decade by decade / Christina Reed.
p. cm. — (Twentieth-century science)
Includes bibliographical references and index.
ISBN-13: 978-0-8160-5533-3
ISBN-10: 0-8160-5533-5
1. Geology—History. 2. Earth sciences—History. I. Title.
QE11.R44 2008
509'.04—dc22   2007017545

Facts On File books are available at special discounts when purchased in bulk quantities for businesses, associations, institutions, or sales promotions. Please call our Special Sales Department in New York at (212) 967-8800 or (800) 322-8755.

You can find Facts On File on the World Wide Web at
http://www.factsonfile.com

Text design by Dorothy M. Preston and Kerry Casey
Cover design by Dorothy M. Preston and Salvatore Luongo
Illustrations by Bobbi McCutcheon
Photo research by Elizabeth H. Oakes

Printed in the United States of America

VB FOF 10 9 8 7 6 5 4 3 2 1

This book is printed on acid-free paper and contains 30% post-consumer recycled content.

Contents

Preface

The 20th century witnessed an explosive growth in science and technology—more scientists are alive today than have lived during the entire course of earlier human history. New inventions including spaceships, computer chips, lasers, and recombinant deoxyribonucleic acid (DNA) have opened pathways to new fields such as space science, biotechnology, and nanotechnology. Modern seismographs and submarines have given earth and ocean scientists insights into the planet's deepest and darkest secrets. Decades of weather science, aided by satellite observations and computer modeling, now produce long-term, global forecasts with high probabilities (not certainties) of being correct. At the start of the century, science and technology had little impact on the daily lives of most people. This had changed radically by the year 2000.

The purpose of *Twentieth-Century Science*, a new seven-volume book set, is to provide students, teachers, and the general public with an accessible and highly readable source for understanding how science developed, decade by decade, during the century and hints about where it will go during the early decades of the 21st century. Just as an educated and well-informed person should have exposure to great literature, art, and music and an appreciation for history, business, and economics, so too should that person appreciate how science works and how it has become so much a part of our daily lives.

Students are usually taught science from the perspective of what is currently known. In one sense, this is quite understandable—there is a great deal of information to master. However, very often a student (or teacher) may ask questions such as "How did they know that?" or "Why didn't they know that?" This is where some historical perspective makes for fascinating reading. It gives a feeling for the dynamic aspect of science. Some of what students are taught today will change in 20 years. It also provides a sense of humility as one sees how brilliantly scientists coped earlier with less funding, cruder tools, and less sophisticated theories.

Science is distinguished from other equally worthy and challenging human endeavors by its means of investigation—the scientific method—typically described as

a) observations

b) hypothesis

c) experimentation with controls

d) results, and

e) conclusions concerning whether or not the results and data from the experiments invalidate or support the hypothesis.

In practice, the scientific process is not quite so "linear." Many related experiments may also be explored to test the hypothesis. Once a body of scientific evidence has been collected and checked, the scientist submits a paper reporting the new work to a peer-reviewed journal. An impartial editor will send the work to at least two reviewers ("referees") who are experts in that particular field, and they will recommend to the editor whether the paper should be accepted, modified, or rejected. Since expert reviewers are sometimes the author's competitors, high ethical standards and confidentiality must be the rule during the review process.

If a hypothesis cannot be tested and potentially disproved by experiment or mathematical equations it is not scientific. While, in principle, one experiment can invalidate a hypothesis, no number of validating experiments can absolutely prove a hypothesis to be "the truth." However, if repeated testing, using varied and challenging experiments by diverse scientists, continues to validate a hypothesis, it starts to assume the status of a widely accepted theory. The best friend a theory can have is an outstanding scientist who doubts it and subjects it to rigorous and honest testing. If it survives these challenges and makes a convert of the skeptical scientist, then the theory is strengthened significantly. Such testing also weeds out hypotheses and theories that are weak. Continued validation of an important theory may give it the stature of a law, even though it is still called a theory. Some theories when developed can revolutionize a field's entire framework—these are considered "paradigms" (pronounced "paradimes"). Atomic theory is a paradigm. Advanced about 200 years ago, it is fundamental to understanding the nature of matter. Other such paradigms include evolution; the "big bang" theory; the modern theory of plate tectonics, which explains the origin of mountains, volcanoes, and earthquakes; quantum theory; and relativity.

Science is a collective enterprise with the need for free exchange of information and cooperation. While it is true that scientists have strong competitive urges, the latter half of the 20th century witnessed science's becoming increasingly interdisciplinary. Ever more complex problems, with increasing uncertainty, were tackled and yet often eluded precise solution.

During the 20th century, science found cures for tuberculosis and polio, and yet fears of the "dark side" of science (e.g., atomic weapons) began to mount. Skepticism over the benefits of science and its applications started to emerge in the latter part of the 20th century even as its daily and positive impact upon our lives increased. Many scientists were sensitive to these issues as well. After atomic bombs devastated Hiroshima and Nagasaki, some distinguished physicists moved into the life sciences and others started a magazine, now nearly 60 years old, *The Bulletin of the Atomic Scientists*, dedicated to eliminating the nuclear threat and promoting peace. In 1975, shortly after molecular biologists developed recombinant deoxyribonucleic acid (DNA), they held a conference at Asilomar, California, and imposed voluntary limits on certain experiments. They encouraged adoption of regulations in this revolutionary new field. We are in an era when there are repeated and forceful attempts to blur the boundaries between religious faith and science. One argument is that fairness demands equal time for all "theories" (scientific or not). In all times, but especially in these times, scientists must strive to communicate to the public what science is and how it works, what is good science, what is bad science, and what is not science. Only then can we educate future generations of informed citizens and inspire the scientists of the future.

The seven volumes of *Twentieth-Century Science* deal with the following core areas of science: biology, chemistry, Earth science, marine science, physics, space and astronomy, and weather and climate. Each volume contains a glossary. Each chapter within each volume contains the following elements:

- background and perspective for the science it develops, decade by decade, as well as insights about many of the major scientists contributing during each decade
- black-and-white line drawings and photographs
- a chronological "time line" of notable events during each decade
- brief biographical sketches of pioneering individuals, including discussion of their impacts on science and the society at large
- a list of accessible sources for Additional Reading

While all of the scientists profiled are distinguished, we do *not* mean to imply that they are necessarily "the greatest scientists of the decade." They have been chosen to represent the science of the decade because of their outstanding accomplishments. Some of these scientists were born to wealthy and distinguished families, while others were born to middle- and working-class families or into poor families. In a century marked by two world wars, the cold war, countless other wars large and small, and unimaginable genocide, many scientists were forced to flee their countries of birth. Fortunately, the century has also witnessed greater access to the scientific and engineering professions for women and people of color, and ideally all barriers will disappear during the 21st century.

The authors of this set hope that readers appreciate the development of the sciences during the last century and the advancements occurring rapidly now in the 21st century. The history teaches new explorers of the world the benefits of making careful observations, of pursuing paths and ideas that others have neglected or have not ventured to tread, and of always questioning the world around them. Curiosity is one of our most fundamental human instincts. Science, whether done as a career or as a hobby, is after all, an intensely human endeavor.

Acknowledgments

Writing this book gave me an excellent opportunity to read about many grand adventures that Earth scientists have embarked upon during the last century. Some of these stories are reproduced here and it is my hope that readers of this book will be inspired to find the original testimonies, narratives, and reports listed in the further readings and resources sections to learn more. In the process of writing this book I have gained a greater appreciation of the current quiescence of Mount Rainer, the bravery of Alfred Wegener, the patient determination of Inge Lehmann and Marie Tharp, and the eye of every geologist who can spot a fossil, an unconformity, a dropstone, and see a story of life and death and how different the world once looked. My fascination with exploring the world led me to obtain an advance degree in Earth sciences from Columbia University, where I learned from some of the most renowned minds in their fields: Wallace Broecker, Walter Pitman, Bill Ryan, Peter deMenocal, Richard Fairbanks, Nick Christie-Blick, and the late Gerard Bond. These men are my heroes and I want to thank them for their leadership and for encouraging me to strive for great achievements in my own way as a science journalist. I would also like to thank my mentors in this process: Marguerite Holloway, Kim Kastens, and Dean McManus.

I am extremely grateful to editor Frank K. Darmstadt, without whom this project would not have happened, and to Bill Cannon for originally asking me to join the team of science history writers for this set. I would also like to thank the art directors Bobbi McCutcheon and Beth Oakes and the rest of the Facts On File staff who had a hand in seeing this project to completion.

I appreciate the legwork those such as Katherine Anderson and others at the press offices of *Nature*, *Science*, and AGU did to dust off and send me old articles not yet archived online. I would especially like to thank all the scientists who volunteered their time in answering questions for this book. I would like to specifically acknowledge: Charles R. Bentley, Chris Newhall, Pamela Matson, Mark D. Zoback, Mary Lou Zoback, Shana Pimley, David Hanych, Bruce Malfait, David P. Stern, T. J. Blasing, Greg Marland, Gustaf Arrhenius, Rick Wunderman, Joe Kirschvink, Walter Alvarez, Hiroo Kanamori, Ed Venzke, Bob Uhrhammer,

Won-Young Kim, Sue Keiffer, Bill Melson, Hans Hofmann, David Hindle, and Mattias Linden.

I would also like to thank the many friends who supported and encouraged me during this endeavor, with special thanks to: Harvey Leifert, Rick Lovett, Arthur Edelstein, Josh Fischman, Huichong Chang, and Patt and Dan Crane. Also I would like to give big hugs to Bob, April, and, my niece, Hana, whose birth coincided with the start of this project, and to Merwin Speer, my number one fan, thank you Grandpa for always reading what I write.

Introduction

In examining the history of Earth science decade-by-decade during the 20th century, this book presents a variety of avenues scientists took as they formed the basic principles underlying the field today. The evolution of the field of Earth science began in the 20th century as a compilation of fields examining the Earth's past, present, and future. Earth scientists have an amazing palette from which to choose their pursuits, specifically because of Earth's complicated structure and the comparisons that can be made between Earth and other solid bodies in the universe. Earth scientists may be drawn to a particular environment—the atmosphere, the ocean, or the core-mantle boundary for example—or perhaps to a particular moment in time and find themselves as Walter Alvarez did, following the Cretaceous-Tertiary boundary around the world from Italy to Mexico's Yucatán Peninsula. They might become experts of a technique that has broadscale applications—computer modeling, radioisotope dating, seismology, remote sensing, or information technology. They may find they become intimate with particular Earth processes that correlate to processes seen on other moons and planets in the solar system. Some Mars experts began their career as Earth experts knowing how to analyze fluvial patterns in hydrology and *sedimentary* geology. The lunar astronauts all took field expeditions to the desert in Flagstaff, Arizona, with astrogeologist Eugene Shoemaker before ever stepping foot on the Moon. Planetary scientist Sue Keiffer became mesmerized by the physics of geysers in Yellowstone and applied her knowledge to the eruption dynamics of Mount St. Helens in 1980. She has since explored via *satellite* observations the geyser-like physics of volcanic eruptions on Io, Triton, and Enceladus—moons of Jupiter and Saturn.

Until the space race of the 20th century, scientists studying Earth processes fell into the department of geoscience. The International Geophysical Year of 1957–58 ushered in a global perspective of how Earth's processes interact across the physical boundaries of the atmosphere, oceans, and land. Eventually the fields that traditionally study only one of these boundaries—meteorology, oceanography, and geology—merged as subdisciplines within the field of Earth science.

Geoscience embodied both geophysics and traditional geology. The classical geologists of the 19th and early 20th century mapped the stratification layers of Earth's surface and surveyed the globe for natural resources. The industrial revolution brought sedimentary geologists into high demand in search for coal and later oil. Geologists had the skill of seeing the world in four dimensions (the usual three dimensions plus time as the fourth dimension), but their depth perspective was limited to what could be drilled or mined. The development of seismology in the late 19th century deepened scientific understanding of Earth's internal structure. Physicists fell into the geoscience camp as they worked to understand the why and the how of the patterns the geologists were identifying. Continents, however, cover only 30 percent of the world's surface; most of the globe's geologic formations are underwater. To fully understand the processes that build and shape the planet, geologists would have to venture away from terra firma. Around the 1930s, the new field of marine geology developed and oceanographers quickly embraced and adapted geologic methods to studying the seafloor.

As more subdisciplines of geoscience began to grow, the interdisciplinary nature of the geosciences became imperative. The 20th century ushered in the development of geochemistry, biogeochemistry, marine geology, and paleoceanography. When the National Science Foundation, the premier establishment for science funding in the United States, wanted to support studies that were applicable to understanding the Moon, geoscientists were well-suited to meet this demand. Soon they began to work in the field of planetary science alongside rocket scientists and astronomers. To distinguish the inherent quality of their work geoscientists began considering themselves Earth scientists.

Ask those in the field to define Earth science, however, and inevitably answers will vary depending on the person's age, discipline of study, and the college or university he or she attended. The quagmire of defining Earth science is seen in the inconsistent renaming of university departments and museums during the 1980s and 1990s. In many cases Earth science combined both the solid Earth science or "hard rock" studies with the general environmental "soft rock" science, which includes atmospheric and oceanographic studies. In other cases these two approaches to Earth science remained separate. Geoscience departments at state universities were renamed departments of Earth science, or departments of Earth and environmental sciences, or departments of Earth and ocean sciences. In 1981 Cambridge University amalgamated the departments of geology, mineralogy and *petrology*, and geophysics into the department of Earth sciences. At that time, Cambridge's Sedgwick Museum of Geoscience became the Sedgwick Museum of Earth Sciences. In 1993 the Lamont-Doherty Geological Observatory in New York took a similar course of action and changed its name to the Lamont-Doherty Earth Observatory. With each name change came improved efforts for interdisciplinary research.

It is fair to say that Earth science as a field of study began in the 20th century, but humans have been grappling with the nature of the planet they live on since the dawn of their imagination. The quintessential Earth processes that most people are familiar with are natural disasters such as *earthquakes*, volcanoes, hurricanes, tsunamis, droughts, and floods. These events have scarred the landscape as well as the human psyche. Before written records of events, oral histories were told to warn succeeding generations of the planet's dangers. The mythology surrounding the lost city of Atlantis may have originated with the 17th-century B.C.E. eruption that formed the Santorini archipelago and destroyed most of the island of Thera. The eruption in 1640 B.C.E. resulted in the youngest caldera in the Aegean Sea and left much of the seafaring Minoan civilization literally in ashes. Twenty-first-century Earth scientists continue to dig for clues. A buried forest in Washington State that dates to the year 1700 C.E. led geologist Brian Atwater of the U.S. Geological Survey in the 1990s to crosscheck Native American stories of a large tsunami in the Pacific Northwest with written records of tsunamis kept on the other side of the Pacific. He discovered an orphan tsunami, one without a local earthquake origin, had struck the Japanese coast on January 26, 1700, and computed that it was the likely result of a magnitude 8.0 earthquake off the coast of Washington. The large quake sent a wave of salt water across the Cascade shores that drowned the forests and buried them in sand. Now in the 21st century it is not surprising to learn that some legends are based on local events with far-reaching global consequences. In today's world of rapid, global communication, the rippling effects of a natural disaster are quickly known, although not yet as quickly mitigated. That is still a challenge.

Earth Science tells of the decade-by-decade developments of the field from the first radioactive dating methods of rocks, during a time when the predominate theory held that Earth was getting progressively smaller, to the discovery of 4.56 billion-year-old meteorites and the realization that the continents not only moved but are moving gradually still today on a planet that is susceptible to human interventions. During the 20th century people stood on the Moon; stopped *lava* flows from flowing; formed man-made auroras near the equator; used, then recognized and prohibited, products that damage the ozone layer; and raised the amount of greenhouse gases in the atmosphere above anything the planet has experienced in the last 650,000 years. If anything, the field of Earth science is more complicated now than it has ever been in its development.

The principles of Earth science today hold that the planet is a mobile jigsaw puzzle of plate tectonics full of dynamically interacting processes that extend from its core all the way out to space. Lessons from earthquakes and eruptions show that the past is helpful in interpreting the present but is not always the key. Each volcano is unique, and there are many ways to build an island. Natural hazards are here to stay. People need to understand the risks in order to consciously accept them, move, or develop appropriate measures of protection. Earth scientists are the global watchdogs for how the physical sciences—chemistry, biology, and physics—combine to affect the planet and its inhabitants. This book chronicles the developments that made this field stand apart as an "umbrella" science for the world. Key events include Arthur Holmes's establishment of the geologic timescale, Alfred Wegener's theory of continental drift, the scientific discovery of plate tectonics, seismological discoveries that revealed Earth's inner structures, and geologic and paleontological discoveries that have changed how Earth scientists view the chronology of life's evolution. At the dawn of the 20th century, geoscientists would develop the tools to give accurate dates to the budding geologic timescale of Earth's history. As the 20th century progressed, Earth scientists would draw meaning to this timescale and integrate dynamic processes of evolution with extinction and the motion of the continental plates. This volume in science history monitors the progress of Earth scientists as they continue to piece together the planet's vast history, its current state of affairs, and what all this information means for life in the future.

1901–1910:
Earth Inside Out

Introduction

The beginning of the 20th century was a time of intense global exploration. Scientists were conducting investigations into the history, formation, functions, and governing principles of the planet. They had a wide

Changes in temperature define Earth's atmospheric layers.

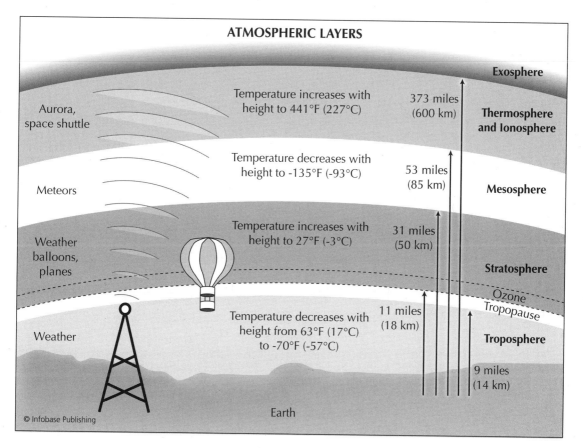

ATMOSPHERIC LAYERS

Exosphere

Temperature increases with height to 441°F (227°C)

373 miles (600 km)

Thermosphere and Ionosphere

Aurora, space shuttle

Temperature decreases with height to -135°F (-93°C)

53 miles (85 km)

Mesosphere

Meteors

Temperature increases with height to 27°F (-3°C)

31 miles (50 km)

Weather balloons, planes

Stratosphere

Ozone

Tropopause

Temperature decreases with height from 63°F (17°C) to -70°F (-57°C)

11 miles (18 km)

Troposphere

Weather

9 miles (14 km)

© Infobase Publishing

Earth

variety of new tools at their disposal, and puzzling discoveries in the lab and in the field to fit in with, or refute, the predominate hypotheses. Chemists examined radioactive elements and learned how to date the age of rocks. Seismologists mapped the shock waves that passed through the planet. Paleontologists and geologists would dig into the earth and pull back time. With volcanoes and earthquakes destroying cities in a matter of minutes, the public was reminded of the urgent need to understand Earth's natural forces.

Introducing *Tyrannosaurus rex*

In the summer of 1900, Barnum Brown (1873–1963) dug a hole 40 feet (12 m) across and 14 feet (4 m) deep into the side of a hill he distinguished only as field site number 12. His goal was to remove a scattering of large dinosaur bones. He and his crew of two men—his assistant, H. M. Smith, and a cook named Armstrong—were camped near the headwaters of Seven Mile Creek, a northern tributary of the Cheyenne River in Wyoming. They had been hoping to find a *Triceratops* skull. What they found was carnivorous. The lower jaw had a row of dagger-like teeth of varying lengths set among smaller serrated teeth. The beast was born to

Santa María in Guatemala erupts on October 24. The eruption lasts for 19 days and on October 25 a *plinian eruption* produces a column of ash and *pumice* that reaches 16 miles (28 km) high

Italian volcanologist Giuseppe Mercalli improves the Rossi-Forel scale for earthquake intensity that M. S. de Rossi and F. A. Forel set in 1883 to describe earthquake damage on a Roman numeral scale from I to X

May 17, an earthquake (recognized today as having had a *magnitude* 4.2) strikes near Portsmouth, Ohio—no fatalities reported

April 19, an earthquake (recognized today as having had a magnitude 7.5) strikes Guatemala—2,000 people die

MILESTONES

1901

1902

American geologist John Hayford (1868–1925), inspector of geodetic work and chief of the computing division at the U.S. Coast and Geodetic Survey, establishes the U.S. Standard Datum of triangulation for conducting topographic and gravity surveys. Canada and Mexico adopt the same standards in 1913

French meteorologist Léon-Philippe Teisserenc de Bort, using balloons, identifies an atmospheric layer (the *stratosphere*) where temperatures do not decrease with altitude as they do in the lower layer (the *troposphere*)

Soufrière on St. Vincent in the West Indies erupts on May 6 killing 1,600. Mount Pelée on neighboring Martinique erupts on May 8. Mount Pelée's *pyroclastic flows* inundate the coastal city of Saint Pierre with its population of nearly 28,000—only two people survive. The large ground-hugging pyroclastic flows became the typical example of a *pelean eruption*

rip and tear its meal. Some of the vertebrae were as round as the belly of the horses that carried the bones out of the hole. The men loaded the fossil into a crate and sent it by train from Edgemont, South Dakota, to the American Museum of Natural History (AMNH) in New York City. After 65 million years, *Tyrannosaurus rex* was once again on the move.

Henry Fairfield Osborn (1857–1935), the founder and curator of the museum's department of vertebrate paleontology, had first hired Brown as a field collector for the summer in 1897. Brown had a year left in graduate school at the University of Kansas at that time but had proven his merit in the field working with his professor Samuel Wendell Williston (1852–1918), who taught anatomy, geology, and paleontology. Williston would go on to become the first dean of the new School of Medicine at the University of Kansas. In 1895 Brown helped Williston retrieve a *Triceratops* skull from Wyoming, the most popular dinosaur for museums to display. "Brown has been with me on two expeditions, and is the best man in the field that I ever had," wrote Williston in his recommendation letter to Osborn. "He is very energetic, has great powers of endurance, walking 30 miles a day without fatigue, is very methodical in all his habits, and thoroughly honest." After Brown graduated, Osborn sent him on a two-year collecting expedition to South America with only three hours notice. Brown wrote in his diary:

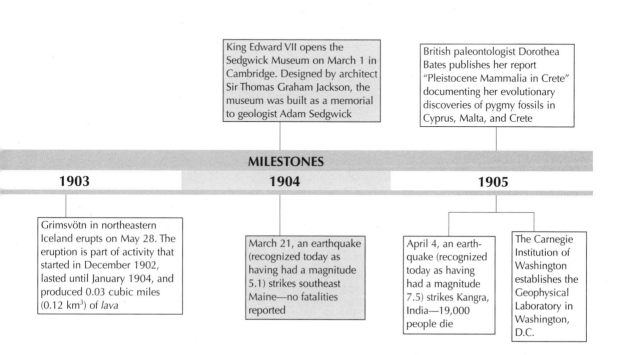

King Edward VII opens the Sedgwick Museum on March 1 in Cambridge. Designed by architect Sir Thomas Graham Jackson, the museum was built as a memorial to geologist Adam Sedgwick

British paleontologist Dorothea Bates publishes her report "Pleistocene Mammalia in Crete" documenting her evolutionary discoveries of pygmy fossils in Cyprus, Malta, and Crete

MILESTONES

1903

1904

1905

Grimsvötn in northeastern Iceland erupts on May 28. The eruption is part of activity that started in December 1902, lasted until January 1904, and produced 0.03 cubic miles (0.12 km³) of *lava*

March 21, an earthquake (recognized today as having had a magnitude 5.1) strikes southeast Maine—no fatalities reported

April 4, an earthquake (recognized today as having had a magnitude 7.5) strikes Kangra, India—19,000 people die

The Carnegie Institution of Washington establishes the Geophysical Laboratory in Washington, D.C.

"Yesterday, about three hours before the *Capac* was to sail I was notified by Prof. Osborn that arrangements had been made for me to go to South America. Four of the dep. [department] men packed up my kit and I took another with me home to pack up. Imagine getting an outfit together in three hours to go on a seven thousand mile journey, and be gone a year or more. Such is the life of a fossil man." Two senior fossil collectors, Olaf Peterson and John Bell Hatcher, joined Brown on the expedition.

When Williston was a graduate student he had worked for O. C. Marsh, one of the country's top paleontologists, at Yale University during a time when natural history museums were being built around the country at an amazing pace. New Haven had the Peabody Museum of Natural History; the Smithsonian Institution in Washington, D.C., had the National Museum; and New York City had AMNH. By the time the first decade of the 20th century arrived, these museums and others needed larger rooms and new buildings to showcase their ever-expanding collections. In 1902 Williston moved to Chicago to take a job as chair of the department of paleontology at the 10-year-old private university in Hyde Park. Chicago's wealthiest man, Marshall Field, had a strong interest in natural history, and in 1905 the Columbian Museum of Chicago would become the Chicago

American mining engineer Daniel Barringer, after three years of reexamining the evidence, reports in the *Proceedings of the Academy of Natural Sciences* that a meteor impact formed the large crater near Flagstaff, Arizona, and not a volcanic eruption as an earlier geology report concluded. The site is now known as the Great Barringer Meteor Crater

April 18, an earthquake (recognized today as having had a magnitude 7.8) strikes San Francisco, California—about 3,000 people die, many from a resulting fire

A 15 megaton airburst from a possible meteor or comet destroys 772 square miles (2000 km^2) of Siberian forest near the Tunguska River

December 28, an earthquake (recognized today as having had a magnitude 7.2) strikes Messina, Italy—an estimated 70,000 to 100,000 people die, many from a resulting tsunami

MILESTONES

1906	1907	1908

August 17, an earthquake (recognized today as having had a magnitude 8.2) strikes Valparaiso, Chile—20,000 people die

After systematically sampling volcanically baked clays, French geophysicist Bernard Brunhes identifies several samples with magnetization aligning with Earth's present magnetic field and others from the Miocene epoch magnetized with their "north" poles pointing south

Bertram Boltwood uses the ratio of lead and uranium in rocks to determine their age. He estimates his samples are 410 million to 2.2 billion years old

Swedish chemist Svante Arrhenius in his book *Worlds in the Making: The Evolution of the Universe* advances the hypothesis of panspermia—that life on Earth is descended from interstellar microorganisms

E. Kalkowsky coins the word *stromatolite* (stromatolith) for Triassic structures in North Germany

Field Museum of Natural History in honor of Field's financial support. Two years later, Andrew Carnegie (1835–1919) in Pittsburgh would finish constructing one of the Carnegie Institution buildings that would host the Carnegie Museum of Natural History (CMNH). By 1911 the National Museum at the Smithsonian in Washington, D.C., would move its fossils, minerals, stuffed mammals, and birds to a new Natural History Museum on the other side of the grassy, open avenue that was the National Mall. The dinosaurs drew the crowds and received prominent displays.

As Carnegie was constructing the future home of CMNH, he lured Osborn's top field collector Jacob Wortman away from New York City to Pittsburgh with the less adventuresome but more prestigious job of working as a curator for the new museum. Upset, Osborn telegraphed Brown and told him to stop what he was doing in Patagonia and go find a *Triceratops* in Wyoming. Brown returned to the states on June 18, 1900, and was on his way up the Cheyenne River by July 1.

Two years later, Brown finally found a crushed *Triceratops* skull near Powder River in Montana. Despite the skull's condition, he returned with the broken bones to Miles City, Montana, on July 2, 1902, and sent the sorted mass by train to New York. Osborn reprimanded Brown for

Based on his gravity surveys and triangulation standards for determining topography, John Hayford establishes that the ocean basins have greater gravitational fields than the continents, indicating that the ocean basins have a higher density than the continents. Using these results he recalculates the figure of Earth's elliptical spheroid, which is adopted as the international reference standard in 1924

Presiding over the eleventh International Geological Congress in Stockholm, Swedish archaeologist Gerard De Geer presented a paper titled *"A Geochronology of the Last 12,000 Years,"* detailing his discovery of *varves*, annual deposits of sedimentary layers. The yearly deposition provided geologists with an influential system for dating rock strata

MILESTONES

1909

1910

On June 12, the Carnegie Institution of Washington launches the nonmagnetic brigantine *Carnegie*, a research sailing vessel built with bronze fittings and machinery instead of iron or steel, to begin conducting magnetic, electric, and gravity surveys around the world

American geologist Frank B. Taylor proposes that mountain chains are the result of colliding continents

Croatian physicist Andrija Mohorovičić identifies a boundary between the Earth's crust and *mantle* where seismic waves increase in velocity and refract. The depth of the Mohorovicic discontinuity, or "Moho" as it is called, varies and is between 3 to 7 miles (5 to 11 km) below the oceans and 16 to 56 miles (25 to 90 km) beneath the continents

shipping what was an almost worthless fossil. "I know you sent the speci-men to us after the best possible methods; but it should have received a more careful examination. I therefore request you to examine all pros-pects and bones pretty carefully, so as to make yourself absolutely sure that we are not bringing on material which will not pay the shipment much less the heavy expenses of collection."

By the time Brown received this letter he had already written to Osborn about a new discovery. He and an assistant, Richard Lutz, had ridden an outfit 130 miles (209 km) northwest of the city and stayed at a ranch in the badlands of one of Montana's now famous fossil-collecting formations: Hell Creek. The tributary to the Missouri River cut a deep canyon that was known for its numerous fossil teeth. Soon it would be known for much more. On their first day out scouting, they immediately discovered *Triceratops* bones and that of an unknown carnivorous dino-saur on a nearby cliff. The collections staff at the museum would catalog the carnivore as AMNH 973. The catalog number is essentially a place-holder that "helps us figure out where it belongs in the collection just like the numbers on library books do," says paleontologist Carl Mehling of AMNH. Museums identify their fossils using the museum's initials and a number corresponding to their collection catalogs. The number usually changes if the fossil is sold to another museum.

After digging the first quarry, Brown and his team soon had three quarries to excavate around Hell Creek. Thankfully, Phillip Brooks, a student from Amherst, joined the crew on July 16 to help. Dinosaur number 973 was proving most intriguing but difficult to extract. Wrote Brown: "the bones are separated by two or three feet of soft sand usually and each bone is surrounded by the hardest blue sandstone I ever tried to work in the form of concretions. There is no question but what this is the find of the season so far for scientific importance. From the pubic [bone] one would think it a Jurassic Dinosaur. It is necessary to shoot [dynamite into] the bank from now on and as it is not accessible to horses, work goes slow. I sent the pubic [bone] and femur in last load in one block which made nearly all the team could pull. Cook just returned and reports safe arrival at Miles [City]." By the end of the summer they had prospected Snow Creek, Hell Creek, Crooked Creek, and the Missouri River, and they had 21 boxes of bones, including 15 skulls to ship by train from Miles City to New York City.

That same summer, Olaf Peterson and John Bell Hatcher were by then collecting for the Carnegie Museum. Peterson had discovered another large carnivorous dinosaur in Wyoming that the Carnegie Museum would catalog as CMNH 1400. It would take time for both museums to chisel their respective fossil treasures out of their matrix in preparation for accu-rate identification at the genus and species level. In three years, Peterson had succeeded in uncovering "the skull, both lower jaws, two dorsal, seven caudal vertebrae, ribs, chevrons, pubis, ilium, femur, and associated frag-mentary bones." By then, Brown had provided Osborn with one femur and part of the pelvis (the ilium and the pubis or pubic bone are both different parts of the pelvis) from the carnivorous dinosaur in the hill over Hell Creek; and the lower jaw, vertebrae, some ribs, and dermal plates (body armor) from the carnivorous dinosaur found near Seven Mile Creek in Wyoming. The differences in the skeletons led Osborn to conclude that the dinosaurs belonged to different genus and species, but there were still more bones for Brown to dig out of the Hell Creek quarry.

As the summer of 1905 progressed, Brown wrote to Osborn. He had recovered the other femur, more of the pelvis, two small humeri, the shoulder blade, several ribs, skull bones, and both lower jaws. The quarry gaped open about 100 feet (30 m) top to bottom, 20 feet (6 m) deep, and 15 feet (5 m) wide into the hard sandstone. The tiny little forearms indicated by the size of the humerus bones seemed strange in comparison to this giant of a dinosaur, which Osborn had started calling *Tyrannosaurus rex* (*tyrannos* in Greek means "tyrant" and *sauros* in Greek means "lizard," while *rex* in Latin means "king"). He wrote to Brown about his doubts: "I hardly believed it possible that the humerus you have found belongs to this animal. It will upset absolutely all that is known of the *osteology* [bone structure] of these carnivorous animals. Of course it will give *Tyran[n]osaurus* a very clear and marked separation, but considering the many points of close resemblance between this animal and *Allosaurus* I hardly think it possible that it has a long fore arm. If you strike another animal in this quarry you will of course have a somewhat less clear path ahead of you, so I hope you will prove to be right and the bone you have found will prove to belong to *Tyran[n]osaurus*, paradoxical as it may appear." Brown wrote back with a response in August: "There is no question regarding the association of the humerus for the only other animal in this quarry is the little carnivore of which we have the humerus and end of the femur."

In the same note, Brown also compared the large Hell Creek carnivore with the carnivorous dinosaur, which had contained a number of dermal plates, from the hillside of Seven Mile Creek in Wyoming. "This specimen is entirely distinct from the carnivore secured in Wyoming and will prove a different genus as I remember the shape of teeth and femur? in that specimen. Moreover, I have not found any plates with this animal and the other is a plated dinosaur. I am confident it is a mistake to combine the remains of the two." The jaw and skull of the fossil from Montana were still in their matrix when Osborn wrote the authoritative description identifying the Hell Creek fossil (AMNH 973) as the *holotype Tyrannosaurus rex.*

"I propose to make this animal the type of the new genus *Tyrannosaurus*, in reference to its size, which greatly exceeds that of any carnivorous land animal hitherto described," he wrote in the Bulletin of the American Museum of Natural History in 1905. A drawing accompanying the report compared the *T. rex* skeleton to that of a human, but Osborn cautioned his readers that, "The association of the small forearm is probably incorrect."

Brown would go on to recover another *T. rex* (AMNH 5881) from the Hell Creek formation in the summer of 1905 and find his fourth and

A Dinosaur Identity Crisis

In the 1905 report entitled "*Tyrannosaurus* and other Cretaceous carnivorous dinosaurs," Osborn named the carnivorous fossil Brown found in 1902 in Hell Creek, Montana, "*Tyrannosaurus rex*." The carnivorous fossil from Seven Mile Creek, Wyoming, he named "*Dynamosaurus imperiosus*." It was a mistake; the animals were the same. In his haste to beat the Carnegie Museum with an identification of the largest discovered carnivorous dinosaur, Osborn did not yet have all the evidence on hand to compare the fossils properly. In 1906 he wrote a correction to the report changing the identity of the Wyoming fossil and making it a *T. rex* as well. Why did he opt to change the identity of the Wyoming fossil instead of the identity of the later discovery? As the first reviser and publisher of both names he could choose which he wanted as the true name, and although the names were both published for the first time in the same report, the description of the Hell Creek fossil as a *T. rex* came in the paragraphs before the description of the Seven Mile Creek fossil—so AMNH 973, even though it was discovered two years later, set the holotype precedent. The fossil formerly known as *D. imperiosus* would eventually make its way to the Natural History Museum of London in 1960. The holotype fossil, in an ironic fate that would have made Osborn cringe, was sold to the Carnegie Museum of Natural History (CMNH) in 1941. The museum gave the fossil a new specimen catalog number (CMNH 9380) to fit with its own catalogs.

The issue of dinosaur identity brings up another interesting historical note regarding the *T. rex* name. Osborn's 1906 report made the Wyoming skeleton the first dinosaur renamed as a *T. rex*. In 1916 Osborn would catalog for the museum the neck bones that Edward Drinker Cope had found in the Laramie Formation of South Dakota and rename them as belonging to a *Tyrannosaurus*. In 1892 Cope had classified the bones as belonging to *Manospondylus*

gigas, meaning "giant, thin vertebra." In 2000 fossil hunters with the Black Hills Institute of Geological Research dug up what they thought was the rest of Cope's *M. gigas* dinosaur. The result was a brief public identity crisis regarding the naming rules for fossil species.

Paleontologists recognized that perhaps the earliest discovery of a *T. rex* bone dates back to 1874 when fossil collector A. Lakes found a "Fossil Saurian Tooth" near Golden, Colorado, that he sent to O. C. Marsh at Yale. In 1888 J. B. Hatcher collected for Marsh some postcranial (below the skull) skeleton bones of a large *theropod* dinosaur from either the Laramie Beds (now called Lance Formation) of eastern Wyoming or the Eagle Sandstone Formation in Fergus County, Montana. Based on the foot bone in the collection, Marsh identified the dinosaur as a larger species (*grandis*) of his newly identified genus *Ornithomimus*, an ostrich-like omnivore with a long tail, which Marsh called a "bird mimic." Other theropod bones that Hatcher discovered in the 1890s and which Marsh classified as *O. grandis* have since been renamed as *Tyrannosaurus* bones. With such a list of *T. rex* fossils previously identified as something else, what was a paleontologist to do? The rules of the International Commission on Zoological Nomenclature (ICZN) clearly stated that the priority of a name went to the first published identity. Paleontologists were still reeling from the upholding of this rule in the 1970s, when all previously known *Brontosaurus* were renamed as *Apatosaurus*, but then on January 1, 2000, ICZN started a new naming rule, which gave a committee the authority to judge whether changing an established name to a name that had precedence in the literature would in fact cause more confusion than it would stability. The new rule allowed for the conservation of names under "extraordinary circumstances." Under this rule, *T. rex* remained taxonomically seated as "king of the tyrant lizards."

more complete *T. rex* skeleton from Big Dry Creek, Montana, in 1908. The Big Dry Creek specimen (AMNH 5027) would stand 18.5 feet (5.6 m) tall and measure 47 feet (14 m) from tip to tail when mounted for display at the American Museum of Natural History in 1915. The plans for the display had included mounting the holotype specimen (AMNH 973) in a crouching position over a fossil of a *Trachodon* as if the two were fighting over a meal. In an article for *Scientific American,* Brown described the scene: "It is early morning along the shore of a Cretaceous lake four million years ago. A herbivorous dinosaur *Trachodon* venturing from the water for a breakfast of succulent vegetation has been caught and partly devoured by a giant flesh-eating *Tyrannosaurus.* As this monster crouches over the carcass, busy dismembering it, another *Tyrannosaurus* is attracted to the scene. Approaching, it rises nearly to its full height to grapple the more fortunate hunter and dispute the prey. The crouching figure reluctantly stops eating and accepts the challenge, partly rising to spring on its adversary. The psychological moment of tense inertia before the combat was chosen to best show positions of the limbs and bodies, as well as to picture an incident in the life history of these giant reptiles."

The museum's Cretaceous Dinosaur Hall, however, did not have the space in 1915 to display both skeletons. The bones of the crouching dinosaur were used to build the casts for the missing limbs, the tiny forearms and long legs, of the more complete Big Dry Creek specimen. Afterward, the bones of the holotype specimen, which Osborn had rushed to name as the first *T. rex,* were then stored in a warehouse where the giant skeleton crouched in the dark until the onset of World War II. At that time, Brown met with curator J. Leroy Kay of the Carnegie Museum to arrange a fossil exchange. Carnegie had on display the skull of CMNH 1400, which Olaf Peterson had found in 1902 in Wyoming, but the curators both agreed it was important that the holotype specimen of *T. rex* leave New York. "We were afraid the Germans might bomb the American Museum in New York as a war measure, and we hoped that at least one specimen would be preserved," wrote Brown later in life.

In 1995 the American Museum of Natural History would renovate the Hall of Dinosaurs and change the stance of the famous *Tyrannosaurus* that had been rearing up from an invisible adversary for 80 years. The new stance has *T. rex* positioned the way the other would have been displayed: with its head low and tail high, in a streamlined crouch. It is likely that *T. rex* both hunted its prey and scavenged the prey from other predators with such a stance.

In 1990 Sue Hendrickson, a fossil hunter with the Black Hills Institute of Geological Research found a *T. rex* skeleton in South Dakota that proved to be the most complete *T. rex* fossil yet discovered. In 1997 sponsors for the Field Museum in Chicago purchased the *T. rex* named "Sue," for $8.4 million during an auction at Sotheby's in New York City. Then in 2000, a hundred years after Barnum Brown first discovered *Tyrannosaurus* for the American Museum of Natural History, the Field Museum revealed its *T. rex* to the public. Casts of "Sue" now travel around the world.

Naming Geologic History

Brown's 1915 article entitled "*Tyrannosaurus*, a Cretaceous carnivorous dinosaur, the largest flesh-eater that ever lived" for *Scientific American* depicted the *Tyrannosaurus* as it might have lived during the Cretaceous period "four million years ago." How did he make this determination? Today's geologists would agree *T. rex* existed during Cretaceous period, but they now know the Cretaceous ended 65 million years ago. Brown was working from knowledge gained during the 19th century, when geologists had worked out a detailed outline of the order in which events in Earth's history had happened, even though the age of the Earth, and the exact dates of the geological periods, was still under much discussion.

Geologists throughout the 19th century had named individual formations or stratigraphic layers and groups of layers that occurred together. In 1822 "Le Terrain Cretace" was the name for chalk deposits throughout northern France that occurred below the Tertiary deposits. The Carboniferous was the name for coal seams in England and Wales. In 1830 Charles Lyell in his book *Principles of Geology* recognized that the order of deposition correlated with the timing of that deposition. The Cretaceous was not just below the Tertiary system; it was older than the Tertiary rocks as well. Geologists began mapping the Cretaceous in other regions of the world and the term *Cretaceous* went from being the name of one specific type of formation to a period in Earth's history identified by its stratigraphic layers.

Italian geologist Giovanni Arduino (1714–95) was the first European to start naming periods in Earth's history by their stratigraphic layers. He began simply with Primary (for primitive or oldest), Secondary, and Tertiary. The Quaternary represented the most recent deposits. By the 20th century the basic periods in Earth's history could be ordered from most recent to oldest: Quaternary, Tertiary, Cretaceous, Jurassic, Triassic, Permian, Carboniferous, Devonian, Silurian, Ordovician, Cambrian, and Pre-Cambrian. Of course, starting at the surface and working deeper

(Opposite page) *Prior to radiometric dating, only relative dates (placement of fossils and correlation of similar rock layers) were used to identify geologic history. Today many factors, including radiometric dating, relative dating, climate change, ice ages, fossil assemblages, and extinctions, mark the onset of various geologic eras, periods, and epochs. The Hadean is an astronomical term for Earth's early formation when asteroid impacts bombarded the planet, not a recognized geologic time period. The International Commission on Stratigraphy has no lower limit for the Archean.*

GEOLOGIC TIMESCALE

Era	Period	Epoch	First life-forms	Geology	Start of Age (millions of years, plus or minus)
Cenozoic	Quarternary	Holocene			0.0118
		Pleistocene		Ice age	1.806
	Neogene	Pliocene	Mastodons	Cascades	5.332
		Miocene	Saber-toothed tigers	Alps	23.03
	Paleogene (Tertiary)	Oligocene			33.9±0.1
		Eocene	Whales		55.8±0.2
		Paleocene	Alligators, horses	Rockies	65.5±0.3
Mesozoic	Cretaceous	(upper)			99.6±0.9
		(lower)	Birds	Sierra Nevada	145.5±4.0
	Jurassic	(upper)	Mammals	Atlantic	161.2±4.0
		(lower)			199.6±0.6
	Triassic	(upper)			228.0±2.0
		(lower)	Dinosaurs		251.0±0.4
Paleozoic	Permian	(upper)	Reptiles	Appalachians	260.4±0.7
		(lower)			299.0±0.8
	Carboniferous	(Pennsylvanian)	Trees	Ice age	318.1±1.3
		(Mississippian)	Amphibians	Pangaea	359.2±2.5
	Devonian	(upper)	Insects		385.3±2.6
		(lower)	Sharks		416.0±2.8
	Silurian		Land plants	Laurasia	443.7±1.5
	Ordovician		Fish	Ice age	488.3±1.7
	Cambrian		Shelled animals	Gondwana	542.0±1.0
Proterozoic Eon	Ediacaran-Siderian		Invertebrates		
			Sea plants	Ice age	2500.0
Archean Eon			Metazoans		Lower limit unknown
			Earliest life		ca. 3,800.0
Hadean Eon				Zircon minerals	ca. 4,400
				Meteorites	4,567.17±0.7

Phanerozoic Eon

Precambrian

Humans

geologists had to deal with rock layers that were frequently missing, folded, faulted or struck by an intrusion from another rock layer (a geological feature James Hutton in the 18th century had identified as an unconformity). To determine which period in time they were digging into, geologists had to look carefully at identifying patterns in the various rock layers. They examined the color, composition, and grain size of the rocks as well as the minerals and fossils found in each layer. They compared rock layers against each other and determined their relationships. For example in an unconformity the younger rock layer is the one that has intruded upon the older rock layer. Geologists became expert surveyors and mapped every region they could explore. Fossil hunters relied on geological maps to dig in the right locations.

A geologist in the late 19th century could identify the time period as the Tertiary and say with confidence even the epoch and still have questions as to how many millions of years ago that happened. The problem was that no dating method existed yet to specifically identify the planet's age in more than a relative way. To determine the age of the Earth, geologists and physicists considered a number of different hypotheses that could explain the planet's rate of cooling since its original formation, the rate of erosion and deposition on the surface, and even Earth's relationship to the Sun and Moon. Different hypotheses yielded different rates. Conflicting opinions resulted in such vast disagreements that scientists between 1885 and 1902 variously categorized the base of the Cambrian Period as having occurred 3, 18, 28, 600, 794, and 2,400 million years ago. Then came the discovery of radioactivity: Earth's built-in clock.

Dating a Radioactive Planet

French physicist Antoine Henri Becquerel (1852–1908) had a passion for light that ran in the family. He and his father, Alexander Edmond Becquerel (1820–91), both experimented with the glow of *phosphorescence* and had a number of *crystals*, minerals, and rock fragments that they exposed to bright lights and then examined in dimly lit or dark rooms to see if the samples would glow. Some of their uranium salts, for example, phosphoresced naturally when exposed to light. In January 1896, Henri Becquerel was discussing with French mathematician Henri Poincaré (1854–1912) the discovery that German physicist Wilhelm Röntgen (1845–1923) had made in November: *X-rays*. Röntgen had induced a type of phosphorescence in a vacuum tube with his mysterious X-rays. Now Becquerel rushed to the lab to see if his uranium salts shared other similar properties with X-rays; namely, the ability to penetrate paper, clothes, skin, and even human tissue (but not bones) to shine on a photographic plate. He took his father's uranium salts and put them next to paper that was covering a photographic plate. The photographic plate fogged as though exposed directly to light. The natural radiation from the uranium had passed through the paper. Unlike X-rays, however, electric and magnetic fields could deflect the "Becquerel rays" as they were called in 1896. Because all uranium salts shared this property, even those that did not phosphoresce, Becquerel concluded they were a special feature of the uranium atom.

Becquerel had discovered radioactivity and Pierre (1859–1906) and Marie Curie (1867–1934) developed the methods for testing its properties. The Curies showed though their experiments with Becquerel radiation that *radium* salts released heat continuously. Their results fascinated the public and scientists. How was this energy being produced? In 1903 Becquerel received half of the Nobel Prize in physics and the Curies shared the other half. The romance of wedded Nobel Prize winners elevated the prestige of this newly founded award in the eyes of the public and consequently the subject of radioactivity. The Curies became the first celebrity science couple of the century. Marie Curie was especially interested in how radioactivity could be used in medical practices and worked with her daughter, Irene, in using radium to help alleviate suffering among injured soldiers during World War I. Besides its believed therapeutic benefits, radium also gave off light naturally like uranium. Radium mining and production intensified during World War I to meet the growing demand for glow-in-the-dark paint, instrument panels, and watch dials. After the war, demand for radium plummeted during the Great Depression. The consequences of too much radioactive exposure also became better understood. In the United States, the Environmental Protection Agency at the turn of the 21st century would still be working with businesses to help clean up radioactive wastes from ore processing sites abandoned in the 1920s.

The discovery of radioactivity changed human history in the 20th century; it led to the development of the atomic bomb, nuclear energy, and chemotherapy for cancer patients to name a few well-known examples. In the history of Earth science, radioactivity would lead to methods for age-dating just about everything from rocks to bones to even the age of the oldest ocean currents. Fallout of radioactive carbon during nuclear testing after World War II left a distinctive signature in the seafloor sediments around the world that oceanographers use as baseline for identifying the 1950s in their core samples, much the same way ash from historical volcanic explosions is used to mark certain years in ice cores.

Seeing the amazing properties being revealed in the atom at the turn of the 20th century, American geologist Thomas C. Chamberlain (1843–1928), in 1899, challenged the prevailing hypothesis that the Earth had begun as a molten body and was still cooling. He suggested cold accretion from the start, concluding that the atom could account for Earth's internal heat. If the atom had secrets left to discover, then so did the planets and stars.

At McGill University, in Montreal, Canada, in 1902, British chemists Sir Ernest Rutherford (1871–1937) and Frederick Soddy (1877–1956) worked together to discover that radioactivity was the result of atomic disintegration. Specifically, they found alpha particles with enormous energies emitted from the nucleus of radioactive atoms. The association of radioactivity with heat led Rutherford, who grew up in New Zealand, to consider the geological ramifications. He soon concluded radioactivity could be used to date the age of the Earth. In the spring of 1904, the Royal Institution in London asked Rutherford to give a presentation on his findings. Wrote Rutherford:

> *I came into the room, which was half dark, and presently spotted Lord Kelvin in the audience and realised [sic] that I was in for trouble at the last part of the speech dealing with the age of the Earth, where my views conflicted with his. To my relief, Kelvin fell fast asleep, but as I came to the important point, I saw the old bird sit up, open an eye and cock a baleful glance at me! Then a sudden inspiration came, and I said 'Lord Kelvin had limited the age of the Earth, provided no new source of heat was discovered. That prophetic utterance refers to what we are now considering tonight, radium!' Behold, the old boy beamed upon me.*

The Scottish physicist William Thomson (1824–1907), knighted the Baron Kelvin of Largs (Lord Kelvin), had dominated the debate over the age of the Earth for 40 years prior to Rutherford's talk. Kelvin supported the hypothesis that the Earth and Sun had formed as molten bodies and had been cooling steadily ever since. According to studies in mines at the time, the Earth's surface temperature increased a degree every 50 feet (15 m) below ground. To measure how much time had passed for a molten Earth to obtain that surface temperature gradient, Kelvin needed to calculate the transfer rate of heat through rocks. In 1820 the French Academy had finally published a mathematical equation Joseph Fourier had written in 1807 to calculate heat transfer rates, but without knowing the conditions of Earth's interior, Kelvin made some large assumptions to solve Fourier's equation. He heated several rock types to determine their ability to conduct heat and deduced the early molten Earth had a temperature of 7,000°F (about 4,000°C). His first answer gave Earth an age of 98 million years old, but because of the uncertainty in his estimates, he later changed his answer to a possible range. Earth, he said, was something between 20 million and 400 million years old, but as he revised his calculations, he found reasons to embrace the younger side of that age range.

Critics of Kelvin supported the theory behind the calculation but shook their heads at his numbers. Engineering professor Fleeming Jenkin (1833–85) of the University of Edinburgh, a friend of Kelvin's, wrote that the great physicist "savors a good deal of that known among engineers as 'guess at half and multiply by two.'" Others challenged Kelvin to consider meteorite impacts as providing more heat than he was accounting for during the planet's cooling period. However meteorites alone were not enough to extend Kelvin's calculation significantly, and his method dominated academic discussions. (Kelvin did raise the heat on the debate over Darwin's theory of evolution at the time, despite giving great weight to the impacts of meteorites in seeding life on Earth.)

Rutherford was mistaken to take Lord Kelvin's beaming for approval. Lord Kelvin did not immediately embrace radium's ability to emit heat and went so far as to publish a note rejecting the idea. He did not publicly abandon his assumptions until later that year and then only in conversation with a colleague at the British Association meeting. By not publishing a retraction, Kelvin maintained his authority on the methods to date the age of the Earth and few challenged him. As Rutherford turned to other fields of interest, Bertram Boltwood (1870–1927) in the United States and Robert John Strutt in England picked up the investigation.

In 1906 Strutt (1875–1947, the fourth Baron Rayleigh) showed that the amount of radioactive *igneous* rocks in Earth's crust provided more heat than what Kelvin had calculated the planet was losing. This was evidence that Kelvin's supporters could not ignore. The Earth indeed had its own heat source and might not be cooling as quickly as they thought—if it was cooling at all.

Radioactivity involves the nuclear disintegration of atoms of one element into atoms of another. This graph shows the decay of a parent element and the production of its daughter element over time, as measured in half-lives. In many cases the daughter product is also radioactive and undergoes further decay (see Uranium 238).

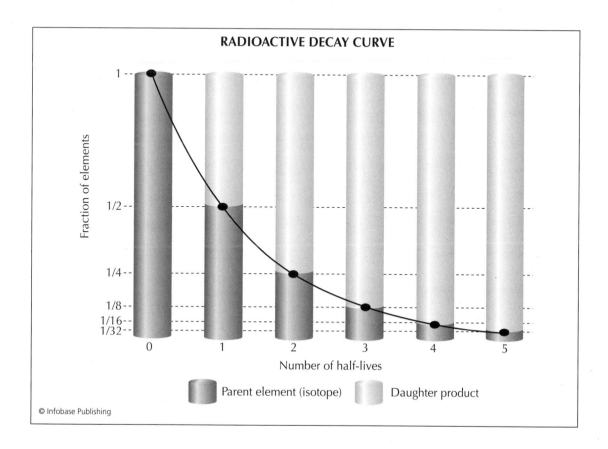

RADIOACTIVE DECAY CURVE

Fraction of elements

Number of half-lives

Parent element (isotope)   Daughter product

© Infobase Publishing

After years of experimenting and sharing ideas (and even radioactive samples) via letters with Rutherford, Boltwood knew that as the nucleus in the atoms of the radioactive element changed, the element itself, uranium or thorium for example, broke down into other elements or *daughter elements* in a series of decay steps. In 1907 Boltwood revealed that through this radioactive decay, uranium gradually and steadily turned to lead. (If it had turned to gold this would have been the alchemist's dream come true.)

Radioactivity was Earth's atomic clock and Boltwood showed the world how to tell time. The breakdown of uranium into lead happens at

The nucleus of unstable radioactive elements gives off alpha or beta particles, and sometimes also gamma rays, during their conversion to a daughter element, which can undergo further decay as pictured here for Uranium 238.

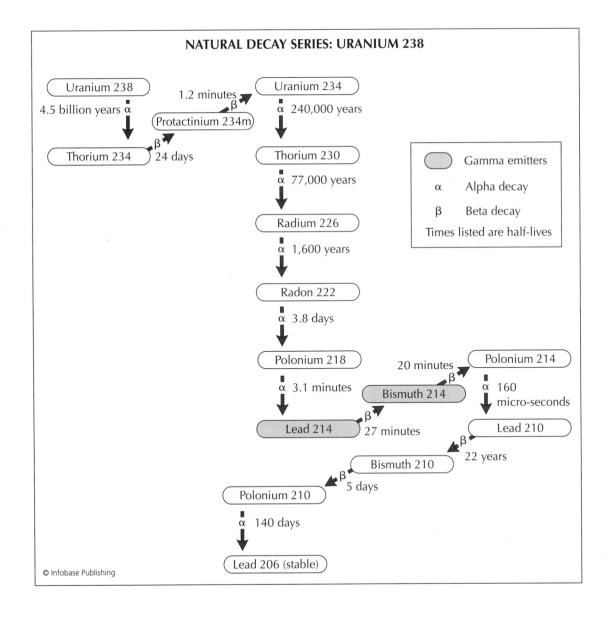

NATURAL DECAY SERIES: URANIUM 238

© Infobase Publishing

a steady rate. By measuring that rate, and the ratio of uranium to lead, Boltwood identified minerals of up to 2.2 billion years old. The minerals were from the Pre-Cambrian, and Earth had to be at least as old as its minerals.

The 20th Century's Deadliest Eruption

Later in the 20th century, dating methods using radioactive *isotopes* of carbon would reveal the timing of events in Earth's more modern Holocene record. For example, volcanologists in New Zealand would investigate lava flows from eruptions that occurred in 9850 B.C.E. Earth scientists modeling the frequency of eruption events now rely on the ancient lava flows deposited around every volcano. They combine the history of eruptions with modern seismic studies to monitor the volcano's activity in real time. Such advances have helped volcanologists better understand the immediate risk of an eruption and to warn civil authorities when an evacuation is warranted. Such cooperation and advances in volcanological studies, however, came only after devastating consequences.

In the Lesser Antilles of the Caribbean, otherwise known as the West Indies, volcanic islands sit like jewels in a necklace between Puerto Rico and Trinidad. The islands—including Saba, Statia, St. Kitts, Nevis, Montserrat, Guadeloupe, Dominica, Martinique, St. Lucia, St. Vincent, and Grenada—form a shield between the Caribbean Sea and the Atlantic Ocean. The homes and businesses that thrive on trade between the islands are painted coral pinks, yellows, whites, and blues. On Saba the roofs are all the same hue of red. Trade between the islands keeps the cities alive. Covered with lush vegetation and fertile soils are steamy, sulfur-emitting volcanoes. Nevis has Nevis Peak. Montserrat has Soufrière Hills. Guadeloupe and St. Vincent also have their own Soufrière volcanoes. Dominica has four volcanoes: Diable, Diablotins, Micotrin, and Patates. St. Lucia has Qualibou. Grenada has St. Catherine and, off its coast, Kick-'em Jenny. In the middle of this arch of islands is the island of Martinique, home to the deadliest volcano of the 20th century: Mount Pelée.

Early in the morning on Thursday, May 8, 1902, the cathedral bell in St. Pierre rang out to commemorate Christ's ascension into heaven. The rum ships sat idle in the harbor as the Roman Catholic merchants took to prayer. Instead of thanks for the spices, fish, and sugarcane that helped make their businesses profitable, the prayer that morning focused on deliverance. They prayed specifically for relief from the ash that had rained on the city for a week, asphyxiated their horses, and forced shops to close. Many residents had fled south to Fort-de-France, but others with homes closer to the volcano sought refuge in St. Pierre. They thought the hills between the harbor city and the volcano would direct any lava flows down the valleys further north.

Only three days earlier, the rim of the crater wall had given way to rising hot water inside the volcano. The resulting mudflow down the valley of the Blanche River killed 23 workers in a rum distillery. The governor, who was campaigning with conservative voters for an upcoming election on May 11, returned to St. Pierre with his wife on May 7. They had no idea what was about to strike.

On May 8 more mudflows cascaded down the valley, this time striking the town of Prêcheur at dawn and carrying 800 people out to sea. At 8 A.M., as the governor knelt in prayer, a dark cloud emerged from the crater. Witnesses hiking the far southeastern hills heard an explosion, looked at the volcano, and saw a glowing avalanche of black smoke and dust consume the landscape, roll down the valley, jump over the flanking hills above St. Pierre, broil through the city, and tumble out over the sea. The ships full of rum exploded and burned. The cathedral bell melted. The city lay in ruins. The victims, more than 28,000, died within minutes. Only two people in St. Pierre survived the eruption, dubbed a *nuée ardente* or pyroclastic flow. Instead of lava, the volcano had sent a cloud of deadly gas, hot ash, and rock careening down its flank at speeds between 426 and 492 feet per second (130–150 m/sec), about 310 miles per hour (500 km/hr), and with temperatures of 392° to 932°F (200°–500°C). Those trapped breathing the mixture seared their lungs and suffocated while their skin burned faster than their clothes. The two survivors were Leon Compère-Léandre and Auguste Ciparis.

Compère-Léandre, a cobbler at 28, was sitting on his doorstep when he saw the cloud. In the seconds it took to turn around and run inside his legs and arms suffered severe burns. He ran to his basement for shelter and escaped the suffocating ash. The second survivor became a circus legend. Auguste Ciparis, 25, survived because he was incarcerated in the city's small jail: a hand-lain stone cave with a heavy door. The jail behaved like a kiln during the pyroclastic flow and started to cook Ciparis alive, but the poor ventilation ultimately protected the prisoner of St. Pierre, keeping his lungs free of pyroclastic gases and glassy ash. He survived for three days on his remaining bowl of water before he was rescued and pardoned. He went on to tour with the Barnum and Bailey circus.

The disaster ignited a global response to better monitor volcanoes. French geologist Alfred Lacroix (1868–1948) built an observatory on the higher southeastern hills of Martinique for volcanologists to keep an eye on Mount Pelée. It was the world's second such volcano observatory, the first having been built in 1847 by the Italians to watch Vesuvius. Thomas Jaggar of the Massachusetts Institute of Technology also visited Martinique and the neighboring island St. Vincent, where Soufrière volcano killed 1,600 people in 1902. Jaggar wanted an American volcano observatory in a place where scientists could safely watch eruptions happening all the time.

The first decade of the 20th century had experienced a number of large eruptions. The eruption of Santa María in Guatemala in 1902 would stand as the century's largest eruption in terms of material ejected. The volcano killed 6,000 people after sending about 5 cubic miles

(20 km^3) of *tephra* into the sky. Karthala Volcano on Grand Comore Island in the Indian Ocean in 1903 killed 17 with its eruption, and Vesuvius in Italy in 1906 killed 350 people. Some large eruptions occurred far from human populations and despite their size remained free of fatalities: Grímsvötn in Iceland in 1903; Lolobau off the island of New Britain in Papua New Guinea in 1905; and the eruption of Ksudach in the Kamchatka Peninsula in 1907. The north rim of the Kilauea caldera with its slow moving lava field proved ideal for Jaggar's purposes. Construction began in 1912. The station would become the U.S. Geological Survey's Hawaiian Volcano Observatory, and its first monitoring instrument was a seismograph.

Seismic Solutions Reveal Earth's Core

Considering the material erupting out of volcanoes, many scientists concluded that the Earth contained a labyrinth of lava tubes connecting chambers of *magma* and gas. Much discussion also focused on how this inner material influenced another natural hazard: earthquakes. For example, John Mitchell in the late 1700s had first proposed a link between gas inside Earth and earthquakes at the surface. He believed earthquakes resulted from gas that rose out of the interior and rolled under the crust until a fracture appeared to release it. Charles Lyell in the 1830s supported this view, arguing for a liquid gaseous interior topped with a thin floating crust.

Lord Kelvin, however, argued that tides disproved this idea. He claimed that if Lyell's model held true, then people on Earth would not notice the tides because, "the solid crust would yield so freely to the deforming influence of the Sun and Moon that it would simply carry the waters of the ocean up and down with it, and there would be no tidal rise and fall of water relative to land." Kelvin, as mentioned earlier, supported the theory of a cooling Earth, and his calculations called for a much thicker and sturdier crust, perhaps even a completely solid Earth. Neither Kelvin nor William Hopkins, who also argued in favor of a thicker crust, offered an alternative model to explain the occurrence of earthquakes. If the crust was too thick for gas to lift, what was causing the upheavals?

English engineer Robert Mallet offered a solution in 1848. In his report published in the *Transactions of the Irish Academy*, he wrote that earthquakes were "the transit of a wave of elastic compression in any direction, from vertically upward to horizontally, in any azimuth, through the surface of Earth's crust." Perhaps, he suggested, instruments around the world could measure the ground motion in action.

Chinese philosopher Chang Hêng is known to have built the first device for detecting earthquakes in 132 B.C.E. The monitoring device was an urn-shaped sculpture with eight carved dragons along the top and a corresponding number of openmouthed toads along the bottom. The animals represented the various points on a compass: north, northeast, east, southeast, south, southwest, west, and northwest. Legend states

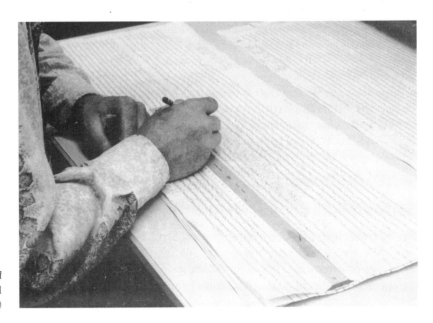

A seismogram being read and interpreted. (U.S. Geological Survey)

that if an earthquake struck within 300 miles (500 km), marbles inside the urn would drop from the mouth of one of the dragons into the maw of a toad—with the sound of the ball clanging in the toad's belly acting as the earthquake alarm. Observing which toad held the marble provided the clue as to which direction one should travel to find evidence of the earthquake. Presumably that was also the direction to send help, in case it was needed. Imagine multiple Hêng dragon pots located throughout the region. Earthquake monitoring is easier when results can be checked and compared with records of movement from neighboring areas.

By the mid-1800s, the science of seismology emerged with new technology monitoring the movements of Earth's surface. *Seismometers*, also called seismographs, could sketch ground motion on paper records, called *seismograms*. Multiple seismometers could pinpoint earthquake *epicenters*. British seismologists teaching as visiting professors at the Imperial College of Engineering in Tokyo founded the Seismological Society of Japan in 1880. John Milne, James Ewing, and Thomas Gray all made significant design improvements and led the field of seismology into the 20th century.

In 1883 Milne (1850–1913) suggested a global network of monitoring stations. "It is not unlikely that every large earthquake might with proper appliances be recorded at any point of the globe," he said. The first recognition of this capability came when Ernst von Rebeur-Paschwitz (1861–95) noticed his data showed seismic waves arriving in two distant German cities an hour after a large earthquake struck Tokyo at 2:07 A.M. on April 18, 1889. To get to Germany, the seismic waves had traveled through the Earth.

In 1891 the Mino-Owari earthquake in Japan led Bunjiro Koto (1856–1935) to contemplate the nature of earthquakes and redefine the *focus*. He concluded that earthquakes happened on fault lines, because the fault line moved to cause the earthquake. The earthquake did not cause the fault line, the fault line was already there. It was a subtle but distinctive difference between cause and effect and turned scientific attention onto faults. It also proves prescient insight when considered in light of today's modern theory of plate tectonics. All around the world, seismologists in the late 19th century were poised for a seismological breakthrough.

Irish geologist Richard Dixon Oldham (1858–1936) would give them one. His first major contribution came in investigating one of the world's largest earthquakes in known history at the time. He was working for the Geological Survey of India, when on June 12, 1897, an earthquake that today is recognized as having been a magnitude 8.7 struck the Assam region at 5:15 P.M. Not since 1755 in Lisbon had an earthquake spurred seismologists around the world to such an extent. Only this time seismometers were stationed nearby; unfortunately, many fell over during the shaking. "Lasting about two and a half minutes, it had not ceased at Shillong before an area of 150,000 square miles [390,000 km²] had been laid in ruins, all means of communication interrupted, the hills rent and cast down in landslips, and the plains fissured and riddled with vents, from which sand and water poured out in most astounding quantities; and ten minutes had not elapsed from the time when Shillong was laid in ruins before about one and three quarter millions of square miles [4.5 million km²] had felt a shock which was everywhere recognized as one quite out of the common," wrote Oldham in his 1899 report of more than 300 pages entitled "The Great Earthquake of June 12, 1897." Witnesses he and others of the Survey interviewed identified both vertical and horizontal motion. They described "loose stones lying on the surface of roads being tossed in the air 'like peas on a drum,'" Oldham reported. This vertical movement was followed by a back-and-forth motion that witnesses described as being "shaken like a rat by a terrier." Oldham identified the first and second motions as preliminary tremors (later recognized as *P* and *S waves*).

In a preface to his report, he also described the motions of waves already understood to occur through liquids and solids and compared these to the experiences felt from seismic waves. Sometimes nausea-inducing surface undulations gyrated underfoot like sea swells. Oldham noted that John William Strutt, third baron Rayleigh (Lord Rayleigh [1842–1919]), had in 1885 predicted the occurrence of such ground waves. Called *Rayleigh waves*, they caused elliptical motion of any particle caught in the ground roll. "It does not appear that the existence of waves of this nature has ever been demonstrated, and they have certainly not as yet been separated in the complicated disturbances of an earthquake, but the possibility of their existence may be taken as demonstrated, and time and the collection of fuller details will doubtless lead to their recognition," Oldham wrote, cautioning that there were at least two types of surface waves in addition to the preliminary tremors. Mathematician Augustus E. H. Love would model the second type, *Love waves*, in 1911 as surface waves that traveled slightly faster than Rayleigh waves in a side-to-side shearing motion. Oldham's report synthesized the type of damage a large earthquake could cause.

From Japan, Milne began keeping track of what was happening at other monitoring stations around the world. He used the difference in time between the arrival of the preliminary waves and that of the surface waves from at least three different stations to draw arcs across the globe and triangulate an earthquake's origin. Following the protocols of seismology, he measured the distance from a recording station to the earthquake's origin in degrees using Earth's center as a fixed reference point. Thus, a large earthquake that originated on the South Pole would have a distance of 90° to a recording station on the equator. More northerly stations detecting the earthquake would have larger angles—up to 180°, which would indicate an earthquake's anticenter at the North Pole. The trend was set, and the catalog of earthquakes that Milne and others recorded launched the 20th century's global seismic monitoring efforts.

In 1900 Oldham recognized that the preliminary tremors, now called primary (P) and secondary (S) waves, traveled through Earth's interior. When transit times of the P and S waves were plotted against their angular distance they tended to result in a smooth curve. For example, a wave might travel 45° in 15 minutes, another 45° in less than five minutes, and finally reaching 120° in a little less than 30 minutes, so the curve looks like it is leveling out.

Seismologists would have expected a station 130° from the source to receive the seismic waves about a half hour after the earthquake struck, but as measuring earthquake origins and the time between waves improved, Oldham noticed that a station at around 130° would receive the S wave 10 minutes later than expected. Something in the middle of the Earth was causing the S wave to slow down. On February 21, 1906, the Geological Society of London read Oldham's report "The Constitution of the Interior of the Earth, as Revealed by Earthquakes." In it, Oldham summarized the working knowledge of Earth's interior at the time:

"Of all regions of the Earth, none invited speculation more than that which lies beneath our feet, and in none is speculation more dangerous; it is little that we can say regarding the constitution of the interior of the Earth. We know, with sufficient accuracy for most purposes, its size and shape; we know that its mean density is about 5½ times that of water, that the density must increase towards the

SEISMOLOGICAL EVIDENCE OF EARTH'S CORE

Earth

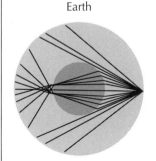

Paths of seismic waves through the Earth assuming a core of radius of 0.4R, in which the speed is 3 km/sec, while the speed outside it is 6 km/sec.

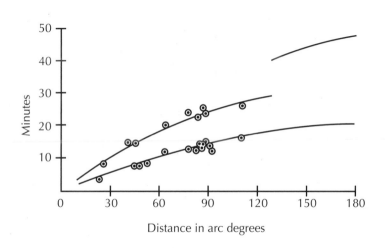

Distance in arc degrees

Time curves of the first and second phases of preliminary tremors. The marks surrounded by circles are averages.

Seismological evidence of Earth's core: In 1906 Richard Oldham explained the 10-minute delay shown in the graph as S-waves at 130° encountering a central core, and slowing their rate to half of that in the surrounding shell.

centre, and that the temperature must be high, but beyond these facts little can be said to be known. Many theories of the Earth have been propounded at different times: the central substance of the Earth has been supposed to be fiery, fluid, solid, and gaseous in turn, till geologists have turned in despair from the subject, and become inclined to confine their attention to the outermost crust of the Earth, leaving its centre as a playground for mathematicians."

A cross section of Earth made in Germany in 1902 showed four different layers: a dense large solid core, surrounded by an elastic mantle, and topped with a crust that made up the continents and the basins that supported the fourth layer, the oceans. The concept that Earth had a distinct core and perhaps other layers was not new. Emil Wiechert, who in 1901 established one of the first formal academic institutes of geophysics at Göttingen University, supported this view, but in 1906 Oldham gave the first seismological evidence that indicated the core's existence.

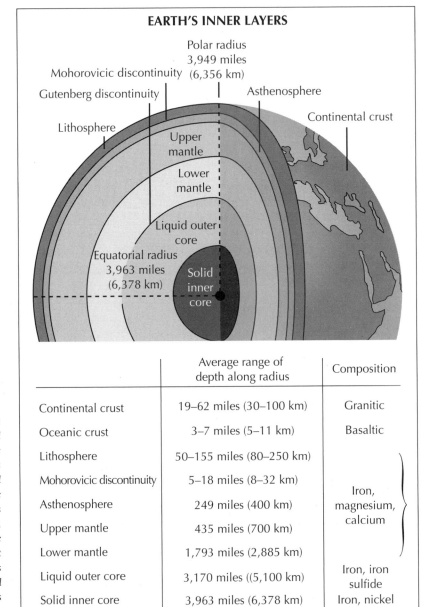

EARTH'S INNER LAYERS

	Average range of depth along radius	Composition
Continental crust	19–62 miles (30–100 km)	Granitic
Oceanic crust	3–7 miles (5–11 km)	Basaltic
Lithosphere	50–155 miles (80–250 km)	Iron, magnesium, calcium
Mohorovicic discontinuity	5–18 miles (8–32 km)	Iron, magnesium, calcium
Asthenosphere	249 miles (400 km)	Iron, magnesium, calcium
Upper mantle	435 miles (700 km)	Iron, magnesium, calcium
Lower mantle	1,793 miles (2,885 km)	Iron, magnesium, calcium
Liquid outer core	3,170 miles ((5,100 km)	Iron, iron sulfide
Solid inner core	3,963 miles (6,378 km)	Iron, nickel

© Infobase Publishing

In 1909 Croatian physicist Andrija Mohorovičić discovered the change in earthquake waves that occurs about 5 miles (8 km) below the seafloor and 18 miles (32 km) under the continents. This is known as the Mohorovicic discontinuity, or "Moho," and represents the boundary between Earth's crust and the mantle. Seismic studies in the 20th century provided an outline of the Earth's inner structure and chemical makeup.

He wrote, "Just as a spectroscope opened up a new astronomy by enabling the astronomer to determine some of the constituents of which distant stars are composed, so the seismograph, recording the unfelt motion of distant earthquakes, enables us to see into the Earth and determine its nature with as great a certainty, up to a certain point, as if we could drive a tunnel through it and take samples of the matter passed through."

Oldham hypothesized that a distinct fluid core inside Earth slowed down S waves traveling around 130° from their source. He went on to measure the radius of the core using seismic waves and their predicted refractions off of the core. He estimated that the core boundary occurred at 1,584 miles (2,550 km) deep. In 1913 German-American seismologist Beno Gutenberg (1889–1960) used the data from the extensive number of stations recording seismic waves at that time and revised the depth of the core's boundary to 1,802 miles (2,900 km). The Gutenberg discontinuity marks the boundary between the mantle and the core. British seismologist (Sir) Harold Jeffreys (1891–1989) would make the definitive statement in 1926 that the core was liquid. Less than a decade later, Danish seismologist Inge Lehmann would report the existence of an even deeper, solid inner core.

The 1906 California Earthquake

In less than two months after the Geological Society read Oldham's report on seismic waves, a perplexing and devastating event would lead geologists to even greater insights on the nature of earthquakes. At exactly 5:12 A.M. on Wednesday, April 18, 1906, the northernmost 267 miles (430 km) of the San Andreas Fault ruptured. The strong shaking liquefied foundations under San Francisco, and although it took less than a minute for the seismic waves from the earthquake to pass, the city would burn for days. The quake had snapped electricity lines and damaged the water mains; fires ignited and firefighters were left without their primary resource to put them out. Although the city had seen its share of both quakes and fires in the past, it was unprepared for the devastation now at hand. The death toll, originally underreported as being around 700, is now recognized to have reached 3,000—making it one of the worst natural disasters to strike the United States of America during the 20th century.

Harry Fielding Reid (1859–1944), a professor of geology and physics at Johns Hopkins University, joined the California State Earthquake Investigation Commission shortly after the quake to survey the land. They looked at the damage for clues. Reid traveled north and south, and found evidence of the rupture miles away from the city. He talked to the residents who showed him bent fences and broken roads. The ground on the western side of the San Andreas Fault had moved almost 15 feet (5 m) northward relative to the land east of the fault. He kept a detailed

Scientist of the Decade: Bertram Borden Boltwood (1870–1927)

Otto Hahn in 1967 recalling the "good old days of early radioactivity research" called Rutherford "the leader in radiophysics" and Boltwood "the leader in radiochemistry." Boltwood looked to Rutherford as a mentor, and the two corresponded extensively about the radioactive nature of the material they were studying. Boltwood indeed would send letters containing uranium salts and other radioactive minerals to Rutherford, as this was long before the health implications of alpha and beta particles were understood.

The first decade of the 20th century was Boltwood's most important period for scientific achievement. At this point in his life, he had just established himself as an exceptional instructor at Yale in the fields of analytical chemistry and physical chemistry. He had spent two years in Germany studying inorganic chemistry between his time as an undergraduate and graduate at Yale. When he

began teaching physical chemistry, textbooks in English did not meet his expectations and, at the age of 27, he translated two German textbooks for his students to use. In 1900 he left Yale to work with Joseph Hyde Pratt (1870–1942) consulting mining engineers and chemists. He returned to Yale College in 1906 as an assistant professor of physics, a position he held until 1910.

Working with Pratt, a geologist, Boltwood analyzed radioactive minerals and established an impressive collection of uranium minerals from around the world. In 1902 Rutherford and Soddy reported that atoms of radioactive elements disintegrate into other elements, emitting radiation energy in the process. Boltwood in turn verified the process demonstrating that uranium disintegrated into radium. In every geological sample containing uranium that Boltwood had found, as long as the sample was from an old geological

record of his observations, and when the commission was done with its survey, he compared it to earlier geological surveys of the region done in the 1860s and 1880s.

*Destruction caused by the 1906
San Francisco earthquake.*
(U.S. Geological Survey)

formation and the mineral remained unaltered, the ratio of uranium to radium was consistent. "Boltwood was a careful and indefatigable experimenter, repeating his analyses and experiments many times to make certain of his results," wrote Alois F. Kovarik in 1929.

He knew that to really prove that the radium was born from uranium, he had to begin with a uranium mineral free of radium, wait, and see if indeed radium sprung forth. After 390 days of waiting with no radium to show for his time, Boltwood reassessed the nature of the disintegration process. He proposed that uranium disintegrated into an intermediate element and that this element lasted longer than 390 days before it also disintegrated to form radium. Now he had to find that element and indeed his research led him to the discovery of Ionium. In the process of chemically isolating this element, Boltwood discovered it was nearly identical to another element: thorium. Once the two were mixed together it became impossible for Boltwood to again separate the elements. He suggested that their atomic weights were so close as to be almost indistinguishable. Soddy took this discovery further and coined the word *isotopes* to describe elements with the same chemical and physical properties, but with different atomic weights. It was soon discovered that radioactive elements disintegrated into different isotopes. Ionium would later prove to be an isotope of thorium (Th-227). Prior to this discovery, Boltwood had determined that the ultimate disintegration of uranium led to lead. He concluded that by, "knowing the rate of disintegration of uranium, it would be possible to calculate the time required for the production of the proportions of lead found in the different minerals, or in other words the ages of the minerals." His minerals turned out to be between 410 million and 2.2 billion years old, establishing a minimum age for the Earth that others would continue to push back with even older minerals over the next 50 years.

The earlier surveys showed the land had begun to move even before the earthquake. Reid noticed that even further away from the actual rupture the land on either side of the fault had shifted in opposing directions, albeit not as much as at the fault itself. The Farallon lighthouse, for example, had moved northwest from its original place of construction in 1855. In his report to the commission, Reid proposed that an elastic rebound theory would explain the geophysical dynamics involved.

The theory of elastic rebound still stands as a reasonable explanation for strike-slip earthquake deformation along the upper six to 12 miles (10 to 20 km) of Earth's crust. Reid had proposed that forces far away from the fault were acting in opposite directions, slowly moving the land elastically in opposite directions as well. The fault line occurs in the area where the stress accumulates and finally exceeds the breaking point for the rocks. The rocks fracture, causing an earthquake. The land on either side of the fault rebounds to compensate for the forces that had acted upon it and establishes a new baseline. The fault is then the weakest point between the forces and will fracture again when pressures accumulate—creating a cycle of earthquakes that will continue in the region for millions of years as long as the forces remain in operation. Decades

Harry Reid helped to survey the San Andreas Fault after the 1906 earthquake that destroyed San Francisco. After comparing the survey's findings to ones in the past, Reid concluded that the earthquake was the result of the fault fracturing under built-up stress from opposing forces farther away. The fault would be the weakest point between the two forces. (Adapted from U.S. Geological Survey)

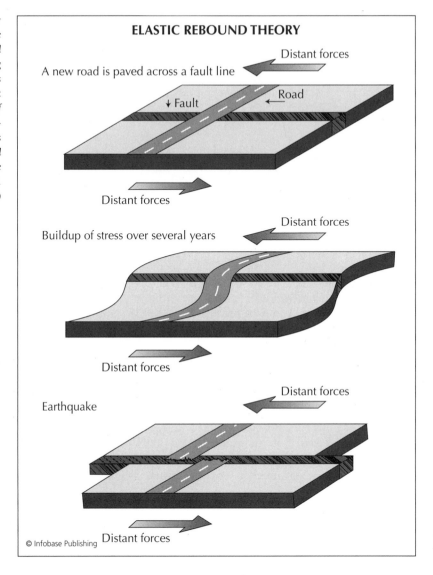

ELASTIC REBOUND THEORY

A new road is paved across a fault line

Distant forces

↓ Fault   Road

Distant forces

Buildup of stress over several years

Distant forces

Distant forces

Earthquake

Distant forces

© Infobase Publishing   Distant forces

would pass before anyone realized California west of the San Andreas Fault was slowly drifting north relative to the rest of the country. The San Andreas Fault is still under pressure.

Further Reading

American Museum of Natural History. "The Division of Paleontology." This Web site chronicles the history of the museum and famous paleontologists from 19th to 21st century. Available online. URL: http://paleo.amnh.org/ Accessed April 24, 2006.

————. *"Tyrannosaurus rex."* This Web site chronicles the story of the first *T. rex* specimens discovered. Available online. URL: http://paleo.amnh. org/projects/t-rex/ Accessed April 24, 2006.

Arrhenius, Svante. *Worlds in the Making: The Evolution of the Universe.* New York and London: Harper, 1908. This book discusses possible theories on the origin of the universe.

The Barringer Crater Company. "The Barringer Meteorite Crater." This interactive Web site provides a history of the crater and the Barringer Crater Company. Available online. URL: http://www.barringercrater. com/ Accessed April 24, 2006.

Bates, Dorothea. "Pleistocene Mammalia in Crete." Geol. Mag., n. s. December 5, 2 (May 1905): 193–202. Bates' report documents her discoveries of dwarfed fossils during the Pliocene and Pleistocene in the islands of Malta, Cyprus, and Crete.

Bolt, Bruce A. *Inside the Earth: Evidence from Earthquakes.* San Francisco: W. H. Freeman, 1982. Bolt provides an introduction to the field of seismology.

————. *Earthquakes and Geological Discovery.* New York: Scientific American Library, 1993. Following the stories in earthquake science, Bolt introduces readers to geological formations around the world.

Brochu, Christopher A. "Osteology of *Tyrannosaurus rex:* Insights from a nearly complete skeleton and high-resolution computed tomographic analysis of the skull," *Society of Vertebrate Paleontology Memoir* 7 (2003): 1–138. Using advanced computer models, this paleontologist produced 3-D images of the inside of a *T. rex* skull.

Brown, Barnum. "*Tyrannosaurus,* a Cretaceous carnivorous dinosaur, the largest flesh-eater that ever lived." *Scientific American* 63, no. 15 (1915): 322–323. Although the bones of a *Spinosaurus* dethroned the king of lizards in the 21st century, this report established *T. rex* as the 20th century's largest known carnivorous dinosaur fossil.

Davison, Charles. *The Founders of Seismology.* Cambridge, England: The University Press, 1927. Reprinted in 1978 by New York, Arno Press, this book provides a historical examination of seismologists from the works of John Bevis, Elie Bertrand, and John Michell after the Lisbon earthquake of 1755 to the works of Seikei Sekiya, Grove Karl Gilbert, Harry Fielding Reid, Fusakichi Omori, and Richard Oldham of the late 19th and early 20th centuries.

De Geer, Gerard. "A Geochronology of the Last 12,000 Years." *Congr. Géol. Int. Stockholm 1910, C.R.,* (1912): 241–253. This report introduced a new dating method using sedimentary deposits, called varves.

Dewey, James, and Perry Byerly. "The Early History of Seismometry (to 1900)." *Bulletin of the Seismological Society of America* 59, no. 1 (February 1969): 183–227. This report provides a detailed analysis of the development of science of seismology. Available online. URL: http://earthquake. usgs.gov/learning/topics/seismology/history/ Accessed February 28, 2007.

Geikie, Sir Archibald. *Founders of Geology.* Baltimore: The Johns Hopkins Press, 1901. Sir Geikie discusses the work of influential geologists including George Huntington Williams (1856–94) and others. Originally published in 1897, New York, Dover Publications provided the second edition again in 1962.

Goodstein, Judith R. "Waves in the Earth: Seismology Comes to Southern California." *Historical Studies in the Physical Sciences* 14 (1984): 201–230. This report documents some of the seismological studies in Southern California.

Greene, M. T. *Geology in the Nineteenth Century: Changing View of a Changing World.* Ithaca, N.Y.: Cornell University Press, 1983. This book provides a history of geosciences during the 19th century.

Hallam, Anthony. *Great Geological Controversies.* Oxford; New York: Oxford University Press, 1989. Hallam writes a widely acclaimed account of the most celebrated controversies in the history of geology, such as uniformitarianism and continental drift.

Hayford, John F. *The Figure of the Earth and Isostasy from Measurements in the United States.* Washington, D.C.: Government Printing Office, 1909. The Hayford Spheroid becomes the international reference standard for Earth's figure in 1924.

Hellman, Hal. *Great Feuds in Science.* New York: John Wiley & Sons, Inc., 1998. A modern look at scientific debates in history.

Howell, Benjamin F., Jr. *An Introduction to Seismological Research.* Cambridge: Cambridge University Press, 1990. Howell writes about the history of the field of seismology as divided into four periods: prior to the 1755 Lisbon earthquake; mid-18th to late 19th century advances in seismometers; early 20th century studies; and the modern era with digital rather than paper records of seismic waves.

Istria on the Internet. "Andrija Mohorovičić." This Web site of prominent Istrians offers a biography on the discoverer of the Moho. Available online. URL: http://www.istrianet.org/istria/illustri/mohorovicic/ Accessed February 28, 2007.

Kalkowsky, E. "Oolith und Stromatolith im norddeutschen. Buntsandstein." (*Oolites* and stromatolites in north Germany, new red sandstone.) *Z. dt. geol. Ges.* 60 (1908): 68–125. This German report is the first to name stromatolite fossils.

Kovarik, Alois F. "Biographical Memoir of Bertram Borden Boltwood 1870–1927." *Biographical Memoirs of the National Academy* 14 (1929): 69–96. "Published since 1877, *Biographical Memoirs* is a monograph series that features the life histories and selected bibliographies of deceased National Academy of Sciences members."

Lloyd, Robin. "The Biggest Carnivore: Dinosaur History Rewritten." This online news report posted on March 1, 2006, covers the dethroning of the tyrant king of lizards. Available online. URL: http://www.livescience.com/animalworld/060301_big_carnivores.html. Accessed February 28, 2007.

Montel, Alfredo. *Building Structures in Earthquake Countries.* Translated from the Italian, with additions by the author. London: C. Griffin & Company, limited, 1912. This book reports on earthquake intensity scales and the effects of earthquakes on different building structures.

Oldham, Richard D. "The Great Earthquake of June 12, 1897." *Memoirs of the Geological Survey of India volume 19:* His Excellency the governor general of India in Council, 1899. Oldham's report on the Great Earthquake of June 12, 1897. Available online. URL: http://books.google.com/books?vid=OCLC38637112&id=Ht8PAAAAIAAJ&dq=Oldham+seismology. Accessed February 28, 2007.

———. "The Constitution of the Interior of the Earth, as Revealed by Earthquakes." *Quarterly Journal of the Geological Society,* 62 (1906): 456–475. This report documents the first seismic evidence for Earth's core.

The Origins and Early History of Earth Sciences at Yale. This Web site provides an excerpt of short biographies of influential Earth scientists at Yale University from "Earth Sciences," by Karl K. Turekian and Barbara L. Narendra, in *Science at Yale*, edited by S. Altman, Yale University, 2002. Available online. URL: http://www.geology.yale.edu/graduate/history.html. Accessed April 24, 2006.

Osborn, Henry F. "*Tyrannosaurus* and other Cretaceous carnivorous dinosaurs." *Bulletin of the American Museum of Natural History* 21 (1905): 259–265. This report introduces the world to *T. rex.*

———. "*Tyrannosaurus,* Upper Cretaceous carnivorous dinosaur (second communication)." *Bulletin of the American Museum of Natural History* 22 (1906): 281–296. This report corrects a misidentification of another fossil.

———. "Crania of *Tyrannosaurus* and *Allosaurus.*" *Memoirs of the American Museum of Natural History* 1 (1912): 33–54. This report discusses the skulls of different dinosaurs.

———. "Skeletal adaptations of *Ornitholestes, Struthiomomus, Tyrannosaurus.*" *Bulletin of the American Museum of Natural History* 35 (1917): 733–771. This report discusses some of the unique skeletal differences among three kinds of dinosaurs.

Reed, Christina. "Mount Pelée, Martinique 1902–2002," *Geotimes* May 2002. The author traveled to Martinique and reported about the history of the 1902 eruption that killed 28,000 people and the lessons learned. Available online. URL: http://www.geotimes.org/may02/geophen.html. Accessed April 24, 2006.

Rutherford, Ernest, and Bertram Boltwood. *Rutherford and Boltwood, Letters on Radioactivity.* Edited by Lawrence Badash. New Haven: Yale University Press, 1969. This book documents the letters of correspondence between Rutherford and Boltwood.

Shindler, Karolyn. *Discovering Dorothea: The Life of the Pioneering Fossil-Hunter Dorothea Bate.* United Kingdom: HarperCollins Publishers Limited, 2006. This book documents the early work of explorer and paleontologist Dorothea Bates who traveled around the world exploring ancient history and in the later half of the century worked closely with anthropologist Mary Leakey. "Dorothea Bate, palaeontologist, geologist, archaeologist and ornithologist, established archeo-zoology as a serious scientific subject. She became one of the outstanding personalities and scientists in the Natural History Museum [of London], but she made her name exploring, alone, the fossil remains in Cyprus, and discovering previously unheard-of species—such as pigmy hippos and elephants—and her travels and explorations ranged thereafter throughout the Mediterranean and beyond to China."

Skoko, Dragutin. "Andrija Mohorovicic." This Web site provides a biography of the discoverer of the Moho. Available online. URL: http://earthquake.usgs.gov/learning/topics/people/mohorovicic.php. Accessed February 28, 2007.

Smith, Crosbie, and M. Norton Wise. *Energy and Empire: A Biographical Study of Lord Kelvin.* Cambridge, England: Cambridge University Press, 1989. This book provides a biography on one of the most influential scientists of the 19th century.

Taylor, Frank B. "Bearing of the Tertiary Mountain Belt on the Origin of the Earth's Plan." *Bulletin of the Geologic Society of America* 21 (1910): 179–226. The geologic community took little notice of this paper when Taylor first proposed a type of continental drift.

Walcott, Charles D. *Cambrian Geology and Paleontology.* City of Washington: Smithsonian Institution, 1910–28. This five-volume book covers the Cambrian history of the planet.

Zittel, Karl A. von. *History of Geology and Palæontology to the End of the Nineteenth Century.* Translated by Maria M. Ogilvie-Gordon. London, W. Scott; New York, C. Scribner's Sons, 1901. This book first published in German in 1899 provides a history of the major geoscience fields during the 19th century.

2

1911–1920:
Crustal Dynamics

Introduction

The second decade of the 20th century was a time of great change and new ideas for geologists. Charles Doolittle Walcott discovered tiny fossils with a big influence on Earthly life. Engineer Percy Bridgman invented a way to examine minerals deep in Earth's interior without leaving the lab, and a young Arthur Holmes advanced the field of *geochronology* and began to fill in the missing dates to the layers of geological history. As evidence from fossil distribution, geologic density of materials, and radio-dating of rocks accumulated, geologists started to question the predominant hypothesis that Earth was cooling and contracting—its surface buckling like the skin of a drying apple. Controversy ensued over how mountains had achieved such heights, and how the same species of plants and animals had come to exist on distant continents. Some still supported the contraction hypothesis and developed alternative methods other than cooling to justify how the process worked. Many paleontologists in Europe favored the idea that former continents and land bridges had existed in the past and were later lost to the seas.

In the United States, a growing number of geologists and physicists promoted the idea of permanency. This hypothesis held that the continents and oceans had always maintained their current locations, fluctuating only in terms of their elevations. This idea relied on a developing principle called *isostasy* that considered the density distribution of Earth's surface and subsurface. For permanency to work, alternative theories such as rafting were needed to address the issue of biological dispersal, but many unanswered questions remained. In this scientific milieu, meteorologist and geophysicist Alfred Wegener launched what would become an international debate to try to resolve these complex problems. Looking to find consensus between conflicting paleontological and geological data, he began championing a theory of continental drift.

The World Under Pressure

Increase temperature and ice melts; continue to raise the temperature to 212°F (100°C) and the water turns to a vapor or gas. Simple enough, but increase the pressure slightly and the molecules of H_2O whether they start as solid ice or as a vapor of steam begin to behave as a liquid. One of the fascinating aspects of physics is how various materials react under changes in temperature and pressure. Earth's atmosphere at sea level applies a force of about 14.7 pounds per square inch (1 kg/cm²). This measurement is known as one atmosphere of pressure and provides a baseline for comparison. To understand the physical properties occurring deep in the Earth, scientists needed to apply the equivalent of hundreds of thousands of atmospheres to their materials. In 1908 the best a physicist could produce was 6,500 atmospheres of pressure. The problem was leakage.

Percy Williams Bridgman (1882–1961), a graduate of Harvard in 1908, invented a collar for his pressure container that became tighter as the pressure increased. By constructing the container from a single piece of heat-treated alloy steel, he was consistently able to reach 12,000 atmospheres and on occasion as much as 20,000. By making the exterior of the

British geophysicist Augustus Love publishes *Some Problems of Geodynamics,* which includes descriptions of seismic waves called Love waves that travel horizontally across the surface like Rayleigh waves but cause ground motion perpendicular to the direction of the wave. Love waves have a slower velocity than P or S waves but are faster than Rayleigh waves, which propagate along the surface causing elliptical patterns of motion

German meteorologist Alfred Wegener first describes his theory of continental drift at a meeting of the Geological Association of Frankfurt

Swedish soil scientist Albert Atterberg classifies fine-grained soils based on their ability to retain moisture

Colima in western Mexico erupts January 18–24, destroying the summit and sending 0.14 cubic miles (0.6 km³) of tephra over the surrounding towns

MILESTONES

1911

1912

1913

The world's largest eruption of the 20th century, Novarupta on the Alaska Peninsula explodes on June 6, sending 6.7 cubic miles (28 km³) of tephra into the sky and draining magma from under Mount Katmai, 6 miles (10 km) to the east

Austrian physicist Victor Hess, in the course of a balloon flight, notes increasing radiation above 5,000 feet (1,500 m) and proposes an extraterrestrial source, later termed *cosmic rays*

British physicist Frederick Soddy discovers that chemically indistinguishable elements can have different atomic weights. Following the suggestion of a family friend, he coins the term *isotope,* from the Greek *topos* or place, since the different isotopes of an element occupy the same place in the periodic table

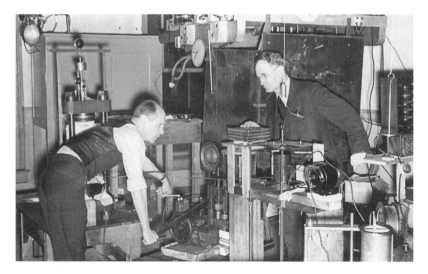

Percy Bridgman (right) conducting high pressure experiments in his lab in Cambridge, Massachusetts. Bridgman won the 1946 Nobel Prize in physics for discoveries he made with his invention of an apparatus to produce extremely high pressure. (AIP Emilio Segrè Visual Archives, Physics Today Collection)

container conical and building an external support, or collar, around the pressure vessel, he bumped his experiments up to 30,000 atmospheres. His investigations yielded important information about the nature of

German seismologist Beno Gutenberg (1889–1960) publishes his discovery of a discontinuity in the behavior of seismic waves at a depth of about 1,800 miles (2,900 km). This "Gutenberg discontinuity," as it becomes known, marks the Earth's core-mantle boundary

Sakura-jima in Kyushu, Japan, erupts on January 12 with explosions that last until May 1915 and litter the region with 0.14 cubic miles (0.57 km³) of tephra and 0.4 cubic miles (1.6 km³) of lava

January 13, an earthquake (recognized today as having had a magnitude 7.0) strikes Avezzano, Italy—30,000 people die

MILESTONES

1914

1915

Lassen Peak of the Lassen Volcanic Center in California erupts on May 30 with *phreatic explosions,* lava, pyroclastic flows, and mudflows or *lahars* that continue until June 29, 1917

Canadian geologist Reginald Aldworth Daly publishes his work *Igneous Rocks and Their Origin*

German paleontologist Von Ernst Freiherr Stromer von Reichenbach (1871–1950) publishes a book on fossil animals accounting for their geologic distribution with time. The same year he also identifies the only known fossil theropod of *Spinosaurus aegyptiacus* from carnivorous dinosaur bones he found in Egypt. Based on the legs, he reports that the animal was bigger than *T. rex*. In 2006 the bipedal, crocodile-mimic and an ancestor to birds is confirmed as having been a larger carnivore than *T. rex*

materials. Most solids are composed of densely packed molecules, and when they melt those molecules expand their distance between one and another. Molecules of H_2O are unusual; ice is less dense than water, hence why it floats. Adding pressure to ice compacts the molecules together, putting the solid in a liquid state or, in effect, lowering its melting point. Bridgman discovered that high enough pressures could reverse the process.

In his own words, Bridgman explained, "It is possible to show thermodynamically that if a substance expands when it melts, its melting temperature must rise with increasing pressure and, conversely, it falls. There are only three substances which belong to the later category in the ordinary range, water, bismuth, and gallium." Bridgman went on to say that "such a state of affairs apparently cannot continue indefinitely. Nature extricates itself from the dilemma by the 'liquidating' of such abnormal substances. Above a certain pressure the lattices in which these substances initially crystallize become unstable, and the lattice collapses into another lattice. The new lattice has a volume so much less than the former lattice that the solid phase is now more dense than the liquid, and from here on the melting curve rises as for other substances."

Structural collapse occurs at a pressure of about 2,000 atmospheres for water, 12,000 for gallium, and 25,000 for bismuth. This change in

Dutch-born physical chemist Peter Debye demonstrates that the powdered form of a substance can be used instead of its solid form for X-ray study of its crystal structure

Tungurahua in Ecuador erupts explosively on April 5 during a period of activity that lasts from 1916 to 1925

Following earlier work of J. J. Thomson, British physicist Francis Aston builds the first mass spectrograph, which allows him to separate ions or isotopes of the same element. The mass *spectrometer* later becomes an important tool in stable isotope geochemistry

MILESTONES

1916	1917	1918

American Association of Petroleum Geologists (AAPG) is founded

October 11, an earthquake (recognized today as having had a magnitude 7.5) strikes Mona Passage, Puerto Rico—116 people die, many from a resulting tsunami. The quake and tsunami cause an estimated $4 million in property damage

Paleontologists Gertrude L. Elles and Ethel M. R. Wood Shakespear complete their 18-year expedition throughout Great Britain identifying the distribution of fossil marine animals called graptolites. The Elles and Wood three-volume *Monograph of British Graptolites* is heralded as "indispensable" a century later. Elles and Wood are the only women to have won the Geological Society of London's Murchison Medal

crystal lattice structure explains why ice deep in a glacier is sometimes transparent and warmer than the ice at the surface. Bridgman continued to improve his pressure vessel. Replacing the steel piston with one made of a newly developed substance called carboloy, an alloy formed from cementing a fine powder of tungsten carbide with cobalt, he could expand his range to 50,000 atmospheres of pressure. By making the pressure vessel and the pistons of carboloy and emerging the whole thing in liquid, he was able to reach 100,000 atmospheres of pressure on material measuring a few cubic millimeters in volume. Ultimately, he would reach 400,000 atmospheres.

Bridgman found that such extreme pressures changed the crystal lattice structure for many types of materials, creating in a way new materials from the same molecules. This type of phase change is called *polymorphism*. "Under pressure, polymorphism is a very common phenomenon; the number of instances increases with increase in the experimental pressure range and with increasing sensitiveness in the methods for detecting small discontinuities of volume. In the range from room temperature to [392°F] 200°C and up to pressures of [700,000 pounds per square inch] 50,000 kg/cm², roughly one-third of the substances examined have proved to be polymorphic. In the much greater range of conditions encountered in the crust of the Earth, the presumption seems to be that no substance exists in the lattice with which we are familiar

| The National Research Council establishes the American Geophysical Union (AGU) as part of the National Academy of Sciences | British astrophysicist Arthur Eddington records data on the Sun's gravitational deflection of starlight during a solar eclipse and confirms Einstein's general theory of relativity | Yugoslavian meteorologist and mathematician Milutin Milankovitch shows that the amount of energy, or heat, Earth receives from the Sun varies with long-term changes in Earth's orbit. Decades later, scientists will correlate fluctuations in global temperature to his "Milankovitch cycles" |

English physicist Frederick Soddy suggests that isotopes can be used to determine geologic age

MILESTONES

1919

1920

American environmental engineer Abel Wolman and chemist Linn Enslow standardize the methods used to chlorinate municipal drinking-water supply

December 16, an earthquake (recognized today as having had a magnitude 7.8) strikes Gansu, China—200,000 people die, most from resulting landslides

Kelut's crater lake in Java, Indonesia, erupts on May 19 killing more than 5,000 people in a rush of lahars and pyroclastic flows that produce 0.05 cubic miles (0.19 km³) of tephra. Volcanic activity stops on May 20. Engineers dig a tunnel to drain the water from the lake and succeed in lowering the lake level more than 164 feet (50 m). Repair and additional construction follow the fatal eruptions of 1951, 1966, and 1990

Norwegian meteorologists Vilhelm and Jacob Bjerknes show the atmosphere is made up of air masses differing in temperature and marked by sharp boundaries called fronts

Maintaining Gravitational Equilibrium

In 1883 Eduard Suess (1831–1914) published *Das Antlitz der Erde* ("The Face of the Earth"). In the book, Suess based his explanation for the origin of mountains on the popular idea that Earth began as a molten mass and had been cooling ever since its formation. Many believed this cooling caused Earth to contract. What was originally seafloor would be uplifted to form mountains. The typical analogy was to compare mountain ranges with the wrinkles formed on the skin of a drying apple. Some geological evidence, such as marine fossils high above sea level, made sense because of this idea of thermal contraction. Suess provided geologists with a framework for applying the hypothesis to geological and paleontological problems. He suggested that fractured coastlines were the result of the partial collapse of former continents or land bridges. He surmised that two ancient continents, separated by a great sea, sank to form the Atlantic Ocean. The northern continent he called Atlantis and the southern continent he named Gondwanaland, after a region in India. Land bridges and former continents offered paleontologists an explanation as to why the same species of plants and animals existed on now distant continents. In Gondwana, India, abundant fossils of a fernlike plant were found that matched fossils in South America, Australia, and South Africa. Suess offered a way the hypothesis of a cooling and contracting Earth could account for widespread geographic abundance of similar fossils. A few problems, however, contradicted this continental contraction hypothesis: The mountains were higher than the math could raise them and the lower density of the continents kept them afloat.

At the start of the 20th century, geophysicists were finding favor with a principle called *isostasy*, which stated that Earth's crust responded to changes in equilibrium and provided an explanation for the gravitational anomalies found in geographic surveys as well as challenging the idea that continents had sunk to form ocean basins. The principle originated from careful examination of what seemed like a mistake. In 1847 the Surveyor General George Everest (1790–1866), was in charge of the Great Trigonometrical Survey of India to map the "jewel in the crown" for Britain. Using a quadrant (often a wooden instrument in the shape of a T) attached with a weighted string or *plumb line*, Everest could measure the angular height of the Sun at noon over the horizon or the North Star, Polaris, at night. Once the latitude of a position was known, his surveyors would map out a series of triangles along the meridian and measure the angles and the length of one side to triangulate for the distance between two locations. This method of triangulation allowed for accurate measurements of distance over varied terrain. (The first triangle did not need to be very large.) Such astronomical latitude measurements had shown during the 18th century that the ellipsoid shape of the Earth was flatter at the poles than at the equator. This knowledge about the curvature of the Earth gave Everest a reference formula to use to calculate geodetic latitude based on his triangulation measurements, but when he compared the astronomical observations with the calculated geodetic ones, his latitude for two stations Kaliana and Kalianpur on the Ganges Plain was off by 5 degrees and 23 minutes (323 nautical miles). He assumed the error was a result of his calculations, but John Pratt (1800–71) thought the Himalayan Mountains might be to blame.

Pratt was the Archdeacon of Calcutta at the time and a Cambridge-trained mathematician. The two stations, Kaliana and Kalianpur, were south of the Himalayan foothills. It seemed reasonable to think that the gravitational attraction of such a tremendous mountain range would deflect the plumb line north away from its normal position. The astronomical observations assume the plumb line hangs perpendicular to the horizon, but if the local plumb-line direction was off due to gravitational effects from the mountain range itself, then that could introduce error into the astronomical observations.

Such concerns were not new. In the 1700s, Sir Isaac Newton (1642–1727) and Jacques Cassini (1677–1756) debated whether the elliptical Earth was flatter at the poles as Newton believed or at the equator as Cassini thought. French surveyors—sent by King Louis XV to settle the matter, hopefully in Cassini's favor—traveled the world measuring meridians. In Quito, Ecuador, mathematician Pierre Bouguer (1698–1758) was concerned about the Andes influencing their plumb lines, but the local gravitational pull was insignificant in its influence on the astronomical observations, and the French teams conceded that Newton had won the debate. An Italian astronomer R. G. Boscovich (1711–87) deemed in 1755 that the surprising lack of gravitational influence from the Andes was perhaps the consequence of thermal expansion producing a void within the mountain, considering that perhaps the surface was a shell over a hollow center. Little else was discussed about the issue until Pratt brought it up again 100 years later.

Pratt decided to calculate the expected deviation, but calculating the mass of the Himalayas was no small feat. He relied on interviews of anyone who had traveled through the mountain passes to gain a sense of the topography. He broke this information down into sections and calculated the gravitational attraction for each section of the Himalayas, based on the premise that the interior density of the mountain range was consistent throughout. His calculations took up 75 pages, and when he summed up the results he found the Himalayan gravitational attraction should have deflected the plumb line almost 16 degrees—more than three times what Everest had observed. He published his results in the *Philosophical Transactions of the Royal Society* in 1855, noting that additional investigation into the problem was needed to explain why the Himalayas did not actually deflect the plumb line as much as their mass seemed to indicate they should.

One of the peer-reviewers of Pratt's report was Sir George Biddell Airy (1801–92), the Astronomer Royal of the United Kingdom. Airy published a three-page follow-up article suggesting the missing gravitational effect could be explained if Earth's crust, including the Himalayas, was composed of a low-density material that floated on a high-density substrate. Airy made the analogy to a raft of logs. "If we remark one log whose upper surface floats much higher than the upper surfaces of the others, we are certain that its lower surface lies deeper in the water than the lower surfaces of the others."

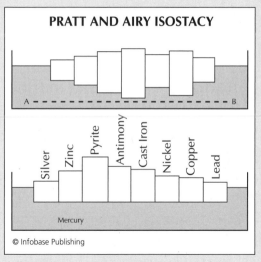

PRATT AND AIRY ISOSTACY

© Infobase Publishing

William Bowie in 1927 simulated both the Airy (above) and the Pratt (below) models of isostasy. Airy envisioned the crust as a low-density material of different thickness floating in a dense substrate. Pratt assumed the crust was made of material with different densities. The models yielded mathematically equivalent results in calculating for the lower than expected gravitational effect seen near mountains and the higher than expected gravity near the ocean. Alfred Wegener favored a combination of the different models. Wegener relied on a thin, dense ocean crust and less dense mountains with deep roots to support the theory of continental drift.

(continues)

(continued)

EXISTENCE OF MOBILE SUBSTRATE

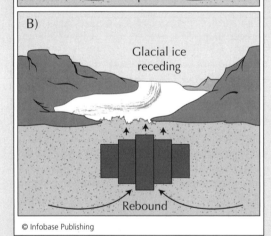

A)

Glacial ice advancing

Compression

B)

Glacial ice receding

Rebound

© Infobase Publishing

During the Pleistocene a tremendous glacier had covered much of Norway, Sweden, and Finland. Since the glacier retreated, the land, especially in the central region where the glacier was largest, had been experiencing uplift. Geologists recognized that processes such as glacier advance (A) above and sedimentation caused the crust to move down, and predicted the substrate flowed outward and away from the roots of the continent as a consequence. Erosion and glacial retreat (B) below allowed the crust to rise, and the substrate to flow back below the crust for support. Wegener argued that it was possible not only for the crust to move vertically and the substrate to flow horizontally around it but for the crust itself to move horizontally through the substrate.

The same analogy applies to icebergs at sea, where much of their ice remains hidden below the water's surface. Airy's model suggested that the Himalayas had mountainous roots of material creating a gravitational deficit of low-density material in the high-density matrix that would in effect balance out the above low-density crustal material seen "floating" on the surface. Such crustal equilibrium would explain the surprisingly little gravitational influence large mountains had on plumb lines.

Three years later, Pratt responded with his own explanation. He criticized Airy for proposing that Earth's matrix under the crust was denser than the crust itself. How would a floating crust in such a matrix sink to form ocean basins? Pratt, who still supported the prevailing contraction hypothesis, suggested that the underlying substrate varied in density. Pratt favored the idea of a crust with constant thickness, which bent or dipped to form mountains or ocean basins according to density differences in the substrate. He calculated that a less dense substrate compensated for the greater density of material seen in mountain ranges and that a high-density substrate fell beneath the oceans. At some great depth this matrix of various densities that supported the crust had to rest on its own level surface in order to make Pratt's calculations work. The geologic literature shows that Airy apparently ignored Pratt's arguments. When the subject came up during a lecture to the Cumberland Association for the Advancement of Literature and Science, Airy referred only to his own model, writes Oxford University geophysicist Anthony "Tony" B. Watts in *Isostasy and Flexure of the Lithosphere*. Watts reveals that Airy's abstract for the lecture was edited and published anonymously in *Nature* in 1878.

A few years later, the Reverend Osmond Fisher (1817–1914)—a fellow of the Geological Society of London, who also favored the contraction theory—investigated the mathematics involved in cooling and contracting Earth's surface. To his astonishment he found that temperature-driven contraction could not produce the change in elevation needed to form the mountains seen around the world; he calculated that contraction could achieve at most 900 feet (290 m) of lift. He published his findings in *Physics of the Earth's Crust*. It was in this book that Fisher made a vital distinction about crustal compensation theories in density: "The crust must be in a condition of approximate hydro-statical equilibrium, such that any considerable addition of load will cause any region to sink, or any considerable amount deduced off an area will cause it to rise." Such an observation had been seen in the case of Scandinavia, which had sunk under the weight of a glacier during the Pleistocene and rebounded when the glacier melted back during warmer times. Geologists acknowledged that continents could sink under heavy loads such as glaciers and that instead of forming new ocean basins the sunken continents would rebound back to a level of equilibrium when the glaciers melted.

In an 1882 review of Fisher's book, the American army officer and geologist Clarence Dutton (1841–1912) used the term *isostacy* in a footnote to describe the concept of crustal floata-tion. "In an unpublished paper I have used the terms isostatic and isostacy to express that condi-tion of the terrestrial surface which follow from the floatation of the crust upon a liquid or highly plastic substratum." Dutton would finally publish the paper he referred to in his footnote seven years later, changing the spelling of isostacy to isostasy with an "s".

Long before the discovery of radioactivity would provide a new heat budget and conflict with the cooling aspect of the contraction theory, the scientific community had shown that a new model for explaining the origin of mountains and ocean basins was needed. Dutton in particular had harsh words against the concept of contrac-tion. The hypothesis, he said, was "nothing but a delusion and a snare, and the quicker it is thrown aside and abandoned, the better it will be for geo-logical science." Even with such motivation for a new model, the scientific community would not be quick to embrace a change to the status quo. The new model would undergo equally harsh criticism as the old.

under laboratory conditions, unless perhaps the lattice is of a particularly simple type." This was an important conclusion because it provided for geophysicists with a new way of thinking about the material in Earth's interior.

Bridgman would go on to win the Nobel Prize in physics in 1946, and his comments here are taken from his lecture to fellow laureates at the time. Beginning in the early 1910s, Bridgman made it possible to explore the mysteries that occur below Earth's crust without leaving the laboratory. Prior to his acceptance speech for the Nobel Prize, Sigurd Curman, president of the Royal Academy of Sciences, addressed the laureate: "You, Mr. Bridgman, have succeeded in doing what was once considered impossible. By the use of new alloys and by other ingenious devices you have been able figuratively speaking, to bring into your laboratory parts of the interior of the Earth or of other places where no human being is able to exist, and you have been able there to examine the physical and chemical properties of a quantity of different sub-stances under the enormous pressures you have created. You have thus been able to reveal a number of strange phenomena in the behavior of matter under other circumstances than those which we consider to be normal. Your work has cast new light on nature's great and mysterious treasure-chamber."

Putting the Time into the Geologic Timescale

At 21 Arthur Holmes (1890–1965) was suffering from a serious bout of malaria in Mozambique when his college professor read Holmes's thesis paper to the Royal Society of London. The paper entitled "The Association of Lead with Uranium in Rock-Minerals, and its Application to the Measurement of Geological Time," launched Holmes's career as the leading expert in geochronology and geochemistry using uranium-lead analysis. Holmes was the first to take Boltwood's instructions on how to tell time and apply the method to build a geologic timescale. Holmes experimented with a rock known to be of Devonian age and found that the amount of lead in the rock samples indicated the radioactive element uranium had been decaying in the rock for 370 million years. He almost did not make it back from Mozambique to continue his research. He had been working for six months as a mineral prospector to make money to pay for his education when he got sick. His parents received a telegraph falsely announcing his death. He returned home as soon as he recovered, and although he had been unsuccessful in prospecting, the experience of being in the field, where he saw his first active volcanoes, filled his mind with ideas.

Holmes realized that it was not enough for geologists to know that younger rocks are typically deposited horizontally on top of the older ones. The age of the layers in comparison to each other was the first step in understanding the planet's history. Uranium-lead dating provided a clock that gave the age of the rocks in years. Holmes knew that with enough rock samples he could provide a geologic timescale that correlated the age of rocks with their different stratigraphic locations.

Cherry Lewis in her biography of Holmes reported that he had grown up reading the *Popular Lectures and Addresses* of Lord Kelvin and the work of Swiss geologist Edward Suess, thanks to a thought-provoking science teacher. As a child, Holmes had wondered about the specific date, 4004 B.C.E., given in the family Bible for the origin of

Early in his career, geologist Arthur Holmes (1890–1965) established the field of geochronology—defining the geologic timescale through radioactive dating of rocks in the different stratigraphic layers. Later in his career, he identified convection currents as a possible mechanism for continental drift.
(NOAA/Department of Commerce)

creation. "I was puzzled by the odd '4,' Holmes wrote. "Why not a nice round 4000 years? And why such a very recent date? And how could anyone know?"

When Holmes returned from Mozambique he wrote to the famous geologists of his time, including South African geologist Alexander du Toit (1878–1948) and Johannes Jakob Sederholm (1863–1934), who was known for his work on Finland's Precambrian rocks. Holmes asked them for rock samples he could use. He published his results in 1913 in his book *The Age of the Earth*. The dates he found for the Carboniferous, Devonian, and Silurian, without the use of a computer, mass spectrometer, or knowledge of isotopes, still fit within the age range known today for those periods. His oldest rock sample gave him an indication that Earth was at least 1.6 billion years old.

Still, the controversy reigned among scientists for another decade as the older generation of conservative geologists who doubted the accuracy of the radioactive dates continued to teach their students that Earth was at most 100 million years old. In 1913 Holmes wrote in the journal *Nature* that "the geologist who ten years ago was embarrassed by the shortness of the time allowed to him for the evolution of the Earth's crust is now still more embarrassed by the superabundance with which he is confronted." Much of their reluctance to support the older date stemmed from not understanding the physics of radioactive dating and its significance to the field of geology.

The discovery of isotopes was brand new the year Holmes published his book. The presence of lead isotopes confirmed Holmes's initial estimates and indicated that an even older age was possible. After presenting a talk at the Geological Society of London in 1915, Holmes was verbally attacked by a geologist who "insisted that all atoms of lead must have the same atomic weight." Holmes later lamented that, "isotopes did not seem to have been heard of in that audience . . . and I found myself in an exasperated minority of one." With the Nobel Prize in chemistry in 1921 going to Frederick Soddy, the radiochemist and physicist who discovered isotopes, geologists embraced the evidence that Earth was not just millions of years old, but billions of years old.

With help from his friend Bob Lawson, Holmes delved into the slow and tedious work of chemically isolating lead isotopes from igneous rock. He continued to refine

Frederick Soddy, who won the 1921 Nobel Prize in chemistry for his discovery of isotopes (E. F. Smith Collection, Rare Book & Manuscript Library, University of Pennsylvania)

his calculations and improve upon the geologic timescale throughout his life.

For a number of years after the publication of his book, Holmes was a proponent for the hypothesis that Earth had begun in a molten state and was cooling and contracting in response to the heat being conducted to the surface. He resurrected Kelvin's model with a twist: radioactivity only slowed Earth's cooling rate; contraction was still the primary cause for mountain building. Geophysicist Harold Jeffreys (1891–1989) joined him in advocating this model.

Continental Drift

German-born Alfred Wegener proposed a new model for Earth's geological formations on January 6, 1912, at a meeting of the Geological Association of Frankfurt. His "displacement hypothesis" introduced a mobile view of the continents. The Earth did not need to shrink to form mountains. The continents, he said, had once been connected and had since split apart and drifted to their current positions. He reasoned that the mountains seen along coastlines had been built up along the leading edge of a continent on the move. Mountains further inland, such as the Himalayas, he reasoned, marked the boundary where continents had previously smashed together. The displacement hypothesis regarded most islands as remnants left behind in a continent's wake.

His talk, entitled "Die Herausbildung der Grossformen der Erdrinde (Kontinente und Ozeane) auf geophysikalischer Grundlage" "(The geophysical basis of the evolution of the large-scale features of the Earth's crust [continent and ocean])" marked a year of research into an idea he had not immediately embraced when he first considered it. He was cautious to propose an idea that had already been rejected by others. Osmond Fisher and Alexander von Humboldt (1769–1837) had questioned the jigsaw puzzle-like fit between Africa and South America and proposed means of previous attachment. Like most scientists, Wegener thought it improbable that the continents had previously been together. Frank Taylor (1860–1938) had submitted an idea of continental motion or "drift" to American geoscientists in 1910—but so ingrained was the idea of permanency, a fixed view of the planet's continents and oceans, that while vertical motion could be explained with the principle of isostasy, horizontal motion seemed impossible. Taylor's theory was mostly ignored.

In the meantime, Wegener was uncomfortable with Suess's idea of sinking land bridges as an explanation for species distribution. If the continents did not move laterally but had been connected via landforms that had since sunk into the ocean, then the species crossing the land bridges must have experienced a wide range of climatic conditions during their migration around the globe. Why then, the meteorologist wondered,

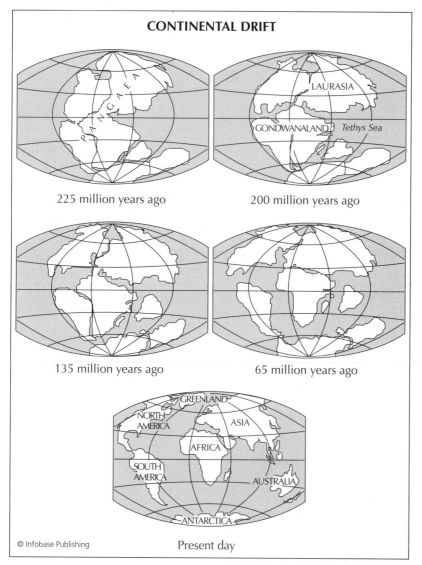

CONTINENTAL DRIFT

225 million years ago

200 million years ago

135 million years ago

65 million years ago

Present day

© Infobase Publishing

Laurasia included what would become North America, Europe, and Asia; Gondwanaland included what would become South America, Africa, Antarctica, Australia, and India. These in turn drifted to modern-day positions, with India colliding with Asia and forming the Himalayas. (Adapted from U.S. Geological Survey)

would some of these species, especially climatically sensitive plants, stop their migration once they crossed a land bridge? What prevented them from being found further inland, instead of just along the coasts of these previously connected continents?

When Wegener came across paleontological evidence for a former land bridge between Africa and Brazil he reexamined the idea of drift. It seemed reasonable now to question whether the two landmasses had once laid side-by-side or if they were indeed linked by a now-missing, long-distance, land bridge. He was careful to find evidence in support of

Scientist of the Decade: Charles Doolittle Walcott (1850–1927)

Charles Doolittle Walcott's discoveries of soft-bodied fossils in the Rocky Mountains of Canada showed just how diverse the earliest history of life was on Earth. In 1928 the *Geological Magazine,* edited by Henry Woodward, recognized Walcott's collection of Cambrian fossils from the Burgess Shale as "the finest and largest series of Middle Cambrian fossils yet discovered, and the finest invertebrate fossils yet found in any formation, including—besides brachiopods and trilobites—merostomes, holothurians, medusae, annelids, brachiopods, malacostracans, etc. Many of the forms are not yet described and illustrated."

Walcott categorized these strange creatures from another time as ancestors of modern animals. "My own investigations have been mainly in the Cambrian and pre-Cambrian strata, and have involved new and somewhat startling discoveries that helped to show how very much earlier life was developed on our planet than we had previously supposed," Walcott wrote in a 1915 report "Evidences of Primitive Life." The animals found in the Burgess Shale represented the earliest known fossil arthropods, the most prolific animal on Earth today. Walcott clearly recognized body plans similar to those of the known four major types of arthropods: ancient and now extinct trilobites, shrimp-like crustaceans, spider- and scorpion-like chelicerae, and insect-like uniramians. For the 20 or 30 arthropods he did not recognize—those with such strange body plans that they fell outside anything ever seen in nature or elsewhere in the fossil record—he only briefly described, named, and left to future generations to determine the place of these animals in history.

Charles Schuchert in an obituary for Walcott in 1928 wrote about how Walcott first found the important Burgess Shale:

Paleontologist Charles Doolittle Walcott at the site now known as the Burgess Shale, Walcott Quarry (The Smithsonian Institution)

Burgess Shale trilobites (Yoho National Park, British Columbia, Canada)

One of the most striking of Walcott's faunal discoveries came at the end of the field season of 1909, when Mrs. Walcott's horse slid in going down the trail and turned up a slab that at once attracted her husband's attention. Here was a great treasure—wholly strange Crustacea of Middle Cambrian time—but where in the mountain was the mother rock from which the slab had come? Snow was even then falling, and the solving of the riddle had to be left to another season, but next year the Walcotts were back again on Mount Wapta, and eventually the slab was traced to a layer of shale—later called the Burgess shale—3,000 feet [900 m] above the town of Field, British Columbia, and 8,000 feet [2,400 m] above the sea. A quarry operated in this shale from 1910 to 1913 and again in 1917 has brought to light what is probably the most interesting and strangest of all invertebrate assemblages. The many thousands of specimens taken from these diggings include algae, sponges with spicules, an array of annelids showing the ventral anatomy, brachiopods, and, most numerous of all, phyllocarids and trilobites with appendages and internal structures. Walcott has described 70 genera and 130 species of Burgess forms, but a vast mine of knowledge still lies buried in these most difficult of fossils.

Paleontologist Stephen Jay Gould (1941–2002) in the last quarter of the 20th century followed in Walcott's footsteps as an advocate for natural history and evolution. (Columbia University)

Schuchert's story passed on to generations of paleontologists. In 1989, however, Stephen Jay Gould in his book *Wonderful Life* disputed Schuchert's story as an exaggeration. Reading Walcott's journal entries of his time on Mount Wapta, Gould was convinced Walcott found the Burgess Shale in 1909 but only began quarrying the site in 1910:

The canonical tale is more romantic and inspiring, but the plain factuality of the diary makes more sense. The slope is simple and steep, with strata well exposed. Tracing an errant block to its source should not have been a major problem, for Walcott was more than a good geologist—he was a great geologist. He should have located the main beds right away, in 1909, in the week after he first discovered the soft-bodied fossils. He did not have an opportunity to quarry in 1909—the only constraint imposed by limits of time—but he found many fine fossils, and probably the main beds themselves. In 1910, he knew just where to go, and he set up shop in the right place as soon as the snow melted.

In the 1911 *National Geographic* article "A Geologist's Paradise," Walcott writes "Nature has a habit of placing some of her most attractive treasures in places where the average man hesitates to look for them." Walcott ultimately found the Burgess Shale the same way he had found other fascinating geological discoveries earlier in

(continues)

(continued)

his life, by going and searching in regions where no one else had looked. As a young boy, Walcott started collecting bird's eggs, fossils, minerals, and other specimens of natural history. He did not incorporate his hobby into a career until much later in life. He attended public schools in Utica, New York, from the age of eight to the age of 18. When he was 20, he moved to Trenton Falls, New York, and took a job as a farmhand. A year later he married the farmer's daughter, Lura Ann Rust. Their farm happened to have an extensive number of fossil trilobites nearby. Walcott's first foray into the professional world of paleontology occurred in 1873 when he sold the trilobites that he and his father-in-law had quarried to Switzerland-born paleontologist Louis Agassiz (1807–73). Agassiz, famous for his work on fossil fishes, was then a professor at Harvard University and looking to add to his collection of specimens for his Museum of Comparative Zoology. On their first meeting, Walcott discussed the appendages and evidence of soft tissue he had noticed in some of the trilobites. Impressed with this young fossil collector's eye for inquiry, Agassiz urged Walcott to pursue a career in paleontology.

Charles Doolittle Walcott (above) succeeded John Wesley Powell as director of the U.S. Geological Survey, serving as director from 1894 to 1907. (U.S. Geological Survey)

He published his first scientific papers in 1875 describing two new species of trilobites: *Hypodicranotus striatulus* and *Sphaerocoryphe robusta*. In January 1876 Lura died. Ten months later, Walcott started working as the assistant to the state geologist of New York, James Hall. In 1879 he moved to Washington, D.C., and began his career with the U.S. Geological Survey working as an assistant to geologist and soldier Clarence Edward Dutton. That summer Walcott worked with Dutton on an expedition to the Grand Canyon and the Eureka district in Nevada. Walcott would go on to take charge of the Survey's invertebrate Paleozoic paleontology division.

At 44, Walcott began serving as head of the U.S. Geological Survey. Expectations for the director were high following the leadership of one-armed American explorer and Civil War hero John Wesley Powell (1834–1902), who led from 1881 to 1894 as the Survey's second director since its establishment as a government organization in 1879. The last quarter of the 19th century was a contentious time in the geosciences. Besides debating over how Earth originally formed, its thermal tendencies, and structural topography—identifying geologic periods in Earth's history brought out a variety of opinions regarding conventional standards or rules on how rock layers should be named. Powell also faced congressional pressure to quickly identify areas where irrigation would appease cattle ranchers and farmers who were now competing over water resources in arid regions of newly formed states. From 1877 to 1896, the flag of the United States of America went from having 38 stars to having 45 with the inclusion of Colorado, North and South Dakota, Montana, Washington, Idaho, Wyoming, and Utah. The westward expansion of "public domain" allowed land claims on property without regard to whether the land would be sustainable for crops and cattle through the summer. During the drought of 1886 many farms and ranches became dust bowls—a harbinger of summers to come in the 1930s. Powell had plenty of experienced surveyors to map the topography of the new states, and in 1888, teams of geologists searched for depressions in the flat terrain where catchment basins could be built to collect water for irrigation from not-too-distant rivers and streams. Unfortunately, the Survey at the time did not have many geologists trained in hydrology to measure stream flow or the engineers needed to build catchment basins. A year later, engineer Frederick Haynes Newell, 26, took charge of training a team of 14 geologists about the science of measuring stream flow. By the spring of 1890, however, Congress still did not know which lands should be held aside from the public domain for irrigation use, and so the Acting Attorney General prudently deemed them all off-limits. The ban held for only a few months before Congress bowed to pressure from developers in the west to repeal the ban. The Irrigation Survey was left high and dry without funding to continue. Powell, who in 1878 had identified areas with less than 20 inches of rain a year as the country's arid regions, had lost the favor of the politicians in charge of the Survey's cash flow. Water resources were no longer seen as important to protect as mining resources in the same arid regions. Congress in 1892 also cut funding for geological surveys as well as studies in paleontology, geochemistry, and geophysics. Powell was left to organize the Survey toward charting and developing the nation's mineral resources. He did this halfheartedly and would leave for months at a time to pursue other adventures. Walcott took over as acting director on an emergency basis during these absences.

Twenty years before Mark Twain wrote *Tom Sawyer*, Powell, at the age of 22, obtained a strong desire for studying natural history while surveying the Mississippi River in a rowboat. After exploring the Ohio and Illinois rivers he looked for mollusks as a volunteer with the Illinois State Natural History Society in 1858. Powell saw the interdisciplinary connections between geology, botany, and zoology and vowed to devote his life to teaching and exploring the science of the Earth. His lectures at public schools in southern states convinced him that the disagreements between the North and the South would not be settled peacefully. At the start of the Civil War he immersed himself in studies on military tactics and engineering and quickly earned the rank of second lieutenant. His wife, Emma Dean, attended him on the battlefield so he could continue to fight even after losing his right arm during an attack at Pittsburg Landing, Tennessee. Even in the thick of war, however, Powell continued his examination of natural history and was known for pocketing fossils while digging a trench. Powell returned to teaching geology after the war and used his newly won political influence to secure funding for geological expeditions. In 1868 he headed west to Denver with his wife and brother and several volunteers to explore the Front Range. He returned again in 1869 and by 1973 had explored much of the southwestern United States, navigating the Colorado River and emerging at the mouth of Grand Canyon.

When Congress cut funding for irrigation studies, Powell continued his southwest explorations through his unpaid position as director of the Smithsonian Institution's Bureau of Ethnology, which he established to investigate North American archaeology. Powell had befriended the Pai Utes, the Moki, and other native tribes during his journey along the Colorado River. He shared

(continues)

(continued)

what he learned of their language and cultural with the museum. In 1893 the new Secretary of Interior—head of the U.S. Department of Interior, which oversees the USGS and other agencies—appointed Walcott as Geologist-in-Charge of geology and paleontology. A year later the same Secretary of Interior, M. Hoke Smith, requested to cut Powell's salary as director of the USGS, a move that succeeded in its intention of publicly forcing him to resign from the position. President Grover Cleveland then accepted Smith's recommendation that Walcott lead the USGS.

Walcott lead the Survey into the 20th century working as the director from 1894 to 1907. His administrative skills brought order to the divergent studies and guaranteed that those in charge of the various geologic and topographic surveys had appropriate geological training. He relied on geology as a fundamental element to other investigations in paleontology, hydrology, and mineralogy. Walcott judiciously categorized the importance of geologic exploration as a means for improving the American economy and welfare. In 1895 and again in 1898 the USGS published updated maps of Alaska detailing the gold and coal regions being discovered there during the Klondike Gold Rush. Survey geologist Samuel F. Emmons charted the headwaters in Alaska leading to the Yukon River Valley and Klondike Region of Canada. His maps, first published in 1890, showed where gold-bearing rocks were reachable by foot or by steamship. Walcott also reinstated mining geologist George Becker to conduct experimental geophysical studies for gold in the southern Appalachians.

Becker hired American physicist Arthur L. Day who was working in Berlin at the time to join chemist E. T. Allen in conducting experiments at the Survey's new chemistry and physics lab in Washington, D.C. The two put the most commonly found minerals from igneous rocks, plagioclase, and feldspars under extreme temperatures to see when they would melt.

The Survey's emphasis on gold and minerals helped advance Walcott's political standing. He soon regained funding for irrigation studies, allowing Frederick Newell and his team to continue to install stream gauges on rivers across the country. As Powell had done, Walcott also included Newell's progress reports on stream measurements in his annual report to the Secretary of the Interior. In 1902 Nevada Representative Francis G. Newlands convinced Congress to pass a federal law called the Newlands Reclamation Act to fund irrigation in western states. Secretary of Interior Ethan Allen Hitchcock, who served under Presidents William McKinley and Theodore Roosevelt from 1899 to 1907, authorized the USGS to lead the program. In January 1907 the Smithsonian Institution appointed Walcott as Secretary. He resigned as director of the Survey in April. In March, James Rudolph Garfield took over as Secretary of the Interior and established a new Bureau of Reclamation, independent of the USGS. Newell took charge as director of the new bureau, damming rivers to water the west.

While serving as director of the USGS, Walcott was very active in the politics of Washington, D.C., working to advance the standing of geologists and promote private funding for explorations. He worked with Powell and others to help

drift from paleontological and climatic data before presenting it to the scientific community.

Like Fisher, Wegener believed that the crust followed Archimedes' principle, which states that the weight of a floating object is equal to the volume of the liquid it displaces. With this in mind Wegener set forth to show that drifting continents worked with the theory of isostasy and

establish the Geological Society of Washington in 1893. In 1898 Walcott served as president of the Cosmos Club, which Powell and colleagues had established two decades earlier as a social club for Washington's elite intellectuals. Walcott worked to help establish the Washington Academy of Sciences in 1899 and two years later the Carnegie Institution of Washington. He would escape the city's summer heat traveling to different regions of North America in search of fossils. When the Smithsonian Institution appointed Walcott as Secretary on January 31, 1907, Walcott saw the opportunity to once again focus his time on fieldwork and fossils. That summer he traveled to Mount Stephen, Castle Mountains, Lake Louise, and Mount Bosworth in British Columbia, Canada. In 1908 he traveled to Montana, Alberta, and returned again to British Columbia. In 1909 the Cambrian fossils near Burgess Pass above Field, British Columbia, would draw his attention and become the distinguishing discovery of his career. As Gould wrote:

> Walcott established his quarry in the phyllopod beds of the Burgess Shale and worked with hammers, chisels, long iron bars, and small explosives charges for a month or more in each year from 1910 to 1913. In 1917, at age 67, he returned for a final fifty days of collecting. In all he brought some 80 thousand specimens back to Washington, D.C., where they still reside, the jewel of our nation's largest collection of fossils, in the National Museum of Natural History at the Smithsonian Institution.

Walcott married his second wife, Helena Breese Stevens, in 1888. They raised four children together before she died in 1911 during a train crash in Connecticut. In 1914 he married artist and naturalist Mary Morris Vaux. After Walcott's death in 1927, Vaux established a trust fund through the National Academies of Science to honor paleontologists early in their careers, between the ages of 21 and 48, who have published distinguishing research or made significant discoveries through explorations into the history of the Precambrian world. The Charles Doolittle Walcott Medal is awarded every five years.

After serving as director of the U.S. Geological Survey, Charles Doolittle Walcott was elected the fourth Secretary of the Smithsonian Institution and served a 20-year term from 1907 to 1927. (Smithsonian Institution Archives)

provided a better explanation to the problems facing Earth scientists. For example, continental drift, unlike the theory of thermal contraction, did not conflict with the discovery of radioactivity.

Wegener illustrated the breakup of a supercontinent he called Pangaea. The southern part of this continent—which, in a nod to Suess, he called Gondwanaland—broke apart to form India and today's continents in the

Southern Hemisphere. India it seemed had ultimately traveled north around eastern Africa and crashed into southern Asia. This explained why the same species of lemurs could be found in Madagascar and India, but not in Africa. Madagascar, had in fact detached from India and was left to float along the eastern African shore like a water-skier that has let go of her ski line.

Continental drift allowed Wegener to provide an explanation for not only the puzzle-like fit for the continents but also for the similar geologic features such as folds found in European and North American mountain belts. In this way, Wegener provided a new explanation for the problems contraction had originally solved as well as solve problems it had not. When it came to the two different types of surface elevation—raised continents and lower ocean basins—Wegener suggested that once continents reached their isostatic equilibrium they remained in equilibrium as they moved horizontally across the ocean.

After giving his presentation, he turned his attention back to meteorology. He taught the field at the Physical Institute in Marburg and served as the head of the Meteorological Department for the German Naval Observatory, Deutsche Seewarte. Later in 1912 through 1913, he made an expedition across the ice cap of Greenland to set up weather stations. Upon his return, Wegener again tackled the issues regarding continental drift. He researched the geological and paleontological evidence and organized a carefully detailed theory of drift that aimed to resolve the scientific conflicts of his time. In 1915 he advanced his ideas in the first edition of his book *Entstehung der Kontinente und Ozeane* (*Origin of Continents and Oceans*). Wegener would update the book three more times with revised editions coming out in 1920, 1922, and 1929, but not until 1922 was an English translation of the book available.

Ultimately drift had one testable hypothesis that if proven would guarantee the theory's place in geology (and history) books: perhaps the continents were still drifting. "If continental displacement was operative for so long a time, it is probable that the process is still continuing, and it is just a question of whether the rate of movement is enough to be revealed by our astronomical measurements in a reasonable period of time," Wegener wrote. He would later work to prove this hypothesis, but technology had not yet advanced to the point of precisely measuring the rate of continental drift. The debate over Earth's tectonics would rise strongly among geologists in the coming decades, then draw to a stalemate before rising again in the 1950s when a new generation of Earth scientists turned to the ocean to help solve geologic unknowns.

Further Reading

Anderson, Mary P. "The Wisconsin Roots of Ground Water Hydrology."
    Ground Water 43, no. 1 (2005): 142–145. This historical note on
    Wisconsin groundwater studies describes the contributions of Thomas

Crowder Chamberlin, Franklin H. King, and Charles Sumner Slichter during the later 19th century. Available as a PDF online. URL: http://www.uwex.edu/wgnhs/pdfs/miscpdf/wiscgw.pdf. Accessed February 28, 2007.

Chamberlin, Thomas C. *Introductory Geology.* New York: H. Holt and company, 1914. A textbook on geology for undergraduates.

Daly, Reginald Aldworth. *Igneous Rocks and Their Origin.* New York: McGraw-Hill Book Company, Inc., 1914. A book on the magmatic cooling processes and formation of igneous rocks.

Dellenbaugh, Frederick S. *The Romance of the Colorado River.* New York: G.P. Putnam's Sons, 1903. The epilogue for this book discussing the career of John Wesley Powell is available online. URL: http://www.nps.gov/archive/grca/photos/powell/pages/career.htm. Accessed February 28, 2007.

Elles, Gertrude L., and Wood, Ethel M. R. (Mrs. Shakespear). *A Monograph of British Graptolites.* London: Paleontographical Society of London, 1901–18. This three-volume illustrated work identified the graptolite bearing strata throughout Great Britain.

———. *The Lower Ordovician Graptolite Faunas With Special Reference to the Skiddaw Slates: Summary of Progress of the Geological Society for 1932, Part 2.* London: His Majesty's Stationary Office London, 1933. This work by Gertrude Elles provides further details on the distribution of graptolite fossils.

———. "The Stratigraphy and Faunal Succession in the Ordovician Rocks of the Builthllandrinod inlier, Radnorshire." *Geol. Soc. London Quart. Journ.* 95 (1939): 397. This report further details the stratigraphic distribution of graptolite fossils.

Fisher, Osmond. *Physics of the Earth's Crust.* London: Macmillan and Co., 1881. Fisher presents the theory of crustal equilibrium, later termed *isostasy.*

Gould, Stephen Jay. *Wonderful Life: The Burgess Shale and the Nature of History.* New York: W.W. Norton & Company, 1989. Gould provides a detailed analysis of the discovery of the Burgess Shale and of its importance to paleontology.

Holmes, Arthur. "The Association of Lead with Uranium in Rock-Minerals, and its Application to the Measurement of Geological Time." *Proceedings of the Royal Society of London. Series A, Containing Papers of a Mathematical and Physical Character* 85, no. 578 (June 9, 1911): 248–256. Professor R. J. Strutt read Holmes's thesis to the Society on April 6, 1911, while Holmes was in Mozambique.

———. *The Age of the Earth.* London and New York: Harper and Brothers, 1913. Holmes presents the first radio-dated geological timescale.

———. "Radium and the Evolution of Earth's Crust." *Nature* 91 (1913): 398. Holmes argues that life has had a superabundant amount of time to evolve on Earth.

———. When Will Lassen Peak Again Erupt? *The Scientific Monthly* 40, no. 1 (January 1935): 21–32. In this article, Holmes predicts the next eruption will occur in 1980 based on the work of Japanese geologist Fusakichi Omori and Lassen's 1915 eruption. Although the volcano that erupted that year was not Lassen, Holmes had made the comment in this article that "It adds to the fascination of the region not to know exactly where to look for the next outburst of activity." Based on Omori's hypothesis that volcanic periodicity for the Pacific region happens in 65- and 130-year intervals, the next eruption should strike sometime around 2045.

Jeffreys, Harold *The Earth: Its Origin, History and Physical Constitution.* Cambridge, England: University Press, 1924. A prominent British geophysicist, Jeffreys raises questions over the mechanism for drift and supports the theory of permanency.

Joly, John. *Radioactivity and the Surface History of the Earth; Being the Halley Lecture, Delivered on 28 May, 1924.* Oxford: The Clarendon Press, 1924. Joly suggests a new solution to the problem of a mechanism for continental drift.

Lewis, Cherry L. E. *The Dating Game: One Man's Search for the Age of the Earth.* New York: Cambridge University Press, 2000. This biography of Arthur Holmes details how this geochemist began determining the age of Earth's rocks and minerals.

———. and Knell, S. (editors). *The Age of the Earth: from 4004 B.C. to A.D. 2002.* London: Geological Society of London, special publications 190, 2001. This book provides a historical perspective of geologic time from philosophers in the 17th century to geochronologists in the 20th century.

———. "Arthur Holmes: An Ingenious Geoscientist." *GSA Today* (March 2002): 16–17. Lewis provides a brief biography of Holmes for the Geological Society of America's Rock Stars anthology.

Nothdurft, William E. *The Lost Dinosaurs of Egypt.* New York: Random House, 2002. This book—written with paleontologists Josh Smith, Matt Lamanna, Ken Lacovara, Jason Poole, and Jen Smith—chronicles Ernst Stromer's original expedition in Egypt and the graduate students' adventures retracing the footsteps of his discovery of *Spinosaurus* and other fossils.

Oreskes, Naomi. *The Rejection of Continental Drift: Theory and Method in American Earth Science.* New York and Oxford: Oxford University Press, 1999. This book chronicles the negative reaction to Wegener's theory in early 20th-century America.

PBS. "Explore the Challenges" This Web site challenges viewers to measure latitude and longitude. Available online. URL: http://www.pbs.org/weta/roughscience/series1/challenges/latlong/ Accessed February 28, 2007.

Pisani, Donald J. "Conflict over Conservation: The Reclamation Service and the Tahoe Contract." *The Western Historical Quarterly* 10, no. 2 (April 1979): 167–190. This historical report discusses the U.S. government's efforts to reclaim desert lands in Nevada for farming through irrigation from the waters in Lake Tahoe.

Pratt, John. "On the Attraction of the Himalaya Mountains, and of the Elevated Regions Beyond Them, Upon the Plumb-Line in India." *Philosophical Transactions of the Royal Society* 145 (1855): 53–100.

Reisner, Marc. *Cadillac Desert: The American West and Its Disappearing Water.* New York: Penguin Books, 1993. This book addresses the long-term effects of policies established during the early 20th century in the rush to develop the American West.

Schuchert, Charles. "Charles Doolittle Walcott (1850–1927)" *Proceedings of the American Academy of Arts and Sciences* 62 no. 9 (1928): 276–285.

Shindler, Karolyn. *Discovering Dorothea: The Life of the Pioneering Fossil-Hunter Dorothea Bate.* HarperCollins Publishers Limited, 2006. This book documents the early work of explorer and paleontologist Dorothea Bates who traveled around the world exploring ancient history and in the later half of the century worked closely with anthropologist Mary Leakey.

Smithsonian Institution Archives. "Charles D. Walcott Collection." This Web site provides biographical information and details the contents of archival material. Available online. URL: http://siarchives.si.edu/findingaids/faru7004.htm. Accessed February 28, 2007.

Stromer von Reichenbach, Ernst, Freiherr, von. *Lehrbuch der Paläozoologie* (Textbook on paleontology). Leipzig, Berlin: B. G. Teubner, 1909–12. This textbook provided one of the first examinations of fossil distribution over geologic time.

Suess, Eduard. *The Face of the Earth (Das Antlitz der Erde).* Translated by Hertha B. C. Sollas. Oxford: Clarendon Press, 1904–24. This five-volume work reports on the varied topography and physical geography of the planet.

Taylor, Frank Bursley. "Bearing of the Tertiary Mountain Belt on the Origin of the Earth's Plan." *Bulletin of the Geologic Society of America* 21, no. 2 (1910): 179–226. The geologic community took little notice of this paper when Taylor first proposed continental collision for the origin of mountains.

U.S. Geological Survey. "Our History." This Web site provides photos of the directors of the USGS and links to relevant periods in the Survey's history. Available online. URL: http://www.usgs.gov/aboutusgs/who_we_are/directors.asp. Accessed February 28, 2007.

———. "3D Photography of the Powell Survey (1870–1879) of Colorado River Canyon Country." A 3D tour of stereoscopic images John Wesley Powell took on his second expedition through the canyons of the American southwest. Available online; 3D viewing glasses needed. URL: http://3dparks.wr.usgs.gov/3Dcanyons/ Accessed February 28, 2007.

———. "The Gold and Coal Fields of Alaska." Maps from the explorations of S. F. Emmons during the 1890s are available online. URL: http://www.davidrumsey.com/maps5795.html. Accessed February 28, 2007.

Walcott, Charles D. "Description of a New Species of Trilobite." *Cincinnati Quarterly Journal of Science* 2 (1875): 273. In this report, Walcott describes the differences that set his discovery apart from other trilobite species.

———. "New Species of Trilobite from the Trenton Limestone at Trenton Falls, New York." *Cincinnati Quarterly Journal of Science* 2 (1875): 347–349. Walcott establishes his credentials as a paleontologist.

———. "Abrupt appearance of the Cambrian fauna on the North American continent." *Smithsonian Miscellaneous Collections* 57, no. 1 (1910): 145–228. This report provides a discussion on the locality of the Burgess Shale fossils.

———. "A Geologist's Paradise." *National Geographic* (June 1911). A three-year Smithsonian Institution expedition studying the rock formations of the Rocky Mountains and Canadian Rockies has found Cambrian rocks, containing superb fossils of prehistoric marine invertebrate life. Also included are panoramic photographs of the mountain range.

———. "Evidences of Primitive Life." *Smithsonian Report for 1915*, (1916): 235–255. Walcott reports on the Burgess Shale fossils found in Canada.

———. *Eminent Living Geologists.* London: Dulau and company, 1919. This book celebrates the work of geologists during the early 20th century.

Watts, A. B. *Isostasy and Flexure of the Lithosphere.* Cambridge: Cambridge University Press, 2001. Part of chapter one, "The Development of the Concept of Isostasy," is available as a PDF online. URL: http://www.earth.ox.ac.uk/~tony/watts/downloads/chap1_part.pdf. Accessed April 24, 2006.

Yochelson, Ellis L. "Discovery, Collection, and Description of the Middle Cambrian Burgess Shale Biota by Charles Doolittle Walcott." *Proceedings of the American Philosophical Society*, 140, no. 4 (December 1996): 469–545. This report details Walcott's legacy to paleontology.

Yoder, Hatten S., Jr. *Centennial History of the Carnegie Institution of Washington Volume III The Geophysical Laboratory.* New York: Cambridge University Press, 2005. "This volume documents the contributions of the Carnegie Institution's Geophysical laboratory over a century of research dedicated to learning about the Earth. Areas of interest range from studying mineral formation beneath the surface to searching for the origins of life, and exploring space to study the chemical evolution of the interstellar medium. Field work has taken researchers from active volcanoes to ocean floors in the course of global mapping expeditions." Sections of this book are available online. URL: http://books.google.com.

1921–1930:
Evolution and Opposition

3

Introduction

Anthropologist Raymond Dart names a fossil hominid from Africa as a new genus and species. Other *Australopithecus* fossils will prove vital in the search for human ancestry, but generations of American students will not learn of such discoveries. The 1920s saw the launch of a fundamentalist political movement that eschewed biological evolution and brought about a ban on the subject in Tennessee schools.

The result was an inconclusive "trial of the century" that set the stage for debates that have continued into the 21st century over the standards of science education in America. Despite the fame of the "Scopes Monkey Trial," not until the 1960s did the U.S. Supreme Court finally determine that bans against teaching evolution were unconstitutional. At that time fundamentalists argued for teaching "Creationism science" in the classrooms.

Today's lexicon has become an overlapping mix of "Young Earth Creationists," "Old Earth Creationists," and "Intelligent Design" advocates, but the battle is inherently the same as that which was fought in the 1920s in a sweltering July courtroom in a small town in Tennessee. Prosecutors during the trial accused Darwinists and evolutionists of being atheists, those who do not believe in God. The defense tried to make the case that evolution did not contradict Christianity. They put on the witness stand religious scholars and Christian scientists who believed in their faith and in the science of evolution. The judge, a Christian fundamentalist, threw out their testimonies, but the majority of religious scholars and scientists even today still see no conflict between the science of evolution and religion. "Theistic evolutionists" believe God created the universe and that evolution in this universe is a fact of life.

The opposition to evolution comes from fundamentalists. "Young Earthers" continue to believe in a literal interpretation of the Bible, with many adhering to an 18th-century establishment that the first day of creation in the story of Genesis happened on Sunday, October 23, 4004

B.C.E., as determined by Bishop James Ussher (1581–1656). "Old Earth" Creationists also believe that God created humans in their present form, but agree with the geologic evidence for deep time and interpret "days" in the Bible to mean extensive periods of time longer than 24 hours. Both groups are primarily considered antievolutionists.

The modern "Intelligent Design" movement teaches that life is too complex to have evolved due to random or naturally selected genetic mutations passed along to offspring over successive generations. The philosophy proposes that biological organisms are creations of an unknown "intelligent designer," perhaps God or possibly aliens from another planet. Toward the later part of the 20th century, a creationist movement to "teach the controversy" rose to include lectures, qualifying statements, and disclaimers against evolution in schools, and, this time, teach as an alternative to evolution the idea of "Intelligent Design." Earth scientists tend to believe that "Intelligent Design" is primarily a philosophical viewpoint, not a scientific one. The seeds of some of these debates date to before the 1920s, but it was in the 1920s that they blossomed into a national fervor that has never truly abated.

One of the decade's other great Earth sciences contributions also had "evolutionary" roots, albeit only tangentially. During his voyage on the

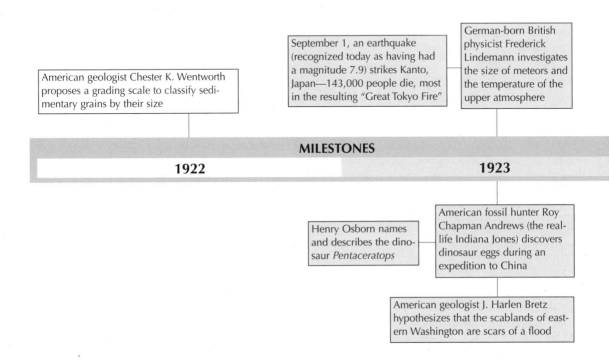

American geologist Chester K. Wentworth proposes a grading scale to classify sedimentary grains by their size

September 1, an earthquake (recognized today as having had a magnitude 7.9) strikes Kanto, Japan—143,000 people die, most in the resulting "Great Tokyo Fire"

German-born British physicist Frederick Lindemann investigates the size of meteors and the temperature of the upper atmosphere

MILESTONES

1922

1923

Henry Osborn names and describes the dinosaur *Pentaceratops*

American fossil hunter Roy Chapman Andrews (the real-life Indiana Jones) discovers dinosaur eggs during an expedition to China

American geologist J. Harlen Bretz hypothesizes that the scablands of eastern Washington are scars of a flood

Beagle, Charles Darwin was not only interested in the diversity of life. He was also looking at subtle divergences in igneous rocks. In 1995, geologist Paul Pearson of the University of Bristol, in the United Kingdom reported, "Darwin hypothesized that density differences among crystals within a mass of partially molten rock would result in their physical separation by sinking and floating. Such a process, he proposed, could be responsible for the separation of compositionally distinct lavas from a single source." The idea of a single source for igneous rocks continued to fascinate petrologists (those in the field of geology who study rock compositions and their origins). One of the great contributions of the 1920s came when Norman Bowen described how a single magma source can provide a diversity of igneous rock types. He would base his work on experiments in the lab, creating a bridge between field geologists and theoreticians.

Other notable Earth scientists during this decade include Harold Jeffreys and Andrew Douglass. Jeffreys used his mathematical knowledge to study geophysics and calculated that the Earth's core was liquid. He also worked as an astronomer, studying the origin of the solar system and the structure of the outer planets. Douglass was an astronomer with an interest in solar cycles. He invented a new field in the Earth sciences called dendrochronology, which uses tree rings as a tool for dating past

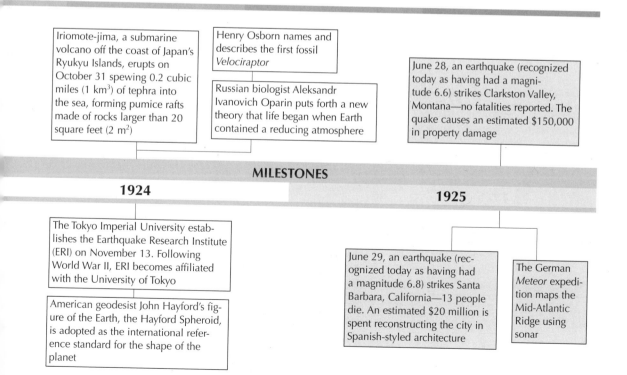

Iriomote-jima, a submarine volcano off the coast of Japan's Ryukyu Islands, erupts on October 31 spewing 0.2 cubic miles (1 km³) of tephra into the sea, forming pumice rafts made of rocks larger than 20 square feet (2 m²)

Henry Osborn names and describes the first fossil *Velociraptor*

Russian biologist Aleksandr Ivanovich Oparin puts forth a new theory that life began when Earth contained a reducing atmosphere

June 28, an earthquake (recognized today as having had a magnitude 6.6) strikes Clarkston Valley, Montana—no fatalities reported. The quake causes an estimated $150,000 in property damage

MILESTONES

1924

1925

The Tokyo Imperial University establishes the Earthquake Research Institute (ERI) on November 13. Following World War II, ERI becomes affiliated with the University of Tokyo

American geodesist John Hayford's figure of the Earth, the Hayford Spheroid, is adopted as the international reference standard for the shape of the planet

June 29, an earthquake (recognized today as having had a magnitude 6.8) strikes Santa Barbara, California—13 people die. An estimated $20 million is spent reconstructing the city in Spanish-styled architecture

The German *Meteor* expedition maps the Mid-Atlantic Ridge using sonar

events and climate cycles. The Earth scientist that perhaps best depicts this decade is Alfred Wegener, whose theory on continental drift received worldwide recognition and tremendous criticism during this time.

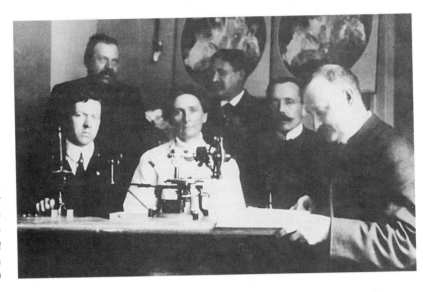

Florence Bascom (1862–1945) in 1906 was regarded among the country's top 100 geologists for her work in crystallography, mineralogy, and petrography. She taught at Bryn Mawr College and was the first woman geologist to work for the U.S. Geological Survey. In 1924, she became the first woman elected to the Council of the Geological Society of America (GSA) and in 1930 became the first woman officer of GSA when she was elected vice president. (Sophia Smith College)

Avachinsky, a *stratovolcano* rising above the city of Petropavlovsk on Russia's Kamchatka Peninsula, erupts explosively on April 5 during a period of activity that lasted a year and spewed out 0.0008 cubic miles (0.0035 km³) of lava and 0.04 cubic miles (0.18 km³) of tephra

Scottish engineer Sir Robert Alexander Watson-Watt proposes the name *ionosphere* for the atmospheric layer characterized by ionization of gases

May 22, an earthquake (recognized today as having had a magnitude 7.9) strikes Tsinghai, China—200,000 people die

MILESTONES

1926

1927

1928

Dutch geodesist Vening Meinesz discovers a large gravity anomaly during a submarine cruise along the Puerto Rico Trench and later again along the Java Trench

The Scott Polar Research Institute opens in Cambridge, England, to conduct Antarctic research

Groundwater hydrologist O. E. Meinzer of the U.S. Geological Survey establishes a classification system for springs based on their discharge rate. A magnitude-one spring discharges 65 million gallons a day or more, whereas a magnitude-eight spring discharges less than 0.65 million gallons a day

American geochemist Norman L. Bowen publishes *The Evolution of the Igneous Rocks*

Taung Child

Raymond Dart (1893–1988) was 29 years old when he was appointed head of the department of anatomy at the University of Witwatersrand in Johannesburg. An Australian with additional training in London, Dart had a reputation as an iconoclast, a young scientist willing to challenge the status quo. He did not disappoint. In the mid-1920s, when the focus for the origin of human evolution was on Asia, Dart examined the first fossil from Africa that showed a common linkage between human and primate ancestry—a fossil that also suggested that walking upright occurred prior to the cranial advances seen in later human species. With one skull, Dart would put forth a new perspective for human origins: Africa as the cradle for humanity. The geographical attention shift would spur a 30-year-long debate in anthropology and draw Earth scientists to the scene to investigate the paleoclimatology of Africa and the links between climate and human evolution.

The skull was that of a child who had lived in a cave during the Pleistocene. When dynamite blasted the pink sandy deposits at the Buxton *limestone* quarry near the village of Taung, the skull emerged from the debris as a round, pink rock. The quarryman M. de Bruyn recognized that the fossil was much larger than the baboon skulls he

A gasoline explosion destroys the research vessel *Carnegie* in Samoa. The Carnegie Institution of Washington's nonmagnetic sailboat had logged 342,681 miles (551,492 km) on its journey around the world conducting oceanographic, magnetic, electric, and gravity surveys

The Woods Hole Oceanographic Institution (WHOI) is established in Woods Hole, Massachusetts

Society of Exploration Geophysicists is founded in Houston, Texas

Swiss-born Norwegian chemist Victor Moritz Goldschmidt produces the first table of ionic radii useful for predicting crystal structures

After searching the night sky for close to a year, American astronomer Clyde Tombaugh at age 24 discovers Pluto outside Neptune's orbit

MILESTONES

1929

1930

November 18, an earthquake (recognized today as having had a magnitude 7.3) strikes Grand Banks, Nova Scotia, Canada—28 people in Newfoundland die from a resulting tsunami that struck two-and-a-half hours after the earthquake

The Carnegie Institution of Washington establishes a department of geophysics headquartered at the Pasadena Seismological Laboratory in California

Komaga-take on Hokkaido, Japan, explodes in a plinian eruption on June 17 sending 0.05 cubic miles (0.19 km³) of tephra into the air and pyroclastic flows and lahars down its slopes. Eruptive activity continues through September

Japanese geologist Motonori Matuyama (1884–1958) independently identifies rocks of different strata with reversals in the alignment of their magnetic fields

On June 11, American zoologist William Beebe and engineer Otis Baron descend in the first bathysphere, a spherical steel craft for undersea exploration, to 1,428 feet (435 m)

had seen before, so he gave it to his manager, A. E. Spiers, who passed it on to a geologist who knew Dart was looking for fossil skulls. On November 28, 1924, Dart received the skull and knew immediately it was special.

As he carefully extracted the skull from its limestone matrix he saw that the fossil consisted of a face, the jaw of a juvenile whose first molars had just started to erupt and several pieces of the cranial bone. The fossil also had a natural *endocranial cast*—an impression of the brain's outer surface where the minerals had replaced the contents of the skull during the process of fossilization. Dart recognized that he was not holding another baboon skull as he had expected to receive, but something entirely different. After extensive measuring, photographing, and drawing of the morphological details of the skull, he compared the Taung child to pictures of other ancient human skulls. On January 6, 1925, Dart submitted a typed manuscript to the prestigious journal *Nature* naming the newly identified skull *Australopithecus africanus*. His identification of the child as a "southern ape of Africa" rather than a "southern man," which would have been "*Australanthropus,*" placed the skull in a new evolutionary branch in the animal kingdom: outside of those of the great apes, but as a potential ape-like ancestor to *homo sapiens*. Anthropologists were livid. The fossil did not fit their idea of a missing link.

British anatomist Sir Arthur Keith (1866–1955) was among the many prominent scientists in the field who hypothesized that humans developed a larger brain first and then the ability to stand and walk upright; have complex thoughts; use tools; and rely less on canine teeth for hunting. A skull found in England, called the Piltdown skull, looked like such a fossil with its larger human-like cranium and ape-like jaw, but the Piltdown skull was a fake, unknown at the time. The skull was made from ape and human bones painted and stained to look old, supposedly to bolster England as the birthplace of human ancestry. The Taung child contradicted the predominant anthropologic hypothesis in every way. The key features of *Australopithecus* included a smaller, ape-like brain; human-like canine teeth; a brain cast indicating an advanced cerebrum in what seemed to be an "ultra-simian" or "pre-human" direction; and, most importantly, a hole in the base of the braincase closer to the front, indicating that the skull sat poised on an upright spinal column. The Taung child walked on two legs. The spinal cord on apes connects to the brain through a hole in the skull that is further back, pointing their nose and eyes naturally toward the horizon (and potential predators) rather than straight down on the ground as they knuckle through the forest. If such a skull were placed on a person they would walk with their nose pointed skyward and crane their necks to look down. Human ancestors it seemed started walking before they started thinking.

In making his discovery, Dart recalled Charles Darwin's 1871 prediction: "it is somewhat more probable that our early progenitors lived on the African continent than elsewhere." The juvenile status of the Taung child however diminished it from being viewed as a major discovery in the 1920s. Not until Robert Broom in the late 1930s found adult *Australopithecus* skulls did other paleontologists begin to seriously regard the possible implications of an African origin for humans and a more gradual evolution in body form and function. The Taung child was "the first of all Africa's testimonies to the dawn of humankind," wrote Phillip Tobias, head of Witwatersrand's department of anatomy in 1985. He added that his predecessor had "the insight to realize the Taung skull was relevant to the discussion of hominid origins and evolution." Other fossil species of *Australopithecus* found during the 20th century—*anamensis, afarensis, aethiopicus, garhi, robustus,* and *boisei*—would reveal a complex and rich history for human evolution from Africa.

The Scopes Monkey Trial

While scientists around the world were debating the nuances of human evolution, politicians and lawyers in America were debating the legality of teaching evolution in schools.

Between 1922 and 1924 the state legislatures of Kentucky, South Carolina, North Carolina, Florida, Texas, and Georgia all had bills introduced that either called for an end to the teaching of evolution, or demanded a withdrawal of financial support to schools that continued to teach the science. The wording of the bills made it clear that this was an attack on science for religious purposes.

The Kentucky bill aimed to ban "Darwinism, atheism, agnosticism or the theory of evolution insofar as it pertains to the origin of man." The Florida legislature passed a resolution recommending teachers avoid teaching "Darwinism or any other hypothesis that links man in a blood relationship to any other form of life." High schools in North Carolina removed biology books with references to evolution, even though no law required it. In Oklahoma the law did. Teachers were afraid of losing their jobs if they brought up the subject of evolution in their classrooms. In California, the State Board of Education in 1924 issued a directive that teachers should present evolution "as a theory only," an ironic twist on a scientific term traditionally used to dignify hypotheses that have been convincingly established and carefully peer-reviewed.

Then, in 1925, the state of Tennessee passed the Butler Act, which made it unlawful for any public school teacher, including those at universities, "to teach any theory that denies the story of Divine Creation of man as taught in the Bible, and to teach instead that man has descended from a lower order of animals." Any teacher found guilty of violating the act would be fined a minimum of $100—nearly two months' pay for the average Tennessee teacher.

An Ordovician gastropod or snail: Maclurites *from the Middle Ordovician Galena Group limestone, near Wyckoff, Minnesota* (North Dakota State University)

The result was the Scopes Monkey Trial, still heralded at law schools as the trial of the century. On the first day, Friday, July 10, 1925, a standing-room crowd of nearly a thousand people crammed into a courthouse in the tiny town of Dayton to hear three-time presidential candidate William Jennings Bryan lock horns with famed defense attorney Clarence Darrow before Judge John T. Raulston, a conservative Christian who insisted on beginning the proceeding with a prayer. The defendant was John Scopes, a well-liked football coach and substitute science teacher at the local high school who had volunteered to stand trial when other townsfolk convinced him that it would help bring attention to Dayton. His legal bills were paid by the American Civil Liberties Union, which had offered to do so for any teacher willing to stand trial for teaching evolution.

The result was a mixture of camp revival and media circus. It lasted eight days, during which it was not only the theory of evolution that was under fire but the entire geological concept of deep time, although much was obscured by the fact that Bryan was a conservative Christian, while Darrow was an avowed agnostic. That difference made for great media publicity but fanned the controversy by appearing to send the message that evolution was at odds with Christianity.

The legal issue was the constitutionality of the law under the Tennessee constitution, which stated that "it shall be the duty of the general assembly to cherish literature and science," that "no preference shall be given to any religious establishment or mode of worship," and that "every citizen may freely speak, write and print on any subject."

In words that echo just as strongly today, Darrow also challenged that the law punished "intelligent, scholarly Christians, who by the millions find no inconsistency between evolution and religion," and he questioned the legal demand that science teachers turn to the Bible for scientific explanations. "The Bible is made up of 66 books written over a period of about one thousand years, some of them very early and some of them comparatively late. It is a book of religion and morals. It is not a book of science. Never was and never meant to be." He reminded the audience that the people who wrote the Bible believed the Earth was the center of the universe. "We know better," he said. The prosecution was "opening the doors for a reign of bigotry equal to anything in the Middle Ages," and throwing the court back to a time when fanatics lit fires to "burn men who dared bring any intelligence and enlightenment and culture to the human mind." The press loved it.

Judge Raulston was unpersuaded. The prosecution then brought forth witnesses who testified that Scopes had admitted to teaching about evolution. In one of the case's most spectacular turns, the defense then argued that the prosecution also had to prove that evolution contradicted the biblical story of creation and paraded a long line of scientists from many Christian faiths who said that it did not. Still, the simple fact remained that Scopes had admitted to violating the law. The jury found Scopes guilty and Judge Raulston sentenced Scopes to a fine of $100.

When asked if he had anything to say, Scopes replied: "Your honor, I feel that I have been convicted of violating an unjust statute. I will continue in the future, as I have in the past, to oppose this law in any way I can. Any other action would be in violation of my ideal of academic freedom—that is, to teach the truth as guaranteed in our constitution of personal and religious freedom. I think the fine is unjust."

Five days later, Bryan, still in Dayton, ate an enormous dinner, lay down for a nap, and died in his sleep. During the final day in court he had given a speech that captured the enormity of the trial, which more than 200 reporters had attended. Said Bryan: "We are told that more words have been sent across the ocean by cable to Europe and Australia about this trial than has ever been sent by cable in regard to anything else happening in the United States. That isn't because the trial is held in Dayton. It isn't because a schoolteacher has been subjected to the danger of a fine $100.00 to $500.00, but I think illustrate how people can be drawn into prominence by attaching themselves to a great cause. . . . Here has been fought out a little case of little consequence as a case, but the world is interested because it raises an issue, and that issue will some day be settled right, whether it is settled on our side or the other side. It is going to be settled right."

A year later, the Tennessee Supreme Court overturned the ruling of the lower court and revoked the fine against Scopes, although not for constitutional reasons. Three of the four judges agreed with the constitutionality of law, although one of the judges in the majority gave the opinion that evolution did not deny Divine Creation and therefore Scopes had not broken the law as it was written. Instead of sending the case back for further action, the state Supreme Court dismissed the case on the technicality that the jury, not Judge Raulston, should have set the fine. "Nothing is to be gained by prolonging the life of this bizarre case," they noted. As a result, the defense could not continue the appeal to the U.S. Supreme Court. The Tennessee law succeeded in limiting the teaching of evolution in classrooms. Publishers revised their textbooks and teachers fearful of the fine or of losing their jobs dropped the subject of evolution or taught students very little about it. By 1928, Mississippi and Arkansas had also passed laws against teaching evolution.

The Butler Act remained on the books in Tennessee until 1967 when Gary Scott of Jacksboro challenged the law that had him fired. A year later, teacher Susanne Epperson won an appeal against the state of Arkansas for upholding its "monkey law." In *Epperson v. Arkansas*, the U.S. Supreme Court ruled that all antievolution laws were unconstitutional for imposing a state-supported religion and eroding the separation of church and state. The court found the laws were merely "an attempt to blot out a particular theory because of its supposed conflict with the Biblical account taken literally."

Evolution of Rocks

"One of the most obvious facts about igneous rocks is that they are extremely variable both in mineralogy and chemical composition. This leads petrologists to think automatically in evolutionary terms, like zoologists and botanists. Yet it is not immediately obvious that inanimate materials have the capacity to evolve, until one contemplates the variety of igneous rocks and asks how the individual types may have come to be created. One is obliged to postulate either that they were all created different, or that some processes exist which have the capacity to generate variety," wrote the authors—Keith Gordon Cox, J. D. Bell, and R. J. Pankhurst—in their 1979 book *The Interpretation of Igneous Rocks*. They were referring to the work of Canadian petrologist Norman Bowen (1887–1956).

In his book *The Evolution of the Igneous Rocks*, published in 1928, Norman Bowen summarized research he had been conducting in the field of igneous petrology for 20 years. Bowen carefully documented common rock-forming minerals and recorded their melting points to show how the minerals changed with temperature. He wanted to know how different types of igneous rocks formed in the Earth's mantle and crust. His graduate adviser at the Massachusetts Institute of Technology (MIT) in 1909 was fellow Canadian geologist Reginald A. Daly (1871–1957).

At the end of the 19th century some investigators of igneous rocks had formed the opinion that the Earth contained different types of magmas that each led to the different types of igneous rocks. Unlike sedimentary or *metamorphic* rocks, both of which are products of secondary processes that have occurred to already existing rocks, igneous rocks are the primary products: the primordial rock type, cooled and solidified magma. Daly hypothesized that Earth had only one parent magma, the same magma that when cooled formed basalt rocks on the ocean floor. He believed that all other magmas were derived from this basaltic liquid. Just how the other magmas formed from this one type of magma, however, remained highly speculative.

Daly turned to the high-pressure studies of Percy Bridgman at Harvard (discussed in chapter two) and worked closely with researchers at the Geophysical Laboratory in Washington to test the properties of minerals and rocks under extreme temperatures. "This planet is essentially a body of crystallized and uncrystallized igneous material. The final philosophy of Earth history will therefore be founded on igneous-rock geology," Daly wrote in his 1914 book *Igneous Rocks*

John Joly (1857–1933), working with John Murray's ocean maps from the 19th century Challenger Expedition, proposed that volcanic activity often took place as a release of radioactive heat built up under the oceanic and continental crusts.

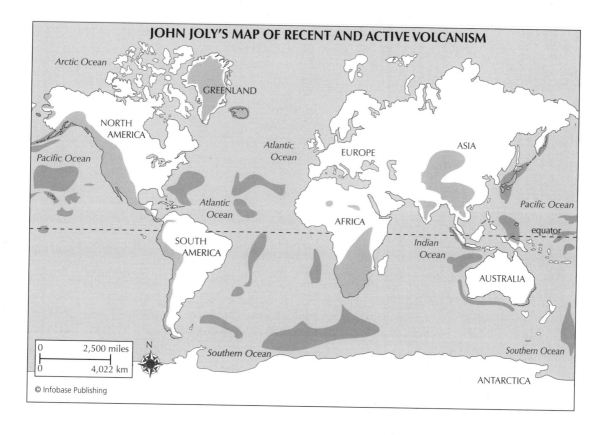

JOHN JOLY'S MAP OF RECENT AND ACTIVE VOLCANISM

Arctic Ocean

GREENLAND

NORTH AMERICA

Atlantic Ocean

EUROPE

ASIA

Pacific Ocean

Atlantic Ocean

Pacific Ocean

AFRICA

equator

SOUTH AMERICA

Indian Ocean

AUSTRALIA

0   2,500 miles
0   4,022 km

N

Southern Ocean

Southern Ocean

ANTARCTICA

© Infobase Publishing

and Their Origin. "The salts of soil, river, and ocean waters, as well as organic matter and the gases of the atmosphere, are largely, if not wholly, derivatives of rock materials once in a state of fusion." Daly confronted a wide range of possibilities. Perhaps other minerals from the surrounding mantle or crust diffused into the basaltic magma to change its composition. Perhaps crystals segregated during formation and caused the magma to split its flow. Or perhaps as a certain fraction of the minerals crystallized, their formation changed the remaining composition of minerals left in the magma to the point that different igneous rock types would emerge when the magma cooled. Bowen followed his lead.

He found camaraderie working with geochemists at the Geophysical Laboratory in Washington where in 1905 Arthur L. Day and E. T. Allen pioneered the study of thermal properties of plagioclase feldspars. Bowen tested the phase equilibrium of different chemicals and learned what kind of environmental conditions turned a solid into a liquid, or vice versa as when a magmatic melt formed a mineral. He discovered rock-forming minerals crystallized at different temperatures, a process called fractional crystallization. This meant that as crystals formed, the magma was left with a different chemical composition. As the magma continued to cool it would form different crystals. Bowen published his report on "The

In the 1920s Norman Bowen proposed a series of reactions for how basaltic magma produces different types of igneous rocks. When the magma is still hot and beginning to cool, calcium, iron, and magnesium crystals are present in large amounts. As the magma rises toward the surface, the temperature decreases and the ratio of silica increases. Identifying the minerals in different types of igneous rocks can provide a guide as to how cool the magma was when the minerals formed. Cooler magma forms quartz, a mineral resistant to erosion and weathering, and one of the most common minerals found exposed on the continents.

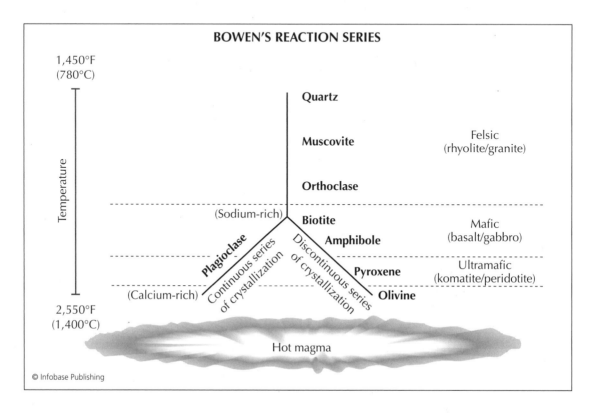

© Infobase Publishing

later stages of the evolution of the igneous rocks" in the *Journal of Geology* in 1915, listing the order of crystallization phases. His work allowed petrologists to form a new understanding of igneous evolution. The first minerals to crystallize out of magmatic solution form the igneous rocks that make up the oceanic crust: mafic and ultramafic basalts, gabbros, komatites, and peridotites with minerals of olivine, pyroxene, amphibole, biotite or calcium-rich plagioclase feldspar. Once these minerals are out of the magmatic solution the chemical composition of the magma has changed, and as it continues to cool it forms the lighter continental crusts: felsic rhyolites and granites with minerals of orthoclase, muscovite and *quartz.*

In 1998, Hatten Yoder, Jr. (1921–2003), then emeritus director of the Carnegie Institution of Washington's Geophysical Laboratory in Washington, D.C., called Bowen "the greatest petrologist of the 20th century." He was being modest. If Bowen was the greatest experimental

The Secret Ancient Life of Trees

In 1894 astronomer Andrew Ellicott Douglass (1867–1962) was riding horseback across the American southwest in search of a location for a new planetary observatory that Harvard graduate Percival Lowell was planning on building. Douglass had just completed the same mission for the Harvard College Observatory, establishing the southern Andean highlands of Arequipa, Peru, as a site for their Boyden Station. He proved astute at observing not only the atmospheric conditions, a necessary protocol for astronomical measurements using a telescope, but also minute details regarding the land around him. In Peru, he measured the movement of crescent-shaped sand dunes, making the first known study of their wind-blown traverse across the high desert.

In the mountain pine forests of Flagstaff, Arizona, where Lowell built his observatory, Douglass again found the landscape as appealing as the sky. His disagreements with Lowell over interpretations of geologic features on Mars led to a dismissal from the observatory in 1901. (Lowell was convinced that Martians had built canals on the Red planet, but he was interpreting fuzzy images with resolution so poor he could convince

himself but not Douglass.) Free to roam through the forests, Douglass spent the summer and winter traveling by wagon and horseback with friends and noting how vegetation increased with altitude in the southwestern deserts. He hypothesized that the concentric tree rings of annual growth would be wider in the higher elevations where rainfall was more plentiful. His purpose was in fact astronomically related. He wanted to know if he could correlate the 11-year cycle of sunspots on the Sun with terrestrial climate changes. As a result of his study, he found a new method for dating both natural and human-caused events through history. He coined the new approach: dendrochronology.

Logging was an important resource for the region, and Douglass spent hours carefully measuring the width of the concentric circles visible on the stumps of felled trees at the Arizona Lumber and Timber Company south of Flagstaff. He convinced the president of the company, T. A. Riordan, to send him sections from the ends of logs. The first six trees that Riordan sent samples from all shared a similar pattern of thickness

(continues)

Andrew Douglass (1867–1962) established the scientific importance of tree-ring dating, a science he called dendrochronology. (AIP Emilio Segrè Visual Archives, Brittle Books Collection)

(continued)

occurring 21 rings in from the bark. Since the trees had been recently cut the event must have happened 21 years earlier. When Douglass found the same pattern on a log 11 years in from the bark he concluded the tree had been cut 10 years ago, an event the property owner confirmed. Because the trees in Arizona were struggling for survival against drought rather than competing against other vegetation for light, as is often the case in rain forests, the pine trees developed rings that reflected the annual rate of precipitation. When Lowell was out of town, Douglass would use the observatory's library to read issues of the *Monthly Weather Review,* paying close attention to Frank H. Bigelow's studies of weather cycles. In one issue, the Smithsonian's Charles Greeley Abbot lamented over the difficulty in correlating rainfall measurements with solar activity. In 1909 Douglass introduced what he hoped would provide a solution to the dilemma with his report "Weather Cycles in the Growth of Big Trees."

The trees Douglass examined, starting with the ponderosa pine, could live for hundreds of years. By keeping detailed records on the width patterns for each tree he was able to cross-date older trees and go back further in time with timber found at archaeological sites. For example, trees with rings dating back to 1851 showed a very narrow ring of growth that year, an indication of drought. Between 1879 and 1889 the rings were compressed together like a tightly wound coil. He traveled to England, Germany, Austria, Norway, and Sweden collecting tree samples for comparison to the Arizona forests as well as sequoias from California and trees from New Mexico, Vermont, and Oregon. His southwestern samples dated back to the early 16th century and tentatively to the late 14th century. In 1914 he revealed the extent of his studies on tree rings in his report "A Method of Estimating Rainfall by the Growth of Trees," published in the *Bulletin of the American Geographical Society.* By that time he had affiliated himself with the University of Arizona. In 1918 he started receiving grants for his work from the Carnegie Institution and writing a series of books on dendrochronology, entitled *Climatic Cycles and Tree Growth.* By this time he had counted some 75,000 rings from 230 trees. Around the world, trees were growing in cycles that seemed to reflect sunspot activity, except for during the mid-17th century, when Douglass could find no distinguishing cycles in the tree rings. He was encouraged to continue pursuing his investigations when E. Walter Maunder asked about any curiosities in his findings between 1645 and 1715, a prolonged period, later nicknamed the Maunder Minimum, when the Sun displayed very few sunspots. Spurred by this revelation, Douglass sought even older wood samples to expand his chronology of tree-ring records. He began investigating pueblo ruins. His work gained the attention of the National Geographic Society, and an expedition to date southwestern Native American ruins began in 1923. From wooden beams excavated from the Aztec and Pueblo Bonita ruins, Douglass in 1929 showed that the trees used to build the structures were cut down 879 years earlier. Archaeologists for the first time had a method for evaluating the accuracy of historical records. Douglass founded the Laboratory of Tree Ring Research at the University of Arizona. By the mid-1930s, cross-correlation of tree ring patterns provided a complete record dating back to 11 C.E.

Dendrochronology is often used to determine major climate shifts, droughts, and forest fire history. Petrified and buried forests tell of the climatic and geologic history of their location prior to their deaths and have even been used to reveal to Earth scientists information about ancient earthquakes and tsunamis. Boring core samples from a tree allows researchers to study the rings without killing the tree, but that is not always the case. The most controversial chopping down of a tree for scientific study occurred in 1964.

That year, the U.S. Forest Service granted a dendrochronologist permission to take several core samples of Bristlecone Pines (*Pinus longaeva*) in what is now Great Basin National Park in Nevada. The trees are famous for their twisting shapes with branches that look like swirled, dark-caramel taffy. The researcher, a graduate student at the University of North Carolina, had difficulty obtaining a core from one particular older-looking tree, which naturalists had earlier nicknamed "Prometheus." The Forest Service then granted him permission to cut down the whole tree. Prometheus, the tree rings proved, had stood for about 5,000 years prior to 1964, making it the oldest known non-clonal organism on Earth. It first sent roots into the ground about the same time the construction of Stonehenge began.

The oldest living organism known on Earth is an 80,000-year-old Quaking Aspen (*Populus tremuloides*) in Utah. The tree started as a seedling that spread out an extensive root system and began cloning itself. The tree trunks, now some 47,000 of them, live for about 130 years before dying, but new clones of the tree are continuously growing to replace the old. This tree—nicknamed Pando, which means "I spread" in Latin—began growing during a time when *Homo sapiens* in Europe and Africa were still relying on hand axes, some 30,000 years before humans began specializing fine stone tools.

Scientist of the Decade: Alfred Wegener (1880–1930)

Alfred Wegener was born in Berlin on November 1, 1880. A man of diverse talents, he was a well-known meteorologist and Arctic explorer. He is best known today as the "father of continental drift." In 1912 he proposed that the continents had been moving for millions of years since their separation from the supercontinent Pangaea. When Wegener died on his fourth expedition to Greenland's inland ice cap, most American and European geologists were divided in their opin-ions, some bitterly so, on the feasibility of such a hypothesis. The debate would continue, albeit with less rancor, for another 30 years.

Alfred, the youngest child of an evangelical preacher, spent his summers in the mountains, where glaciers had shaped the landscape and lakes, and forests fueled his urge to explore. After graduating from a regimented high school

(continues)

German meteorologist Alfred Wegener was responsible for igniting geologic debate against the established theory that the continents permanently maintained their current positions when he published his research on the likelihood of continental drift. (Alfred Wegener Institute for Polar and Marine Research)

(continued)

where lessons in humanities were emphasized over science, he turned to math and astronomy at the University of Berlin. By the time he earned his Ph.D. he had become disillusioned with the opportunities for advancement in the field of astronomy and turned instead to meteorology. There, advances in radio and telegraph communication, plus the completion of the Trans-Atlantic Cable, allowed meteorologists to track storms almost around the world and create more accurate weather forecasts.

Wegener also experimented with instrument-laden kites and lighter-than-air balloons. In 1906 he and his brother Kurt set a new world endurance record for ballooning when they stayed aloft for 52 hours and 30 minutes. The previous record of 17 hours had been a day-trip in comparison.

The brothers' adventure caught the attention of journalist Ludvig Mylius-Erichsen, who needed a meteorologist on an expedition to northern Greenland. In the next two years, Wegener learned to run dogsleds and conducted kite and cabled balloon ascents to study the polar atmosphere. He watched the aurora borealis dance across the sky. He wrote in his diary "I have had a series of small but valuable experiences [including] . . . How one repairs a broken sled, the quickest way to [untangle] the dog lines, how to prevent the dogs from tangling the lines after stops, and so on. The Arctic technical experience I am collecting alone is worth the two years."

The expedition was not without hardship, however. Mylius-Erichsen and two men died on a sledge trip across the uncharted region. It was during the rescue attempt that Wegener and three others heading west made one of the expedition's most startling discoveries: a large ice-free region called a nunatak, a polar version of an oasis. Here, the ice cap ended abruptly with a 90-foot vertical drop. Plants of Arctic white heather and red and gold dwarf birch grew in abundance. Wegener and his team climbed down the ice wall to investigate the plants, rocks, and fossils—most likely marine bivalves, plants, and the bones of musk ox. They called the region Queen Louise Land.

In 1910, two years after his return from Greenland, Wegener first contemplated the idea of continental drift after reviewing a map of the world and considering the shape of the coastlines on either side of the Atlantic Ocean. That same year, in the *Bulletin of the Geological Society of America* Frank Taylor first published a theory that relied on continental drift to explain mountain chains. Taylor had been elected to the American Geographical Society in 1906, but his report received little attention. Wegener originally dismissed his own idea of drift because he "regarded it as improbable." In 1911 he published the book, *Thermodynamik der Atmosphäre* (The Thermodynamics of the Atmosphere), which German universities adopted as their standard textbook for teaching meteorology. Not until after reading about paleontological similarities in fossils found in Brazil and Africa did Wegener give credibility to the idea of continental drift—convincing himself that horizontal motion of the continents drifting over the Earth's surface, not sunken land bridges, held the most promise for explaining geological and paleontological phenomena. It was a whole new way of thinking about the planet. Excited about what this meant for science, he wrote to his future father-in-law, Wladimir Köppen, director of the Meteorological Department of the German Marine Observatory: "if it turns out that sense and meaning are now becoming evident in the whole history of the Earth's development, why should we hesitate to toss the old views overboard?" Two weeks later on January 6, 1912, Wegener presented his theory of drift at a meeting of the Geological Association in Frankfurt. He followed this talk with a similar speech four nights later to the Society for the Advancement of Natural Science. He then published two written reports on the subject before returning to Greenland.

This expedition was a four-man team, led by Johan Peter Koch. The goal was a diagonal east-to-west journey across the widest part of the ice cap. Instead of dogsleds, the explorers relied on Icelandic ponies and were the first team to winter on the margin of the inland ice, although not where they had hoped. Their objective was to camp in Queen Louise Land, but the team encountered great difficulties right from the start. Six of their 16 horses ran away during a stampede, and the team almost died when a glacier they were climbing collapsed. Not until the following April, with only five ponies left alive, did the team begin its 700-mile trek across the ice cap. They made the trip in three months, after enduring blistering sun and snow-blinding blizzards. Wegener experimented with attaching sails to the sleds and using the wind to help carry their supplies over the ice—a technique later used by many for polar crossings. Nearly starved before they were rescued on the western coast, they sailed home loaded with meteorological data from the Greenland's harsh interior.

When Wegener returned after this second trip, he started a family with his new wife Else Köppen, but World War I intervened, and he was drafted as a reserve lieutenant in the infantry, where he was wounded twice, the second time severely enough to take him permanently away from the action. He was transferred to the Army meteorological service and had time to pursue a book about his theory of continental drift: *The Origin of the Continents and Oceans,* published in 1915. The book tied together the fields of geography, paleoclimatology, geophysics, and geology and would undergo three more editions in 1920, 1922, and 1929 in response to criticism.

He had hoped to return to Greenland again with Koch, but his friend died in 1928. The following year, Wegener recruited Johannes Georgi, Fritz Loewe, and Ernst Sorge to help him explore the feasibility of recording a meteorological and glaciological profile of Greenland's inland ice sheet using three yearlong observation stations set up across the island. The plan called for a three-man team to set up an east coast station and a larger contingent of scientists to set up the western and central stations. Seismic readings from set explosions would allow them to calculate the depth of the ice between and at these different locations.

The west coast crew of 18 German scientists, four Icelandic assistants, and 13 Greenlanders got off to a bad start, hampered by harbor ice. By the time they landed in June, they were 38 days behind schedule.

Multiple trips were needed to get the central station up and running 249 miles (400 km) inland. As the summer passed, it became obvious that much of the supplies for building materials would not arrive in time. Two of the scientists hunkered down, sending word back that they could hold the camp until October 20. With a convoy of 15 dogsleds and a

(continues)

(continued)

motor-driven sledge, Wegener raced the oncoming winter in a desperate attempt to provide additional supplies. He hoped to make the roundtrip mission in 30 days, but the weather was already turning disastrous, plummeting down to -65.2°F (-54°C). Then the motor-driven sledge carrying most of their supplies sank deep in newly fallen snow. All but three men turned back. Wegener, Fritz Loewe, and Rasmus Villumsen crawled into the mid-ice station at the end of October after six weeks of travel. Loewe's toes were frostbitten and amputated with a pocketknife and a pair of plate shears—an operation that left him unable to return to the coast. Instead of bringing supplies and encouragement the resupply effort had hampered the inland camp with another crew member to feed over winter, but the three who remained would survive. Wegener and Villumsen would not. They left the inland ice camp on Wegener's 50th birthday to return to the west coast station.

Ultimately the expedition would record seismic readings from 34 locations and find that, like an overfilled bowl of ice cream, Greenland's coastal mountains trap ice in the interior. The coastal mountains rise 5,850 feet (1,783 m), capped with 2,600 feet (800 m) of ice. Inland, central station sat on ice 8,775 feet (2,675 m) thick at a total elevation of 9,700 feet (2,956 m). [For comparison, Greenland's highest mountain, Mount Gunnbjørn, which is located on the eastern coast, reaches a rocky peak of 12,139 feet (3,700 m)]. The team under the guidance of Wegener's brother Kurt completed their expedition, collecting additional information about glacier movement and the accumulation and evaporation of snow across the interior. Meteorological data from kite and balloon surveys of the atmosphere at all three stations provided a look at how weather propagates across the island before heading to Europe. Wegener died of a heart attack 113 miles (182 km) from the coast. Villumsen carefully wrapped blankets around the fur-coat clad expedition leader and buried the body in the snow. He took Wegener's diary and set a ski up as a marker before continuing on his own. No one else knew he had died. The following spring, expedition members found the grave, but Villumsen, the two dogsleds, and the diary had disappeared.

After Wegener's death, the bulk of the geologic community's champions of continental drift came from those who had worked or lived in the Southern Hemisphere, where the geologic record supported a jigsaw puzzle fit of the continents. Paleontologist Kenneth Caster (1908–92) was among the minority in the United States with his support, but he saw the evidence firsthand during his many years traveling extensively through Brazil, Colombia, South Africa, New Zealand, and Australia. In 1956 he was awarded the Gondwana Medal of the Geological Survey of India. British geochronologist Arthur Holmes, whose mentor at Imperial College John William Evans (1857–1930) had read Wegener's book on drift in its original German and provided the forward for the English edition, came to support continental drift after examining the issue of Earth's heat. Holmes would provide the first mechanism for drift with his model of convection currents. Geologist Alexander Logie du Toit (1878–1948) was, after Wegener, the most ardent supporter of continental drift, examining the subject in detail in his 1938 book *Our Wandering Continents*. The book made clear that the subject of drift was worthy of serious consideration. Another geologist in favor of drift was the South African Lester Charles King (1907–89). Other advocates of continental drift included the Australian geologist Samuel Warren Carey (1911–2002), the Brazilian geologist Reinhard Maack (1892–1969), and the Indian geologists Maharajpuram Sitaram Krishman (1898–1970) and Darashaw Nosherwan Wadia (1883–1969). Research in 1935 by Japanese seismologist Kiyoo Wadati (1902–95) followed in 1940 with studies done by California seismologist Hugo Benioff (1899–1968) that introduced evidence of something active and deep presently shifting beneath the continents. The geologic community in the Northern Hemisphere began to evaluate the ideas behind continental drift with a new perspective.

petrologist, it was during the first half of the century with Yoder as the greatest petrologist during the second half. Bowen's legacy, wrote Yoder, "is the construction of an experimental and theoretical basis for the interpretation and documentation of the diversity of igneous and metamorphic rocks."

In his 1928 book, Bowen listed six steps for problem-solving in petrology:

- use field observations to identify patterns and relationships in the rocks
- establish laboratory experiments that re-create the natural conditions believed needed for these patterns to arise
- conduct the experiments carefully and unambiguously
- look for inconsistencies when comparing the principles learned through the experimental results with the field observations
- test the principles again with additional field observations
- repeat the above steps to create new experiments using the new observations and results from the field tests of the principles until a satisfactory solution is found.

Such lessons allowed geologists to establish universal methods for testing their theories in the laboratory. "The greatness of Norman Levi Bowen stems from his clear exposition of physicochemical principles and their application to major, complex geological field problems," Yoder wrote. "After half a century, it is clear that his philosophy had been successful even though new interpretations of the details were required."

Further Reading

Abbot, Charles Greeley. "The Relation of the Sun-Spot Cycle in Meteorology." *Monthly Weather Review* 30 (1902): 178–181. This report discusses the difficulties of correlating rainfall with solar activity.

Adams, L. H., and E. D. Williamson. "The Composition of the Earth's Interior." *Journal of the Washington Academy of Sciences* 13 (1923): 413–428. This report provided an early analysis of the geology of the Earth's interior.

The American Civil Liberties Union. "Frequently Asked Questions About 'Intelligent Design.'" This Web site offers explanations about the philosophy of "Intelligent Design." Available online. URL: http://www.aclu.org/ReligiousLiberty/ReligiousLiberty.cfm?ID=17204&c=139. Accessed April 24, 2006.

Antievolution and the Law. This Web site provides a timeline of the legal activities regarding the teaching of evolution. Available online.

URL: http://www.antievolution.org/topics/law/ Accessed April 24, 2006.

Bowen, Norman L. "The Later Stages of the Evolution of the Igneous Rocks." *Journal of Geology* 23 supplement (1915): 1–89. Bowen's doctoral thesis introduced a new way of thinking about magma.

———. *The Evolution of the Igneous Rocks.* Princeton, New Jersey: Princeton University Press, 1928. Bowen presents an explanation for the diversity of igneous rock types that is based on the cooling rates of minerals.

Cox, Keith Gordon, J. D. Bell, and R. J. Pankhurst. *The Interpretation of Igneous Rocks.* London and Boston: G. Allen & Unwin, 1979. This book discusses the evolution of igneous rocks.

Cranford, Garry (editor). *Not Too Long Ago.* St. John's, Newfoundland: The Seniors Resource Centre, 1999. This book provides firsthand accounts of the 1929 Grand Bank tsunami and is available online as a PDF. URL: http://www.nald.ca/clr/ntla/ntla.pdf. Accessed February 28, 2007.

Daly, Reginald A. *Igneous Rocks and Their Origin.* New York: McGraw-Hill Book Company, Inc., 1914. This is one of the first books to address the possible geochemical reasons for the diversity of igneous rocks on the planet. Available online. URL: http://books.google.com/books?vid=0I5LbCFrI-QUvr&id=obb8aFRgb8EC&pg=PA1&lpg=PA1&dq=Reginald+Daly. Accessed February 28, 2007.

Dart, Raymond A. "*Australopithecus africanus*, the man-ape of South Africa." *Nature* 115 (1925): 195. This report introduces an African hominid as the missing link in human evolution.

Douglass, Andrew Ellicott. "Weather Cycles in the Growth of Big Trees." *Monthly Weather Review* 37 (June 1909): 225–237. The first report on measuring tree rings as a method for tracking terrestrial climate.

———. "A Method of Estimating Rainfall by the Growth of Trees." *Bulletin of the American Geographical Society* 46, no. 5 (1914): 321–335. A more detailed analysis on the new science of dendrochronology.

———. *Climatic Cycles and Tree Growth.* Washington, D.C.: Carnegie Institution of Washington, 1919–36. This three-volume book illustrates the relationship between periodicities in climate, solar activity, and annual tree-ring growth.

Jeffreys, Harold (Sir). *The Earth: Its Origin, History and Physical Constitution.* Cambridge, England: University Press, 1929. This book examines Earth and lunar theory within the structure of the evolution of the solar system.

———. *Earthquakes and Mountains.* London: Methuen & Co., 1935. The preface reads: "To a large extent [this book] summarizes my larger book *The Earth* (1929)."

Lovett, Richard. "Histories: The Wave from Nowhere." *New Scientist* no. 2592 (February 24, 2007): 53. This report discusses the history of the 1929 Grand Banks tsunami. A discussion of the accompanying photo is available online. URL: http://www.newscientist.com/article/mg19325950.700-ship-of-fools.html. Accessed April 11, 2007.

The National Center for Science Education. This organization is dedicated to defending the teaching of evolution in public schools. Available online. URL: http://www.ncseweb.org/ Accessed April 24, 2006.

Natural History Museum. "Piltdown Man." This Web site provides images of the excavation and skull reconstruction in 1912 and compares the methods then to how scientists work today. An online quiz questions viewers on their own skills. Available online. URL: http://www.nhm.ac.uk/nature-online/life/human-origins/piltdown-man/index.html. Accessed February 28, 2007.

Natural Resources Canada. "The Magnitude 7.2 1929 'Grand Banks' Earthquake and Tsunami." This Web site provides archived news accounts and *isoseismal* maps of the deadly event that struck northeast North America. Available online. URL: http://earthquakescanada.nrcan.gc.ca/historic_eq/20th/1929/1929_e.php. Accessed February 28, 2007.

Pearson, Paul N. "Charles Darwin on the Origin and Diversity of Igneous Rocks." *Earth Sciences History* 15 (1996): 49–67. Pearson writes that Darwin hypothesized the diversity of igneous rocks, based on density differences in crystals.

The Peking Man World Heritage Site. This Web site describes Swedish geologist Johann Gunnar Andersson and Austrian paleontologist Otto Zdansky's discovery of the Peking Man fossil, the first ancient human found in Asia. Available online. URL: http://www.unesco.org/ext/field/beijing/whc/pkm-site.htm. Accessed April 24, 2006.

The Roy Chapman Andrews Society. "Just Around the Corner." This Web site chronicles the adventures of Roy Chapman Andrews as well as distinguishing scientists and explorers of today. Available online. URL: http://www.roychapmanandrewssociety.org/ Accessed February 28, 2007.

The Scopes Trial: An Introduction. Douglas Linder, a law professor at the University of Missouri-Kansas City, provides a detailed account of the famous trial. Available online. URL: http://www.law.umkc.edu/faculty/projects/ftrials/scopes/scopes.htm. Accessed April 24, 2006.

Smiley, Terah L. "Obituary: Andrew Ellicott Douglass." *Geographical Review* 52, no. 4 (October 1962): 612–614. This obituary chronicles the life of Andrew Douglass.

Taylor, Frank B. "Bearing of the Tertiary Mountain Belt on the Origin of the Earth's Plan." *Bulletin of the Geologic Society of America* 21 (1910): 179–226. The geologic community took little notice of this paper when Taylor first proposed a type of continental drift.

Tilley, C. E. "Norman Levi Bowen 1887–1956" *Biographical Memoirs of Fellows of the Royal Society* 3 (November 1957): 6–22. A biography on Bowen.

Time. "Teaching Evolution." A collection of excerpts from *Time* magazine articles about evolution. Available online. URL: http://www.time.com/time/archive/collections/0,21428,c_evolution,00.shtml. Accessed April 24, 2006.

Webb, George E. "Solar Physics and the Origins of Dendrochronology." *Isis* 77, no. 2 (June 1986): 291–301. This report examines how the field of tree ring science arose from Douglass's experiments in searching for a relationship between 11-year solar cycles and terrestrial climate.

Wegener, Alfred. *Thermodynamik der Atmosphäre.* (The thermodynamics of the atmosphere.) Leipzig, Germany: J. A. Barth, 1911. Germany's standard textbook on meteorology at the time.

————. *The Origin of Continents and Oceans.* London: Methuen & Company, 1924. Translated by John Biram, from the 4th revision. New York: Dover Publications, 1966. This book is a late English translation of Wegener's book on continental drift.

Wentworth, C. K. "A Scale of Grade and Class Terms for Clastic Sediments." *Journal of Geology* 30 (1922): 377–392. This report classifies sediment grains by size.

Yoder, Hatten S. Jr., editor. *The Evolution of the Igneous Rocks: Fiftieth Anniversary Perspectives.* Princeton, New Jersey: Princeton University Press, 1979. This book examines issues in the field of igneous petrology.

————. "Norman L. Bowen (1887–1956), MIT Class of 1912, First Predoctoral Fellow of the Geophysical Laboratory." *Earth Sciences History,* 11, no. 1 (1992): 45–55. Available online. URL: http://vgp.agu.org/bowen_paper/bowen_paper.html. Accessed April 24, 2006.

————. "Norman L. Bowen: The Experimental Approach to Petrology." *GSA Today* (May 1998): 10–11. Available online as a PDF with Adobe Reader. URL: http://gsahist.org/gsat/gt98may10_11.pdf. Accessed April 24, 2006.

Young, Davis A. *Mind Over Magma: The Story of Igneous Petrology.* Princeton, New Jersey: Princeton University Press, 2003. Young, an igneous petrologist, provides a modern analysis about the history of his field, reminding readers of the difficulties geologists faced in solving concepts taken for granted today.

————. *N. L. Bowen and Crystallization-Differentiation: The Evolution of a Theory.* Washington, D.C.: Mineralogical Society of America, 1998. A history of Norman Bowen's contribution to igneous petrology.

4

1931–1940:
Exploring Inner Earth

Introduction

From the 1920s through the 1930s seismologists around the world worked together to build better seismographic instruments and analyze the incoming seismic records for understanding the planet's most mysterious layers: those unreachable depths of the core and mantle. Society turned to the earthquake experts for help and advice on surviving the damages wrought by building cities on ground liable to move. Americans redefined the European intensity scale to take into consideration the new world's construction habits—and new construction codes in California began setting a higher standard for acceptable risk of building failure during an earthquake, especially in public schools. The decade of the 1930s opened with seismologists confident of their deduction that the Earth's core was fluid, and it closed with the same seismologists now confident that they still had much to learn, based on Inge Lehmann's discovery of the inner core. Although seismology represents only one of many fields in the Earth Sciences, during the 1930s it was one of the most influential fields for those working to understand the nature of the planet Earth.

A Fluid Core

After Richard Oldham's early 20th-century identification of Earth's core using seismicity, and Beno Gutenberg's determination that a discontinuity in seismic wave behavior marked the core-mantle boundary, the two seismologists diverged in their analysis of the data as to whether the core was liquid or solid. The disagreement stemmed from missing S waves.

Rigidity is important in the physics and mathematics involved in wave propagation. S waves, also called transverse or shear waves, propagate by vibrating the medium they are in from side-to-side or perpendicular to their advancing direction. If the material is not rigid enough to provide an elastic rebound and perpetuate the side-to-side or transverse motion of the wave, than the wave will not advance. P waves advance their direction by means of compression, and can in fact travel faster given a less rigid medium. While S waves can travel through solid material, only P waves, also called compressional waves, such as sound waves, can travel through solids, liquids, and gases.

Oldham originally favored a solid mantle and a denser solid core to explain the perceived slowdown in the P waves, but as seismologists began to scrutinize the seismological records more carefully they noticed the S waves they thought they had missed because of difficulties in reading the seismographic records, were in fact missing.

Russian seismologist Leonid Leybenzon (1879–1951) in 1911 was the first to hypothesize that the core was fluid, or at least not rigid enough to support S waves. Oldham independently came to the same conclusion in 1913, and others, including Prussian-German geophysicist Emil Wiechert in 1924, supported this new theory based on the change in velocity at the Gutenberg discontinuity. Wiechert (1861-1928) had, before the turn of the century, originally proposed a solid iron core and stony mantle structure for Earth's inner layers and later had taught Gutenberg as a student at the University of Göttingen in Germany.

Gutenberg remained unconvinced that the lack of S wave observations implied a fluid core. Others too were not yet convinced that the seismographic records were devoid of S waves passing through the core, as a few records at least seemed to indicate otherwise. As historian Steven Brush discusses in his book *A History of Modern Planetary Physics: Nebulous Earth,*

Kliuchevskoi, Russia's highest and most active volcano on the Kamchatka Peninsula, erupts explosively throughout the decade drawing the attention of the volcanological community to this remote region. Eruptions continue sporadically throughout the century, reaching the same explosivity again in the late 1980s

Fuego in Guatemala erupts explosively on January 21 spewing out 0.05 cubic miles (0.2 km³) of tephra in a single day

U.S. Coast and Geodetic Survey initiated a program of strong-motion recording in California

MILESTONES

1931

1932

Aniakchak, on the Alaska Peninsula, erupts explosively on May 1 spewing out 0.1 cubic miles (0.4 km³) of tephra accompanied by pyroclastic flows, lava flows, and debris avalanches that continue for a month

December 25, an earthquake (recognized today as having had a magnitude 7.6) strikes Gansu, China—70,000 people die. The quake causes an estimated $150,000 in property damage

American seismologists Harry O. Wood and Frank Neumann modify a scale for identifying earthquake intensity, called the Modified Mercalli (MM) Intensity Scale

American chemist Harold C. Urey discovers deuterium, a heavy isotope of hydrogen (denoted as: D or ²H). His discovery ushers in the modern field of stable isotope geochemistry

Cerro Azul in central Chile erupts explosively on April 10 punctuating a long period of activity, which began in 1916, and including phreatic explosions, pyroclastic flows, and 2.3 cubic miles (9.5 km³) of tephra

Gutenberg published in German a review of six methods for determining Earth's rigidity. The first four involved evaluating the effect of: ocean tides; the gravitational attraction from the Sun and Moon; Earth's own gravitational changes as a result of changes in topography; and the small circular oscillation the poles of the Earth make as the planet rotates around its axis (otherwise called the Chandler wobble, after American astronomer Seth Carlo Chandler who discovered the phenomena in 1891). Gutenberg concluded that these events called for a high rigidity. He also stressed a recent calculation by Swiss mathematician Ernst Meissner that claimed a minimum rigidity was needed in the core to maintain Earth's structural stability. The lack of S waves was the only factor that remained problematic for Gutenberg, and he argued that the core boundary might be to blame. In 1926 a report by British mathematician and geophysicist Harold Jeffreys (1891–1989) changed Gutenberg's opinion on the subject.

In his article "The Rigidity of the Earth's Central Core," Jeffreys provided a detailed critique of Gutenberg's list of methods showing how the events could indeed occur even with low rigidity in the core. He also compared the rigidity of the Earth as a whole to the rigidity indicated by the seismic wave velocities in the mantle. Jeffreys found that the rigidity of the whole Earth was less than what the seismic wave velocities in the mantle indicated. A region of low rigidity had to exist to compensate for this inequality. The core was the only solution. The seismic community breathed a sigh of

March 11, an earthquake (recognized today as having had a magnitude 6.4) strikes Long Beach, California—115 people die. The quake causes an estimated $40 million in property damage

Shin-dake on Japan's Kuchinoerabu-jima Island in the northern Ryukyus experiences its largest eruption since 1840 on December 24, causing fatalities and property damage to local villages

March 2, an earthquake (recognized today as having had a magnitude 8.4) strikes Sanriku, Japan—2,990 people die, many from a resulting tsunami

MILESTONES

1933

1934

Kharimkotan, one of Russia's northern Kuril Islands, erupts explosively on January 8 causing a tsunami, fatalities, and property damage along with debris avalanches, pyroclastic flows, and lava flows. The volume of lava released during the four-month period of activity was 0.02 cubic miles (0.1 km³); 0.2 cubic miles (1 km³) of tephra was released as well

Suoh on Sumatra, Indonesia, erupts explosively on July 10 spewing out 0.05 cubic miles (0.21 km³) of tephra

March 12, an earthquake (recognized today as having had a magnitude 6.5) strikes Kosmo, Utah—2 people die

November 20, an earthquake (recognized today as having had a magnitude 7.4) strikes Baffin Bay, Canada—no fatalities reported. The quake is the largest in the 20th century to strike north of the Arctic Circle

relief. It seemed the major questions regarding the structure of the inner layers of the Earth had been solved, like seeing a map of the world for the first time with all major continents identified. Now, they could focus on evaluating some of the more peculiar discrepancies in the seismic record and work on the finer details of the planet's inner map. Little did they know that one particular discrepancy would lead to the discovery that their map was missing a critical and very large continent: the inner core.

Earthquake Intensities

In 1929 the Carnegie Institution of Washington was planning a new department of geophysics at the Seismological Laboratory in Pasadena, California. Gutenberg traveled to Pasadena and contributed significantly to the department's conception. Within a year, he had joined both the Pasadena Seismological Laboratory and the nearby California Institute of Technology, where he met American seismologists Harry O. Wood (1879–1958), Charles Richter (1900–85), and Hugo Benioff (1899–1968).

Wood, director of the Seismological Laboratory from 1921 to 1946, invented a specific type of seismograph in 1922 with John August Anderson (1876–1959), Executive Officer of the Caltech Observatory Council. Their Wood-Anderson torsion seismograph was designed especially for recording the short-period horizontal vibrations of local

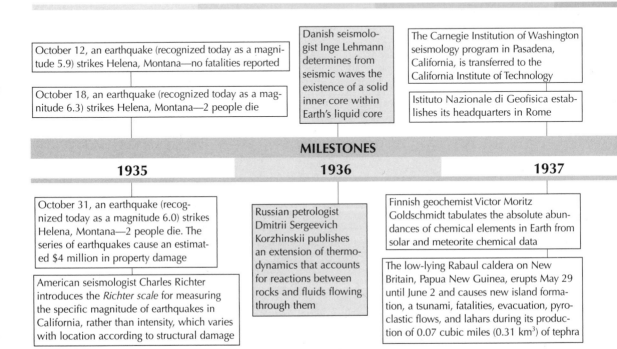

October 12, an earthquake (recognized today as a magnitude 5.9) strikes Helena, Montana—no fatalities reported

October 18, an earthquake (recognized today as a magnitude 6.3) strikes Helena, Montana—2 people die

Danish seismologist Inge Lehmann determines from seismic waves the existence of a solid inner core within Earth's liquid core

The Carnegie Institution of Washington seismology program in Pasadena, California, is transferred to the California Institute of Technology

Istituto Nazionale di Geofisica establishes its headquarters in Rome

MILESTONES

1935   **1936**   **1937**

October 31, an earthquake (recognized today as a magnitude 6.0) strikes Helena, Montana—2 people die. The series of earthquakes cause an estimated $4 million in property damage

American seismologist Charles Richter introduces the *Richter scale* for measuring the specific magnitude of earthquakes in California, rather than intensity, which varies with location according to structural damage

Russian petrologist Dmitrii Sergeevich Korzhinskii publishes an extension of thermodynamics that accounts for reactions between rocks and fluids flowing through them

Finnish geochemist Victor Moritz Goldschmidt tabulates the absolute abundances of chemical elements in Earth from solar and meteorite chemical data

The low-lying Rabaul caldera on New Britain, Papua New Guinea, erupts May 29 until June 2 and causes new island formation, a tsunami, fatalities, evacuation, pyroclastic flows, and lahars during its production of 0.07 cubic miles (0.31 km^3) of tephra

earthquakes. In 1931 Benioff, still a Caltech graduate student at the time, started engineering his own seismometers. The vertical component Benioff seismometer measured the amplification of vertical ground motion better than previous designs and became a standard piece of equipment for earthquake monitoring stations. Coupled with the Wood-Anderson seismograph, the Benioff seismometer became a standard piece of equipment for earthquake monitoring stations.

Also in 1931 the U.S. Department of Commerce Coast and Geodetic Survey (C&GS) received funding from Congress to begin an engineering seismology program and establish a national strong-motion monitoring network. The 1929 World Engineering Congress in Tokyo inspired American engineers to develop *accelerographs* that could be placed close to known faults and triggered to record the strong earthquake motions that would typically damage other seismographs. The National Bureau of Standards in the Department of Commerce modified a Wood-Anderson seismograph for their design of the first accelerograph. By the summer of 1932 Caltech and the Seismological Laboratory had collaborated to build a network of six seismographic stations around Southern California installed with accelerographs.

A devastating test of the equipment struck Long Beach, California, on March 10, 1933. Just two years earlier, Wood collaborated with seismologist Frank Neumann (1892–1964) to modify and publish in English

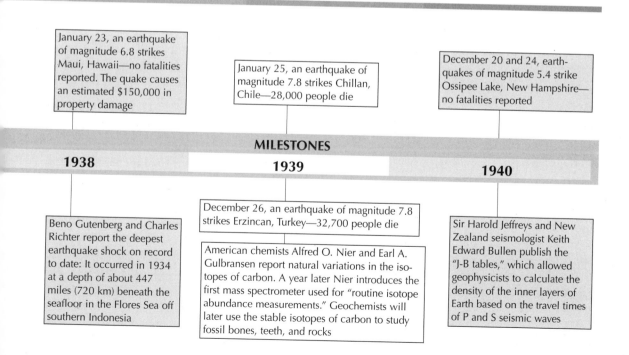

January 23, an earthquake of magnitude 6.8 strikes Maui, Hawaii—no fatalities reported. The quake causes an estimated $150,000 in property damage

January 25, an earthquake of magnitude 7.8 strikes Chillan, Chile—28,000 people die

December 20 and 24, earthquakes of magnitude 5.4 strike Ossipee Lake, New Hampshire—no fatalities reported

MILESTONES

1938   **1939**   **1940**

Beno Gutenberg and Charles Richter report the deepest earthquake shock on record to date: It occurred in 1934 at a depth of about 447 miles (720 km) beneath the seafloor in the Flores Sea off southern Indonesia

December 26, an earthquake of magnitude 7.8 strikes Erzincan, Turkey—32,700 people die

American chemists Alfred O. Nier and Earl A. Gulbransen report natural variations in the isotopes of carbon. A year later Nier introduces the first mass spectrometer used for "routine isotope abundance measurements." Geochemists will later use the stable isotopes of carbon to study fossil bones, teeth, and rocks

Sir Harold Jeffreys and New Zealand seismologist Keith Edward Bullen publish the "J-B tables," which allowed geophysicists to calculate the density of the inner layers of Earth based on the travel times of P and S seismic waves

the standard intensity scale being used in Europe at the time. Intensity scales had been used throughout history to describe the type of damage an earthquake had caused to buildings. Like topography maps indicating the peak of a mountain, isoseismal maps used increasing intensity scales to pinpoint the epicenter of an earthquake.

In 1883 Italian seismologist Michele Stefano Conte de Rossi (1834–98) and Swiss limnologist François-Alphonse Forel (1841–1912) combined their own earlier intensity scales and established the Rossi-Forel scale for intensity. The area farthest from the epicenter that could still trigger a local record of activity on a seismograph was given the Roman numeral I. The scale had 10 levels, with X indicating complete destruction. When Japanese seismologist Omori Fusakichi (1868–1923) visited Italy to observe earthquake-damaged cities he immediately recognized that the European buildings were far more susceptible to earthquake damage than Japan's infrastructure, which relied heavily on wood rather than brick and mortar—a testament to Japan's seismically aware society.

In 1900 Omori published his own intensity scale. Historian Gregory Clancey of the National University of Singapore writes in *Historical Perspectives on East Asian Science, Technology, and Medicine*, that: "In re-writing the Rossi-Forel Scale to Japanese specifications, Omori had written the survivability of 'Japanese' buildings and the fragility of 'foreign' ones directly into the content of seismology. Their unequal relationship was now fixed in Japanese practice as scientific fact. . . . The ratio (in some cases the percentage) of destroyed 'Japanese' and 'foreign' structures was now to be the normative sign of a particular acceleration of seismic waves, the principle calculation by which seismic waves were to be seen and explained over very large areas."

In 1902 Italian volcanologists Giuseppe Mercalli (1850–1914) updated the Rossi-Forel scale to include how witnesses of an earthquake responded to the danger and described the event. Soon after, Italian physicist Adolfo Cancani (1856–1904) proposed expanding the Mercalli to XII. German geophysicist August Heinrich Sieberg (1875–1945) followed his suggestion and the Mercalli-Cancani-Sieberg (MCS) Intensity Scale dominated Europe. When Wood and Neumann introduced their intensity scale, which also had XII levels, they dropped Cancani and Sieberg's names and called it the Modified Mercalli (MM) Intensity Scale. This remained as the standard for describing the intensities of earthquakes in America until 1956, when Charles Richter updated the scale for modern structural designs but continued to call it the Modified Mercalli (MM) Intensity Scale. Today when seismologists refer to the Modified Mercalli Scale, they are typically referring to the 1956 version.

In 1933, shortly after the Long Beach earthquake, Wood provided a preliminary report to the Seismological Society of America. He explained that the earthquake manifested a grade VIII on the 1931 scale, in numerous places. "Serious damage to bad construction resulted in many places inside an area of about [450 square miles (1,200 km²)], with the greatest concentration in and near Compton, and in and near Long Beach." Newspapers reported 115 people had died during the earthquake, most from falling debris as they ran outside their homes and buildings. The cost of the damage was upward of $50 million in depression-era dollars. Wood compared the intensity of the Long Beach earthquake to earlier damage from a nearby shock: "All the evidence indicates a fairly strong, moderately large shock in the local earthquake class, manifesting about the same intensity over an area of about the same size as the shock in Santa Barbara in 1925." He ends the report with a critical assessment of city's infrastructure: "The disastrous consequences of the shock were due chiefly to poor construction on bad natural ground in a rather densely populated district." The lesson learned was an ancient one, and often ignored: Earthquakes do not kill people; poorly constructed buildings built on earthquake fault lines kill people.

One of the more surprising reactions to the devastation of San Francisco after the earthquake of 1906 was California's limited restructuring of its building laws. The California Building Standards Commission, established in 1953, reports that California's first public building law was enacted in 1909 and addressed State Tenement Housing. Not until 1927 did the state have a uniform building code. The Long Beach earthquake struck at 5:54 P.M. on a Friday and left 70 schools in ruins, 120 schools severely damaged, and 300 schools with minor damage. If the earthquake had happened earlier in the day, the loss of young lives would have been horrendous. The public demanded action and California Assembly Member Charles Field rapidly pushed forward a bill through legislature to make schools resistant to earthquake damage. One month after the earthquake, the governor signed into action the California Field Act authorizing the Division of Architecture of the California State Department of Works to review, approve, and supervise the construction of all public schools in the state.

Determining Earthquake Magnitude: The Richter Scale

Wood's language in his preliminary analysis of the Long Beach Earthquake exemplifies the widespread use of intensity scales for establishing how damaging an earthquake had been and the extent of damage done in comparison to previous earthquakes in neighboring cities where construction is often assumed to be similar. The levels designated are arbitrary (hence the multiple scales used by varying nations), subjective (the damage seen is not indicative of the energy from the earthquake, but of the quality of the construction), and provide no mathematical or quantifiable measurement for identifying how much energy the earthquake distributed to ground motion. Intensity scales were useless for comparing earthquakes that struck in areas with no people or no buildings—such as land under consideration for development, on farmland, or in the ocean.

Seismologist Charles Richter provided a mathematical means for comparing the amplitude of seismic waves when he introduced the concept of magnitude. (AIP Emilio Segrè Visual Archives)

That changed in 1935 when Richter introduced the astronomical term *magnitude*, which referred to a star's brightness, into the lexicon of seismologists. Richter had joined the Seismological Laboratory in 1927 as he was completing his Ph.D. at Caltech. Wood gave the eager physicist the task of locating earthquake epicenters from the burgeoning network of seismometers in order to establish a catalog of earthquake events and when they occurred. In a 1980 interview, Richter explained that he suggested to Wood that they "might compare earthquakes in terms of the measured amplitudes recorded at these stations, with an appropriate correction for distance." After some struggle, Richter began looking for assistance. He read the comparisons Japanese seismologist Kiyoo Wadati (1902–95) made of large earthquakes by graphically plotting the maximum ground motion recorded during an earthquake against the seismometer's distance to the epicenter. In a seismic record of a local earthquake, the P wave strikes first and is followed within seconds by the S wave. The further away a station is located from the epicenter, the more time passes before an S wave is recorded and the less the S wave's amplitude—which is one reason why seismologists did not at first question the lack of S waves for stations recording earthquakes located on the other side of the planet. They assumed the amplitudes faded into the noise from the P wave.

Richter, however, was still stumped over the vast range in differences between the largest and smallest earthquakes and did not know how to graph them in a manageable way. That was when "Dr. Beno Gutenberg then made the natural suggestion to plot the amplitudes logarithmically," he said. A logarithm converts large numbers into small numbers (the logarithm of 100 to the base 10 is 2; written $\log_{10}100=2$); it is the mathematical inverse of exponentially raising a number to a power (10

Richter's calibration of seismic magnitude on a Wood-Anderson seismograph. After measuring the amplitude of the seismic wave on the seismograph and the time between the P and S waves, a line drawn between the amplitude and the elapsed time between seismic waves points to the earthquake's Richter magnitude.

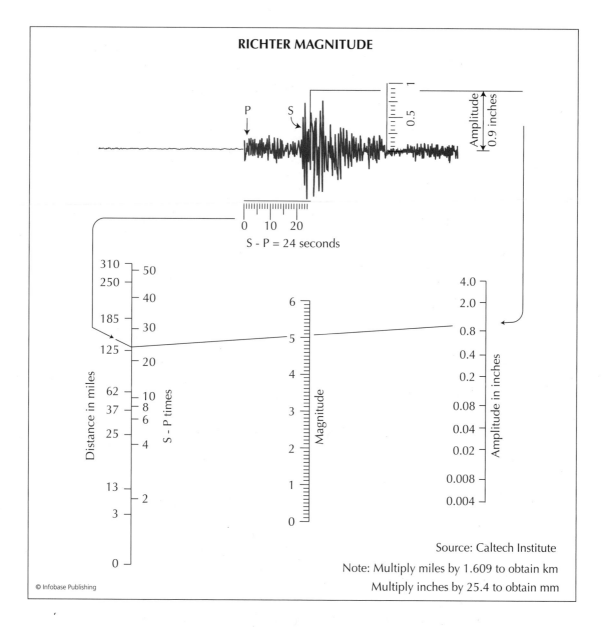

RICHTER MAGNITUDE

Source: Caltech Institute

Note: Multiply miles by 1.609 to obtain km

Multiply inches by 25.4 to obtain mm

to the exponent 2 is 100; written $10^2=100$). Using a millimeter scale for measuring the maximum amplitudes of the S wave as recorded on the Wood-Anderson seismographs and calculating the difference in travel times between S and P waves, Richter quantified the seismic energy of an earthquake by taking the logarithm of the amplitude and adding a distance correction factor—which in the case of the Southern California seismometers, Richter calculated to be: $3\log_{10}[8\Delta t(s)] - 2.92$, where $\Delta t(s)$

RICHTER SCALE COMPARISON

Magnitude	TNT for seismic energy yield	Approximate example
-1.5	6 ounces (170 g)	Breaking a rock on a table
1.0	30 pounds (13.6 kg)	Large blast at a construction site
1.5	320 pounds (145 kg)	WWII conventional bombs
2.0	1 ton	Large quarry or mine blast
2.5	4.6 tons	WWII blockbuster bombs
3.0	29 tons	Massive ordinance air blast bomb
3.5	73 tons	Chernobyl nuclear disaster, 1986
4.0	1,000 tons	Small atomic bomb
4.5	5,100 tons	Average tornado (total energy)
5.0	32,000 tons	Nagasaki: atomic bomb
5.5	80,000 tons	Little Skull Mountain, Nevada, quake, 1992
6.0	1 million tons	Double Spring Flat, Nevada, quake, 1994
6.5	5 million tons	Northridge, California, quake, 1994
7.0	32 million tons	Kobe, Japan, quake, 1995
7.5	160 million tons	Landers, California, quake, 1992
8.0	1 billion tons	San Francisco, California, quake, 1906
8.5	5 billion tons	Anchorage, Alaska, quake, 1964
9.0	32 billion tons	Chilean quake, 1960/Indian Ocean quake, 2004

Note: Multiply tons by 0.9072 to obtain metric tonnes

is the change in time (Δt) between S and P waves in seconds (s). Wood recommended naming the calculated seismic energy scale something new to differentiate it from earthquake intensity. Richter, who had an affinity for astronomy chose the word "magnitude." The full Richter equation for magnitude or M, where A stands for the Amplitude in millimeters (mm) read: $M = \log_{10}A(mm) + 3\log_{10}[8\Delta t(s)] - 2.92$. Richter, who was not a fan of logarithmic plots, considered himself lucky when the mathematics of his system yielded a robust and objective means for comparing earthquakes. Suddenly, each earthquake had a unique fingerprint that distinguished it from all others regardless of the extent of damage it produced. With Gutenberg's help, Richter was able to apply the system of calculating earthquake magnitudes to other seismometers around the world.

Earth's (Solid) Inner Core

On Monday June 17, 1929, a strong earthquake struck New Zealand at 10:17 A.M. The epicenter was located close to the small town of Murchison near the northwest end of the South Island, but people from as far south as Dunedin and as far north as Auckland reported feeling the seismic waves. Many of the 300 townsfolk in Murchison lost their homes and became refugees after the quake, but the devastation to the road along the Bullen River and Gorge made providing emergency assistance difficult. Most of the damage and many of the 17 casualties resulted from flooding and landslides, as the hills in the region were already soaked with winter rains.

On the other side of the planet, seismometers in Europe began recording the P wave from the earthquake as it finished traveling through Earth's interior—reaching Copenhagen just after 11:17 P.M. on Sunday June 16. The record from the network of seismometers tracking this particular earthquake sparked Danish seismologist Inge Lehmann's curiosity. Lehmann (1888–1993) had been analyzing the subtle variations in the seismic records as they came off seismometers from all over the world, including her own seismometers in Copenhagen, rather than relying on the published work from other seismologists who may or may not be paying attention to the same type of irregularities that she wanted to track. "I preferred to read phases from borrowed records or from copies of records that had been obtained. It meant a lot of work, but the published readings were not always satisfactory, especially when the movement was complex," she wrote in a 1987 article reflecting on her achievements in the field.

When Lehmann compared the European records of the New Zealand quake, she recognized two branches of P waves in the time curves that should have been deflected by the core given the epicentral position of the stations in comparison to the origin of the earthquake. Remember from Chapter 1 that a station located directly on the opposite point of

Scientist of the Decade: Inge Lehmann (1888–1993)

Denmark is not known for its earthquakes, but it is known for its seismologist Inge Lehmann. In her later years she wrote of the first time she felt the ground shake: "I may have been 15 or 16 years old, when, on a Sunday morning, I was sitting at home together with my mother and sister, and the floor began to move under us. The hanging lamp swayed. It was very strange. My father came into the room. 'It was an earthquake,' he said. The center had evidently been at a considerable distance, for the movements felt slow and not shaky. In spite of a great deal of effort, an accurate epicenter was never found. This was my only experience with an earthquake until I became a seismologist 20 years later."

As a child, Lehmann attended a coed school that was run under the guidance of Hannah Adler—an aunt of Niels Bohr, the 1922 Nobel Physics Laureate. In this environment Lehmann grew up without the typical societal constraints of the time regarding women in the fields of science. She is often quoted saying that, at the school, "no difference between the intellect of boys and girls was recognized, a fact that brought some disappointment later in life when I had to recognize that this was not the general attitude." She began studying at the University of Copenhagen in 1907 and after passing examinations in math, physics, chemistry, and astronomy gained acceptance to spend her junior year at Newnham College in Cambridge—where coincidently Harold Jeffreys was also a student but failed to make Lehmann's acquaintance. Lehmann returned home in December 1911 and started working in an actuary's office. In 1918 she returned to the University of Copenhagen to finish her undergraduate studies.

Lehmann's work in seismology officially began in 1925 when N. E. Norlund hired her as an assistant to help him implement seismographic stations in Denmark and Greenland. Bruce Bolt in his biography of Lehmann quotes her as describing this time in her life thusly: "I began to do

seismic work and had some extremely interesting years in which I and three young men who had never seen a seismograph before were active installing Wiechert, Galitzin-Wilip, and Milne-Shaw seismographs in Copenhagen and also helping to prepare the Greenland installations. I studied seismology at the same time unaided, but in the summer of 1927 I was sent abroad for three months. I spent one month with Professor Beno Gutenberg in Darmstadt. He gave me a great deal of his time and invaluable help."

A year after her time with Gutenberg and other foremost seismologists, Lehmann obtained her master's degree in *geodesy* and seismology from the University of Copenhagen. She went on to become chief of the Royal Danish Geodetic Institute's seismological department, managing until her retirement in 1954 Denmark's top (and only) seismic monitoring stations. As Bolt wrote, each of the stations had a "caretaker" that Lehmann instructed, but the Scoresbysund station's caretakers were "a special concern." Keeping in mind that Denmark is surrounded by waterways, the only way to reach the Scoresbysund station was in those days by boat "calling in once a year."

Lehmann, working out of the Copenhagen observatory, established a system early on in her career of evaluating the various seismic records by eye for similarities in wave patterns. In a memorial essay about his aunt, Niles Groes wrote in 1994: "I remember Inge one Sunday in her beloved garden . . . with a big table filled with cardboard oatmeal boxes. In the boxes were cardboard cards with information on earthquakes and the times for these and the times for their registration all over the world. This was before computer processing was available, but the system was the same. With her cardboard cards and her oatmeal boxes, Inge registered the velocity of propagation of the earthquakes to all parts of the globe. By means of this information, she deduced new theories of the inner parts of the Earth."

the planet from the focus or origin of the earthquake is said to have an epicenter of 180°. Because the core changes how P waves travel through Earth, Oldham had found the P-wave shadow using time curves when he first identified the core seismically.

Evaluating the travel time of seismic waves was still a very difficult problem in the 1930s, and many seismologists were tackling the issue. They would frequently plot seismic waves vertically side-by-side on a graph with time on the Y-axis and the distance from the epicenter of the earthquake on the X-axis. A curve connecting the arrival of each wave would yield the velocity or travel time of that wave, also equal to the change in distance divided by the change in time. Explained Lehmann, "If the observations of a group of stations were all read by one and the same person who paid attention to the shape of the curves, it might be possible to trace a phase from one station to another and in this way determine a time curve that was not otherwise obtainable. A very critical attitude is required in order to avoid reading phases where they are expected to be. If the readings are adapted to time curves that already exist, they are not very useful."

In 1930 Lehmann published her unusual finding of the two branches of P waves traveling through the Earth but continued to wonder about their meaning. In her reflections she wrote, "The rays are bent when they leave the mantle and enter the core, in which the velocity is much smaller. Thus the time curve has two branches. The first wave through the core (the one with the smallest angle of incidence) emerges at the surface of the Earth at considerably greater epicentral distance and later than the wave that just touches the core. . . . The upper branch had not been indicated in Gutenberg's time curves and does not seem to have been observed before." This upper branch she labeled P-prime, written P´.

Six years after her discovery, she provided a reason for the strange P-wave behavior in one of the shortest titles for an article in seismological history: *P´*. The waves she reasoned were deflected only after traveling some distance within the core—meaning the core itself had an inner layer. The implications of her finding supported the theory that while the outer layer was fluid and affected shear waves as Jeffreys had concluded, a solid inner layer changed the direction of compressional waves. In 1980 historian Stephen Brush wrote: "Lehmann's 'inner core' hypothesis, soon accepted and elaborated on by other seismologists, is one of the most important advances in our knowledge of the Earth's interior over the past 50 years."

Further Reading

Adams, Frank Dawson. *Birth and Development of the Geologic Sciences.* New York: Dover Publications, Inc., 1954. Originally published by Williams & Wilkins in 1938, this book examines the history of the geologic field.

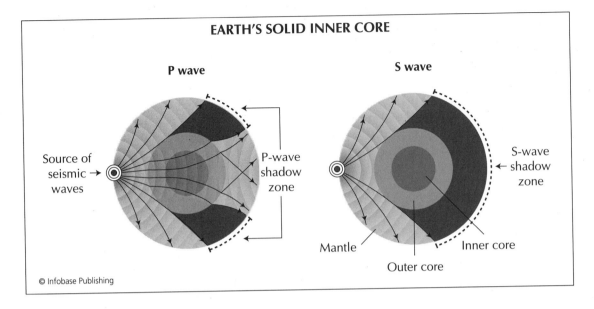

EARTH'S SOLID INNER CORE

P wave

S wave

Source of
seismic →
waves

P-wave
shadow
zone

S-wave
← shadow
zone

Mantle

Inner core

Outer core

© Infobase Publishing

Because S waves do not travel through the liquid core, a shadow zone forms on the other side of the Earth after an earthquake. Some P waves that passed through the core but were then deflected remained a mystery. Inge Lehmann explained the strange seismic P-wave observations as the result of a small solid core in the innermost part of the Earth.

Adams drew from original texts published in medieval times to provide insight into little known and discarded ideas about the mineral kingdom and how the field of geology evolved from Greek and Roman times through the Middle Ages and the Renaissance and into the modern era of the early 20th century.

Bolt, Bruce A. "Inge Lehmann." *Biographical Memoirs of Fellows of the Royal Society* 43 (1997): 285–301. This biography provides a detailed look at the professional and personal life of Inge Lehmann from a renowned seismologist and historian.

——— and Erik Hjortenberg. "Memorial Essay Inge Lehmann (1888–1993)." *Bulletin of the Seismological Society of America* 84 (1994): 229–233. Includes eulogies from Lehmann's nephew Niles Groes.

Brush, Stephen G. "Chemical History of the Earth's Core," *Eos* 63, no. 47 (1982): 1,185–1,188. A look at how scientists investigated a subject they could not see.

———. *A History of Modern Planetary Physics: Nebulous Earth*. Cambridge: Cambridge University Press, 1996. Brush discusses the impacts and evolutions of the scientific theories regarding Earth's early formation.

Clancey, Gregory. "The Science of Eurasia: Meiji Seismology as Cultural Critique." In: *Historical Perspectives on East Asian Science, Technology, and Medicine*. Gregory K. Clancey, Alan Kam-leung Chan, Hui-Chieh Loy. (eds.) Singapore: World Scientific, 2001. A chapter on how Omori Fusakichi revolutionized intensity scales for Japan and influenced European seismologists.

Contributions of 20th Century Women to Physics. This University of California Los Angeles library archive details the lives of 83 women who contributed significantly to fields in physics during the 20th century.

Available online. URL: http://cwp.library.ucla.edu/Phase2/Lehmann,_ Inge@81234567.html. Accessed April 24, 2006.

Davison, Charles. *A Manual of Seismology*. Cambridge: The University Press, 1921. An early look at the story of the inner Earth.

du Toit, Alex L. *Our Wandering Continents: An hypothesis of continental drifting*. Edinburgh: Oliver and Boyd, 1937. South African geologist du Toit provides detailed geological observations favoring the argument for continental drift but puts forth the hypothesis that instead of a single supercontinent, Pangea, the Tethys Ocean separated a former northern continent, Laurasia, and a southern continent, Gondwanaland.

———. *The Geology of South Africa*. Edinburgh: Oliver and Boyd, 1926. The first chapter of this book provides a brief historical record of the general principles of geology during the 1920s as treated from a South African standpoint. Chapter XVIII provides a guide to human tools and bones found in the South African geologic record.

Faul, Henry, and Carol Faul. *It Began with a Stone: A history of geology from the Stone Age to the Age of Plate Tectonics*. New York: John Wiley & Sons, 1983. A geologist and his wife team up to describe the people and events that influenced the geologic field.

Gutenberg, Beno, and Charles F. Richter. "Magnitude and Energy of Earthquakes." *Science* 83 (February 21, 1936): 183–185. A classic paper on seismology.

Jeffreys, Harold. *The Earth: Its Origin, History and Physical Constitution*. 6th edition. Cambridge: Cambridge University Press, 1976. A 20th-century perspective on the formation of the Earth from an influential voice in seismology.

———. "The Rigidity of the Earth's Central Core," *Monthly Notices Roy. Astron. Soc. Geophysical Supplement* 1 (1926): 371–383. Jeffrey's definitive argument for a fluid core.

Lehmann, Inge. "'P' As Read From the Records of the Earthquake of June 16, 1929." *Gerl. Beitr. Geophys.* 26 (1930): 402–412. An introduction to a curious feature in the seismological record.

———. "P'," *Publications du Bureau central seismologique international, serie A, Traveaux Scientifiques* 14 (1936): 87–115. A revolutionary paper in classic seismology identifying the Earth's inner core.

———. "Seismology in the Days of Old." *Eos* 68, no. 3 (1987): 33–35. Lehmann recollects her past achievements.

Longwell, Chester, Adolph Knopf, Richard Flint, Charles Schuchert, and Carl O. Dunbar. *Textbook of Geology*. New York: J. Wiley & Sons, Inc.; London: Chapman & Hall, Limited, 1932–33. This book is a successor to Louis Valentine Pirsson and Schuchert's 1929 *Textbook of Geology*, two-part volume covering physical and historical geology.

Mathez, Edmond A. (editor). *Earth: Inside and Out*. New York: The New Press, 2001. Essays answering the questions posed in the American Museum of Natural History's Gottesman Hall of Planet Earth: How has the Earth evolved? How do scientists read the rocks? Why are there ocean basins, mountains, and continents? What causes climate and climate change? Why is the Earth habitable? This book profiles histori-cally significant Earth scientists and highlights case studies of present-day researchers.

Montel, Alfredo. *Building Structures in Earthquake Countries.* London: Charles Griffin & Co., 1912. A comparison of lessons learned from vari-ous earthquakes at the turn of the century and the intensity scales used at the time to describe their impact on society.

National Information Service for Earthquake Engineering. "The Long Beach Earthquake of 1933." This Web site provides a brief history of the structural damage and building codes that followed. Available online. URL: http://nisee.berkeley.edu/long_beach/long_beach.html. Accessed February 28, 2007.

Oldroyd, David. *Thinking about the Earth: A History of Ideas in Geology.* Cambridge, Massachusetts: Harvard University Press, 1996. A look at the development and evolution of ideas in the geologic field.

Omori Fusakichi, "Seismic Experiments on the Fracturing and Overturning of Columns," *Publications of the Imperial Earthquake Investigation Committee*, no. 4, (1900): 138–141. A revolutionary paper that redefined the Rossi-Forel intensity scale for Japan and set in motion a revision of the scale in Europe.

Spall, Henry. "Charles F. Richter—An Interview." *Earthquake Information Bulletin* 12, no. 1 (1980). The U.S. Geological Survey provides biogra-phies of influential geologists, in this Web site: an interview of Richter in a Question and Answer format. Available online. URL: http://neic. usgs.gov/neis/seismology/people/int_richter.html. Accessed April 24, 2006.

Wood, Harry O., and F. Neumann. "Modified Mercalli Intensity Scale of 1931," *Bull. Seismol. Soc. Am.* 21 (1931): 277–283. A revision of the European intensity scale for North America.

———. "Preliminary report on the Long Beach earthquake." *Bulletin of the Seismological Society of America* 23, no. 2 (1933): 43–56. Wood provides a short preliminary report on the intensity and problems resulting from the 1933 earthquake.

5

1941–1950:
The Atomic Age

Introduction

Physicists who made connections between disparate fields of study exemplify the history of Earth science during this decade. Serbian astrophysicist and mathematician Milutin Milankovitch (1879–1958) exemplified this technique in 1941 when he published his book *Kanon der Erdbestrahlung und seine Anwendung auf das Eiszeitenproblem* (*Canon of Insolation and the Ice-Age Problem*) calculating the effect of the planet's orbit, tilt, and wobble on global climate cycles, specifically *ice ages*. German theoretical physicist Walter Elsasser (1904–91) provides another example when, after escaping Nazi Germany, he finds work in the United States helping with the war effort in the field of meteorology and winds up developing a theory explaining the production of Earth's magnetic field. American nuclear physicist Willard Libby (1908–80) finds time during his work on the Manhattan Project investigating uranium isotopes to research carbon's radioisotope. Carbon-14 is itself a prime example of how important it is to science to understand the interactions between fields of research. The strength of Earth's magnetic field influences the amount of cosmic rays that enter Earth's atmosphere. To correlate radiocarbon dates with calendar dates, researchers have turned to dendrochronology and paleoceanography. The use of primordial *radioisotopes*, those stellar born elements with half-lives of billions of years that contributed their weight to the formation of the planet, provides a check and balance on dating done with the unusual atmospheric-born carbon radioisotope. As discussed in Chapter 2, Arthur Holmes was the geologist principally responsible for applying radioisotope dates to the geologic record. As the author of the 1944 book *Principles of Physical Geology*—which discusses dating the geologic timescale using radioisotopes and proposing a convection model for the Earth's thermal distribution, a model that as a by-product provided a mechanism for continental drift—Holmes is recognized in this chapter as the scientist of the decade.

Milankovitch Cycles

While interned as a foreign enemy during part of World War I, Serbian astrophysicist Milutin Milankovitch spent most of his time in a library under the watch of the Austro-Hungarian army. By the end of the war, he had developed a mathematical model comparing variations in solar radiation across Earth's surface. Wladimir Köppen and Alfred Wegener incorporated his work in deducing past climates over drifting continents. This brought a great deal of publicity to Milankovitch, not all of it positive.

To improve the accuracy of modeling past climates, Milankovitch spent decades carefully calculating by hand how wobbles in Earth's orbit and rotation around its axis would have changed over the last 600,000 years.

(Opposite page) Milutin Milankovitch (1879–1958) calculated the changes over time to Earth's orbit around the Sun and Earth's own daily rotations. He proposed that variations over thousands to hundreds of thousands of years affect how much solar energy is reaching different parts of the planet influencing the onset of ice ages. A) Eccentricity: The shape of Earth's orbit around the Sun changes from slightly circular to more elliptical and back. B) Obliquity: The angle of Earth's tilt on its axis in relation to its plane of orbit around the Sun changes from 21.5 to 24.5 degrees (currently at 23.5 degrees) with a periodicity of 41,000 years. C) Precession: Over a period of 23,000 years, the axis of rotation traces a circle in the northern celestial sphere from Polaris, the current North Star, to the star Vega and back again to Polaris.

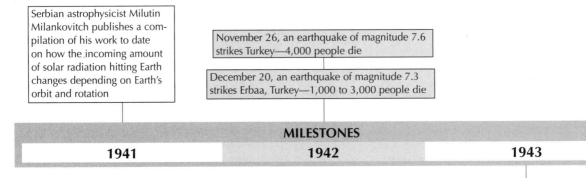

Serbian astrophysicist Milutin Milankovitch publishes a compilation of his work to date on how the incoming amount of solar radiation hitting Earth changes depending on Earth's orbit and rotation

November 26, an earthquake of magnitude 7.6 strikes Turkey—4,000 people die

December 20, an earthquake of magnitude 7.3 strikes Erbaa, Turkey—1,000 to 3,000 people die

MILESTONES

1941	1942	1943

A farmer in Mexico plowing his field with his family witnesses the birth of a new volcanic cinder cone erupting in his cornfield on February 20. Parícutin's formation in the Michoacán-Guanajuato volcanic region causes fatalities (from lightning), evacuations, explosive eruptions, and lava flows accompanied by 0.3 cubic miles (1.3 km³) of tephra. Within a week the cinder cone is 300 feet (90 m) high. Within a year it has climbed to 1,100 feet (335 m) high. The eruption continues until 1952 with 0.2 cubic miles (0.7 km³) of slow moving lava flows engulfing the surrounding villages

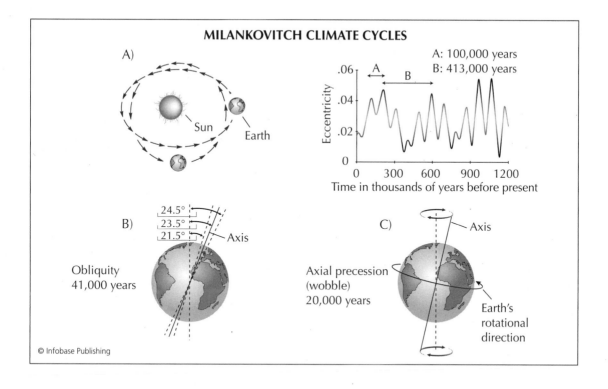

MILANKOVITCH CLIMATE CYCLES

A)

Sun
Earth

A: 100,000 years
B: 413,000 years

Eccentricity

.06
.04
.02
0

A
B

0   300   600   900   1200
Time in thousands of years before present

B)

24.5°
23.5°
21.5°
Axis

Obliquity
41,000 years

C)

Axis

Axial precession
(wobble)
20,000 years

Earth's
rotational
direction

© Infobase Publishing

MILESTONES

1944

1945

September 5, an earthquake of magnitude 5.8 strikes between Massena, New York, and Cornwall in Ontario, Canada—no fatalities reported. The quake causes an estimated $2 million in property damage

January 12, an earthquake of magnitude 7.1 strikes Mikawa, Japan—1,900 people die

December 7, an earthquake of magnitude 8.1 strikes Tonankai, Japan—1,223 people die

Avachinsky on Russia's Kamshatka Peninsula erupts on February 25 spewing out 0.07 cubic miles (0.3 km³) of tephra accompanied by lahars

November 27, an earthquake of magnitude 8.0 strikes off the coast of Pakistan—4,000 people die

Scientists knew that solar radiation varied due to slight changes in Earth's orbit on the order of tens of thousands of years. Milankovitch found that the gravitational influence from Jupiter and other planets gradually shifted the shape of Earth's orbit, its *eccentricity*, around the Sun from circular to more elliptical and back again on cycles of 100,000 and 400,000 years. He found that the tilt of Earth's axis—or *obliquity*, long known to cause the difference in seasons between the Southern and Northern Hemisphere—changed its tilt from 24.5° to 21.5° and back about every 41,000 years, and, like a spinning top that is winding down, Earth also traces a small circle in the celestial sky as its axis of rotation changes direction over a period of about 20,000 years. (This *precession* is responsible for why sailors look to Polaris in the constellation Ursa Minor as the North Star. In the Northern Hemisphere, measuring the angle of the North Star from the horizon provides the equivalent degree of latitude. Navigators typically use a sextant to measure the angle of a star above the horizon. A reading of 45° for the North Star would correspond to latitude 45°N. As the planet's axis traces its circle, the axis drifts away and points to different stars. Currently, the Southern Hemisphere's polestar, Sigma Octantis, is too far away to see easily with the naked eye.)

American chemist Willard Frank Libby develops the idea of *radiocarbon* dating

Sarychev Peak on Russia's Kuril Islands erupts explosively on November 9 with pyroclastic flows and lava flows

German-American geophysicist Walter Maurice Elsasser expands on the dynamo model of the Earth, which proposes that eddy currents in the Earth's molten iron core cause magnetism

American geophysicist William Maurice "Doc" of Columbia University sails the *Atlantic* on a two-month expedition over the Atlantic Ocean. Cores of the seafloor reveal modern plankton deposits sitting on top of fossil marine shells from the Eocene. The missing layers indicate unknown disturbances occurring on the seafloor. His oceanographic investigation provides the impetus for Columbia University to build a new geological observatory

MILESTONES

1946

1947

April 1, an earthquake of magnitude 8.1 strikes Unimak Island, Alaska—165 people die from the resulting tsunami. The tsunami provides the catalyst for a Seismic Sea Wave Warning System that is established on August 12, 1948, and later called the Pacific Tsunami Warning System

June 23, an earthquake of magnitude 7.3 strikes Vancouver Island in British Columbia, Canada—2 people die: one of a heart attack in Seattle and the other from drowning when an earthquake-generated wave capsizes a small boat

Russian-born Belgian chemist Ilya Prigogine publishes theories on nonlinear and irreversible thermodynamics (the study of the motion of atoms and molecules to produce heat), useful for predicting rates of geochemical processes, traffic problems, and for explaining how biological systems and other ordered structures can develop from disorder. For his theories, Prigogine is awarded the 1977 Nobel Prize in chemistry

After calculating the changes in solar radiation that hit Earth during different periods in eccentricity, obliquity, and precession—Milankovitch published the culmination of his work entitled *Kanon der Erdbestrahlung und seine Anwendung auf das Eiszeitenproblem (Canon of Insolation and the Ice-Age Problem)* in 1941. If the factors contributing to climate change coordinated perfectly, the graph representing the history of Earth's glacial and interglacial periods might have looked very similar to a heartbeat, but as Milankovitch discovered, the contributing factors overlap. This complexity brought mixed responses to his theory. To test his model, scientists needed an accurate means for determining when ice ages had occurred in the past. Their search led to radioisotopes.

In 1968 American oceanographer Wallace S. Broecker of Columbia University's Lamont Geological Observatory in Palisades, New York, with researchers from Massachusetts and Rhode Island, published a report in the journal *Science* titled "Milankovitch Hypothesis Supported by Precise Dating of Coral Reefs and Deep-Sea Sediments." Their work relied on uranium and thorium dating of corals around the Barbados Islands and of sediment cores taken from the seafloor. As research continued, the correlation between the work of Milankovitch and the dates

British physicist Patrick Blackett wins the Nobel Prize in physics for his modifications to the Wilson chamber, which allowed him to track cosmic rays with both positive and negative electrons occurring at the same time. Blackett later turns to the study of Earth's magnetism and reconsiders the physics that might yield a magnetic field from a large rotating mass of nonconducting material. His work has possible applications to the production of magnetic fields on other planets in the solar system

April 13, an earthquake of magnitude 7.1 strikes Puget Sound, Washington—8 people die. The quake causes an estimated $25 million in property damage

August 15, an earthquake of magnitude 8.6 strikes Assam, India, and Tibet—1,526 people die. The quake causes an estimated U.S. $25 million in property damage. American seismologist Bruce Bolt in 1993 reports in his book *Earthquakes* that Anders Kvale in 1955 coined the term seismic *seiche* to describe oscillations of lake levels in Norway and England caused by the Assam earthquake

MILESTONES

1948   **1949**   **1950**

June 28, an earthquake of magnitude 7.3 strikes Fukui, Japan—5,390 people die

Columbia University establishes the Lamont Geological Observatory on the former estate of Thomas W. Lamont in Palisades, New York, overlooking the Hudson River. Maurice Ewing takes charge as the observatory's first director

October 5, an earthquake of magnitude 7.3 strikes Ashgabat, Turkmenistan—110,000 people die

American seismologist Hugo Benioff identifies deep earthquakes occurring along ocean trenches and extending beneath South America and volcanic islands in the South Pacific. In the 1920s and 1930s, Japanese seismologist Kiyoo Wadati had independently identified similar faults extending under Japan. Later recognized for its role in the process of plate tectonics, the Wadati-Benioff zone delineates the top of the *lithosphere* during subduction

of past glacial and interglacial periods led scientists to dub the changes in eccentricity, obliquity, and precession as they contribute to Earth's climate the Milankovitch cycles. A variety of other contributing factors both natural and, more recently, man-made, also account for periodicity in and impacts to climate.

Currently Earth is in the midst of an interglacial period, which began about 11,000 years ago. Predictions using the Milankovitch model for when the next great ice age should return show Earth again cooling down after 25,000 to 50,000 years from now. In the meantime, human activities are contributing to the warming trend. Just how hot this interglacial period becomes is now in the hands of the dominant emissions-generating species.

Finding the Source of the Magnetic Field

In 1936 a nuclear physicist from Germany, Walter Elsasser, moved to Pasadena, California, and began a foray into the physics of meteorology. Having attended the University of Göttingen as a graduate student, Elsasser had known and worked with many of the most esteemed and burgeoning theoretical physicists of his time, including American physicist Robert Oppenheimer (1904–67), who also obtained a Ph.D. from the German university.

Elsasser's switch from nuclear physics to atmospheric physics came as a surprise to his friends and colleagues, but Elsasser was able to successfully apply his knowledge of quantum mechanics to some unsolved mysteries in the field—namely, the effects of infrared radiation. Biographer Harry Rubin wrote that at Caltech, Elsasser "learned that the Earth's atmosphere is full of unpredictable contingencies on every level of its scale, which gives the meteorologist a feeling for reality that is radically different from that of the laboratory scientist who can minimize contingencies."

Earth's rotation drives one of the prime examples of variations that meteorologists must take into account: that of the *Coriolis effect*. This is the deviation away from a straight line that a moving object makes on a rotating body, as seen from the reference frame of that rotating body. On Earth the deflection is to the right in the Northern Hemisphere and to the left in the Southern Hemisphere. As Elsasser's acquaintance Carl-Gustav Rossby, head of the department of meteorology at MIT, determined mathematically, the importance of Earth's rotation on moving objects is based on the speed of the object, and the distance and location it travels on Earth. The Coriolis effect is seen on such things as air currents and ocean currents, airplanes and long-range missiles—and more so in midlatitude regions and on objects traveling at high speeds for long distances. The Coriolis effect does not, as urban legend would claim, influence the direction a toilet flushes. (Instead, the shape of the

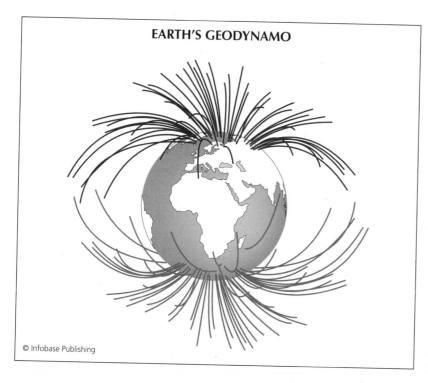

EARTH'S GEODYNAMO

© Infobase Publishing

In 1995 Earth scientist Gary Glatzmaier and mathematician Paul Roberts produced a 3-D computer model showing the internal and external magnetic lines of force, the geodynamo, generated by Earth's core. They modeled how the magnetic field changes during its course from a normal period, as it is today, to a period of reversal, when the north magnetic pole is located in the geographic south. This image diagrams parts of the external magnetic field lines near Earth's surface as they extend out into space from the Northern Hemisphere and return to Earth via the Southern Hemisphere. Glatzmaier and Roberts's model shows that in the core the magnetic field lines become jumbled and look like pasta in a boiling pot of water.

basin and the direction of the incoming water determine in which direction the water drains.)

Flow travels from high-pressure systems to low-pressure systems and that starts a current in motion. The Coriolis effect sets up interesting dynamics in air and ocean currents. In both hemispheres, currents moving toward the equator deviate to the west; those moving toward the west deviate to the closest pole; those moving toward a pole deviate to the east; and those moving toward the east deviate to the equator. The predominate directions of the trade winds and westerlies follow this pattern and influence the direction of ocean gyres, such as the Gulf Stream, and the path of hurricanes and cyclones, but the storms themselves spin counterclockwise in the Northern Hemisphere and clockwise in the Southern Hemisphere.

One of the earlier known curiosities in meteorology, described as Buys-Ballot's law after the Dutch meteorologist who recognized the phenomena in 1857, is that if a person in the Northern Hemisphere stands with her back to the wind, the low-pressure system will be on her left. This general rule of thumb works well at high latitudes but does not reach right-angle accuracy in the lower latitudes. When air flows rapidly toward a low-pressure area, it can set in motion a vortex. The Coriolis effect counters the direction of the pressure gradient and the airflow instead of leveling out the pressure gradient spins in a circle of equal pressure around the low-pressure system in the direction opposite to the Coriolis effect. The faster the wind speeds, the stronger the Coriolis effect and the more circular the eye of the storm.

Not long after arriving in California, Elsasser applied his knowledge of theoretical physics and meteorology to geophysics. He considered the Coriolis effect on flow in the mantle and liquid core. Arthur Holmes championed *convection currents* in the mantle as a mechanism for continental drift. Like Holmes, Elsasser considered radioactive heat as a means for setting currents in motion. Only instead of focusing on the mantle and surface he turned his attention to how currents in the liquid iron outer core could drive Earth's magnetic field. "Radioactive impurities which are very small compared to the total radioactivity of the Earth are sufficient to maintain thermally driven convective motions in the metallic core," wrote Elsasser in a 1939 article "On the Origin of the Earth's Magnetic Field" published in the journal of the American Physical Society.

For centuries, those puzzling over the magnetic properties of Earth had wondered about magnetic forces, magnetic fluids, and magnetic elements. The physicists questioned the nature of Auroras, of magnetic storms, and whether Earth had two or four magnetic poles. They debated as to whether the magnetism formed internally in the planet or formed because of some interaction with the Sun or, like the tides, with the Moon.

Then in 1820, Danish physicist Hans Christian Oersted (1777–1851) discovered he could induce a magnetic field using the flow of an electric current. Within two decades, Carl Friedrich Gauss (1777–1855) determined how to represent a magnetic field mathematically. This helped terrestrial physicists (or geophysicists, as they starting calling themselves in Europe at the turn of the century) determine that Earth's magnetic field spread internally from the planet out into space. Scottish physics mathematician James Clerk Maxwell (1831–79) provided the reasoning behind why an oscillating electric field generates an oscillating magnetic field, which in turn generates an oscillating electric field. Maxwell's equations proved that as these fields move they form an electromagnetic wave traveling at the speed of light. With this clue electromagnetism provided a new way of questioning terrestrial magnetism and the field of geophysics emerged from the 19th century as a quantitative pursuit.

Iron was a suspected mineral in Earth's core long before seismologists determined the planet's inner structure, but until the arguments for a liquid or solid core could be resolved, most geoscientists studying the magnetic field focused on whether the planet could produce a permanent magnetic field. They were at a loss however because the type of magnetic material, such as iron, that can hold a permanent magnet without an electric charge, loses its capability to maintain a permanent magnet at the high temperatures that exist within Earth's mantle and core. They also had to account for the magnetic field's tendency to drift westward; the magnetic north, which compass needles point to, moves several degrees per century relative to the geographic North Pole—an observation first recorded in the 1600s.

In 1912 German-British physicist Arthur Schuster (1851–1934) suggested that a planet's very rotation might establish a magnetic field. This set about a search for a mathematical link between a large rotating mass and magnetization. In 1905 Albert Einstein had introduced his theory on *special relativity*, concluding that mass (m) and energy (E) were related to the speed of light (c) in the equation $E=mc^2$. Special relativity, applied to electromagnetism, unified the electric and magnetic fields even further than Maxwell's equations. Einstein showed that each field was essentially the same phenomena, only observed differently. With this new perspective, physicists could apply mathematical explanations for Michael Faraday's 1830s experiments generating an electric current from a moving magnetic field. With his theory on general relativity in 1915, Einstein then brought gravity into the equations. This seemed promising for Schuster's theory, but the relationship, if any, between a large rotating mass and magnetism remained difficult to determine. Even Einstein, who embraced the idea, could not find the math necessary to support it.

In 1919 Joseph Larmor offered a different approach. He suggested a series of possibilities for explaining a persistent magnetic field on a celestial body, favoring the idea that convective motion within electrically conducting fluids on the Sun could continuously regenerate a magnetic field. This idea was dubbed the dynamo theory and immediately considered for its application on Earth, but anti-dynamo critics dismissed the idea because Earth's magnetic field is irregular: the magnitude of the magnetic field is different over different parts of the globe. The field's formation remained an enigma through the 1920s and '30s leading geophysicists to lament that "it cannot be said that at present any satisfactory explanation of the Earth's main field is available."

Elsasser's interdisciplinary approach to science provided a much needed perspective. He relied on the physics of the Coriolis effect and equations used to describe the motion of fluids. Turbulence in the system was key. By applying the physics of the dynamo theory to Earth's core and the importance of the rotation of the planet in establishing a Coriolis effect within the convecting metallic fluids of the outer core, he explained the formation of the magnetic field—the result of a self-excited (or self-sustaining) magneto-hydro-dynamic dynamo. The field remained stable for eons yet variable because of feedback in the system. Convection causes the conducting metallic fluid to flow; the Coriolis effect introduces turbulence in the flow and generates electric currents in an asymmetric pattern. These thermoelectric currents produce a changing magnetic field. The changing magnetic field in turn produces electric currents and, as the process continues, reinforce and cause variations to the original magnetic field.

Elsasser continued to develop the dynamo theory through the 1940s, moving with his wife to the east coast where he jumped from the Blue

Hill Meteorological Observatory of Harvard University to Columbia University's Division of War Research in New York during World War II—ultimately landing at the Radio Corporation of America Laboratories in Princeton, New Jersey. In 1946 *Physical Review* published the first of Elsasser's three-part report entitled "Induction Effects in Terrestrial Magnetism." The reports presented Elsasser's dynamo theory for Earth's magnetic field. With this paper he introduced the feasibility that the electrical currents in the outer core likely flow in a toroidal or doughnut-shaped electric field, significantly due to the Coriolis effect. He also concluded that the magnetic field flows in a poloidal pattern— that of larger circles linked through the middle of the toroidal electric field and extending like skinny hula hoops out beyond Earth and deep into space, but in the middle, the hole in the doughnut-shaped electric field, the magnetic field becomes twisted. Modeling these twists and turns would require advanced computers. The reports sparked new interest in analyzing the formation magnetic field.

Cosmic Rays

In 1925 Nobel physicist Robert Millikan (1868–1953), head of Caltech until 1946, introduced the term *cosmic rays* to describe the radiation that Victor Hess in 1912 had discovered entering the upper atmosphere from the cosmos. At first, cosmic rays were considered part of the *electromagnetic spectrum*. They were grouped together with other oscillating electric and magnetic fields, which Einstein identified as streams of light quantum, later called *photons*, which in a vacuum travel in waves at the speed of light. The electromagnetic spectrum includes radio waves, microwaves, infrared radiation, visible light, ultraviolet light, X-rays, and gamma rays, but cosmic rays, it turned out, were not part of the electromagnetic spectrum. Photons are considered particles with no mass and no electric charge. Experiments in 1929 determined that cosmic rays were actually electrically charged particles traveling at the speed of light. With particle physics awash in more questions than answers in the 1930s, cosmic rays took on celebrity status.

In 1920 Lord Ernest Rutherford (1871–1937) proposed the existence of the neutron; he had

already discovered the atomic nucleus and the positively charged *proton* inside hydrogen's atomic nucleus. The neutron would be a subatomic particle with slightly more mass than the proton, but no net electric charge—essentially, he considered it a closely coupled electron and proton that had joined so tightly as to form a new subatomic particle rather than staying separate as they do in the common hydrogen atom. Neutrons, he argued, would provide the building blocks for the nuclei of atoms heavier than hydrogen. It would also later explain the existence of isotopes, nearly identical chemical elements with the same electric charge but different atomic weight. The search was on, but the neutron was elusive.

In the meantime, British theoretical physicist Paul Dirac (1902–84) predicted the existence of antimatter: that every particle has a corresponding antiparticle, which has the same mass as the particle but the opposite charge. At first, Dirac considered protons as the antimatter to electrons, but their differences in mass ruled out that idea. What he needed to find were positrons. Neutrons, and also photons perhaps, because they have no

English nuclear physicist Sir Edward "Teddy" Bullard, who, like Elsasser, also became a geophysicist during the Depression, used an early digital computer to investigate the dynamo theory as it applied to Earth's magnetic field. During World War II, Bullard (1907–80) had helped save British submarines from German magnetic mines by neutralizing each ship's induced magnetization with wires that carried currents through the steel hulls. His work on the dynamo theory coupled with Elsasser's provided geophysicists with the first working mathematical and theoretical physics model of Earth's magnetic field. Discoveries of variations in the magnetic field that correlated with variations in atmospheric radiation provided a new method for identifying the mystery of cosmic rays.

Radiocarbon Dating

Cosmic rays are not actually "rays" in the beam-of-light meaning of the word. A more accurate description for the phenomena would be:

net charge, might actually be their own antimatter if such a thing is possible. The idea of antimatter itself seemed very strange but mathematically explained some discrepancies in quantum physics. Dirac split the 1933 Nobel Prize with Austrian physicist Erwin Schrödinger.

In February 1932, James Chadwick (1891–1974), who had worked for Rutherford, used laboratory experiments to finally obtain proof of the existence of neutrons. That same year, cosmic ray scientist Carl Anderson (1905–91) at Caltech discovered the positron, the positive twin to the negative electron. He had used a cloud chamber, a device that Scottish physicist Charles T. Rees Wilson (1869–1959) invented at the turn of the century, that allowed physicists to study electrically charged particles in a chamber of moist air. When flown to high altitudes, the cloud chamber captured cosmic rays and allowed scientists to investigate their composition and behavior. It was a cloud chamber experiment in 1929 that first tipped off scientists to consider cosmic rays as charged particles.

Millikan had also flown instruments thousands of feet up in the atmosphere to study cosmic rays, but instead of dropping the photon hypothesis entirely, he proposed that a fraction of cosmic rays

remained as photons. Millikan in 1909 had been the first to calculate the electric charge of an electron using an oil-drop experiment, which earned him a Nobel Prize in 1923. His status as an expert on electrically charged particles, however, did not intimidate Ohio-born Arthur Compton, who shared the 1927 Nobel with Wilson. Compton (1892–1962) had provided key insight into the light-scattering behavior of X-rays that Wilson's cloud chamber verified by following the tracks of electrons that the X-ray photons hit. Compton also later provided a significant revision to Millikan's calculations regarding the electron charge. When Compton began studying the intensity levels of cosmic rays around the world he found himself again at odds with Millikan. The evidence Compton collected in 1930–40 showed that variations in Earth's magnetic field correlated with variations in the intensity levels of cosmic rays, another indication that they behaved as particles rather than photons. Anderson had discovered that cosmic rays carried positrons, and he split the Nobel in physics with Victor Hess in 1936, the year after Chadwick won for his discovery of the neutron. Did cosmic rays carry neutrons as well? Millikan did not think so, but that did not stop others from investigating.

"Sub-atomic cosmic particles pelting the planet at the speed of light." Or more simply: "Space shrapnel." The explosions of supernova are thought to generate the nonsolar particles or "galactic cosmic rays" that bombard Earth's atmosphere; explosions on the surface of the Sun provide the "solar cosmic rays" of solar particles that rain on the planets in the solar system, but to move away from rays, physicists typically use the no less confusing synonym "cosmic radiation," with the understanding that radiation can come in different forms even when the source is the same. For example, the sun delivers photon or *electromagnetic radiation* in the form of light waves, and this is referred to as solar radiation. The Sun also delivers particle radiation, in the form of protons from blown up bits of atoms of hydrogen—in other words: solar shrapnel. Today astronomers also refer to these particles from the sun as solar wind.

When scientists in the 1930s began investigating the type of particles pelting the planet from space, the results yielded a wealth of fascinating tiny atomic bits that had only recently been theorized to exist in nature. Anderson in 1932 first identified positrons, the antimatter electrons that Dirac had proposed existed. Then working with other scientists on cosmic radiation, Anderson in 1937 identified the first meson subatomic particle called the muon. Three years earlier, Japanese physicist Hideki Yukawa (1907–81) had predicted the existence of mesons from his studies of nuclear forces acting on the atomic nuclei. Particle physicists all over the world were picking the atom apart into smaller and smaller pieces. When Anderson confirmed his theory, Yukawa reinvigorated his focus and later received a Nobel for his work. Cosmic rays and the inner secrets of the atom were still sweeping Sweden in 1949.

Rutherford and Chadwick's neutron contained immense power. It could split atoms, destroy molecules, collide, and form new chemical elements. The neutron fascinated atomic scientists. Those with the proper equipment looked to the sky for signs of neutrons from cosmic rays. The highest balloon flown in 1935 was the *Explorer II*. (The *Explorer I*, filled with hydrogen and air, ripped and partly exploded the previous year. Captain Albert Stevens and his two aeronauts escaped via parachutes during the descent.) Filled with helium, equipped with one less copilot, a wider manhole in the sealed, spherical gondola for escape, and a lighter science payload—the *Explorer II* succeeded in reaching 72,395 feet (22,066 m) high. Captain Stevens provided scientists with the first photographs of the stratosphere. Proton tracks in the emulsions from the second mission gave scientists the first clue that neutrons were colliding with protons and sending them scattering through the atmosphere.

Using a sensitive neutron detector that could transmit from a balloon via shortwave radio, physicist Serge Korff (1906–89) of New York University counted two neutrons hitting less than a square inch (cm^2) of space every second. The cosmic ray collisions in the upper atmosphere were resulting in neutron debris. In 1939 Korff noted that these energetic bits of atomic nuclei were then knocking out a proton from every nitrogen-14 they hit and forming radioactive carbon-14 in its place.

This discovery started American chemist Willard Frank Libby thinking about carbon's role as a basic building block for life. Carbon is in the air, the water, and the soil. Every living creature consumes carbon, absorbs carbon, and respires carbon in one form or another. Commonly used carbon compounds include: CO_2 (carbon dioxide), H_2CO_3 (carbonic

Willard Libby, discoverer of the radiocarbon dating process, received the Nobel Prize in chemistry in 1960. (AIP Emilio Segrè Visual Archives, Segrè Collection)

acid or carbonate: water and carbon dioxide mixed together—which is why the ocean and carbonated drinks are slightly acidic), $C_{55}H_{72}MgN_4O_5$ (Chlorophyll a: used in photosynthesis), $C_6H_{12}O_6$ (the most common carbohydrate: glucose), $CaCO_3$ (calcium carbonate: for strong bones and shells), and CH_4 (methane: gas from bacteria). Life on Earth's surface is solar driven and carbon built.

The most universal and stable form of carbon is carbon-12, having six protons and six neutrons. The other stable carbon isotope (discovered in 1946) is carbon-13 with six protons and seven neutrons. Could carbon-14, a naturally formed radioactive isotope of carbon with six protons and eight neutrons, survive long enough in the environment to find its way into the carbon cycle? Libby wondered, but thought the possibility unlikely. He gave carbon-14 a half-life of four months.

Then in 1941, chemists Martin Kamen and Samuel Rubin working at Berkeley's Radiation Laboratory (now Lawrence Berkeley Laboratory) in California showed that the half-life for carbon-14 was at least 1,000 years. That gave Libby the time he needed to set his idea into action. He hypothesized that radioactive carbon, like stable carbon, made its way into every living organism. Once the organism died, the continuously decaying radioactive carbon would not have any new source of radioactive carbon to replace it and the radioactive countdown would begin. Knowing the half-life he could calculate how much radiocarbon he should expect to find for any given time. Measuring how much radioactive carbon was left in a fossil, a bone, a shell, a leaf, a piece of wood, a tooth, hair, nails, any part of any once living thing, would show how long its radioactive clock had been counting down to zero. If the half-life was 1,000 years, then a human skeleton that was 1,000 years old would be half as radioactive as a human alive today. The bones would have half of their original radioactive carbon still decaying back into stable nitrogen-14. After two thousand years, the bones would have a quarter of their radioactive carbon remaining; then in another thousand years still 12.5 percent; then 6.25 percent; then 3.1 percent; then 1.5 percent; then .78 percent; then .4 percent; then .2 percent; then .09 percent; then .04 percent; then .02 percent; then .01 percent; then .006 percent and so on. With a half-life of 1,000 years the perpetual cutting of each half could continue for 10,000 to 15,000 years or more before the amount of radioactive carbon remaining would be so low as to be undetectable.

Imagine the possibilities Libby considered when he found out that carbon-14 has a half-life closer to 5,600 years. That pushed the potential for dating back at least 40,000 years. Radioactive elements were nature's timekeepers, but most of the clocks were locked in the rock record. Could radioactive carbon track the history of humanity? Libby was so nervous about the implications of his idea that he held off discussing it with anyone until after World War II.

From 1941 to 1945, Libby worked on separating uranium isotopes at Columbia University under the leadership of Harold Urey, who had

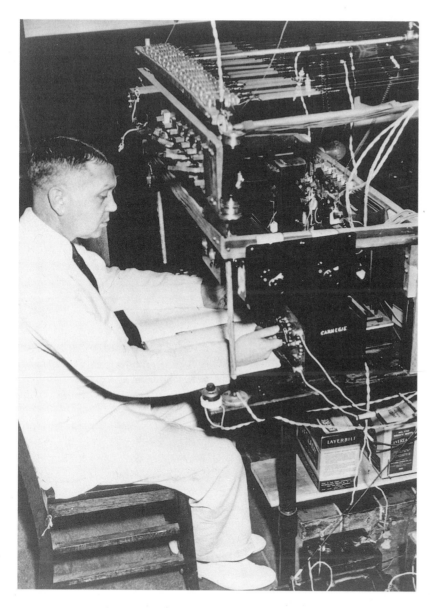

Harold Urey (1893–1981) won the 1934 Nobel Prize in chemistry for his discovery of the isotope deuterium, or heavy hydrogen. (Argonne National Laboratory; AIP Emilio Segrè Visual Archives)

discovered a method for identifying hydrogen's isotope. Their work was part of the start of the Manhattan Project, which ultimately led to world's first nuclear bomb. As a side project, Libby continued to toy with the idea of radiocarbon as a dating method.

In 1945 both Urey and Libby left Columbia to work at the University of Chicago. Libby focused on radiocarbon, but only Urey figured out why. Then in 1946, Libby shared his ideas with his colleagues at a party and also formally in an article published in *Physical Review* entitled "Atmospheric Helium Three and Radiocarbon from Cosmic Radiation."

Using radiocarbon as a dating technique was originally seen as a tool that would revolutionize the field of archaeology and anthropology much the same way tree-ring dating had done. Word and rumor spread quickly between 1947 and 1948 as Libby worked to develop the technique. Few grasped the importance radiocarbon would have on the geosciences. Historian Greg Marlowe in his article entitled "Year One: Radiocarbon Dating and American Archaeology, 1947–1948" published in *American Antiquity* in 1999 examines the communicative efforts, what he calls "truncated dialogue," that took place during this formative period about the implications of Libby's investigations. Some archaeologists, he writes, "exhibited ambivalence, if not resistance, to the prospect of 'physics' intruding into their domain."

Historian R. E. Taylor in 1985 quoted physicist Leona Woods Marshall Libby (1919–86) as explaining Willard's secrecy, "He did not tell anyone of his final goal of proving radiocarbon dating would be able to reveal the history of civilization because he felt that if he talked about such a crazy idea he would be labeled a crackpot and would not be able to get money to fund his research nor students to help him." Leona had worked on the Manhattan Project under Enrico Fermi at the University of Chicago and was present when the first nuclear chain reaction occurred. Her first husband was John Marshall. She married Willard Libby in 1966. (Willard's first wife was Leonor Hickey, with whom he had twin daughters born in 1945.)

To test his idea, Libby collaborated with his graduate student and four researchers from Pennsylvania. One of the researchers, ironically named Aristide von Grosse, had the unenviable chore of collecting methane gas from the sewage disposal plant in Baltimore, Maryland. The biomethane, as they called the gas, showed close to the predicted decay rate for carbon-14. They also tested methane from oil wells and, as they expected, found the long-since-dead petroleum carbon source free of radiocarbon. They concluded that the biomethane exemplified an all-natural source of radioactivity in living organisms. This was the 1940s, though. What were the chances of contamination? Libby checked with the Atomic Energy Commission to ensure that no one in Baltimore had received a radioactive dose of carbon from nuclear tests. He considered his precaution redundant: "The possibility of its origin from the atomic piles or bombs is excluded when one realizes that our activity corresponds to the existence in nature of some 10^8 curies, or 20 metric tons—an amount far larger than any synthetic source could have produced to date."

Before the dating method progressed any further, Libby received a package from the Metropolitan Museum of New York. Archaeologists would be the first to embrace the new dating tool and Museum Director Ambrose Lansing wanted to put the tool to the test. He sent Libby acacia wood from the coffin belonging to the third-dynasty Egyptian King

Zoser (Djoser), who according to historical records died in 2750 B.C.E. In 1949 Libby and colleagues dated the pharaoh's tomb to be approximately 4,650 years old, placing the age of the wood within 50 years of the pharaoh's death. This was an impressive feat, and they tested their dating adeptness with a variety of other historically important pieces:

- pine flooring from a Syrian palace
- Douglas fir excavated along with wooden flutes from an Anasazi cave in Arizona
- an Egyptian mummy's coffin
- cedar planking from an Egyptian warlord's funeral boat
- the linen wrapping of one of the Dead Sea Scrolls found in Palestine
- bread carbonized in Pompeii, Italy, during the volcanic eruption of Vesuvius in 79 C.E.
- part of the stump from an American giant sequoia felled in 1874 and nicknamed the "Centennial Stump," which Andrew Douglass had dated using his tree-ring method

Libby worked together with the American Anthropological Association and the Geological Society of America to determine what samples of known age would be best to use for testing. They established a committee to investigate dating questions regarding the history of early humans; pollen chronology; the first Native American cultures; the history of Mesopotamia, Western Asia, Scandinavia, Western Europe, the Yukon, Peru, and the Valley of Mexico. As samples for testing began to accumulate, however, so too did evidence of errors. Libby was shocked to learn that dates for civilization were accurate only back to 5,000 years. In his 1960 Nobel lecture, he says:

> We had thought initially that we would be able to get samples all along the curve back to 30,000 years, put the points in, and then our work would be finished. You read statements in books that such and such a society or archaeological [sic] site is 20,000 years old. We learned rather abruptly that these numbers, these ancient ages, are not known accurately; in fact, it is at about the time of the First Dynasty in Egypt that the first historical date of any real certainty has been established. So we had, in the initial stages, the opportunity to check against knowns, principally Egyptian artifacts, and in the second stage we had to go into the great wilderness of prehistory to see whether there were elements of internal consistency which would lead one to believe that the method was sound or not.

Libby also noted in his lecture that the premise of the dating method relied on the assumption that the movements of the winds and ocean currents would uniformly distribute radiocarbon throughout the world: in the form of carbon dioxide in the air and carbonate in the water.

Scientist of the Decade: Arthur Holmes (1890–1965)

Earth scientists who want to go back farther in time use stratigraphy and, thanks to Arthur Holmes, a radioisotope-dated geologic timescale. Finding and telling those stories from the geologic record takes diligence.

Holmes and his young wife Margaret "Maggie" Howe moved with their baby boy to Burma for two years in 1920. Nothing good came of this. Holmes went bankrupt working for an oil company and his three-year-old son caught dysentery and died. In 1924 Maggie gave birth to another son and Holmes landed a job as the head of a new Geology Department at Durham University.

In 1922 the leading Alpine geologist from Switzerland, Émile Argand (1879–1940) presented to the International Geological Congress in Belgium a unified synthesis of Eurasian tectonics that called for support of a mobile substrate. On his extensive mountaineering excursions, he had mapped a number of overthrusts and interpreted their presences as a result of episodic horizontal crustal motion—local response to global action. When Holmes learned of this he considered how it fit with what he knew of Earth's thermal properties. John Joly (1857–1933), a leader in the application of radioactivity to Earth's internal dynamics (who nevertheless balked at an expanding timescale that reached into the billions and preferred his own "salt" clock, which indicated that salt had been eroding into the oceans for 90 million years), had in 1908 and 1909 speculated as to whether Earth was indeed cooling. Joly was convinced that radioactivity at depth produced more heat than conduction alone could conceivably carry away. Holmes now agreed.

Joly hypothesized that the added heat would periodically melt Earth's basaltic substrate along the base of the crust and cause a rift in the seafloor. He predicted that lava would flood out from these rifts, separating the continents from the oceans, and cause regional crustal deformations. For examples of where this had happened in the past,

he pointed to the famous Deecan traps of India where Late Cretaceous age basalt covers 200,000 square miles and to the Tertiary basalt columns of the Giant's Causeway in Northern Ireland. In 1924 Holmes's former mentor at Imperial College, John William Evans (1857–1930), would write the foreword to the first English translation of Wegener's *Origin of Continents and Oceans*. In 1925 Joly published his ideas in his book *The Surface-History of the Earth*. Holmes followed with an article in 1926 elaborating on the probability of thermal cycles. Cooling alone was no longer a reasonable option, and heating up was not likely either: "That we are here at all to investigate the problem is sufficient proof that the Earth is not continuously growing hotter," he wrote sarcastically. That left a third option: The Earth was accumulating and discharging heat. He linked the clues together and reasoned that Joly's melted substrate intrusion into the upper crust played a role in forming Argand's Alpine overthrusts. Holmes saw convection as the most reasonable explanation. His new model for the dissipation of radioactive heat to the surface called for the material in Earth's mantle to slowly churn.

He depicted the mantle as having convection currents that rose when warmed by radioactive decay from Earth's core, and then cooled as the mantle currents traveled across the surface and sank back down to the base of the mantle. With this hypothesis Holmes also provided a mechanism for continental drift, persuading him of the possibility that the continents were still in motion. Wegener had proposed that the continents plowed through the oceanic crust. With Holmes's model the crust of the oceans and continents rode along the top of the mantle passively. The convection cells provided energy from below to break up the continents and expand the oceans.

Around 1930, he debated the merits of his convection cell model for the mantle with geophysicist Harold Jeffreys (1891–1989) in a series

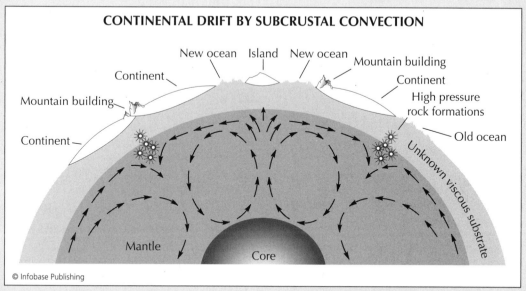

CONTINENTAL DRIFT BY SUBCRUSTAL CONVECTION

In 1929 Arthur Holmes proposed a mechanism for continental drift using convection currents below the crust.

of letters published in British scientific journals that "reads like an extended dialogue on the thermal history of the Earth," wrote science historian Alan Allwardt. The Geological Society of London would award the Murchison Medal to Jeffreys in 1939 and to Holmes in 1940. Sir Roderick Impey Murchison, before he died in 1871, had founded the University of Edinburgh with a leading role in the field of geology and mineralogy. In October 1943, Holmes became the Regius Professor of Geology and Mineralogy at the University of Edinburgh, where he achieved worldwide recognition as the "Father of the Geological Timescale."

Holmes included a chapter on continental drift in his 1944 book the *Principles of Physical Geology,* in which he summarized the geologic knowledge gained since Charles Lyell's influential 1830 *Principles of Geology.* In the 1940s, Holmes achieved some of his most important work on the geologic timescale with a new wife by his side. Maggie died in 1938 and Holmes married geologist Doris Reynolds, one of the few women geologists

with a Ph.D. at the time. Reynolds had worked as a research assistant at Queen's College investigating the origin of granites in Northern Ireland. Holmes incorporated much of her work in his book. He further investigated rocks of Precambrian age and the geology of Africa, fulfilling a lifelong dream he had started in Mozambique. He received the Wollaston and Penrose medals in 1956 and the Vetlesen Prize in 1964. Holmes is quoted as having said in 1956 that, "despite appearances to the contrary, I have never succeeded in freeing myself from a nagging prejudice against continental drift; in my geological bones, so to speak, I feel the hypothesis to be a fantastic one." He was alive when Harry Hess of Princeton University hypothesized a similar model for seafloor spreading that envisioned the edges oceanic crust subducting into the mantle to form oceanic trenches, and in the second edition of *Principles of Physical Geology,* published months before his death in 1965, Holmes wrote that "mantle currents are no longer regarded as inadmissible."

Libby was well aware of the variation in production of radioactivity, due to the variation in cosmic rays, which Compton showed correlated with variation in the strength of Earth's magnetic field over different latitudes. Preliminary studies still had indicated that living organisms all over the world had the same radiocarbon content per gram of carbon despite their locations, but even a decade of research can just begin to scratch the real story.

Starting in the 1960s, errors in radiocarbon dating changed from being annoying irregularities to calculated concerns for older dates where less radiocarbon is available in the sample to test. As dated samples fell slightly off from the curved line of time versus estimated radiocarbon activity, the margin of error increased with the age of the sample—widening the curve into a ribbon. The distribution of radiocarbon has been uniform since the end of the last ice age about 11,000 years ago, but the production has varied in that time due to changes in the solar magnetic field. The deep waters in the ocean underwent massive circulation changes as the last ice age began receding, influencing the carbon cycle and perhaps changing the radioactive carbon distribution. For samples older than 15,000 years, the calibration for radiocarbon has to account for a dramatic change in the strength of the Earth's magnetic field. To solve the controversy over the dates, scientists turned to tree-ring studies.

Many researchers began radiocarbon dating each ring to determine an accurate count for radiocarbon activity in a given year. A calibration curve for radiocarbon dating was born. Since then, researchers have continued to work to improve accuracy and push back the dates using fossil corals as well. Like trees that experience cycles of growth and mark their progress with a new ring of wood each year, corals also grow in spurts: they mark their progress with a new layer of calcium carbonate shell.

In 2006 researchers had multiple calibration curves to choose from, including one made from three different curves fitted together: one for marine samples and one each for terrestrial samples from the Northern and Southern Hemispheres. The most robust calibration evidence from tree-ring dating goes back 12,410 calendar years before the present. The farthest-reaching calibration curve today is one done by American paleoceanographer Richard Fairbanks and colleagues at Columbia University's Lamont-Doherty Earth Observatory. Fairbanks calibrated radiocarbon dates on fossil corals from the Atlantic and Pacific oceans with uranium and thorium radioisotope dates on the same corals and provided a calibration curve that goes back 55,000 years. Tree-ring researchers in Australia are working to match that expanse of time with overlapping studies of fossil kauri trees that each live as long as 1,000 years. Generations of these trees are preserved in New Zealand swamps.

During the last 50,000 years, a meteor struck Arizona, the last ice age began to thaw, ocean circulation patterns changed, Earth tilted on its axis from 24.5° to 21.5° and back continuing on to today's 23.5° tilt, and across Europe humans hunted mammoths and cave bears into extinction. *Homo sapiens, H. neanderthalensis,* and *H. floresiensis* all existed during much of this time, but not all in the same place. Footprints in Central Mexico put humans in the Americas as early as 40,000 years ago. Following the radiocarbon trail from the atmosphere to the ocean through the life cycle of organisms and back to the atmosphere as nitrogen-14 is an ongoing pursuit.

Further Reading

Balter, Michael. "Radiocarbon Dating's Final Frontier." *Science* 313, no. 5793 (2006): 1,560–1,563. This article discusses the status of the calibrations scientists are making to extend accurate radiocarbon dating back 50,000 years.

Benioff, Hugo. "Seismic Evidence for the Fault Origin of Oceanic Deeps." *GSA Bulletin* 60, no. 12, Part 1 (1949): 1,837–1,856. This paper presents evidence for deep faults dipping below the continental crust of South America and the volcanic islands in the South Pacific north of New Zealand called the Tonga-Kermadec region.

Bolt, Bruce A. *Earthquakes.* New York: W. H. Freeman and Company, 1993. This book is a revised and expanded edition of a book first published in 1988.

Broecker, Wallace S., David L. Thurber, John Goddard, Teh-lung Ku, R. K. Matthews, and Kenneth J. Mesolella. "Milankovitch Hypothesis Supported by Precise Dating of Coral Reefs and Deep-Sea Sediments." *Science* 159, no. 3812 (1968): 297–300. The report explains that the radioisotopic evidence "show a parallelism over the last 150,000 years between changes in Earth's climate and changes in the summer insolation predicted from cycles in the tilt and precession of Earth's axis."

Chapman, Sydney, and Julius Bartels. *Geomagnetism.* Oxford: Oxford University Press, 1940. The authors conclude: "It cannot be said that at present any satisfactory explanation of the Earth's main field is available."

Daly, Reginald A. "Origin of the Moon and Its Topography." *Proceedings of the American Philosophical Society* 90, no. 2 (1946): 104–119. This obscure paper first introduced the idea that an impact event striking Earth led to the formation of the Moon.

Dunham, K. C. "Arthur Holmes: 1890–1965." *Biographical Memoirs of Fellows of the Royal Society* 12 (November 1966): 290–310. A biography on the life and work of Arthur Holmes.

Elsasser, Walter. "On the Origin of the Earth's Magnetic Field." *Physical Review* 55 (1939): 489–498. Elsasser's first article on the dynamo theory introduces the effect of the *Coriolis force* on convection currents in the core.

———. "Induction Effects in Terrestrial Magnetism Part I. Theory." *Phys. Rev.* 69 (1946): 106–116. In this report, Elsasser concludes that the shape of the electric field is toroidal, whereas the magnetic field is poloidal.

————. "Induction Effects in Terrestrial Magnetism Part II. The Secular Variation." *Phys. Rev.* 70 (1946): 202–212. This article discusses how the dynamo theory can account for irregularities in Earth's magnetic field.

————. "Induction Effects in Terrestrial Magnetism, III. Electric Modes." *Phys. Rev.* 72 (1947): 821–833. Elsasser interprets his analysis of the relationship between magnetic and electric modes as a "feed-back amplifier whereby the field can be maintained through the power delivered to it by the fluid motion." He further identifies the "rotational energy lost by the Earth as it is slowed down through the action of the lunar tide" as a possible source of power for maintaining the field.

Holmes, Arthur. *Principles of Physical Geology.* London: T. Nelson and Sons Ltd., 1944. This textbook is now a classic in the field of geophysics with the third and last edition published in 1978.

Lewis, Cherry. *The Dating Game: One Man's Search for the Age of the Earth.* New York: Cambridge University Press, 2000. This biography of Arthur Holmes details how this geochemist began determining the age of Earth's rocks and minerals.

Libby, W. F. "Atmospheric Helium Three and Radiocarbon from Cosmic Radiation." *Physical Review* 69 (1946): 671–672. In this short paper, Libby proposes his ideas regarding radiocarbon dating.

————, E. C. Anderson, and J. R. Arnold. "Age Determination by Radiocarbon Content: World-Wide Assay of Natural Radiocarnon." *Science* 109 (1949): 227–228. This report discusses the results of the first radiocarbon dating done on Egyptian tombs.

Marlowe, Greg. "Year One: Radiocarbon Dating and American Archaeology, 1947–1948." *American Antiquity* 64, no. 1 (1999): 9–32. This report examines the early influence of radiocarbon on the field of archaeology, and how archaeologists responded to this new physics method of evaluating historical dates.

Milankovitch, Milutin. *Canon of Insolation and the Ice-Age Problem (Kanon der Erdbestrahlung und seine Anwendung auf das Eiszeitenproblem) Belgrade, 1941.* Translated from German. Royal Serbian Academy. Jerusalem: Israel Program for Scientific Translations, 1969. This book provides an English translation of Milankovitch's cumulative work up to 1941.

Rubin, Harry. "Walter M. Elsasser: (1904–1991)." *Biographical Memoir of the National Academy of Sciences* 68 (1995): 103–166. This biography details Elsasser's contributions to geophysics. Available online. URL: http://newton.nap.edu/html/biomems/welsasser.html. Accessed April 24, 2006.

Schopf, J. William. "Solution to Darwin's Dilemma: Discovery of the Missing Precambrian Record of Life." *Proceedings of the National Academy of Sciences* 97, no. 13 (2000): 6,947–6,953. Schopf details the history of the search and discovery of Precambrian fossils since the days of Darwin.

Sprigg, Reginald C. "On the 1946 Discovery of The Precambrian Ediacarian Fossil Fauna in South Australia." *Earth Sciences History* 7, no. 1 (1988): 46–51. Sprigg recounts the geological survey that lead to his 1946 discovery.

Taylor, R. E. "The Beginnings of Radiocarbon Dating in American Antiquity: A Historical Perspective." *American Antiquity*, 50, no. 2 Golden Anniversary Issue (1985): 309–325. This article traces the impact of radiocarbon dating on archaeology.

Time. "The Philosophers' Stone." *Time* (August 15, 1955). The cover story in this issue profiles Willard Libby and his work at charting a postwar map "away from national preoccupation with the destructive atom to international cooperation for harnessing the atom's untold goodness." Available online. URL: http://www.time.com/time/magazine/article/0,9171,807508-1,00.html. Accessed April 24, 2006.

University of Washington. "1946 Aleutian Tsunami." This Web site tells of the deadly tsunami that devastated Hilo, Hawaii, killed five in a lighthouse in Alaska and one person in California. Available online. URL: http://www.geophys.washington.edu/tsunami/general/historic/aleutian46.html. Accessed February 28, 2007.

6

1951–1960:
Earth and Space

Introduction

The 1950s represent a decade in transition. The fear that drove scientists working on the Manhattan Project to use their knowledge of nuclear chemistry and particle physics to help the U.S. military build a nuclear bomb before anyone else could use such power was spent. The bombs dropped on Hiroshima and Nagasaki, Japan, in August 1945. The genie as they said was out of the bottle and a new fear gripped the world. The scientists abandoned their military housing units and returned to their universities, many determined to use nuclear science only for nonmilitary applications. Willard Libby with his development of radiocarbon-dating methods had led the way. With him, a generation of nuclear geochemists came to the aid of the older geochronologists who had established radioisotopic dating techniques long before the war. The methods had improved at such an accelerated rate that a graph of the age of the Earth as calculated each year would trend upward almost linearly. The problem now was that the rocks had reached their plateau—leaving geochronologists with a mystery as to how much time had passed between the formation of the Earth and the formation of the oldest rocks still on the surface today. Tied with the oldest rocks was also a mystery as to their fossil assemblage. For more than a century, paleontologists had searched for the missing Precambrian fossils. Many believed they had succeeded in identifying such fossils, only to have their findings not unequivocally supported by the entire scientific community—a must for such a milestone in Earth's history.

The 1950s bring with them a decade of tremendous human accomplishments: the launch of *Sputnik*; the establishment of a South Pole station and a successful trans-Antarctic crossing; solving the mystery of the Earth's age during formation; establishing a Precambrian fossil assemblage on both the microscopic and macroscopic levels; and gaining a new understanding of how Earth's magnetic field interacts with the Sun. These are only a sample. Despite the growing shadow of cold war fear, this decade draws a new map to success in scientific achievements—one that follows the route toward international cooperation.

Man-made Moons

Broadcasting stations interrupted their regular Friday night radio and television programs on October 4, 1957, to play an ominous noise to Americans during the height of the cold war: the sound of Soviet success in space. The high-pitched chirp of the electronic radio signal transmitting from Earth's first artificial satellite, or man-made moon as it was also called, inspired amazement and shock. Many Americans feared that the 183-pound (83 kg) *Sputnik*, Russian for satellite, orbiting the planet every 96 minutes, indicated the Soviets had the technological prowess for building an intercontinental ballistic missile (ICBM): the same type of missile capable of dropping a nuclear bomb on American cities from space. Moscow's rocket had launched the satellite 560 miles (900 km) into orbit above the Earth. Anyone looking to

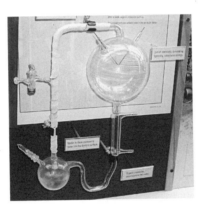

Harold Urey's student, American biochemist Stanley Miller (b. 1930), experimented with Urey's hypothesis that Earth's early atmosphere was rich in ammonia, methane, and hydrogen. When sparked with electricity, a simulated version of the early atmosphere yielded amino acids and other organic molecules, the building blocks of life. (Denver Museum of Nature and Science)

The forested peak of Mount Lamington in Papua New Guinea erupts on January 17 with pyroclastic flows surging down all sides of the volcano and killing 2,942 people. Volcanic activity—including lahars, pyroclastic flows, and debris avalanches—lasts until 1956

Rachel Carson publishes *The Sea Around Us*

American geophysicist Francis Birch estimates how depth effects mineralogy in Earth's mantle

American geophysicist Marie Tharp identifies a valley in the middle of the Mid-Atlantic Ridge

MILESTONES

1951

1952

Kelut on Java, Indonesia, experiences a crater lake eruption on August 31 that spews out water and 0.05 cubic miles (0.2 km³) of tephra, and causes pyroclastic flows, lahars, debris avalanches, fatalities, and evacuations in a single day. Repairs are made on the drainage tunnels to the lake, but the eruption leaves the crater 230 feet (70 m) deeper, and 1.8×10^9 cubic feet (50 million m³) of water remains

British geophysicist Edward C. Bullard publishes a description and the results of an instrument probe using an O-ring as a seal to measure Earth's heat flow through the seafloor in the Atlantic Ocean

the horizon with a pair of binoculars at sunrise or sunset might see a glint of the basketball-sized aluminum sphere as it crossed overhead at 18,000 miles (29,000 km) per hour, its four antennas projecting out like a comet's trail. At its closest approach during its elliptical orbit, the instrument skimmed through the stratosphere at about 130 miles (210 km) from the surface.

The Russian scientists had said very little to their American counterparts prior to the launch. After World War II, the Soviet Union's defense of socialism conflicted with the British, French, and American policy that capitalism was the ideal means for governing the divided Germany and its capital. The first cold war confrontation came in 1948 when the Soviet Union blocked ground traffic from entering West Berlin. The United States and its allies responded with an airlift of food and supplies that they flew into the city for more

The world's first human-made satellite, Sputnik I, *in the assembly shop in Russia* (NASA)

Spurr in southwestern Alaska erupts explosively on July 9 for the first time in more than 300 years—scattering ash over the streets of Anchorage	American chemists Stanley Miller and Harold Urey demonstrate experimentally how organic compounds might have begun on Earth. They expose a warm, gaseous mixture of inorganic compounds to electrical discharges. The gases are meant to represent the prebiotic atmosphere, the proverbial primordial soup

MILESTONES

1953   **1954**

American chemist Loring Coes invents an apparatus for obtaining high temperatures at high pressures in the laboratory. He uses this apparatus to grow high-pressure minerals, including a new form of dense silica that bears his name (coesite)	The U.S. Geological Survey splits the Carboniferous Period in the Geologic Time Scale into two epochs: Mississippian and Pennsylvanian	American geologist Stanley Tyler and paleobotanist Elso Barghoorn announce the discovery of Precambrian microfossils

than a year until the crisis was resolved. As the Soviet Union and its allies continued to support communism throughout Eastern Europe, geopolitical tensions and economic sanctions ensued. The Russians worried considerably about the American military stations all over Western Europe that were outfitted with intermediate-range ballistic missiles (IRBM) and the same type of airplanes that dropped the nuclear bombs on Japan. With the launch of *Sputnik I*, the nuclear arms race that had been developing between the two superpowers escalated into a space race, especially in the eyes of politicians. Scientists on both sides of the "iron curtain," however, considered their work less a race per se and more an international challenge to achieving goals that were previously only imagined.

As the 3,000 cherry trees, a gift of friendship from Japan in 1912, began to bloom again around the tidal basin of Washington in the spring of 1950, American radio physicist and engineer Lloyd Berkner (1905–67) received a call from rocket scientist James Van Allen (1914–2006) to come by his house for a visit. British astronomer Sydney Chapman (1888–1970) was in town and Allen was getting a few other

American geophysicists Bruce Heezen and Marie Tharp present evidence of a network of oceanic ridges and rifts that extend around the globe for 37,000 miles (60,000 km)

American geochemist Clair Cameron Patterson, using lead isotopes in a Canyon Diablo meteorite fragment from Barringer Crater, calculates that the Earth is about 4.5 billion years old

The International Geophysical Year (IGY) begins on July 1. Sixty-seven countries participate in a coordinated study of Earth sciences, including geomagnetism, the physics of the ionosphere, oceanography, Antarctic exploration, seismology, and meteorological research. IGY continues to the end of 1958

The Soviet Union launches the world's first artificial satellite, *Sputnik*

American physicist Eugene Parker discovers solar wind, a stream of charged particles from the Sun

MILESTONES

1956

1957

1958

Previously thought extinct, Bezymianny on Russia's Kamchatka Peninsula erupts explosively on March 30 punctuating a period of activity that lasts from October 22, 1955, to March 1, 1957. The eruption spews out 0.7 cubic miles (2.8 km³) of tephra and causes debris avalanches, a tsunami, pyroclastic flows, and lahars. The eruption marks the end of 1,000 years of quiescence and leaves a distinguishing horseshoe-shaped crater from a lateral blast that exploded when the summit collapsed. Dome-growing activity continues into the 21st century

March 9, earthquakes of magnitude 8.6 and 7.1 strike Andreanof Islands and Fox Islands, Alaska—no fatalities reported. The resulting tsunami causes an estimated $5 million in property damage to Oahu and Kauai Islands of Hawaii and minor damage to San Diego Bay, California. Mount Vsevidof on Umnak Island, Alaska, erupts after being dormant for 200 years

Using data from the *Explorer I* satellite, American physicist James Van Allen discovers a belt of radiation around the Earth. The Van Allen belts consist of two fields where charged particles from the Sun are trapped in Earth's magnetic field

colleagues in the geophysics and atmospheric science community together to meet him. Soon the discussion at the party turned to the studies of geophysics during the International Polar Years when scientists in the 1880s and again 50 years later teamed together to explore the planet's coldest climate regions. They had investigated weather patterns, the aurora light displays, the electricity in the atmospheric, snow and ice flows, the geomagnetic field, and ocean currents and tides. The third international research year was scheduled for 1982, but Berkner suggested that the geophysics community should act sooner to take advantage of the sunspots reaching a maximum in their 11-year cycle in 1958. Enthusiasm for an International Geophysical Year spread quickly from Van Allen's living room in Silver Spring, Maryland, to scientists around the world.

In 1952 the International Council of Scientific Unions, a nongovernmental organization, began preparations and fundraising for the International Geophysical Year (IGY) that would start in July 1957 and last through December 1958. The logo for the research year showed a satellite in orbit around Earth. The United States originally planned to

---

Seismologists examine the use of seismographs for detecting underground nuclear detonations

A group within the National Academy of Sciences requested funds of $2.5 million to begin Project Mohole, the plan to drill through Earth's crust to the Mohorovicic discontinuity

May 22, an earthquake of magnitude 9.5 strikes Chile—5,700 people die. The earthquake is designated the largest earthquake in the world and leaves 3,000 injured and 2 million people homeless.

After two years, the National Academy of Sciences' committee on oceanography chaired by Harrison Brown publishes the report "Oceanography 1960" identifying important questions in the field that needed investigation and advocating a 10-year program of large-scale expansion of scientific research and teaching about the ocean

American Air Force launches the *Discoverer* satellite into a low polar orbit where it photographs the entire surface of the Earth every 24 hours. The exposed film is returned to Earth in a capsule

MILESTONES

1959   **1960**

American satellite *Explorer 6* takes the first television pictures of Earth's cloud cover from space

Mary Leakey discovers fossil remains of an early hominid 1.75 million years old in Kenya

February 29, a shallow earthquake of magnitude 5.7 strikes Agadir, Morocco—c. 10,000 to 150,000 people die. The quake causes an estimated $70 million in property damage

Swiss engineer Jacques Piccard and U.S. Navy lieutenant Don Walsh descend on January 23 to the bottom of Challenger Deep in the Mariana Trench off the Pacific Island of Guam in the bathyscaphe *Trieste,* setting a new record of 35,813 feet (10,916 m)

American geologists Marion Hubbert and William Rubey demonstrate that fluids in rocks reduce friction and allow for overthrusting of large horizontal slabs, resulting in folding and uplift

launch what the Russians called a small grapefruit-sized satellite. The U.S. Naval Research Laboratory's Project *Vanguard* began under the Department of Defense, but after the launch of *Sputnik I*, the United States had the Army begin a second satellite program. On January 31, 1958, the United States successfully launched its first Earth satellite, *Explorer I*, into orbit. James Van Allen led the mission, which confirmed the existence of charged particles above the upper atmosphere and the extension of Earth's magnetic field deep into space. The *Vanguard* satellite, the first solar-powered satellite, was successfully launched in March 1958.

Four months later, President Dwight D. Eisenhower signed into force the National Aeronautics and Space Act, which established the National Aeronautics and Space Administration (NASA). The act was done to improve America's standing in space. "That the Soviet Union was first in this project is due to the high priority which the Soviet Union gives to scientific training . . ." wrote Secretary of State John Foster Dulles in a letter to the White House after the launch of *Sputnik*. The countries had taken very different approaches to neutralizing their perceived political threats. The United States in the 1940s and 1950s had given high priority to identifying and discrediting Americans with communist sympathies. Under the leadership of Presidents Franklin Roosevelt, Harry Truman, and Eisenhower, new laws enabled employers to fire anyone they suspected was a communist, or someone who supported a socialized system for governance over capitalism and democracy, out of fear that such people would try to violently overthrow the government. People who lost their

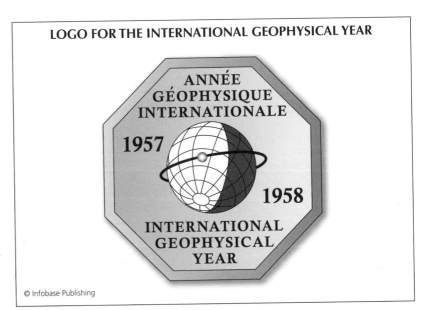

LOGO FOR THE INTERNATIONAL GEOPHYSICAL YEAR

ANNÉE GÉOPHYSIQUE INTERNATIONALE
1957
1958
INTERNATIONAL GEOPHYSICAL YEAR

© Infobase Publishing

During IGY, the launch of Russia's Sputnik *satellite on October 4, 1957, heralded a new era in Earth science.*

jobs under these new laws were given restrictions on their appeals process; some were detained, had their passports revoked, or were put in prison. Senator Joseph McCarthy (R-Wisconsin), in 1950 publicly supported this action, hence the term McCarthyism. The list of suspected citizens who lost their jobs included scientists and college professors; even students were scrutinized and subjected to political harassment.

NASA logo (NASA)

After the successful launch of *Vanguard*, those running the project were transferred to a new NASA space facility in Greenbelt, Maryland, to continue to monitor the satellite and build new spacecraft. In 1959 NASA named this new facility the Goddard Space Flight Center. Whereas the other original satellites eventually burned up in the atmosphere, *Vanguard* is heralded as the longest running satellite in history. In 2008 the grapefruit-sized satellite will celebrate 50 years in orbit.

Radiation Belts

Van Allen, the mission leader for the 1958 *Explorer I* satellite, quickly established that charged particles of radiation, soon called the Van Allen Radiation Belts, were trapped in Earth's extensive magnetic field well beyond the upper atmosphere. In 1957, Nicholas Constantine Christofilos (1916–72) working at the Lawrence Radiation Laboratory in Livermore, California, had predicted that the magnetic field would act as a trap for electrons, raising the question as to whether such a band of radiation might have military applications. After Van Allen confirmed the radiation's natural existence, the U.S. military decided to test the possibility of artificially inducing a radiation belt using nuclear bombs. From August 1 to September 6, 1958, the U.S. Navy conducted top secret tests under the code name Argus.

The world learned of Project Argus on March 19, 1959, when two reporters, Walter Sullivan (1918–96) and Hanson W. Baldwin (1903–91), with the *New York Times* finally broke the story they had been sitting on for nine months. The U.S. Navy's missile ship *Norton Sound*, situated off the Falkland Islands in the South Atlantic Ocean, had launched three rockets during the summer of 1958 with atom bombs that detonated as high as 300 miles (483 km) above the Earth. *Time* magazine, on March 30, 1959, reported the test was likely influencing U.S. strategy for "above-the-atmosphere warfare," the first effort to develop an antiballistic missile initiative. "Van Allen has stated that neutrons from a nuclear charge exploding in a vacuum might detonate or inactivate an incoming enemy warhead, 'if there were enough of them,'" the newsmagazine reported, clarifying that Van Allen had not specified how much of a nuclear charge was needed to be "enough" to hinder an incoming missile.

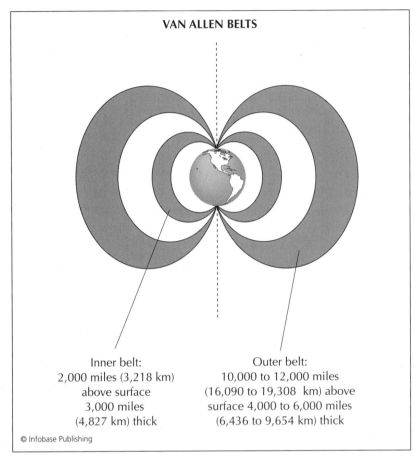

VAN ALLEN BELTS

Inner belt:
2,000 miles (3,218 km)
above surface
3,000 miles
(4,827 km) thick

Outer belt:
10,000 to 12,000 miles
(16,090 to 19,308 km) above
surface 4,000 to 6,000 miles
(6,436 to 9,654 km) thick

© Infobase Publishing

Physicist James Van Allen (1914–2006) with the University of Iowa in 1958 confirmed the existence of charged particles caught in Earth's magnetic field using Geiger counters on America's Explorer satellites. Colorful auroras result when the particles strike the Earth's atmosphere and fluoresce.

Seen from the *Norton Sound*, part of the explosion of electrons cut into the top of the atmosphere where they collided with atoms and colored the sky in a display of artificially induced auroras just south of the point of detonation. Observers positioned at the corresponding point north of the magnetic equator, on a ship near Bermuda, witnessed the electrons that had spiraled along the magnetic field deep into space come careening back down to form a second aurora. Nine ships were reportedly used during the operation, stationed at various positions around the world. The *Times* article cites "unofficial Pentagon information," claiming the electrons traveled along the magnetic fields at the speed of light, and then switched direction upon hitting the upper atmosphere to travel back to the other hemisphere. The electrons that did not annihilate into auroras followed a slightly different path back along the magnetic field toward the opposite magnetic pole, such that after an hour a doughnut-shaped shell of traveling electrons had surrounded the Earth. The *Times* reports that the Pentagon was not revealing how long the shell lasted. "Presumably it died away in a few days as its electrons got mired in the atmosphere. But according to some accounts, the Argus shell was stronger for a short time than even the Van Allen natural radiation."

Crossing Antarctica and the Treaty of 1959

Polar missions again played a key role during the International Geophysical Year. After 99 days, starting on November 24, 1957, a team under the leadership of British polar explorer Vivian Fuchs (1908–99), whose surname rhymes with "books," completed the first successful trans-Antarctic crossing. Starting from the Shackleton Base on the Weddell Sea, his team conducted seismic recordings and geomagnetic surveys. They had a dogsled but relied primarily on tracked vehicles called Tucker Sno-Cats® for transportation. Instead of sending scouts ahead and back to stock depots, they kept their food supply in good shape via constant communication with an aerial support team that, weather permitting, could fly out and drop supplies as needed. Not quite halfway through the expedition, they reached the Amundsen-Scott Base at the South Pole, where Sir Edmund Hillary of New Zealand and his men were waiting to help guide Fuchs's team the remainder of the way across the continent. In 1953 Hillary (b. 1919) and Nepalese Sherpa Tenzing Norgay (1914–86) made history as the first climbers to reach the top of Mount Everest. Hillary and his team in Antarctica loaded New Zealand's Scott Base on the Ross Sea with supplies and then traveled on tractors to the South Pole station, setting up depots as they went in preparation for the return trip back with Fuchs and his men.

American geographer Paul Siple (1908–68) wrote about the activities that took place under his command at the South Pole Station during IGY in his 1959 book *90° South*. By the end of the decade, 12 countries had staffed 55 research stations. The need to rely on international cooperation to outfit the stations trumped territorial claims during the research year and led to a treaty to keep the area south of 60° South latitude as a natural reserve "devoted to peace and science." By 1961 all the representative countries with stations on the ice had ratified the Antarctic Treaty of 1959:

- United Kingdom with 15 stations ratified the treaty on May 31, 1960.
- Argentina with eight stations ratified the treaty on June 23, 1961.
- Soviet Union with seven stations ratified the treaty on November 2, 1960.

Drill rig in full operation pulling an ice core. Juneau Ice Fields. Juneau Ice Field Research Project, Summer 1950 (G. J. Wasserburg. Courtesy University of Miami Rosenstiel School of Marine and Atmospheric Science)

- United States with six stations, plus one shared with New Zealand, ratified the treaty on August 18, 1960.
- Chile with four stations ratified the treaty on June 23, 1961.
- Australia with three stations ratified the treaty on June 23, 1961.

- France with three stations ratified the treaty on September 16, 1960.
- South Africa with three stations ratified the treaty on June 21, 1960.

The Buildup to Success in Antarctica

In 1977 Poland built a permanent research station on King George Island and named it after one of their prestigious Antarctic explorers: Henryk Arctowski (1871–1958), who was on board the *Belgica* when in February 1898 the ship became stuck in the pack ice of the Bellingshausen Sea and unintentionally became the first winter-over expedition to Antarctica.

Arctowski at the time took full advantage of the situation for oceanographic and meteorological observations. He dropped weighted lines overboard to measure the water depth and used the soundings to map the bathymetry during their drift. Polar explorers Roald Amundsen (1872–1928) of Norway and American surgeon Frederick Cook (1865–1940) were also on board and helped Captain Adrien Victor Joseph de Gerlache (1866–1934) keep most of the crew alive. In May the trapped sailors watched as the Sun set and did not rise again for 10 weeks. Their main source of light became the Moon and the auroras. At least one man died from madness. The crew finally freed the ship in February 1899. Fifteen years later, British Antarctic explorer Ernest Shackleton (1874–1922) encountered similar conditions in the Weddell Sea. Ironically, he was sailing a ship originally built in 1912 for de Gerlache, who due to financial difficulties had to pull out of the boat deal. His financier, Lars Christensen, sold their ship, *Polaris,* below cost to Shackleton, who renamed her *Endurance.* The name was more apt for the crew than the ship. The ice crushed the *Endurance* as the crew watched, leaving them stranded with lifeboats and a leader who would eventually rescue them all.

Studying sea ice, icebergs, and ocean currents around Antarctica became a priority during the later international research years. Shackleton's 1914 expedition had been planned as the first trans-Antarctic crossing from the Weddell Sea to the Ross Sea via the South Pole. Shackleton had given the responsibility of setting the depots along the route from the Ross Sea to Beardmore Glacier near the South Pole to Captain Aeneas Lionel Acton Mackintosh, who with a small team managed to set the first depot in 1915. They returned to the Ross Sea to find their ship the *Aurora* missing, blown away during a storm and blocked from returning by pack ice. The 10 marooned explorers consolidated the rest of their supplies and, still under the belief that Shackleton and his men would die if they did not succeed in laying all the depots, continued with their plan. When the *Aurora* returned in January 1917 with Shackleton on board, the depots were set, but three men, including Mackintosh (1879–1916), and most of the sled dogs had died.

By the time Hillary and Fuchs attempted the same journey, radio communication, tracked snow vehicles, airplanes, and steel-hulled ships made the trans-Antarctic crossing a complete success for the first time. In preparation for the IGY, the United States in 1955 began building an airfield on McMurdo Sound for a fleet of C-130 Hercules cargo planes. Operation Deepfreeze as it was called continued in 1956 to establish a permanent South Pole station, using planes to deliver much of the needed supplies. When Fuchs's team arrived at the South Pole, Hillary and his men as well as the scientists stationed at the Amundsen-Scott station were there to greet them. Operation Deepfreeze continues today with the New York Air National Guard flying retractable ski-equipped LC-130 planes and landing on groomed ice-runways at various international stations around Antarctica and on the summit of Greenland.

Greenland ice core (Photo by
M. G. Hastings, University of
Washington, Seattle)

- New Zealand with two stations ratified the treaty on
  November 1, 1960.

- Belgium with one station ratified the treaty on July 26,
  1960.

- Japan with one station ratified the treaty on August 4,
  1960.

- Norway with one station ratified the treaty on August 24,
  1960.

Poland ratified the treaty on June 8, 1961. It was the only country without a research station on Antarctica at the time that still ratified the treaty prior to its enforcement on June 23, 1961. Since that date, 32 other countries have signed the treaty with 15 of those taking on significant research projects to gain consulting status on decisions under the treaty.

Precambrian Fossils

Paleontologists have referred to the Cambrian Explosion as Darwin's Dilemma. Having so many fossils emerge on the geological record in the Cambrian from apparently nothing remained inexplicable to Charles Darwin. He wrote in *On the Origin of Species* that the lack of fossils in the Precambrian "may be truly urged as a valid argument against the views here entertained." The missing fossils became the Achilles heel for the otherwise august observations supporting the evidence for evolution.

For a century, paleontologists scoured what are called *shield formations* in the interior of the continents where the oldest preserved rocks of Precambrian age can still be found. Knowing where to look helped, but the search resulted in many Precambrian strata discoveries of more rocks rather than fossils. Part of the problem was nobody knew what a Precambrian fossil looked like, and there were plenty of differing opinions on the matter. Imagine running the evolutionary clock backward with only the information from species in existence today. What might a fossil from the Cretaceous look like? It is easy perhaps to think of a small shrewlike creature, but a dinosaur? Evolution is not necessarily linear.

As Charles Walcott (1850–1927) discovered across the United States and most famously in the Canadian Burgess Shale, soft-bodied fossils and trace fossils—the impressions, tracks, and signatures of organisms—can be extraordinarily complex. Most fossils are mineralized skeletons, or, in the case of the king of the Cambrian fossils: exoskeletons. Trilobites reigned supreme in the fossil record from the Cambrian to the Permian. Growing an exoskeleton made survival sense. With the abundance of carnivorous appetites in the Cambrian ocean, soft was a meal. Trilobites diversified their basic body shape—a head, thorax, and tail—with curly spines, straight spines, long spines, short spines, no spines, bigger armor, bigger bodies, better eyes, big eyes, little eyes, tiny bodies, and more. Radical and incremental changes abound in the fossil record. The main component of arthropod exoskeletons is chitin, made from a combination of ammonia and sugar, specifically glucose.

Plenty of other creatures never evolved exoskeletons or any hard shell and survived. Some species of modern sea cucumbers, for

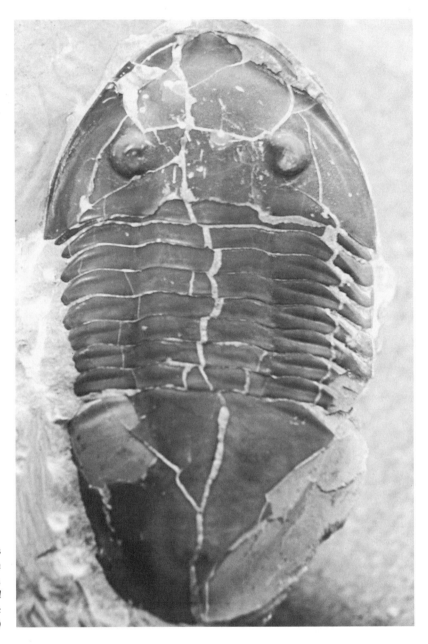

Ordovician trilobite Isotelus *from a Decorah Formation limestone, Spring Grove, Minnesota. Specimen collected by A.C.A.* (North Dakota State University)

example, have toxins in their skin. If this does not deter an attack, a sea cucumber under duress will use hydrostatic pressure to compress its body and eventually excrete its entire intestine into the sea with the hope that the predator will snatch up the food offering as it drifts away in the current and leave the poor sea cucumber alone to heal internally. Sea cucumbers take about a month to regenerate their intestines. In the meantime, they try to avoid another attack by not eating or moving much.

All modern and fossil sea cucumbers, which date back to the Silurian 400 million years ago, have microscopic skeletal structure called *spicules* that look like tiny hooks, barbs, and burrs. Linked together in the tissue these spicules provide strength and support for the inverte-

Pygidium of the Upper Cambrian trilobite Uncaspis *from the Eau Claire Formation, Willow River, Wisconsin.* (North Dakota State University)

brates. The same skeletal structure is also found inside sponges and is even used by some carnivorous sponges to capture small crustaceans. Following the trail of spicules through the fossil record leads to the Cambrian. Here along with the sponges in the phylum Porifera are spicule-free sponges in the phylum called Archaeocyatha, whose *calcareous* sponges came in two types: some with no spicules and some with spicule-like rods. Sir Raymond Priestley (1886–1974), a British-born Antarctic geologist on both the Shackleton expedition (1907–09) and the Scott expedition (1910–12) was familiar with Archaeocyatha from Cambrian limestone deposits near the Ross Sea. These ancestors of sponges and coral reefs marked a warmer time in Antarctica's history.

In neighboring Australia, the signs of a comparable climate change were also embedded in the sedimentary record. On March 27, 1946, geologist Reginald "Reg" Sprigg (1919–94) discovered round jellyfish impressions and other soft-bodied fossils in what he thought were Cambrian deposits lying just above a distinct period of glaciation. His surprising findings of an ancient sea of macrofauna were dismissed, however, like so many other questionable rock patterns, as being inorganic in nature—an impression made perhaps by the wind. Walcott had encountered similar reactions when he surveyed the Grand Canyon and distinguished Precambrian from Cambrian deposits both containing fossil patterns that have been described as looking like cabbage. He believed, as many did, that bacteria or algae in warm shallow seas had formed these fossils called Cryptozoon, which meant "hidden life." He did not gain the confidence, however, of leading paleobotanist Albert Charles Seward (1863–1941) of the University of Cambridge. In his 1931 book *Plant Life Through the Ages*, Seward wrote a stinging critique of Precambrian Cryptozoon: "We can hardly expect to find in Pre-Cambrian rocks any actual proof of the existence of bacteria." Until a definitive fossil assemblage could stand up to the skepticism as both Precambrian and biological in origin, Darwin's dilemma remained unsolved.

After a century of searching, false hopes, and mistaken identities from generations of paleontologists, the person who succeeded in this venue was not originally looking for fossils. He was fishing. In 1950 geologist Stanley Tyler (1906–63) at the University of Wisconsin had a grant to study outcrops of iron—an important component for making steel at the steel mills in Gary, Indiana—that is then used for making cars at the auto plants in Detroit, Michigan. Tyler had taken the afternoon off from mapping the Precambrian Gunflint iron formation along the north side of Lake Superior, when he saw something strange. As he navigated his boat toward Schreiber Beach he saw an outcrop of black chert. Banded iron formations like the one he was surveying are zebra-striped sedimentary rocks of red chert and black hematite or magnetite. He took a sample of the black chert back to his laboratory, where he made a *thin section* to study under a microscope. What he saw looked oddly organic.

At the next meeting of the Geological Society of America, Tyler turned to paleontologist Robert Shrock (1904–93) for advice. Shrock, a former colleague now at the Massachusetts Institute of Technology, jokingly suggested Tyler might have fungi of the sort that "cover the top of a jam jar left open too long." He recommended Tyler contact paleobotanist Elso Barghoorn of Harvard. Barghoorn (1915–84) had recently published an article on marine fungi that digest cellulose in wood. Tyler wondered if the same type of relationship might occur with these microorganisms and iron. Collaboration between the two was quickly established, with Tyler sending Barghoorn more and more samples to study and mapping the Gunflint Cherts extensively throughout the Precambrian rocks of the Canadian Shield around Lake Superior. Their first paper on the subject, published April 30, 1954, in *Science*, stated that: "As far as we are aware, these plants are the oldest structurally preserved organisms that clearly exhibit cellular differentiation and original carbon complexes which have yet been discovered in pre-Cambrian sediments and, as such, are of great interest in the evolutionary scheme of primitive life." As Earth scientist J. William Schopf wrote, Tyler's discovery "set the course for modern studies" of Precambrian life, even though, as Tyler's friend and colleague Robert Dott wrote, Tyler often joked that he only knew 10 fossils, all of which were microscopic.

The macroscopic Precambrian fossils had actually already been discovered—only misidentified or dismissed as inorganic. In the late 1950s, paleontologist Martin Gleassner (1906–89) of the University of Adelaide, working with Mary Wade (1928–2005), who in 1971 became Curator of Paleontology at the Queensland Museum, took a second look at the jellyfish fossils Sprigg had found in the Ediacaran Hills of the Flinders Range in South Australia. The formation that Sprigg and others had thought was Cambrian was actually late Precambrian; the soft-bodied fossils were creatures preserved in the sediments of an ancient warm shallow sea. In the Geologic Time Scale, the Ediacaran is now identified as the name of the last period before the Cambrian Period.

By the 1960s, the preconceived notions about the Precambrian were replaced with a tour de force of recognition for microbial mats as living fossils. Walcott had been right, and although still most widely known for his discovery of the Burgess Shale, he is now also heralded within the paleontological community for his distinctive Precambrian fossil discoveries. The attention to Cryptozoons actually revealed an international identity crisis. For hundreds of years, the circular fossil patterns have adorned the walls of churches and been polished into jewelry, but the history of the fossil's scientific nomenclature is much more recent. In 1825 J. H. Steel introduced into the scientific literature a description of an *oolite* formation near a quarry in Saratoga Springs, New York. Working near the same location 60 years later, paleontologist James Hall (1811–98) in 1883 named the fossils he found at Beekmantown in Saratoga, New York, cryptozoon, meaning: "hidden life." Two years later, German geologist Johannes Walther (1860–1937) identified ancient rock-forming algae in limestone sediments. In 1906 G. Gürich identified examples he found in Belgium as spongiostromids. Two years later, E. Kalkowsky coined the term *stromatolith* to describe fossils from the Triassic in northern Germany.

The word *stromatolite* would ultimately become the prevailing term for the microbial mats. Walcott and others compared the fossil patterns to the growth of freshwater blue-green algae, which themselves

Stromatolites in the Helena Formation along Highline Trail in Glacier National Park, Montana, July 4, 1979 (USGS)

Scientist of the Decade: Clair Cameron Patterson (1922–1995)

That nothing on Earth seemed to last longer than 3.3 billion years frustrated geochronologists in the 1950s. In September 1953 a team of American geochemists announced at a meeting in Wisconsin a new method for estimating the age of the Earth. Erosion-plagued rocks had their limits. The time had come to turn to meteorites. These remnants of broken asteroids and fallen meteors had hit the Earth relatively recently, but their ages were unknown.

Nuclear chemist Harrison Brown (1917–86) and others at the University of Chicago who had worked on the Manhattan Project wanted to "focus their attentions on new concepts for developing scientific knowledge in fields as far from military applications as possible," wrote Brown's contemporaries in his biography. They turned to planetary and Earth sciences, in particular the work of Arthur Holmes in geochronology, and applied their knowledge to develop studies in nuclear geochemistry. The key to obtaining better age dates for older material was in refining the amount of sample needed for measuring parent-daughter decays.

The early 20th century development of the mass spectrometer gave scientists the ability to separate and identify the different components of any sample based on the mass and charge of the electrically charged particles, or ions, it emits when turned into an ionized gas. As light through a prism bends and produces the visible spectrum of light in the form of a rainbow, ionized gas through the electric or magnetic field of a mass spectrometer bends, the lighter ions travel faster than the heavier ions, and produces a mass spectrum. Prior to World War II, mass spectrometers required tens of milligrams of a sample (10 milligrams = .01 gram). Brown brought together two students at the University of Chicago, George Tilton and Clair Patterson, to begin working on ways to measure microscopic-sized mineral samples (1 microgram = .000001 gram).

In a 1995 interview, Patterson described how Brown approached him with the idea. Clair, who went by the nickname "Pat," had worked on separating Uranium 235 from Uranium 238 using mass spectrometers during the war. He and his wife Laurie McCleary Patterson had returned from working on the Manhattan Project in Tennessee to Chicago, where Clair could complete his Ph.D. at the University of Chicago while Laurie supported them financially with her job as a spectroscopist at the Illinois Institute of Technology. Brown learned of Clair's experience and, according to Clair, said to him one day: "Hey Pat, you're familiar with mass spectrometers. Now, there's this other youngster, George Tilton. What we're going to do is learn how to measure the geologic ages of a common mineral that's about the size of a head of a pin. It's called zircon."

Zircon minerals crystallize during the formation of igneous rocks, when magma reaches the Earth's crust and cools. The amazing resiliency of zircon allows it to remain in existence long after an igneous rock is eroded into sedimentary material or reconstituted through heat and pressure into metamorphic stone. When the zircon is formed it contains trace amounts of uranium, only a few parts per million, and no lead. With time, the uranium decays to lead and it was this minute amount of lead that Brown wanted Patterson to measure. Tilton would measure the uranium. As Patterson explained, Brown had a master plan and zircons were the first step: "So Brown said, 'Pat, after you figure how to do the isotopic composition of these zircons, you will then know how to get the lead—you will have it all set up. You just go in and get an iron meteorite—I'll get it for you. We'll get the lead out of the iron meteorite. You measure its isotopic composition and you stick it into the equation. And you'll be famous, because you will have measured the age of the Earth.' I said, 'Good, I will do that.' And he said, 'It will be duck soup, Patterson.'"

Atomic physicist Alfred Nier (1911–94) and colleagues conceived the equation Brown was referring to for estimating the age of the Earth. Only they were missing the critical component. "If we only knew what the isotopic composition of primordial lead was in the Earth at the time it was formed, we could take that number and stick it into this marvelous equation we had. And you could turn the crank and, *blip,* out would come the age of the Earth," Patterson said. Brown was counting on him to do just that.

They were making two assumptions. The first was that on Earth the only change to the ratio of lead to uranium found at the surface came from the radioactive decay that had occurred since the time the minerals in the crust had formed. (Evidence for this being, for example, that younger lead ore is more radiogenic than older lead ore.) The second assumption they made was that the isotopic composition of lead in iron meteorites represented the same isotopic composition of lead at the time of Earth's formation. They had no evidence to support that assumption at the time, and for the assumption to work they needed to investigate a meteorite that did not have a significant concentration of uranium to contribute to its lead mix. Brown had learned from his studies of trace elements in meteorites that unlike silicate meteorites, iron meteorites had essentially no uranium. (Either they had little to no uranium to start with or they were old enough for the uranium to have been depleted.) The stable lead isotopes on Earth today are a mixture of primordial lead and lead formed as the result of ongoing radioactive decay:

- Uranium 238 decays to lead 206
- Uranium 235 decays to lead 207
- Thorium 232 decays to lead 208

If they could determine the isotopic composition of lead in an iron meteorite, then they could compare this number with the isotopic composition of lead in the crust today and calculate the rate of change, giving them the age of the planet since the time of the meteorite's formation. This would also presumably equate to Earth's original birth year, give or take a few tens of millions of years.

Step one, however, identifying the radioisotope dates for zircons, took five years. Patterson had been able to reduce the sample size by a factor of a thousand within the first year. The problem then became contamination. As Tilton writes in Patterson's biography, "Patterson started lead measurements in 1948 in a very dusty laboratory in Kent Hall, one of the oldest buildings on campus" at the University of Chicago. "In retrospect it was an extremely unfavorable environment for lead work. None of the modern techniques, such as laminar flow filtered air, sub-boiling distillation of liquid reagents, and Teflon containers were available in those days."

Patterson became aware of the problem because the amount and type of lead he detected was wrong for what should be there, given the stratigraphy where the rock was found and the uranium measurements Tilton had done. "We could calculate how much lead there should be and what its isotopic composition should be. And it kept coming up with the wrong number, so I had to figure out why—to go to all these sources for different possibilities. That's how I found out all about this contamination—that there was lead coming from everywhere," Patterson said. To correct the problem, Patterson built a clean lab when none of the other spectroscopists he knew had even considered the option. "Only a few nuclear geochemists understood what was being done there. And they were all busily working in these two other methods: potassium-argon dating and rubidium-strontium dating. None of them knew how to isolate lead without getting it dirty." Visitors to his lab presented a new problem, which he compared to one of Charles Schultz's *Peanuts* comic strip characters: Charlie Brown's infamous friend Pigpen. "You know Pigpen, in Charlie Brown's comic, where stuff is coming out all

(continues)

(continued)

over the place? That's what people look like with respect to lead." In Patterson's superclean laboratory, everyone was a Pigpen with lead from their hair and clothing contaminating the laboratory the moment they stepped inside for a visit. "It was contamination of every conceivable source that people had never thought about before. It was working with those zircons that enabled me to become aware of this enormous contamination problem." Fighting for congressional laws to ban lead from everyday household products, such as gasoline, tin cans, and paint, would become a lifelong pursuit. Before he embarked on that mission though, he still had the age of the Earth to determine.

After Tilton and Patterson published their Ph.D. work on determining the age of zircon crystals in rocks, Patterson began working as a post-doc for Brown. When Brown moved to the California Institute of Technology in Pasadena, Patterson followed him. Tilton took a job in the Department of Terrestrial Magnetism at Carnegie Institution of Washington in Washington, D.C. Because Patterson's new lab in Pasadena was not yet equipped with an appropriate mass spectrometer, he continued to work in Mark Inghram's laboratory at the University of Chicago. Brown had obtained a Canyon Diablo iron meteorite, a remnant of the destroyed meteor that had formed Barringer's Crater in Arizona for Patterson to investigate. In 1953 he had all the measurements in place. He inserted his findings into the equation and calculated that the Earth had coalesced from the solar disk 4.5 billion years ago. Patterson formally announced the discovery at the September conference on the "Application of Nuclear Processes to Geological Problems" in Geneva, Wisconsin. His presentation, coauthored with Tilton and Inghram, was published in the following *Bulletin of the Geological Society of America*.

The impact on the scientific community was immediate. The previously accepted estimate for the age of the Earth at the time had been constrained to 3.3 billion years. German-born physicist Friedrich "Fritz" or "Fiesel" Georg Houtermans (1903–66) at the University of Bern in Switzerland, who was in contact with nuclear geochemists in Chicago, analyzed Patterson's calculations and data on the Canyon Diablo meteorite and came to the same conclusion. In 1953 Houtermans published his report "Determination of the Age of the Earth from the Isotopic Composition of Meteoritic Lead," in volume 10 of Italy's premier journal for physics, *Il Nuovo Cimento*. In 1955 Patterson and his colleagues reported additional meteorite data, including an iron meteorite from the craters in Henbury, Australia, that also resulted in a calculated age date of 4.5 billion years for Earth's formation.

At the time, astronomers had just begun debating over whether the universe was in a steady state, and therefore ageless, or had been expanding since the time of the "big bang," a term coined sarcastically in 1949 by one of the originators of the steady-state model. Patterson's calculated age for the Canyon Diablo meteorite was not only older than the generally accepted estimate for the age of the Earth at the time but also older than the astronomers' estimated age of 2 to 3 billion years for an expanding universe. During the second half of the 20th century, astronomers, like geochronologists during the first half of the century, would find their age date becoming progressively older. Today the universe is thought to be 13.7 billion years old. For Earth, the answer was solved in 1953. During the remainder of the 20th century geochronologists would try to disprove the age date, only to find they were improving its precision of significant figures and reducing the margin of error to between 600,000 and one million years. Investigations in 2005 into oxygen isotopes of meteorite inclusions found indications that the solar nebula rapidly changed between 4.567 billion years ago and 4.565 billion years ago. What was happening to Earth at this time remains a mystery. The oldest zircon mineral found on Earth dates back to 4.4 billion years, indicating the time when magma first began to cool and form the planet's crust.

would later become known as cyanobacteria. With every slight variation of the fossil pattern receiving a new name, the mass confusion led paleontologist Carroll Lane Fenton (1900–69) of the University of Buffalo to write a 29-page report in 1943 on "Pre-Cambrian and Early Paleozoic Algae," in an attempt to organize their nomenclature based on their perceived differences in organic origin. He wrote: "A large part of [this] paper is devoted to stromatolites, which outrank all other Pre-Silurian plant fossils in abundance, variety and importance as rock-builders." When Brian W. Logan of the University of Western Australia reported in 1961 on the existence of modern-day living examples of "*Cryptozoon* and associated stromatolites" in Shark Bay, Western Australia, he confirmed the status of microbial mats as important reef-builders throughout Earth's history. By the 1970s, paleontologist Hans J. Hoffman, who is now with McGill University in Canada, wrote that stromatolites were being used to "determine paleolatitudes, to gauge ancient tidal ranges, to shed light on past rates of rotation of the Earth, and to time the capture or closest approach of the Moon." One of Earth's first organisms to inhabit the planet was finally revealing billions of years of history.

Further Reading

Barghoorn, Elso S., and Stanley A. Tyler. "Microorganisms from the Gunflint Chert." *Science* New Series, 147, no. 3658 (1965): 563–577. This report, published after Tyler's death, describes the algal cherts he discovered in the Canadian Shield and the evidence of their biological origin in the Precambrian.

British Antarctic Survey, National Environment Research Council, "The Antarctic Treaty." A detailed Web site on the history of the Antarctic Treaty, including a list of the countries that have ratified the agreement. Available online. URL: http://www.antarctica.ac.uk/About_Antarctica/Treaty/index.html. Accessed April 24, 2006.

"British Transantarctic Expedition 1957–58" Map and pictures from Sir Vivian Fuchs's expedition. Part of the Voyage of the Scotia Glasgow Digital Library files. Available online. URL: http://gdl.cdlr.strath.ac.uk/scotia/gooant/gooant0206.htm. Accessed April 24, 2006.

Bullard, Edward C. "The flow of Heat through the floor of the Atlantic Ocean." *Proc. R. Soc. Lond.* A 222 (1954): 408–429. A description of the first marine geological instrument equipped with an O-ring and used to measure seafloor temperatures.

Carson, Rachel. *The Sea Around Us.* New York: Oxford University Press, 1951. This book discusses the field of oceanography and the influence of the oceans on society.

Dalrymple, G. Brent. *The Age of the Earth.* Stanford: Stanford University Press, 1991. This book explains radiometric dating and its application in dating the Earth and Moon.

Debenham, Frank. *The Global Atlas: A New View Of The World From Space.* New York, Simon and Schuster, 1958. The first atlas with satellite images of Earth—also published the same year under the title: *The World Is Round*, in London by Macdonald. Both have introductions by Bertrand Russell.

Dott, Robert H. Jr. "Serendipity and Stan Tyler's Precambrian Gunflint Fossils." *The Outcrop* (2000): 25–26. Available online. URL: http://www.geology.wisc.edu/outcrop. Accessed April 24, 2006.

Eklund, Carl R., and Joan Beckman. *Antarctica: Polar Research and Discovery during the International Geophysical Year.* New York: Holt, Rinehart, and Winston, 1963. M. L. Wolbarsht in a 1965 review writes: "This book, revised by Joan Beckman after Carl Eklund's death, is a well-written, simple introduction to all aspects of the Antarctic. It describes earlier exploration; the fauna of the ice and the sea; geology; meteorology; and how research in the Antarctic casts light on many varied problems, such as the shape of the Earth, the origin of the Aurora and cosmic rays."

Fenton, Carroll Lane. "Pre-Cambrian and Early Paleozoic Algae." *American Midland Naturalist* 30, no. 1 (July 1943): 83–111. A detailed description of different algal fossils.

Gamow, George. *Biography of the Earth: its past, present and future.* Rev. ed. New York: Viking Press, 1959. This book, which was translated into at least three languages, discusses the origin of Earth, its formation and past climates. Gamow (1904–68) is the author of a number of introductory math and science books, including the fictional *Mr. Tompkins* series.

Hofmann, Hans J. "Stromatolites Characteristics and Utility." *Earth-Science Reviews* 9 (1973): 339–373. An extensive report on Stromatolites.

Holmes, Arthur. "An Estimate of the Age of the Earth." *Nature* 157 (1946): 680–684. After Alfred Nier in 1939 used *mass spectrometry* to determine the correct ratio of Uranium 235 to Uranium 238, he calculated an age of 2 billion years for lead minerals by determining the ratio of lead 206 to lead 207. Here Holmes makes the same calculations on older lead minerals and calculates an age of 3 billion years.

Houtermans, F. "Determination of the Age of the Earth from the Isotopic Composition of Meteoritic Lead." *Nuovo Cimento* 10 (1953): 1,623–1,633. The report was published shortly after Clair Patterson's presentation on radioisotopic measurements of lead on the Canyon Diablo meteorite to determine the age of the Earth.

Hyde, Margaret O. *Exploring Earth and Space.* 4th ed. New York: McGraw-Hill, 1967. An introduction to scientific investigations of space, the ocean, Earth's interior and crust, the magnetic field, and the poles.

Krot, Alexander N., Hisayoshi Yurimoto, Ian D. Hutcheon, and Glenn J. MacPherson. "Chronology of the early Solar System from chondrule-bearing calcium-aluminium-rich inclusions." *Nature* 434 (2005): 998–1,001. This report concludes that a meteorite had material added to it during a remelting episode 2 million years after formation 4.567 billion years ago.

Lansing, Alfred. *Endurance: Shackleton's Incredible Voyage.* New York: McGraw-Hill, 1959. This best seller during its time recounts the story of Shackleton's 1914 expedition and was recently republished in 1999.

Lewis, Ricki. "Access to Rare Fossils Preserved." *BioScience* 41 no. 9 (October 1991): 599–601. A story about pending destruction to the Petrified Sea Gardens stromatolite exhibit in Saratoga Springs, New York.

Margulis, Lynn, and Andrew H. Knoll. "Elso Sterrenberg Barghoorn, Jr.: June 30, 1915–January 27, 1984." *Biographical Memoirs of the National Academy of Sciences* 87 (2006): 92–109. This biography on Barghoorn includes details on his work with Stanley Tyler. Available online. URL: http://fermat.nap.edu/openbook.php?record_id=11522&page=92. Accessed April 24, 2006.

"NASA History" This Web site chronicles the major achievements in space since 1957. Available online. URL: http://history.nasa.gov/ Accessed April 24, 2006.

Patterson, Clair. "The Pb 207 /Pb 206 Ages of Some Stone Meteorites." *Geochimica et Cosmochimica Acta* 7 (1955): 151–153. A report on the methods of meteoritic lead dating.

———. "Age of Meteorites and the Earth." *Geochimica et Cosmochimica Acta* 10 (1956): 230–237. A report on the radioisotopic evidence for the ages of meteorites and the Earth.

———. "Contaminated and Natural Environments of Man." *Arch. Environ. Health* 11 (1965): 344–360. A report on the abundant and dangerous use of lead in society.

———, G. Tilton, and M. Inghram. "Age of the Earth." *Science* 121, no. 3134 (January 21, 1955): 69–75. A report on the meteoritic evidence indicating the Earth is 4.5 billion years old.

"Reach into Space." *Time*, May 4, 1959. A biography on James Van Allen. Available online. URL: http://jcgi.pathfinder.com/time/magazine/article/0,9171,892531,00.html. Accessed April 24, 2006.

Revelle, Roger. "Harrison Brown: September 26, 1917–December 8, 1986." *Biographical Memoirs of the National Academy of Sciences* 65 (1994): 44–55. Roger Revelle died on July 15, 1991. This memoir was reviewed and revised in small part by Edward Goldberg, Claire C. Patterson, and George Tilton.

Riding, Robert. "Microbial carbonates: the geological record of calcified bacterial–algal mats and biofilms." *Sedimentology* 47 (2000): 179. Available online. URL: http://www.blackwell-synergy.com/doi/full/10.1046/j.1365-3091.2000.00003.x. Accessed April 24, 2006.

Schopf, J. William. "Solution to Darwin's dilemma: Discovery of the missing Precambrian record of life." *Proceedings of the National Academy of Sciences* 97, no. 13 (2000): 6,947–6,953. Schopf details the history of the search and discovery of Precambrian fossils since the days of Darwin.

Siple, Paul. *90° South: The Story of the American South Pole Conquest.* New York: G.P. Putnam's Sons, 1959. Siple worked as the stationmaster of the South Pole Amundsen-Scott base during the International Geophysical Year.

Sprigg, Reginald C. "On The 1946 Discovery Of The Precambrian Ediacarian Fossil Fauna In South Australia." *Earth Sciences History* 7, no. 1 (1988): 46–51. Sprigg recounts the geological survey that led to his 1946 discovery.

Sullivan, Walter. "Called 'Greatest Experiment'; Radiation Spread." *New York Times,* March 19, 1959. Front Page. Sullivan breaks the news about a top secret U.S. government project that blew up nuclear bombs in space the previous summer.

———. "The Argus Experiment—Q. and A. on the Basic Science Involved." *New York Times,* March 20, 1959. Review of the Week Editorials, Page E6. A question and answer discussion about the top secret Argus project.

———. "Argus Produced Wide Atom Flash; It and Earlier Tests Showed Possible Blinding Effect Up to 1,000 Miles Away." *New York Times,* March 23, 1959, Page 9. Preliminary results of the Argus tests are revealed, but much remains classified.

———. *Assault on the Unknown: The International Geophysical Year.* New York: McGraw-Hill Book Company, 1961. Sullivan, a *New York Times* science reporter, discusses the work done during the International Geophysical Year.

Taylor, G. A. M. *The 1951 Eruption of Mount Lamington, Papua. Bureau of Mineral Resources, Geology, and Geophysics Bulletin no. 38.* Australia: Australian Government Publishing Service, 1958; second edition 1983. One of the first exhaustive geologic reports of a volcanic eruption.

Tilton, George R. "Clair Cameron Patterson." *Biographical Memoirs of the National Academy of Sciences* 74 (1998): 266–287. This biography discusses the nuclear geochronological work of Clair Patterson. Available online. URL: http://newton.nap.edu/html/biomems/cpatterson.html. Accessed April 24, 2006.

Tyler, Stanley A., and Elso S. Barghoorn. "Occurrence of Structurally Preserved Plants in Pre-Cambrian Rocks of the Canadian Shield." *Science* 119 (1954): 606–608. This report announces the discovery of Precambrian microfossils, called algal cherts.

Tyler-Lewis, Kelly. *The Lost Men: The Harrowing Saga of Shackleton's Ross Sea Party.* New York: Viking Adult, 2006. Following her Emmy-winning work on the PBS/NOVA documentary "Shackleton's Voyage of Endurance," Tyler-Lewis focused on the less known saga of the men who succeeded during their part of the 1914–1917 trans-Antarctic mission but died as a result.

U.S. Geological Survey. "Historic Earthquakes: Chile 1960" This Web site provides information and links to articles about the largest earthquake

of the 20th century. Available online. URL: http://earthquake.usgs.gov/
regional/world/events/1960_05_22.php. Accessed February 28, 2007.

Wilson, John Tuzo. *I.G.Y.: The Year of the New Moons.* New York: Alfred
A. Knopf, 1961. Canadian geophysicist Wilson was president of the
International Union of Geodesy and Geophysics during the IGY and in
this book discusses his expeditions to Romania, the Soviet Union, and
China and the efforts to bridge science in countries that were in conflict
politically.

7

1961–1970:
A New Planetary Perspective

Introduction

The work of oceanographers and marine geophysicists in the 1950s merged with the work of terrestrial paleomagnetists in the 1960s to revitalize the debate over continental drift. Instead of focusing on similarities in geology and fossil assemblages between continental coasts, the new generation of Earth scientists followed the geophysical evidence and cached the debate in terms of polar wanders, magnetic reversals, and the interactions of plate boundaries. Geologists in North America who had for decades shunned the idea of continental drift reconsidered the possibility and embraced the new theory of plate tectonics as a revolutionary concept for modeling how Earth processes operate. A few geologists continued to hold on to the contraction model, but the majority recognized the overwhelming amount of evidence coming in for lateral motion of both the continents and the seafloor. Some researchers swung to the opposite extreme and attributed the horizontal drift to the hypothesis that the Earth was slowly expanding. This idea, difficult to prove, was overshadowed by the realization of how significant the role of subduction was in terms of recycling the oceanic crust back into the mantle. During this decade of changing opinions many scientists returned to Wegener's original idea to determine why the geologic, paleontological, and meteorological data indicating drift had not convincingly swayed a significant portion of the geologic community in North America. The results seem to indicate that the lack of support for drift stemmed from a reluctance to thoroughly consider the iconoclastic model and favoritism for continuing to needle the issues it addressed using the status quo model of permanence. The geophysical evidence coming to light in the 1960s discredited the theory of permanence. The continents in the past as well as the seafloor had definitely experienced lateral change in their positions. The geophysical evidence when combined with the earlier evidence from Wegener, du Toit, Holmes, and others finally convinced the geological community that the pattern of volcanoes and earthquakes was not random. The Earth's crust indeed moved laterally as well as vertically and the stress from the motion produced a dynamic planet.

The Lunar Orbiter shot this first photograph of the Earth from the vicinity of the Moon on August 23, 1966. (NASA)

Earth's Magnetic Reversals

Students studying physics in the 18th century may have burnt clay pots or bricks as a way of testing magnetism. The Honorable Robert Boyle (1627–91), an Irish-born natural philosopher, had first conducted the experiment, one of many, and a collection of his work was published the

American researchers establish *Arctic Research Lab Ice Station II* (*Arlis II*), a drifting sea-ice station

The United States, Soviet Union, and United Kingdom sign the Limited Test Ban Treaty banning nuclear tests from the atmosphere, underwater, and in space. Underground nuclear explosions are still allowed due to a lack of confidence in seismometers being able to monitor underground tests even though few such tests had been carried out. Over the next 30 years, China, the United States, the Soviet Union, the United Kingdom, France, and India would conduct the equivalent of a test a week

MILESTONES

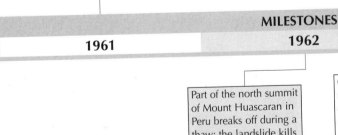

1961   **1962**   **1963**

Part of the north summit of Mount Huascaran in Peru breaks off during a thaw; the landslide kills 3,500 people

American environmentalist Rachel Carson publishes *Silent Spring*

On November 14, a new volcanic island emerges off the coast of Iceland. Surtur is the Icelandic god of fire and the island, which sent black smoke into the sky as its lava broke the surface, was given the name Surtsey

Geologist I. G. Gass identifies the Troodos Massif in Cyprus as a remnant of ancient seafloor uplifted onto continental crust, a geologic feature given the term *ophiolite*

year of his death and widely reproduced. The experiment on magnetism called for heating a brick in a kiln and allowing the brick to cool in the same position. The brick, and other clay ceramics, would become weakly magnetized in the same direction as the Earth's magnetic field. Later in the 18th century, the Italian physicist Giambatista Beccaria (1716–81) reported that the same magnetic polarization happened whenever lightning struck stones containing iron. For a hundred more years, the magnetic alignment in heated clay and *ferruginous* stones remained little more than a curiosity. In the 1860s a survey of antique clayware throughout Italy and Egypt showed that the pottery retained its magnetic alignment. These permanent magnets of ancient history inspired Giuseppe Folgheraiter in 1896 to advance the idea that they could be used as a record of Earth's magnetic field at the time of their construction. He began collecting at archaeological sites of known dates the vases and other items that needed to bake and cool in an upright position. Knowing when and where the vases were made, Folgheraiter could track the changing position of Earth's north and south magnetic poles. Soon others were investigating the apparent polar wander of the magnetic north

American paleontologist John Ostrom uncovers the first fossil of a raptor dinosaur. He compares the fossil *Deinonychus* to modern-day nonflying birds and suggests that dinosaurs and birds may share an evolutionary link

The U.S. National Science Foundation establishes a consortium of four leading institutes, called the Joint Oceanographic Institutions for Deep Earth Sampling (JOIDES), for the purpose of drilling into Earth's ocean floor. Results from the project over the next few years confirm that the oceanic crust subducting back into the mantle is less than 200 million years old

The Large Aperature Seismic Array is established in Montana. The signals from 525 seismometers, dispersed over an area of 11,583 square miles (30,000 km^2) are combined to record seismic events with a high degree of sensitivity

NASA launches *GEOS 1* (*Geodynamics Experimental Ocean* Satellite) to provide a 3-D map of the world accurate to within 30 feet (10 m)

Australian geochemists Alfred Edward "Ted" Ringwood and Alan Major explain the seismic discontinuity at a depth of 250 miles (400 km) to a change in mineral structure from olivine to spinel

MILESTONES

1964   **1965**   **1966**

Shiveluch on Russia's Kamchatka Peninsula erupts on November 12 collapsing the dome and producing 0.2 cubic miles (0.75 km^3) of tephra in a single day

Geologists Jack Oliver, Lynn Sykes, and Bryan Isacks of Columbia University's Lamont-Doherty Geological Observatory identify plate subduction of the oceanic crust

March 28, an earthquake of magnitude 9.2 strikes Prince William Sound, Alaska—125 people die, most from the resulting tsunami. The quake and tsunami cause an estimated $311 million in property damage

Mission specialists controlling the Lunar Orbiter from Earth focus the camera on board the spacecraft away from the Moon's surface features in order to shoot the first photograph of Earth from lunar orbit

The National Science Foundation puts Scripps Institute of Oceanography in charge of the JOIDES project and establishes the Deep Sea Drilling Project (DSDP)

pole. Folgheraiter also supported the ideas of Italian physicist Macedonio Melloni (1798–1854), director of the Vesuvius Observatory during the 1840s, who hypothesized that ancient lava flows from Vesuvius would also contain a record of Earth's magnetic field. The lava rocks might be used to check the growing archaeological data as well as push the record further back in time.

In 1901 French physicist Bernard Brunhes (1867–1910) took charge of systematically testing that idea. He focused much of his work on the baked clays underneath the lava flows from the Central Massif of France. Clay is formed from weathering of rock minerals; after being subjected to intense heat, the iron in the clay becomes magnetized in alignment with the Earth's magnetic field as it cools. Brunhes surveyed several volcanic flows, including a site west of the mountain town of Saint-Flour. Without the synthetic diamond saws of the 1960s, he made slow progress. He finally published his results in 1906 in the report entitled "Recherches sur la direction d'aimantation des roches volcaniques" (Research

The American geophysicist Jason Morgan, a postdoctoral candidate at Princeton University, gives a talk at a meeting of the American Geophysical Union describing the motions of crustal plates as rigid areas each rotating about Earth's spherical surface around a central point or pole. Working together, independently of Morgan, Dan McKenzie and Robert L. Parker, 25-year-old geophysicists of the Institute of Geophysics and Planetary Physics at the University of California at San Diego, publish similar conclusions regarding the motion of the Pacific plate. Their report in the December 30 issue of *Nature* concludes that individual seismic-free areas "move as rigid plates on the surface of a sphere"

A borehole is drilled 7,093 feet (2,162 m) into the Antarctic ice at Byrd Station and reveals that the bottom of the layers are 100,000 years old

The floor of the Fernandina caldera in the Galápagos Islands drops 1,150 feet (350 m) during an explosive eruption from June 11 to July 4 that emits more than 0.02 cubic miles (0.1 km³) of tephra and causes pyroclastic flows, lava flows, and debris avalanches

French geophysicist Xavier Le Pichon, working at the Lamont-Doherty Geological Observatory in New York, describes the motions of Earth's six largest plates using poles of rotation derived from the patterns of magnetic anomalies and fracture zones about mid-ocean ridges

MILESTONES

1967

1968

Fluid geophysicists with Princeton University and the National Oceanographic and Atmospheric Administration, Syukuro Manabe and Richard T. Wetherald, warn that an increase in carbon dioxide from human activities will result in a "greenhouse effect," which combined with water vapor in the atmosphere will raise ground surface temperatures and cause sea levels to rise

U.S. survey ship *Glomar Challenger* starts drilling cores in the seafloor as part of the Deep Sea Drilling Project. Capable of drilling in water up to 19,685 feet (6 km) deep, it can return core samples from 2,460 feet (750 m) below the seafloor

British geochemist Ron Oxburgh and American aeronautical engineer Donald L. Turcotte calculate the thermal consequences of subduction

American biologist Elso Sterrenberg Barghoorn and his associates report the discovery of the remains of amino acids in three billion-years-old Precambrian sedimentary rocks

on the direction of the magnetization of volcanic rocks). The rock layers he collected dated back to the Miocene epoch and presented him with a strange record of the magnetic field. He had expected magnetic drift. What he found was more than that: Earth's magnetic south pole during the Miocene had crept toward the Northern Hemisphere and was then closer to central France than the magnetic north pole. ("Qu'en un moment de l'époque miocène, aux environs de Saint-Flour, le pôle Nord était dirigé vers le haut: c'est le pôle Sud de la Terre qui était le plus voisin de la France centrale." That at one time during the Miocene, around Saint-Flour, the North Pole was directed upward; it is the South Pole of the Earth which was closest to central France.) Geologists in 2002 reinvestigating Brunhes's claims found that their samples from the same site analyzed with new methods produced "virtually identical" results. The geologists wrote that Brunhes had provided "the first suggestion ever reported that the Earth's magnetic field had reversed itself in the geologic past." Damian Kreichgauer (1859–1940) had made a similar suggestion

---

American civil engineer Herbert Saffir and director of the U.S. National Hurricane Center Bob Simpson establish the Saffir-Simpson Hurricane Scale to estimate of the potential property damage and flooding expected along the coast from a hurricane landfall

March 28, an earthquake of magnitude 6.9 strikes Gediz, Turkey—1,100 people die. A report on the event concluded that, "rough rock and weak mortar and adobe are common building materials. These natural materials provide good protection from the heat of summer and the cold of winter; but in strong earthquakes, they virtually ensure the instant burial of their occupants"

MILESTONES

1969

1970

American astronauts Neil Armstrong and Buzz Aldrin walk on the Moon during their successful *Apollo 11* Lunar Lander mission

A meteorite lands in Murchison, Australia, about 60 miles north of Melbourne. The "Murchison meteorite" contains amino acids, but whether they are primordial or terrestrial remains contentious

The U.S. National Oceanic and Atmospheric Administration (NOAA) is established

British geologist John F. Dewey and American geologist John M. Bird relate the positions of Earth's mountain belts, or ranges, to the motions of lithospheric plates

as early as 1902. Brunhes's research at the time examined the geologic record of paleomagnetic reversals.

Paleomagnetism attracted the attention of a number of researchers and around the world they scoured ancient lava, working in France, Italy, Germany, the United States, England, Russia, and Japan. Better analysis of the lava rocks showed they also had minerals of iron that had reversed polarities and aligned in a way that showed the magnetic poles had switched: The magnetic South Pole had traveled so far north as to become the magnetic North Pole and the magnetic North Pole had shifted to the south.

As British physicist Sir Edward Bullard (1907–80) explained in his address to the Royal Society of London in 1967, if *ferromagnetic* materials with randomly oriented crystals are heated above their *Curie points* and cooled in a magnetic field they orient in the direction of the magnetic field. In 1926 glaciologist Paul Louis Mercanton (1876–1963) of the University of Lausanne in Switzerland had stressed the importance of the Curie point in obtaining accurate paleomagnetic records. He also proposed that studies of the past and present positions of the magnetic poles might provide a means to test Alfred Wegener's theory of continental drift. Historian Homer Le Grand of Monash University in Australia argues that others in the field at the time, such as Japanese geophysicist Motonori Matuyama (1884–1958) and French geophysicist Emile Thellier (1904–87) were "less concerned with its applications than with the mechanisms and stability of rock magnetism and with the intriguing phenomena of reversals." Matuyama identified additional polar magnetic reversals in the Miocene and the Quaternary Epochs.

By the 1950s, paleomagnetists had discovered reversals throughout the Phanerozoic Eon. The growing collection of data indicated that a geologist walking on lava flows older than the Holocene had an almost equal chance of walking on normal magnetic or reversed magnetic rocks. With the magnetic poles dancing around from one location to the next over the course of geologic time, suspicions began to mount as to whether these magnetic shifts and reversals were indicative of true polar wander. Astronomers in 1914 had agreed that subtle variation of the poles was a probable occurrence but argued that there was no reason for extensive wandering, let alone reversals, and considered the idea preposterous. At the time, the prevailing theory relied on Earth's axis of rotation to explain Earth's magnetic field; the geologists found the notion of a wandering axis of rotation easier to accept than did the astronomers. With the newly established geomagnetic dynamo theory of the 1940s, the axis of rotation might wobble, but it did not need to wander to explain wandering magnetic poles, or even reversals. Add to the conundrum the question as to whether the continents wander, and determining the exact position of the poles became a great deal more challenging. The geologic community began to doubt their own evidence when some minerals were discovered to self-reverse under the influence of a normal magnetic field.

In the 1950s, paleomagnetists in Cambridge produced a map of the apparent polar wander path recorded in rocks from Great Britain. This did not account for specific reversals but rather averaged them together along with variations in between reversals for intervals that spanned tens to hundreds of thousands of years. Their working hypothesis was that the geomagnetic field when averaged over extensive amounts of time would correspond to a north and south magnetic *dipole* that originated in Earth's core and aligned with Earth's axis of rotation. (They called it the *Geocentric Axial Dipole Hypothesis.*) This hypothesis allows researchers to then estimate the position of the geographic North Pole over geologic time, relative to where the continents are located today. Polar wander maps were not new. The researchers compared their map with the polar wander maps of Damian Kreichgauer in 1902 and Wladimir Köppen in 1940 (Alfred Wegener's father-in-law). Put in perspective of continental drift, however, and the wander of the North Pole became a guide for landmass locations over time. Each of the maps they drew after studying magnetic signatures in lava flows from Australia, India, North America, and Europe showed a unique polar wander path. The clues were accumulating.

As chapter 6 discussed, geochronologists were also developing improved radioisotopic dating techniques in the 1950s. One of these methods included analyzing the ratio of radioactive potassium isotopes to argon isotopes trapped in the lattice of baked clay minerals and volcanic rocks. In the lab, geochemists and geophysicists could determine the ages of the rocks and their polarity, but the duration of a reversed or normal magnetic field typically lasted within the margin of error, a few hundred thousand years, for the estimates of the age of the minerals. The margin of error for radioisotope dating at the time was also greater for older rocks. (The margin of error is also dependent on the abundance of rocks studied, which today is not necessarily the oldest because many geologists since then have sought them out for investigations.) To compensate for the margin of error, one group of paleomagnetists turned to lava flows younger than four million years old.

The team became the first to succeed in accurately dating polarity reversals beyond their known location in the stratigraphic record and announced their achievement in a report to the journal *Nature* in 1963 entitled "Geomagnetic Polarity Epochs and Pleistocene Geochronometry." Like tree ring records, the rocks revealed a repetitive pattern with successive lava flows alternating between normal and reversed magnetic fields within the Pleistocene Epoch. The team included three American paleomagnetists: Allan Cox (1926–87) and Richard Doell (b. 1923) of the U.S. Geological Survey at Menlo Park, California, and G. Brent Dalrymple (b. 1937) of the University of California at Berkeley. All of their samples were from California. The report laid the foundation for the steps needed to identify the timescale and duration for periodic reversals. Subsequent investigations included samples from around the world.

At Berkeley, Dalrymple had learned to use the new all-glass, static mass spectrometer that Berkeley professor John Reynolds (1923–2000) had designed using Westinghouse Research Laboratories physicist Daniel Alpert's invention of a bakeable ultrahigh-vacuum system. Dalrymple discussed his work with Doell and Cox, both Berkeley alums, during a field expedition to the Sierra Nevada mountain range. They agreed a Reynolds spectrometer, as it was called, would be a boon to their paleomagnetic studies and hired Dalrymple to lead the team in dating the age of the rocks. Doell and Cox would focus on the magnetic fields.

After graduating from Berkeley, Dalrymple worked with two technicians to carefully hand-assemble a new mass spectrometer in the Menlo Park lab. James Balsley, chief of the USGS Geophysics Branch, had in 1958 asked Doell, an assistant professor at MIT at the time, to move back to California and establish a paleomagnetic lab. He sold him on the idea by saying how ideally situated the facilities at Menlo Park would be for the delicate magnetic measurements. When Doell came out to visit, the best building available was an old World War II hospital barrack built from tar paper and wood and far from the main road. It was perfect. Doell immediately contacted Cox and the two started assembling a lab ideal for collecting and reading the weak magnetic signals from rocks—a lab with no steel or iron structures and far from other magnetic influencers such as automobiles or a neighboring scientist's equipment.

As the team wrote in their 1963 report, "Palaeomagnetic investigations of reversals would be relatively simple were it not for the phenomenon of mineralogically controlled self-reversals, whereby lava flows containing certain minerals may acquire a reversed remanent magnetization when they cool in a normal field." To resolve this issue, they collected multiple ferromagnetic minerals from each site, being careful at each site to collect from flows that cooled at different rates as well. They purposely avoided minerals known to self-reverse. They collected samples from six different volcanic sites of different ages within the Pleistocene. In the lab they continued to test a variety of minerals to see if any had a tendency to self-reverse and tested their own rock samples as well by heating them gradually to temperatures below their Curie point and letting them cool. They also partially demagnetized representative samples from each flow in alternating magnetic fields to unmask any possible recent magnetization. Through all of their tests the polarity of the rocks remained unchanged until they heated the samples above their Curie points, at which point all the rocks cooled in a normal magnetic field and obtained normal magnetization.

Like Mercanton, the team hoped that paleomagnetism would lead to a test of Alfred Wegener's Continental Drift theory. At Berkeley, Cox had one of the few professors in the United States in the 1950s that supported Drift. In his biography on Cox, Konrad B. Krauskopf quotes Cox as saying: "We sniffed something in the air that we were not hearing about in our lectures and seminars, with the exception of those of John

Verhoogen. So we graduate students formed a Geology Club. . . . At the end of the first year we voted on the question of whether continental drift was likely. For safety we used a secret ballot. Continental drift won, though not by a landslide. Voting as we did on a scientific issue was probably done mainly to annoy the Berkeley faculty. Luckily they had the good judgment not to acknowledge that our club existed." Cox, Doell, and Dalrymple would lead the field of paleomagnetism in the 1960s, dating the reversals of rocks from around the world and further back in time. Little did they know that their work would become the Rosetta Stone for deciphering clues in the seafloor that would revolutionize Earth science for the rest of the century.

Seafloor Spreading

Rear Admiral Harry Hammond Hess (1906–69) was not a submarine commander in World War II as biographies about him sometimes claim. This gaff was first printed in the widely read 1973 book about plate tectonics, *A Revolution in the Earth Sciences*, and corrected in a brief note in response to a letter to the editor of *Science*, months after the book's review in that journal. Oceanographer Bruce Heezen (1924–77) of Columbia University's Lamont-Doherty Geological Observatory in Palisades, New York, reviewed the book in the February 8, 1974, issue of the journal *Science*. He praised the author for his evaluation of the marine science contributions to the theory of plate tectonics during the 1950s (much of which were Heezen's) but criticized the author for neglecting to place Hess's proposed convection theories in historical context. Heezen then went on to call the late Rear Admiral of Naval Reserves and Princeton University professor as being in the 1960s a "then-landlubber Princetonian geologist" and referred to Hess's postwar contributions as those of an armchair critic.

Granted Hess obtained his rear admiral rank serving at the U.S. Naval Hydrographic (later Oceanographic) Office after the war, but calling him a landlubber? Geologist Frank C. Whitmore Jr. (1937–2001) of the U.S. Geological Survey, who worked on identifying the geology of strategic islands in the South Pacific during World War II, wrote a letter to the editor published in the June 14, 1974, issue of *Science*. Whitmore mocked Heezen and defended Hess as being "such a low-keyed man that his modesty probably prevented some 'high-seas' folk from realizing that, during World War II, he [Hess] arranged for the preservation of data from recording fathometers on U.S. naval vessels plying the seas for other than oceanographic purposes."

Hess was captain of the USS *Cape Johnson*, a transport ship that starting in June 1944 began redistributing American troops to various islands in the Pacific during the last stages of the fight against Japan. The vessel steamed across the ocean from California to the Mariana Islands and the South Pacific. In January 1945 she provided support for the initial assault

Revisiting Wegener's Theory

With a new model for Earth processes in development during the 1960s, many geologists and geophysicists turned again to the work of Alfred Wegener and considered the history of his idea. In 1970 science historian Nicolaas A. Rupke then with Princeton University recalled that Wegener's theory had sparked controversy, as opposed to being ignored and left to smolder like earlier drift theories, because Wegener had proposed continental drift in the framework of uniformatarianism. James Hutton and Sir Charles Lyell had in the 19th century advanced the concept of uniformatarianism—which considered geologic processes as ongoing events, continuing today in the same way as they have acted in the past.

Earlier proponents of continental collisions had considered the idea in light of the theory of catastrophism. In 1910 American geologist Frank Taylor, for example, supplied as a mechanism for drift the Earth's capture of the Moon as a satellite, an event which he believed had occurred in the Cretaceous and created the Pacific Ocean. As British marine geophysicist Frederick J. Vine (b. 1939) wrote in 1977, "by the turn of the century the invocation of any sort of catastrophic event to explain geological phenomena was something of an anathema to all right-minded geologists."

The peak of resistance from American geologists against continental drift occurred in 1926 at a meeting of the American Association of Petroleum Geologists titled: "A Symposium on the Origin and Movement of Land Masses, both Inter-Continental and Intra-Continental, as proposed by Alfred Wegener." Two years after the meeting, 14 authors including Wegener and Taylor contributed essays to a 240-page book under the same title as the symposium. About half of the authors were supportive of Wegener, but most had reservations about his theory. Geologist Chester Longwell (1887–1975) of Yale University in his essay for the book wrote in a way that reveals the conflict American geologists had as they struggled to find a new theory for Earth processes other than contraction that would uphold the idea of permanency or uniformatarianism: "The Taylor-Wegener doctrine, on its part, shows little respect for time-honored ideas backed by weighty authority. Perhaps the very completeness of this iconoclasm, this rebellion against the established order, has served to gain for the new hypothesis a place in the sun." In a nod toward having an open mind about the merits of debating the subject, Longwell goes on to list a number of "enigmas" troubling physical geologists at the time that continental drift promised to resolve, such as:

- Missing land bridges or sunken continents that other theories had used to explain similar fossils from the same time period on separate continents
- The difference between the Atlantic and Pacific coastlines
- How mountains formed
- And an explanation for the existence of "rifts, thrusts, folds, and

on Luzon Island and then from February through the end of March offloaded Marine Corps troops and cargo throughout the final battle over Iwo Jima. Hess then returned the *Cape Johnson* to San Francisco where she picked up troops for deployment in Manila. After the bombings on Hiroshima and Nagasaki, the *Cape Johnson* left Manila for Pearl Harbor and then on to Japan to carry Japanese POWs home. From Japan she traveled extensively around the Pacific, this time redistributing American troops back to the United States.

other conspicuous features of crustal deformation"

His essay also reveals that scientists during Wegener's time were already referring to "plates" of continental lithosphere or *sial* as Wegener had termed the continental material. Longwell concedes that "If Wegener or anyone else can throw new light on these baffling problems, he is entitled to a hearing." He then argues that "certain demands" should be made of this "new and romantic speculation before it is admitted into the respectable circle of geologic theories." After 1928 few American geologists considered the subject still worthy of research. This general attitude of American geologists toward continental drift lasted for 30 years. Students were subjected to their professors' biases, but by keeping an eye on the reports coming from Europe, Africa, and the South Pacific; an ear to those few American geologists who disagreed with their colleagues on the importance of drift as an idea; and, as Cox says, a nose in the wind for the scent of change, they began to formulate their own impressions.

In 1929 British geophysicist Arthur Holmes provided support for the concept of continental drift by proposing a plausible mechanism with his subcrustal convection cell model. He proceeded to argue the issue in depth in journal articles but decided not to report his ideas in his 1937 rewrite of his book *The Age of the Earth*. This action surprised readers who were looking for further details on continental drift, convection currents, and thermal cycles. By 1944, however, Holmes had found his internal muse again and included descriptions of his convection cell model in his book *Principles of Physical Geology*. During his discussions he referred to the birth of the South Atlantic Ocean as the result of a rift between Africa and South America as they separated from Wegener's Pangaea. He considered the questions this divergence raised, such as: What caused the rift and why was the crust that emerged between the continents oceanic basalt? What happened to the oceanic crust that had surrounded Pangaea before its breakup? He then built the answers into his model of subcrustal convection currents.

Holmes proposed that convection currents in the mantle directed the motion of the crust and, like a conveyor belt, carried the oceanic belt of basalt and the continents along for the ride. He wrote that innumerable fissures would be found in ocean basins with basaltic magma "spreading out as sheet-like intrusions within the crust, and as submarine lava flows over its surface." He envisioned the dense oceanic crust experiencing intense dynamic metamorphism where the convection currents collided and became dense enough to sink back into the mantle as a highly compressed form of rock. In a review of *Principles of Physical Geology*, published in the September–October 1944 issue of *The Geographical Journal*, British geologist Sydney E. Hollingworth (1899–1966) wrote: "Professor Holmes gives a masterly exposition of the hypothesis of convection currents in the fluid sub-crustal regions, as applied to mountain building and, in a later chapter, to the theory of continental drift. . . . This book, notable for its simplicity of presentation and lucidity of style, represents a real achievement in the portrayal of geology as a science that is full of vitality and of intriguing problems awaiting solution."

Hess obtained his first oceanographic experience under the direction of Dutch geophysicist Felix A. Vening Meinesz (1887–1966) and Princeton geologist Richard Field (1885–1961) in 1932 on board the USS *S-48*. From Panama to the Lesser Antilles of the Caribbean, the researchers on board the U.S. Navy submarine mapped the seafloor and measured gravity anomalies. Vening Meinesz, who was reportedly over 6 feet tall, had began circumnavigating the world's oceans in submarines in the 1920s with his invention of the first gravimeter to measure grav-

Rear Admiral Harry Hess (1906–69) was one of many influential marine geologists who helped reignite the continental drift debate in American geology. Hess focused on the possibility of convection currents in the mantle, an idea first discussed as a mechanism for continental drift by British geologist Arthur Holmes. (Princeton University Library)

ity at sea. His goal was to test if the theory of isostasy, Earth's continual balancing act to find equilibrium under unequal pressures, applied to the oceanic crust as well as it did to the continents. The oceanic crust was still considered stable. Isostasy anomalies were not expected, except in areas of high sedimentation such as a river delta. Vening Meinesz showed quickly with his work that this was not the case. The Nile delta revealed no anomaly, whereas the Java trench in the Philippines provided a negative anomaly as extensive as the positive anomalies of mountain chains. The combination of the oceanic crust's quick rebound behavior under sediment loads and slow response to massive unknown stresses occurring in the deep trenches, sent the geodesists back to the Pratt and Airy models of isostasy. Wegener had relied on the Airy model for his drift theories and now the oceanic crust was proving him right.

When Hess saw the gravity measurements from the trenches off the eastern edge of the Lesser Antilles, he concluded immediately that the Caribbean crust was moving eastward and down-warping at a site of compression. The concave arc of volcanic islands and earthquake epicenters had long since proven the region had strong tectonic activity. Movement of the crust provided an explanation. Hess attributed the negative anomalies from the trenches off the Cayman Islands to the north as faults resulting from the lateral motion of the Caribbean crust. Vening Meinesz and Field incorporated Hess's conclusions into their own presentations of the results of their study and included discussions on convection currents beneath the crust as a possible cause for gravity anomalies. Other geologists began running small-scale laboratory experiments to confirm the theories behind the idea of convection cell driven compression and crustal deformation.

On board the submarine *Barracuda* in 1937, Hess revisited the Caribbean Sea again with geophysicist William Maurice Ewing (1906–74) to flush out further details regarding the region's bathymetry and gravity anomalies. By this time Hess had begun teaching geology at Princeton University. Ewing would go on to help establish and lead Columbia University's Lamont-Doherty Geological Observatory in oceanography. When the Naval Reserves called Hess in for active duty they assigned him to the task of detecting enemy submarines in the West Indies and North Atlantic. He joined the crew of the Q-ship USS *Big Horn*, a tanker the Navy disguised as a merchant ship in order to lure German submarines (U-boats) in closer for an attack. The strategy, effective in World War I, failed in World War II and ultimately only five Q-ships were commissioned. (A U-boat sank the first Q-ship within days of the start of the operation, and the Germans described the details of the battle in the press.) Two years later, Hess found himself navigating the unfamiliar waters of the Pacific. Fascinated with the opportunity to study the bathymetry of the Pacific seafloor during his command of the *Cape Johnson*, Hess ran the ship's echo sounder, the navy's most powerful model at the time, fairly continuously during transit. This lead to Hess mapping hundreds of flat-topped underwater seamounts he called guyots. [Swiss-born geologist and meteorologist Arnold Henry Guyot (1807–84) had taught at Princeton later in life and the geology building there was named in his honor.] Harold W. Murray of the U.S. Coast and Geodetic Survey had mapped flat-topped submarine mountains in the Gulf of Alaska between 1925 and 1939. The features were familiar to marine geologists, but Hess was the first to consider that these underwater structures had once broached as volcanic islands. After the war, Hess hypothesized that the guyots became flat-topped as the result of erosion from wave action.

Throughout the 1950s, as Hess considered the formation of guyots, taught at Princeton, and worked as needed in the oceanographic office for the Navy, he kept up to date with the research being done in the fields of marine geology and also the new work emerging in paleomagnetics. It seemed reasonable that continental drift might provide a very sensible explanation for the variations seen from continent to continent for the path of the magnetic polar wander. He talked with Bruce Heezen about oceanic ridges and saw the maps that Marie Tharp (1920–2006), also at the Lamont-Doherty Geological Observatory, had drawn. Their evidence from soundings of the Atlantic Ocean showed that the ridges had a seismically active rift valley.

When Tharp first identified the valley to Heezen in 1952 he dismissed the indication. Tharp had taken the sounding records from six ship crossings of the Atlantic and plotted separate contour maps of the seafloor for each leg. Granted errors in the data were prone to occur anytime someone on the ship had opened the refrigerator, their echo sounder was limited by its supply of electricity, but such errors appeared as never-ending abyssal fissures because the "sounder" device missed recording the "echo." The valley showed up as a small V-shaped notch in the middle of the ridge. "It cannot be. It looks too much like continental drift," Heezen told her. She wrote later that his comment "was just about the worst thing he could have said, since at the time, he and almost everyone else at Lamont, and the United States, thought continental drift was impossible. North American Earth scientists considered it to be almost a form of scientific heresy, and to suggest that someone believed in it was comparable to saying there must be something wrong with him or her."

Geologist and oceanographic cartographer Marie Tharp (1920–2006) in her office at Columbia University's Lamont-Doherty Earth Observatory (Lamont-Doherty Earth Observatory, Columbia University)

A few days later the two agreed they needed a three-dimensional view of the seafloor and Heezen quickly sketched out how the Atlantic seafloor might look drained of its ocean. Tharp then proceeded to re-plot the sounding records using their new technique for drawing a 3-D map. Tharp combined the map with seismic data an assistant was plot-ting and the earthquake epicenters all fell within the walls of the ridge valley. Charles Richter and Beno Gutenberg had in the 1940s identified the Mid-Atlantic ridge as a source of shallow earthquakes, and seismic charts indicated belts of activity in areas of the seafloor not yet mapped by ships. Tharp now had evidence that the Mid-Atlantic ridge was tear-ing apart. Heezen hypothesized that if they conducted soundings over the areas of seismic activity they would find more ridges. He was not yet

Bruce Heezen, who worked with Marie Tharp in mapping the ocean floor (United States Navy)

convinced of finding the focus of the earthquakes in another ridge valley. To test the idea before going again out to sea Heezen had Tharp prepare maps with a bird's eye view of the African Rift Valley. If the ridges in the ocean were connected like seams in a baseball, then it was possible the continents manifested the same feature, a terrestrial extension of this hypothetical extensive ridge system. When they saw the similarities to the Mid-Atlantic Ridge, Heezen was convinced the Earth was literally coming apart at its seams. He joined a small camp of advocates who thought the Earth was expanding and ripping continents and oceans apart in the process.

Hess had no use for an expansion theory. He had a good idea of where the material was going. In 1956 Heezen shared the discovery he had made with Tharp to geologists outside of Lamont. He had maps and globes for a presentation at a meeting of the National Academy of Sciences that Hess was moderating. Hess found the global network of ridges amazing and invited Heezen to Princeton to discuss his work in more detail. Four years later, Hess incorporated the growing evidence for continental drift in a manuscript he whimsically referred to as "geopoetry."

Hess presented convection currents in the mantle as a mechanism for lateral motion of the continents and oceanic crust. The upwelling mantle material, heated by the core, would rise to the surface where it formed the oceanic crust. The currents in the mantle would buoy up the seafloor and move it laterally with the mantle as it cooled. The seafloor, under tremendous pressures, would become denser and sink back into the mantle following the mantle's own descending current. Such recycling of the oceanic crust neatly explained why no rocks or cores from the seafloor were older than the Jurassic. The Earth was in slow motion, moving at about the same speed as a fingernail grows—little wonder that the movement itself went unnoticed. The results of the movement were far more obvious. Hess was careful though to distance the idea from the theory of continental drift, even though "continental drift" was, from this conveyor belt perspective, more appropriate. "The continents do not plow through the oceanic crust impelled by unknown forces; rather they ride passively on mantle material as it comes to the surface at the crest of the ridge and then moves laterally away from it," Hess wrote. Perhaps if geologists had continued to call Wegener's theory a "displacement theory" as he originally dubbed it, than Hess might have been more comfortable with the "geopoetry" of the term *continental drift*.

In an article published in 1961, oceanographer Robert Dietz (1914–95) of the U.S. Navy Electronics Laboratory in San Diego proposed the "spreading sea floor theory," which quickly became coined as the theory of "seafloor spreading" and was immediately compared to Hess's essay of geopoetry. They were in many ways the same as Holmes's convection model. Hess ultimately published his ideas in a chapter called "History of Ocean Basins," in the book *Petrologic Studies* published by the Geologic Society of America in 1962. Holmes, Hess, and Dietz all considered the seafloor an extension of the mantle. Holmes had included in his model an unknown viscous substrate at the top of the mantle that was rigidly responding to the lower mantle's convection. Like Holmes, Hess had the seafloor forming at the point of upwelling, but attributed a geochemical reaction rather than a physical eruption as the source.

Before starting graduate school, Hess had spent two years working as an exploration geologist in Rhodesia, where some of the oldest volcanic rocks of basalt contain nodules or *xenoliths* of peridotites, which themselves contain a high level of the mineral olivine. In 1954, he published a hypothesis that the oceanic crust forms from seawater mixing with olivine in the mantle. The olivine then converts to serpentinite, a process known as *serpentinization*. This geochemical reaction produces heat and, in addition to mantle upwelling, would contribute to the higher heat flow at the ridges. Again in 1960, Hess predicted serpentinization as the method for producing the seafloor.

Dietz also considered the ridges the surface feature of upwelling but, like Holmes and not Hess, he explained the process of oceanic crust formation in terms of volcanic eruptions. This explained the earthquakes in the rift valley as well as the heat flow. Dietz independently stressed the importance of distinguishing the depth of the Earth's different layers. The crust (both oceanic and continental) had become seismically defined as anything above the Moho. The lithosphere, he reminded his readers, must be considered the rigid layer supporting the crust and riding on the *asthenosphere*—which was the upper layer of the mantle, a region difficult to identify seismically due hypothetically to its uniform composition and tendency to dissipate stress quickly. "If convection currents are operating 'subcrustally,' as is commonly written, they would be expected to shear below the lithosphere and not beneath the 'crust' as the term is now used," Dietz wrote.

Richard Oldham, who seismically identified Earth's core, remarked on the history behind the subject of continental drift and Earth's interior layers during a meeting of The Royal Geographical Society (with the Institute of British Geographers) in 1923. He was surprised at the reaction to Wegener's theory as a novel idea and compared it to the work of British geophysicist Osmond Fisher (1817–1914), who wrote the textbook *Physics of the Earth's Crust*, published in 1889. "He had advocated notions that in those days were rejected unanimously, but had he lived till now he would have seen that under an altered nomenclature we have come round to something not very unlike what he maintained," Oldham said. Fisher had written of convection currents in the Earth's fluid interior as a mechanism for continental motion. In 1923 Oldham acknowledged that the current geologic discussions did not consist of convection currents and fluid interiors, "but we may safely talk of an asthenosphere and of under-tow, which are not so very different in effect." History and conversations tend to repeat in slightly modified ways.

Similar to Taylor's ideas in 1911, Fisher had proposed that the Moon split from Earth leaving behind a cavity in the Pacific Ocean. And like

Wegener would with his theory, Fisher had recognized the similarity between coastlines on either side of the Atlantic. He considered the event with the Moon the trigger for the separation of the continents from a supercontinent and proposed that the Americas were drifting westward into the Pacific. Despite the absurdity of the idea still, Oldham defended the underlying concepts Fisher introduced: "He recognized the general principle that the continents were capable of drifting about in the Earth, and that they have not through all time maintained the same position relative to each other and to the Pole and Equator." He continued to say, "I should like to express a hope that in this discussion of Wegener's theory we will remember that the important question is not whether Wegener is right or wrong in his specific conclusions, but whether the continental masses have throughout all times maintained their present position relative to each other and to the poles." In other words, he said, it was "the doctrine of the permanence of oceans and continents" that was at stake.

Dietz and Hess finally rang the death knell for this doctrine in 1961. Like vultures, the geophysicists had started circling as early as 1889. After Wegener, they began picking it apart bit by bit. During the 1960s a new doctrine emerged—its common ancestors the theories of continental drift and seafloor spreading, and its parentage a diverse mixture of tectonics and paleomagnetic reversals. Some diehards of the old doctrine survived the decade of the sixties, recognized both then and now as a time of revolution in the Earth sciences. By the end of the 1970s, permanency was extinct. The doctrine of plate tectonics stood in its place.

Plate Tectonics

"There is nothing in this field which could not be solved by paleomagnetism if the results were 10 times more numerous and the method 10 times more accurate." The quote is attributed to Sir Edward Bullard, and the results and accuracy soon followed.

After World War I, Lieutenant Patrick M. S. Blackett (1897–1974) resigned from the British Navy to learn physics at the University of Cambridge. In the early 1950s, Blackett switched from his Nobel Prize-winning studies on cosmic rays to the field of geomagnetism. To aid in his experiments on the magnetic properties of a rotating body, Blackett invented an extremely sensitive magnetometer. He soon realized he had the perfect tool for identifying the weak magnetic fields ingrained in the geologic record. He switched his focus, again, this time to paleomagnetism and his instrument became widely used.

In 1955 the Coast and Geodetic Survey ship *Pioneer* on a cruise off the coast of California towed behind it a marine magnetometer, which Scripps oceanographers had designed. The survey identified magnetic anomalies along the seafloor. As on land, the oceanic crust had a paleomagnetic timescale of its own.

In 1961 British marine geophysicist Drummond Matthews (1931–97) of the University of Cambridge joined the International Indian Ocean expedition (1961–63) on board the HMS *Owen.* Matthews ran the instrumentation for the marine magnetometer towed behind the ship, pulling the 1,640-foot (500-m) cable in by hand each time he needed to redeploy the system. The results were worth the effort. He discovered patterns of reversed and normal magnetic fields aligned in parallel along a submarine ridge in the Gulf of Aden.

Back on the west coast of the United States, marine geophysicists of the Scripps Institution of Oceanography identified striped magnetic patterns on the seafloor off the coast of Washington State. They also noticed that the patterns were offset along known strike-slip faults, in some cases showing a slip of almost 1,000 miles (1,420 km). In 1963 Lawrence Morley (b. 1920) of the Canadian Geological Survey proposed that these magnetic patterns marine geophysicists were finding resulted from the seafloor spreading Hess and Dietz had described. Fred Vine, a graduate student of Matthews, came to the same conclusion. In an infamous snub to Morley, however, the editor of the *Journal of Geophysical Research* declined to publish his report, explaining that: "Such speculations make interesting talk at cocktail parties, but it is not the sort of thing that ought to be published under serious scientific aegis." Luckily for Vine and Matthews the editor of *Nature* had a considerably different opinion.

Consensus was growing among oceanographers that the material emerging from the spreading ridges behaved in the same way as lava on land in that it obtained a record of Earth's magnetic field from the time of its deposit. When Dalrymple at the 1965 annual meeting of the Geological Society of America presented the timescale of paleomagnetic reversals that he, Cox, and Doell had determined, Vine was in the audience. Vine immediately recognized that these paleomagnetists at the U.S. Geological Survey in Menlo Park had discovered the Rosetta Stone for interpreting the ages of marine magnetic reversals. Now oceanographers could read the timescale for geomagnetic field reversals horizontally across the oceanic crust. Core samples from the seafloor confirmed the ages as well. The evidence was in agreement from both land and sea and the model of seafloor spreading provided a robust explanation for the fit.

The theory of seafloor spreading relied on two distinct boundaries to achieve the ocean floor dynamics it predicted. The first was oceanic ridges, where the mantle accretes magma to produce the oceanic crust. The second was trenches, later more commonly referred to as subduction zones, where the mantle consumes the oceanic crust producing a zone of deep-focus earthquakes of the type Benioff and Wadati had recognized decades earlier. Accreting ridges and subducting trenches, however, were not the only boundaries marked by earthquakes and faults. That meant a major piece of the continental drift puzzle remained.

Canadian geophysicist John Tuzo Wilson (1908–93) provided the solution. Sir Edward "Teddy" Bullard had invited Wilson to visit Cambridge

MAGNETIC STRIPES

Periods of reversed magnetic polarity

Periods of normal magnetic polarity

New crust development along mid-ocean ridge

Seafloor

Lithosphere

Magma upwelling

© Infobase Publishing

Reversals in Earth's magnetic field are recorded in the crust of the ocean seafloor. When magma cools, the iron crystals in the rock align with the direction of the magnetic field. When paleomagnetic records from land were compared to the magnetic profile taken from the East Pacific Rise, the confusing zebra pattern from the ocean floor made sense if the seafloor was moving away from a zone of origin. Age dating of cores from the seafloor confirmed that older sediments and oceanic crust existed further away from spreading ridges.

during the winter of 1964–65. Hess joined them from Princeton and together with Vine and Matthews the group carried on detailed and lively discussions about ocean crust dynamics and large-scale continental displacement. In a 1965 article published in *Nature*, Wilson referred to the motion of crustal "plates" and identified the missing boundary as one that linked the lithospheric crust to other boundaries, transforming one boundary into another. Because of this Wilson called the new earthquake-riddled boundary transform faults. They are identified as strike-slip faults that are bounded between ridges or trenches.

In a biography on Wilson, G. D. Garland wrote: "It was well known that the major ocean ridges show frequent perpendicular offsets, by fractures which can be mapped bathymetrically and which, in part, are seismically active. Tuzo recognized that the conventional theory of faulting, as applied to a medium that is conserved, must be modified if the ocean floor is characterized by nonconservation. Thus the shear motion across

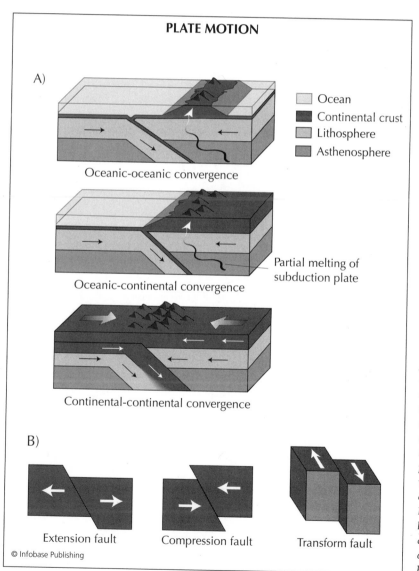

PLATE MOTION

A)

Ocean
Continental crust
Lithosphere
Asthenosphere

Oceanic-oceanic convergence

Partial melting of subduction plate

Oceanic-continental convergence

Continental-continental convergence

B)

Extension fault

Compression fault

Transform fault

© Infobase Publishing

At convergent plate boundaries A) Earth's oceanic or continental crust collides. The subduction of one plate under the other is common for dense oceanic crust—forming volcanic islands or continental volcanoes from the partial melting of the subducting plate. Such subduction may or may not take place during continental collisions. The Rocky Mountains are considered the result of the shallow subduction of the Pacific plate beneath North America, whereas the Himalayas are considered the result of both the Indian and the Eurasian plate buckling together during their collisions. Three different types of faults B) occur along plate boundaries.

Scientist of the Decade: John Tuzo Wilson (1908–1993)

John Tuzo Wilson was in 1946 the only professor of geophysics in Canada. He accepted the position at the University of Toronto as a geologist working in the physics department and headed the country's first Geophysics Laboratory. At the time, he supported the theory of contraction to explain mountain building and proposed models to account for compression in mountains and continental growth. He visited Australia and South Africa in 1950 and years later remarked: "In South Africa all the geologists were disciples of Alfred Wegener and A. L. du Toit, and were anxious to correct my failure to accept continental drift, but I remained inflexible for another nine years." His public disclosure of his changed opinion came in the form of a review article to *Nature* in 1961 regarding Dietz's theory of seafloor spreading. While embracing continental drift, Wilson also veered to the opposite extreme from his opinion in regards to a contracting Earth and allowed that some idiosyncrasies could be explained with expansion. He wrote: "Another possibility is that the Earth is slowly expanding. A rate of a few mm./yr. would suffice to maintain continents above sea level. This would not interfere with and indeed might assist the other orogenetic processes described. . . . this is a matter of fundamental importance in physics and cosmology and one which it is very hard to prove or disprove."

Wilson correctly compared seafloor spreading to the model Hess had developed and brought attention to the earlier model Holmes had proposed as well. Wilson found convection currents and seafloor spreading an acceptable model primarily because it answered many questions that had plagued the contraction theory and, to Wilson's own credit, did not render obsolete the work he had done earlier on continental growth

and compression. The collisions of the oceanic crust with continents explained a great deal about the accumulated material along the continental margins. Subduction of the oceanic crust back into the mantle skimmed material onto the continental crust. For the continent's interiors Wilson still had more questions than answers. These were partially alleviated when others demonstrated how extensive the effect of a subducting oceanic plate has on a continent and uncovered evidence of relict collisions between continents. Wilson had envisioned the effect of such collisions in 1961: "The collision of continents might be expected to produce migrating waves of uplift which could catch klippe of sedimentary rocks on their advancing crests and carry them forward like surfboards on waves, stranding them when the uplift subsided." Even so, seismic histories and mile-high elevations in the continental interiors give geophysicists pause. Another source of geophysical contention in the 21st century involves the interior of oceanic crustal plates. Guyots and island chains present a curious feature in what should otherwise be a featureless abyssal plain. Besides formulating his transform fault hypothesis and identifying the crust as segmented plates, Wilson put forth the explanation of "hot spots" for the formation of the Hawaiian Island chain in the middle of the Pacific Ocean.

Wilson toured Mauna Loa in Hawaii and realized the volcanic islands had to originate as magma rising from the mantle to the seafloor. The islands were distinct features and did not appear to form a new type of crustal boundary. Unlike other oceanic islands that tend to increase in age with distance from a spreading ridge, the Hawaiian Islands are young and still active despite their remote location surrounded

a fault joining two ridge segments ends abruptly at these segments. For this reason he referred to these faults initially as half-shears, but because they can also transform an accreting boundary into a consuming one, or

by Cretaceous seafloor crust. To explain the formation of the Hawaiian Islands, Wilson envisioned a magmatic "hot spot" in the upper mantle pushing through the moving asthenosphere to the spreading seafloor surface. He imagined lying on his back in a river and allowing the flow of water rush over him as he blew bubbles. He pictured the islands on the moving seafloor behaving as bubbles might: breaking the surface and drifting away from their spot of origin as the moving current carried them downstream. Most of his data relied on the fact that the older now extinct Tertiary volcanic islands in the Hawaiian chain were also trapped in the older segments of the surrounding Cretaceous seafloor whereas the younger active volcanoes had popped up in the younger portions of the Cretaceous. This indicated a tendency for the islands to drift with the seafloor once they emerged. His hot spot theory published in 1963 in the *Canadian Journal of Physics* and again that year in an article in *Nature* inspired a flurry of investigations.

Princeton University geophysicist W. Jason Morgan, in an article in *Nature* in 1971, linked Wilson's hot spot to the concept of a deep plume of magma rising to the surface from a location in the lower mantle. Deep plumes, Morgan argued, would explain the geological differences between oceanic islands and oceanic ridge basalts for the plumes likely brought primordial mantle material that would fractionate into two parts, with one part venting to the surface and the rest becoming part of the asthenosphere. He proposed that these "hotspots" pushed the asthenosphere away, influencing the overall direction of plate motion and plate-to-plate interactions.

In a radical break from the convection cell model of plate tectonics where upwelling magma was seen as pushing the spreading ridges or rift valleys apart, Morgan pitched the idea that

the hotspot-driven motion of the asthenosphere resulted in pulling the lithosphere apart, which in turn ruptured along boundaries of greatest stress to form rift valleys that would then fill with magma. He wrote: "The ridge basalts would come entirely from the asthenosphere, passively rising to fill the void created as plates are pulled apart by the stresses acting on them." Thus started the push vs. pull debate on how plate tectonics operate. Morgan considered the hotspot plumes convection driven only in the lower mantle with the movement of the asthenosphere in the upper mantle traveling away from the hotspot plumes. This motion, he claimed, provided the resulting stresses around the plates to form ridges, trenches, and faults. "Hotspots may come and go," he wrote. "But the hotspots would leave visible markers of their past activity on the seafloor and on continents."

Seismically sourcing the depth of hotspot plumes in the 21st century has shown that variations are abundant, with some plumes tending to refute Morgan's theory and reestablish Wilson's original proposal of shallower hotspot activity. While identifying the depths of hotspot plumes will provide further insights into the deep-seated mechanisms of plate motions within the Earth, the existence of the hotspots has helped to identify the surface motion of the plate both in direction and velocity. The bend between the Hawaiian island chain and the Emperor Seamount chain to the northwest, for example, indicates a change in the direction of the Pacific Plate 43 million years ago. Dating the age of the islands provides a measure of plate motion velocity relative to the stable hotspot in the mantle. The hotspot theory continues to inspire geologists to examine other island chains as well as Iceland and its neighboring islands, which outcrop along the Mid-Atlantic Ridge.

vice versa, he modified this to 'transform faults.' In this way was born the most striking example of a new concept in structural geology in many years."

Wilson argued that seismicity defined crustal plate boundaries and that large areas of the interior of the plates remained structurally stable and accordingly free of seismicity despite the movement of the plate

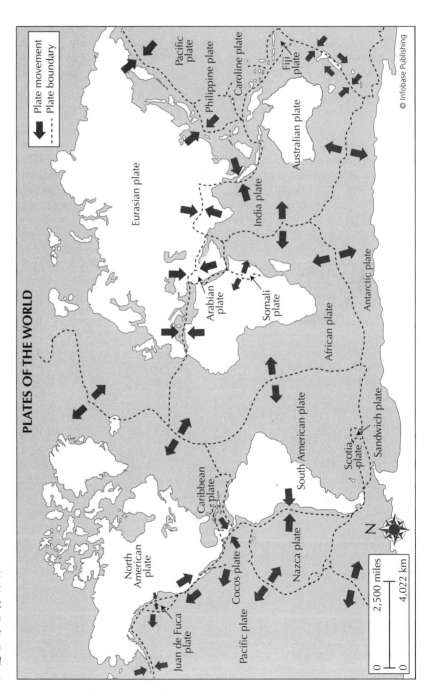

PLATES OF THE WORLD

Plate movement
Plate boundary

© Infobase Publishing

Pacific plate

Philippine plate

Caroline plate

Fiji plate

Australian plate

Eurasian plate

India plate

Antarctic plate

Arabian plate

Somali plate

African plate

North American plate

Caribbean plate

South American plate

Scotia plate

Sandwich plate

Juan de Fuca plate

Pacific plate

Cocos plate

Nazca plate

N

2,500 miles

4,022 km

0

0

Colliding at convergent boundaries, spreading apart at divergent boundaries, or sliding past each other along transform faults, the plates of the world are in constant motion—moving on average at about the same speed as a human fingernail grows.

as a whole. He specified that along the ridges earthquakes would focus in areas of active deformation, and even though the bathymetry maps revealed areas of strike-slip or lateral displacement outside of a spreading ridge valley, these areas were no longer active. The active regions he said should occur only within the spreading ridge and along the transform faults that marked the ridge's offsets. In 1966, at a meeting of the Geological Society of America, 40 years to the month after the New York symposium on Wegener's hypothesis, geophysicist Lynn Sykes of Lamont-Doherty Geological Observatory presented seismic evidence confirming Wilson's "transform-fault" hypothesis. At the same meeting, others presented data supporting the Vine-Mathews hypothesis. The tables on continental drift had turned. Information accumulated on the shapes of the plates, their motions, the tools being used to locate their past and present locations, and the physical constraints that take place when all three boundaries meet at what is called a triple junction. The new generation of Earth scientists in the field also included Tanya Atwater, John Holden, Xavier Le Pichon, Dan McKenzie, W. Jason Morgan, and Walter C. Pitman III. They followed the paleomagnetic clues and relied on geophysics and geometry to reveal the complexities and patterns inherent in a world where continents and oceans were no longer regarded as fixed. By the mid-1970s, most Earth scientists had embraced the new evidence for the revolutionary theory of plate tectonics.

Further Reading

Acton, Gary D., and Katerina E. Petronotis. "Studying Oceanic Plate Motions with Magnetic Data." *EOS* 75, no. 5 (February 1, 1994): 49. The first paragraph of this report provides a definition of the geocentric axial dipole hypothesis. Available online. URL: http://www.agu.org/sci_soc/acton.html. Accessed April 24, 2006.

Allan, D. W. "Reversals of the Earth's Magnetic Field." *Nature* 182 (August 15, 1958): 469–470. A letter to the editor of *Nature* regarding the recent conclusions on rock magnetization and the implications for reversals of Earth's magnetic field.

Barrell, Joseph. "The Status of Hypotheses of Polar Wanderings." *Science* 40, no. 1027 (September 4, 1914): 333–340. This report provides an early history on theories of polar wanderings, including mention of Kreichgauer's 1902 magnetic field reversal report.

Brunhes, Bernard. "Recherches sur la Direction de L'aimantation des Roches Volcaniques" (Research on the direction of the magnetization of volcanic rocks). *J. de Physique* (1906): 705–724. This paper provided an early examination into the field of paleomagnetic reversals.

Bullard, Edward. "The Bakerian Lecture, 1967: Reversals of the Earth's Magnetic Field." *Philosophical Transactions of the Royal Society of London Series A, Mathematical and Physical Sciences* 263, no. 1143 (December

12, 1968): 481–524. Bullard provides a historical prospective into the research of paleomagnetics.

Carson, Rachel. *Silent Spring.* Boston: Houghton Mifflin; Cambridge, Massachusetts: Riverside Press, 1962. This book launches the environmental movement through its investigation into the toxicology of pesticides and effects on wildlife.

Cox, Allan, and Richard R. Doell. "Palæomagnetic Evidence Relevant to a Change in the Earth's Radius." *Nature* 189 (January 07, 1961): 45–47. This report discusses the evidence against an expanding Earth hypothesis.

——, Richard R. Doell, and G. Brent Dalrymple. "Geomagnetic Polarity Epochs and Pleistocene Geochronometry." *Nature* 198 (June 15, 1963): 1,049–1,051. The first accurately dated timescale for magnetic reversals.

——, Richard R. Doell, and G. Brent Dalrymple. "Reversals of Earth's Magnetic Field." *Science* 144, no. 3626 (June 26, 1964): 1,537–1,543. This report provides further details on the timescale of terrestrial magnetic reversals.

Dietz, Robert S. "Continent and Ocean Basin Evolution by Spreading of the Sea Floor." *Nature* 190 (June 3, 1961): 854–857. First published model for seafloor spreading.

——. "Colston Symposium: Marine Geology and Geophysics." *Science* 149, no. 3679 (Jul. 2, 1965): 94–95. A summary of a recent British conference covering marine geological processes, such as *turbidity currents* and seafloor tectonics.

Donnenfield, David, and David Howell. "The Birth of Plate Tectonics Theory." This article, written for the 125th anniversary of the U.S. Geological Survey in 2004, discusses the achievements of Cox, Doell, and Dalrymple in the 1960s. Available online. URL: http://www.usgs.gov/125/articles/plate_tectonics.html. Accessed April 26, 2006.

Fisher, Osmond. *Physics of the Earth's Crust*, 2nd ed. London: Macmillan, 1889. An early discussion on Earth processes, including lateral motion of the continents.

Fiske, R. S., and E. D. Jackson. "Orientation and Growth of Hawaiian Volcanic Rifts: The Effect of Regional Structure and Gravitational Stresses." *Proceedings of the Royal Society of London Series A, Mathematical and Physical Sciences* 329, no. 1578 (August 22, 1972): 299–326. This report provides a map of the Hawaiian Islands in relationship to the age of the surrounding oceanic crust.

Gallant, René. *Bombardment Earth: An Essay on the Geological and Biological Effects of Huge Meteorite Impacts.* London: J. Baker, 1964. A pioneering book on the effect of impact events.

Garland, G. D. "John Tuzo Wilson. 24 October 1908–15 April 1993." *Biographical Memoirs of Fellows of the Royal Society* 41 (November 1995): 534–552. This biography on Tuzo Wilson discusses his contributions to the study of plate tectonics.

Gilluly, James. "Continental Drift: A Reconsideration." *Science* 152, no. 3724 (May 13, 1966): 946–950. This report reviews the published record from the London symposium on continental drift in March 1964.

Glen, William. *The Road to Jaramillo: Critical Years of the Revolution in Earth Science.* Stanford: Stanford University Press, 1982. This book discusses the importance of marine geology in developing the theory of plate tectonics.

Hamilton, Edwin L. "The Last Geographic Frontier: The Sea Floor." *The Scientific Monthly* 85, no. 6 (December 1957): 294–314. This report discusses the advances in the field of marine geology during the 1950s.

Hess, Harry H. "History of Ocean Basins." In *Petrologic Studies: A Volume to Honor A.F. Buddington*, edited by A. E. J. Engel, H. L. James, and B. F. Leonard. Denver: Geologic Society of America, 1962. Originally written in 1960, Hess is credited with developing the model of seafloor spreading.

Hollingworth, S. E. "Principles of Physical Geology: Review." *The Geographical Journal* 104, no. 3/4 (September–October 1944): 119–122. A review of Arthur Holmes's 1944 book.

Hopwood, Arthur. "The Magnetic Materials in Claywares." *Proceedings of the Royal Society of London Series A, Containing Papers of a Mathematical and Physical Character* 89, no. 607 (August 1, 1913): 21–30. This paper discusses the early history of magnetic fields in burnt clays.

Kerr, Richard A. "Plate Tectonics: Hot Spot Implicated in Ridge Formation." *Science* 202, no. 4367 (November 3, 1978): 503–505. An early discussion on the science of hotspot formation.

Krauskopf, Konrad. "Allan V. Cox: December 17, 1926–January 27, 1987." *Biographical Memoirs of the National Academy of Sciences* 71 (1997): 17–32. The accidental death of Cox in 1987, then dean of Earth Sciences at Stanford University, devastated the scientists in the plate tectonic community. "Cox died in a bicycle accident, colliding with a large redwood tree after a steep descent on a stretch of mountain road."

Laj, Carlo, Catherine Kisel, and Hervé Guillou. "Brunhes' Research Revisited: Magnetization of Volcanic Flows and Baked Clays." *EOS* 83, no. 35 (August 27, 2002): 381–386–388. The authors retrace the early evidence for magnetic reversals.

Lamplugh, G. W., Richard D. Oldham, F. Debenham, Harold Jeffreys, John William Evans, and C. S. Wright. "Wegener's Hypothesis of Continental Drift: Discussion." *The Geographical Journal* 61, no. 3 (March 1923): 188–194. A transcript from an early 20th century discussion on the evidence for continental drift with both pro- and anti-drift proponents.

McKenzie, Dan P. and Robert L. Parker. "The North Pacific: An example of tectonics on a sphere." *Nature* 216, no. 5122 (1967): 1,276–1,280. McKenzie and Parker provide the first written report concluding that individual seismic-free areas "move as rigid plates on the surface of a sphere."

Menard, Henry William. *The Ocean of Truth: A Personal History of Global Tectonics.* Princeton: Princeton University Press, 1986. Published posthumously, this book discusses the development of plate tectonics.

Metz, William D. "Plate Tectonics: Do the Hot Spots really Stand Still?" *Science* 185, no. 4148 (July 26, 1974): 340–342. This report begins: "With plate tectonics firmly established . . ." and goes on to discuss geologic features that the theory did not yet fully explain.

Morgan, W. Jason. "Rises, Trenches, Great Faults and Crustal Blocks," *Journal of Geophysical Research* 73 (1968): 1,959. This report details Morgan's presentation at the AGU meeting in 1967 on the motions of tectonic plates as rigid bodies in rotation on Earth's spherical surface.

Rupke, Nicolaas A. "Continental Drift Before 1900." *Nature* 227 (July 25, 1970): 349–350. This report places in context earlier proposals for continental drift before Wegener.

Schopf, J. William, Keith A. Kvenvolden, and Elso S. Barghoorn. "Amino Acids in Precambrian Sediments: An Assay." *Proceedings of the National Academy of Sciences of the United States of America* 59, no. 2 (February 15, 1968): 639–646. This report discusses evidence for Precambrian microorganisms.

Sullivan, Walter. "Trip to Moon Will be Computed on Theories Advanced in 1609." *New York Times*, March 28, 1958. This newspaper report recounts the history of the mathematics involved reaching the Moon.

Sykes, L. R. "Mechanism of earthquakes and nature of faulting on the mid-ocean ridges." *Geological Society of America Annual Meeting Program*, (1966): 216–217. Sykes's presentation at GSA provided evidence confirming Wilson's transform fault hypothesis.

Tharp, Marie, and Henry Frankel. "Mappers of the Deep: How Two Geologists Plotted the Mid-Atlantic Ridge and made a Discovery that Revolutionized the Earth Sciences." *Natural History* 95, no. 10 (October 1986): 49–62. Tharp discusses her role and that of Bruce Heezen's in the history of the development of plate tectonics.

U.S. Geological Survey. "Historic Earthquakes: Prince William Sound, Alaska 1964." This Web site provides information and links to articles about the great earthquake and ensuing tsunami. Available online. URL: http://earthquake.usgs.gov/regional/states/events/1964_03_28.php. Accessed February 28, 2007.

———. "Historic Earthquakes: Gediz, Turkey 1970." This Web site provides an abridged account of a historical report on the earthquake. Available online. URL: http://earthquake.usgs.gov/regional/world/ events/1970_03_28.php. Accessed February 28, 2007.

van der Gracht, W. A. J. M. van Waterschoot. "Theory of Continental Drift—A Symposium on the Origin and Movement of Land Masses both Inter-Continental and Intra-Continental, as Proposed by Alfred Wegener." Tulsa, Oklahoma: The American Association of Petroleum Geologists; London: T. Murby & Co., 1928. The published record of the 1928 symposium.

Vine, Fred J., and Drummond H. Matthews. "Magnetic Anomalies Over Oceanic Ridges." *Nature* 199 no., 4897 (September 7, 1963): 947–949.

This report introduces the Vine-Matthews hypothesis connecting magnetic reversals in the oceanic crust with seafloor spreading.

———— and J. Tuzo Wilson. "Magnetic Anomalies Over a Young Oceanic Ridge Off Vancouver Island." *Science* 150, no. 3695 (October 22, 1965): 485–489. This article provides further evidence for seafloor spreading.

————. "The Continental Drift Debate." *Nature* 266 (March 3, 1977): 19–22. "The controversy within the Earth sciences over the hypothesis of continental drift has been unusually protracted. Here Professor Vine reviews the history of the debate as recorded in the pages of *Nature*."

Whitmore, Frank C., Jr., and Bruce C. Heezen. "Landlubbing Admiral?" *Science* 184, no. 4142 (June 14, 1974): 1,132–1,133. These letters to the editor discuss Harry Hess and his role in the development of plate tectonics.

Wilson, John Tuzo. "A Possible Origin for the Hawaiian Islands." *Canadian Journal of Physics* 41 (1963): 863–870. Wilson proposes the hotspot theory as an explanation for the formation of the Hawaiian Islands.

————. "Hypothesis of Earth's Behaviour." *Nature* 198, no. 4884 (1963): 925–929. A diagram in this article shows the location of a hotspot in relation to the convection cell and spreading ridge.

————. "Evidence from Ocean Islands Suggesting Movement in the Earth." *Philosophical Transactions Royal Society of London* 258, no. 1088 (1965): 145–167. Further development of the hotspot theory.

————. "Transform Faults, Oceanic Ridges, and Magnetic Anomalies Southwest of Vancouver Island." *Science* 150, no. 3695 (October 22, 1965): 482–485. Wilson proposes his transform fault theory.

8

1971–1980:
Fire and Water

Introduction

In comparison to other decades, the 1970s were about average for volcanic activity, perhaps even a bit below average. Only four cataclysmic eruptions with more than 0.024 cubic miles (0.1 km^3) but less than 0.24 cubic miles (1 km^3) of tephra occurred above sea level. During the 20th century, four or more such eruptions, having a volcanic explosivity index (VEI) of 4 on a scale of 0–8, have peppered each decade. Mount St. Helens in 1980 had a VEI of 5: where the amount of tephra is more than 0.24 cubic miles (1 km^3), but less then 2.4 cubic miles (10 km^3). Mount St. Helens released 0.3 cubic miles (1.2 km^3) of tephra. A volcanic eruption with a VEI of 5 happened once in the first decade of the 20th century, twice from different volcanoes in the 1930s, and once every decade starting in the 1950s. The last VEI of 5 was the August 12, 1991, eruption of Cerro Hudson in the Andes of Southern Chile. Upping the explosivity level up another notch to 6 shows that an eruption of this magnitude, with more than 2.4 cubic miles (10 km^3) but less than 24 cubic miles (100 km^3) has struck the 20th century three times: Santa Maria in 1902, Novarupta in 1912, and Pinatubo in 1991.

What made the 1970s exceptional was the amount of global attention drawn to active volcanoes with a foreseeable risk of an eruption. Congress passed legislation in 1974 mandating that the U.S. Geological Survey become the lead federal agency in charge of "providing reliable and timely warnings of volcanic hazards to State and local authorities," according to the David A. Johnston Cascades Volcano Observatory (CVO) Web site. The observatory was built in Vancouver, Washington, after the eruption of Mount St. Helens, to provide a permanent monitoring office for the Cascade region. In 1982 the office was officially dedicated to Johnston, a 30-year-old USGS volcanologist who died observing Mount St. Helens on the morning of May 18, 1980. He was one of 57 victims of the eruption.

The Smithsonian Institution also took responsibility for providing a network of scientists around the world with event notifications of natural and man-made occurrences. During the first half of the 1970s these events varied tremendously, but toward the later half of the decade the institution maintained a focus on volcanic activities. Today the archives of the Smithsonian provide a wealth of volcanological observations from the field dating back to 1968, as well as reports since then that examine the history of hazardous eruptions throughout the Holocene. The Smithsonian's Global Volcanism Program works jointly with the USGS to provide weekly volcanic updates to the public.

In 1973 the eruption on Heimaey along the submarine Vestmannaeyjar volcanic system stands out as one of the most impressive eruptions of the 20th century. Not for its explosivity, however, which was a VEI of 3 with only 0.015 cubic miles (0.065 km^3) of tephra. The eruption is remarkable because for the first time in history, humans fought a volcano and won. Using water hoses and a jury-rigged sprinkler system the Icelanders brought the approaching 0.05 cubic miles (0.2 km^3) of slowly flowing lava to a standstill. They saved much of their town and harbor from destruction and later used the cooling lava as an alternative fuel source for heating their homes and businesses.

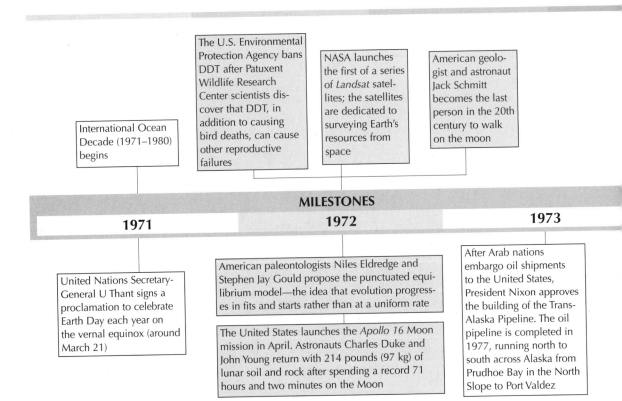

The U.S. Environmental Protection Agency bans DDT after Patuxent Wildlife Research Center scientists discover that DDT, in addition to causing bird deaths, can cause other reproductive failures

NASA launches the first of a series of *Landsat* satellites; the satellites are dedicated to surveying Earth's resources from space

American geologist and astronaut Jack Schmitt becomes the last person in the 20th century to walk on the moon

International Ocean Decade (1971–1980) begins

MILESTONES

1971

1972

1973

United Nations Secretary-General U Thant signs a proclamation to celebrate Earth Day each year on the vernal equinox (around March 21)

American paleontologists Niles Eldredge and Stephen Jay Gould propose the punctuated equilibrium model—the idea that evolution progresses in fits and starts rather than at a uniform rate

The United States launches the *Apollo 16* Moon mission in April. Astronauts Charles Duke and John Young return with 214 pounds (97 kg) of lunar soil and rock after spending a record 71 hours and two minutes on the Moon

After Arab nations embargo oil shipments to the United States, President Nixon approves the building of the Trans-Alaska Pipeline. The oil pipeline is completed in 1977, running north to south across Alaska from Prudhoe Bay in the North Slope to Port Valdez

Working with the new model of plate tectonics for Earth processes, volcanologists in the 1970s reinterpreted the modern dangers of volcanoes. They recognized the importance of both hazard mapping and active monitoring and struggled with estimating when an eruption might strike or determining whether an expensive and unpopular evacuation was needed. Triumphs came when scientists provided authorities and the public the complicated explanations behind their hypotheses for a volcano's behavior. Unnecessary risks and blind faith in past eruptive history helped no one. During this decade many mistakes were made that should never be forgotten. Some would be repeated again, but the lessons of this decade are ones that can still be applied to the future.

Keeping Track of a Changing Planet

The violent eruption of a new island in the North Atlantic Ocean in 1963 eventually drew global attention. The volcano off the southern coast of Iceland began oozing *pillow lava* about 430 feet (130 m) below sea level on November 8. As the volcano's cinder cone grew closer to the surface, the reduced water pressure could not contain the tremendous amount of

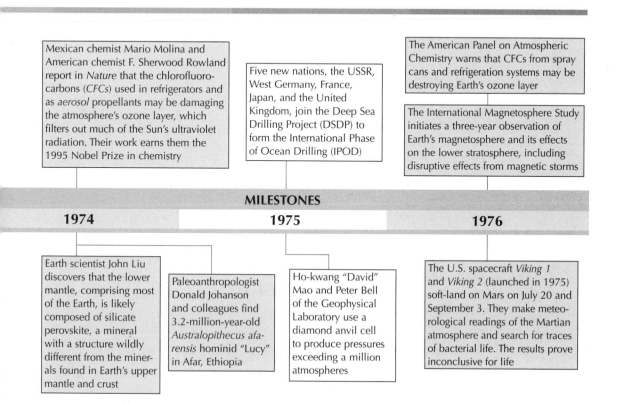

Mexican chemist Mario Molina and American chemist F. Sherwood Rowland report in *Nature* that the chlorofluoro-carbons (*CFCs*) used in refrigerators and as *aerosol* propellants may be damaging the atmosphere's ozone layer, which filters out much of the Sun's ultraviolet radiation. Their work earns them the 1995 Nobel Prize in chemistry

Five new nations, the USSR, West Germany, France, Japan, and the United Kingdom, join the Deep Sea Drilling Project (DSDP) to form the International Phase of Ocean Drilling (IPOD)

The American Panel on Atmospheric Chemistry warns that CFCs from spray cans and refrigeration systems may be destroying Earth's ozone layer

The International Magnetosphere Study initiates a three-year observation of Earth's magnetosphere and its effects on the lower stratosphere, including disruptive effects from magnetic storms

MILESTONES

1974   **1975**   **1976**

Earth scientist John Liu discovers that the lower mantle, comprising most of the Earth, is likely composed of silicate perovskite, a mineral with a structure wildly different from the miner-als found in Earth's upper mantle and crust

Paleoanthropologist Donald Johanson and colleagues find 3.2-million-year-old *Australopithecus afa-rensis* hominid "Lucy" in Afar, Ethiopia

Ho-kwang "David" Mao and Peter Bell of the Geophysical Laboratory use a diamond anvil cell to produce pressures exceeding a million atmospheres

The U.S. spacecraft *Viking 1* and *Viking 2* (launched in 1975) soft-land on Mars on July 20 and September 3. They make meteo-rological readings of the Martian atmosphere and search for traces of bacterial life. The results prove inconclusive for life

eruptive energy pouring forth into the ocean, and the eruptions turned explosive. Icelandic scientists contacted volcanologists, atmospheric scientists, oceanographers, and ecologists around the world to come witness the birth of the new island. An interior mixture of magma and water produced a bomb-like blast of tephra that burst out of the ocean. Plumes of ash and steam rose high into the atmosphere identifying the site of the growing volcano for miles away.

The island, named Surtsey after the fire giant Surtur in Norse mythology, broke free of the sea surface waves on November 15 and continued to rise to a height of 571 feet (174 m) until the volcanic eruptions stopped completely on June 5, 1967. From that time forward the home of the fire giant, emerging a mile (1.5 km) in diameter and a square mile in area (2.8 km²), has been losing territory back to the ocean—the waves slowly eroding its shoreline. Icelandic volcanologist Sigurdur Thorarinsson (1912–83) kept tabs on the immigration of organisms to the island, which was protected as a nature reserve. Starting in 1965 during a lapse in eruptive activity, lichens and moss began to colonize the newly formed basalt rocks. Within a few years, insects, birds, and marine animals had moved to the new land. Their excrement and death helped fertilize the island,

---

Voyager spacecrafts *1* and *2* are launched to take advantage of a rare planetary alignment in the outer solar system. They fly by Jupiter and its moons in 1979 and use the planet's gravity to slingshot their way to Saturn. Powered by radioisotope thermoelectric generators and the gravity assist of the flyby technique, they continue on past the other outer planets on their way to interstellar space, reaching the heliosheath in the early 21st century

Scientists from the project FAMOUS (French-American Mid-Ocean Undersea Study) in the Woods Hole Oceanographic Institution's deep-sea submersible vehicle *Alvin* discover a host of strange life-forms, such as red and white tubeworms, near undersea hot springs heated by ocean-ridge volcanism

The U.S. Geological Survey joins the Advanced Research Projects Agency Network (ARPANet), a forerunner of the Internet

MILESTONES

1977

1978

American paleobotanist Elso Barghoorn discovers fossil bacteria in South Africa dating back 3.4 billion years

American microbiologist Carl Woese and researcher George E. Fox discover and identify Archaea as a separate domain from Eukaryotes and Bacteria, based on their different 16S rRNA sequences, restructuring the evolutionary tree of life

Japanese seismologist Hiroo Kanamori develops the Moment Magnitude Scale for earthquakes

British archaeologist Mary Leakey working with a team that included American volcanic stratigrapher Richard Hay and anthropologist Tim White discover hominid footprints in a 3.7-million-year-old volcanic tuff deposit from the Sadiman Volcano in Laetoli, Tanzania

The U.S. research vessel *Glomar Challenger* extends a drill through a record-setting 4.376 miles (7,044 m) of water to collect core samples of the ocean floor

Originally called an Earth Resources Technology Satellite (ERTS), the Landsat (Land Remote Sensing Satellite) was designed to survey and relay back to Earth masses of data in various ways. (NASA)

America's worst nuclear accident occurs at Three Mile Island, Pennsylvania

The U.S. Geological Survey celebrates its 100th anniversary

Mount St. Helens in southern Washington erupts explosively on May 18 following an earthquake of magnitude 5.0. The subglacial, plinian eruption punctuates the volcanic activity that began on March 27 and lasts until late October 1986. The eruption ejects 0.3 cubic miles (1.2 km³) of tephra and 0.02 cubic miles (0.074 km³) of lava and causes pyroclastic flows, lava dome extrusion, spine extrusion, lahars, debris avalanches, 31 fatalities, evacuations, and an estimated $0.5–2 billion in property damage. Tree ring records indicate this is the volcano's largest eruption since 1800 C.E., when the volcano ejected 0.4 cubic miles (1.5 km³) of tephra. Early settlers in the west coast of the United States reported witnessing explosive activity from the Goat Rocks area on the north flank throughout the 19th century

MILESTONES

1979

1980

Drilling offshore of Brunei leads to a "blow out" of water that will take decades and 20 relief wells to stop the man-made eruption

During the Scripps Institution of Oceanography Rise Expedition to the East Pacific, Fred Spiess and others are the first to discover black smokers: *hydrothermal vent* chimneys on the seafloor that emit dark, sulfur-rich plumes. They take photographs using the deep-diving submersible *Alvin* and *Deep Tow,* an unmanned vehicle

Walter Alvarez, Luis Alvarez, Frank Asaro, and Helen Michel publish their discovery of a thin layer of clay at the Cretaceous-Tertiary boundary enriched with heavy metal iridium, and their hypothesis that an impact event formed the iridium layer (later found to be worldwide). Luis Alvarez also suggests that the impact threw enough dust into the sky to obscure the sun and cause the extinction of the dinosaurs paving the way for other small plants and animals to scratch out a living on the volcanic soil.

From 1963 to 1967 the international cooperation among the Earth scientists monitoring the island's formation established a new sense of global responsibility for up-to-date communication about natural events. Recognizing the role the Smithsonian Institution could play in such situations, Assistant Secretary Sidney Galler chose Robert Citron to direct a new Center for Short-Lived Phenomena. At the time, Citron was developing satellite tracking stations around the world for the Smithsonian Astrophysical Observatory in Cambridge, Massachusetts. He quickly enlisted his extensive network of contacts to help him as he converted his office into the new center. In a time before e-mails, instant messaging, and Web sites—Citron and his secretary, Lee Cavanaugh, sent postcards and relied on the two phones in their shared office space to build up a network of people on the alert for recent volcanic eruptions, major earthquakes, meteorite falls, and other geophysical as well as biological, and even anthropological, events.

Citron and his secretary sent out their first report cards in late January 1968 about the eruption of Metis Island: a submarine volcano that was cresting above sea level among the volcanic Tonga Islands of the South Pacific Ocean. They relied on news stories about the event published in the *Washington Post* on December 14 and in *Science News* on January 6 as well as a report from a local ship's captain who had seen the eruption. By February the eruptions had stopped, and Metis Island had once more sunk below the ocean waves to become Metis Shoal. The formation of the ephemeral island, which has repeated its stunt multiple times throughout history (as have its neighbors, most recently in 2006), was exactly the kind of event that busy scientists might have missed reading about if not given direct notice.

Soon the Center for Short-Lived Phenomena had expanded to include a staff of nine men and women. The team relied on news reports and a network of 2,300 correspondents who would call, write, telegraph, or radio the center with news of an event whenever they saw something. These eyewitnesses included scientists as well as airline pilots, sailors, forest rangers, local merchants, ranchers, and farmers. Each week, Citron and his team would learn of some 200 different events. For example, during one typical week Citron and his staff received reports of 41 earthquakes, 26 volcanic eruptions, 29 fireballs (very bright meteors), 20 major oil spills, 10 animal migrations, and a red tide. Roughly a quarter of the events they learned about would merit an alert on the center's notification postcards. The frequency of earthquakes and volcanic eruptions happening all the time around the world came as a surprise to many people, including some volcanologists. While correspondents received their weekly postcards for free, another 2,000 people around the world each paid $15 a year for the service, with some paying $250 a year to be given immediate updates whenever news broke of an event in a particular region or in their field of study. Many scientists upon reading one of the postcards or getting a phone call from the center would pack up their portable equipment and head to the site of the event. By 1974 Citron was even instructing astronauts on where to aim their cameras from space: for example, pine beetle infestations in North America, an oil spill in a Hungarian river, and the eruption of Kilauea in Hawaii.

In 1974 the center's annual budget reached $120,000, but only a quarter of that was paid for by subscriptions. The rest came from federal money. The number of event reports inundating the small staff and their limited funding contributed to the sad irony that the Center for Short-Lived Phenomena (CSLP) did not last long. In 1975 government funding for the center's operations out of the Smithsonian Astrophysical Observatory ended, and the center was restructured. Citron converted CSLP into a nonprofit organization that would later focus on oil spills. (According to his biography at Kistler Aerospace, Citron would go on to found several companies in the fields of global communications, scientific field research, publishing, and commercial space development.) Many from the center's small staff moved to Washington, D.C., where the Smithsonian established headquarters for a Scientific Event Alert Network (SEAN) at the National Museum of Natural History.

Volcanologists at the museum, William Melson and Tom Simkin, had provided the Center for Short-Lived Phenomena research assistance since its inception. Along with mammalogist Henry Setzer, they now helped advise the coverage of events for the Washington-based alert network. The transition took a month. The Center mailed out its last batch of postcards on August 25, 1975. No event reports were issued in September. In October the new SEAN staff began posting a monthly *Natural Science Event Bulletin* to their network of correspondents, scientists, librarians and other subscribers. By publishing monthly, the SEAN staff lost the immediate alert aspect of their service, but they could now verify and better document events—improving their ability to identify false reports and hoaxes of UFO and sea monsters that had embarrassed them earlier. In January 1978 they changed the name of their publication to the *Scientific Event Alert Network Bulletin*. Biological and geological events continued to dominate the alerts, but the biological events now focused more on beachings of marine mammals. Insect infestations, massive Appalachian squirrel migrations, Malaysian "frog wars," squid strandings, cyanide spills, and oil spills, examples of previously reported events, no longer made the cut. Another round of budgetary reductions in 1982 resulted in complete elimination of the bulletin's coverage of biological events and a narrowing of the focus onto volcanic eruptions.

In 1984 the Smithsonian obtained congressional funding for the Museum of Natural History to formalize a Global Volcanism Program that kept the alert network service running as a strictly volcanic endeavor. In 1987 the program made use of the burgeoning computer-to-computer

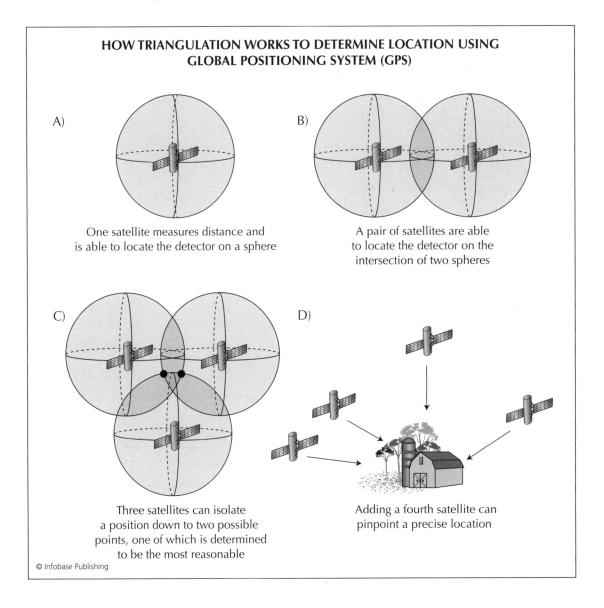

HOW TRIANGULATION WORKS TO DETERMINE LOCATION USING GLOBAL POSITIONING SYSTEM (GPS)

A) One satellite measures distance and is able to locate the detector on a sphere

B) A pair of satellites are able to locate the detector on the intersection of two spheres

C) Three satellites can isolate a position down to two possible points, one of which is determined to be the most reasonable

D) Adding a fourth satellite can pinpoint a precise location

© Infobase Publishing

In 1978 the U.S. military began launching satellites for use in detecting the location of specialized GPS receivers. Geologists affix GPS receivers to seismometers on either side of fault lines, such as the San Andreas, to measure the tectonic movement of plates.

communication advancements by posting its reports on electronic bulletin boards (OMNET and KOSMOS), the ancestors of the Internet. In 1990 the program updated the name of its monthly publication to the *Bulletin of the Global Volcanism Network* to reflect the changes done in 1984. Today only the archives of the volcanic updates from the various incarnations of the alert reports are available online. The rest of the event reports, including the one of the sea monster "that turned out to be a whale with a bone protruding from its head," are filed away in the bowels of the Smithsonian.

Fighting a Volcano

The rumble on the small island of Heimaey (HAY-mah-ay) began at 8 P.M. on January 21, 1973. A delicate needle on a seismograph dutifully recorded the slight tremors as they continued through the night. At first no one noticed. A volcanologist looking at the record from the seismic station, which was located 37 miles (60 km) away from the epicenter, would later count 200 earthquakes of very little magnitude striking between 1 and 3 o'clock on the morning of the 22nd. The largest, still only a magnitude 2.7, struck at 4:16 A.M. Fishermen already awake and working at the docks looked at each other with nervous apprehension. Little activity followed the predawn swarm to indicate impending danger. Given the island's volcanic history, however, even the slightest tremor put authorities on alert. The sun rose at 10:38 A.M. and would set six hours later with some townsfolk jittery and perhaps considering the need to pack an overnight bag as they drifted off to an uneasy sleep. Heimaey was part of the same volcanic archipelago off Iceland's southern coast that had given birth to Surtsey a decade earlier.

With 32 Holocene volcanoes on or around Iceland's main island an eruption is always just a matter of time. After Surtsey quieted down in 1967, the next eruption came in 1970 from Hekla, a stratovolcano on the southern part of the mainland. Throughout the 20th century, Iceland, which is about the size of the state of Virginia, had at least 11 different volcanoes erupt, many of them erupting multiple times. The frequency is not coincidental. The country sits on the Mid-Atlantic Ridge, where the North American plate and the Eurasian plate are spreading apart. For more than 16 million years, the main island has remained on the ridge rather than sliding to one side or another because it is also fed by a hotspot plume from the mantle. The rare combination of hotspot and spreading ridge also contributes to the formation of the Azores off the cost of Portugal and Ecuador's Galápagos Islands. Twenty-first-century Earth scientists are still investigating the tectonics of such regions to determine which feature, ridge or hotspot, has the greater influence over the erupting landforms. On Iceland, the Mid-Atlantic Ridge is a visible tear through the island's middle.

Off the southern coast of Iceland, the Vestmannaeyjar (Vést-mun-ayar) archipelago (Westmann Islands) is made up of basaltic volcanic islands and submarine cones that dot a 40-mile-long (64 km) shelf. In 1973 a population of 5,300 people lived on the island of Heimaey in the harbor town that shared the same name as the volcanic archipelago. The fishing community of Vestmannaeyjar was built on Holocene basalt flows from Mount Helgafell, an extinct volcano with an elevation above sea level of 741 feet (226 m) that last erupted 5,000 years ago. When the earthquakes began to rattle the island, those who felt the slight shaking and the geologists checking the records immediately looked to the supposedly extinct volcano. They would soon learn that the earthquake swarm was the result of magma moving up to form a fissure and a new cinder cone, later named Eldfell, next to Helgafell's northeastern slope.

At 1:55 A.M. on January 23, the ground to the east of Helgafell split apart under the pressure of the rising magma. Through a mile-long fissure (1.6 km) a fountain of lava and tephra shot 375 feet (114 m) into the sky at a rate of 130 cubic yards (100 m³) per second. The Icelandic State Civil Defense Organization had prepared for such a contingency and immediately implemented the evacuation plan for Vestmannaeyjar. The close-knit fishing community also worked quickly to make sure their friends and family made it off the island alive. They expedited the process using their fleet of fishing vessels as ferries to and from the mainland. By 8 A.M., before the sun had even risen, reports of a successful evacuation began hitting the telegraph wires. Only one person reportedly died, having fallen asleep in a basement room that became inundated by volcanic gasses. The community's displacement would last for months.

"Short-term and long-term costs totaled many tens of millions of dollars, a very large amount when compared with Iceland's 1971 gross national product (GNP) of $500 million," a 1983 report on the eruption concluded. "The location and housing and other services for 5,300 people, for example, was equivalent in national impact to finding emergency housing with overnight notice for 5.3 million Americans." As a Hawaiian-like viscous flow of basalt lava crept toward the town and began filling in the harbor, Iceland braced for the possibility that the ongoing catastrophe could mean the end of their premier fishing port. Faced with the economic and societal impacts such a loss would bring, officials acted on the advice of volcanologists from the University of Iceland's Science Institute and agreed to experiment with ways to stop or control the lava. The slow-moving nature of the lava gave them time to act.

Volunteers ventured back to secure corrugated iron panels over windows and sweep heavy ash from the roofs of homes and other buildings. The Icelandic geologists and geophysicists had collaborated on theoretical calculations regarding the cooling effect of water on lava and had done small-scale experiments earlier on Surtsey to test these calculations. On February 6 they began a test using the town's water supply to see if the same cooling effect could work on slowing the lava flow into Vestmannaeyjar. Even with a limited amount of water, they could see the front of the flow thicken and harden as it cooled and then pile up on itself. If the lava had been less sticky to begin with, then instead of piling up, the flow would have likely trickled under the newly hardened barrier, rendering it ineffective. Officials authorized a team to bulldoze a lava barrier around the northwest part of town not already buried or burned. In the meantime, they also sent ships with onboard saltwater pumps to the harbor and asked foreign nations for help obtaining large-capacity pumps that could be used ashore. Equipped with 43 pumps and 19 miles

(30 km) of plastic pipes, Icelandic fire fighters led a disaster-trained volunteer crew of 75 people dressed in protective gear to build the world's first volcanic-emergency saltwater sprinkler system.

To get the lava to stop, the crew needed to cool the flow from its liquid temperature in late February of 1,994°F (1,090°C) to a solid rock forming 1,500°F (800°C). They first attacked the oncoming flow with water using fire hoses, sending steam rising like a fog over the island and joining with the plume of ash and smoke that rose even higher. They continued this firefighting strategy until part of the margin and surface of the flow was cooled deep enough to send a bulldozer through to build a road behind the frontline of the flow. From this strategic point the crew snaked 10-inch diameter plastic pipes punctured with small holes and gushing sprays of water onto the hot lava field. The pipes delivered as much as 26 gallons of seawater per second onto the molten rocks, the heat converting most of the water to steam and the cold water keeping the plastic pipes from melting. The crew worked through March and April to build the branching network of pipes. Each branch of the sprinkler system would soak a spot for two weeks at a time dropping the temperature to 212°F (100°C) before the steam began to dissipate and the crew could safely move the pipe to a higher point on the lava field.

The crew leaders relied on scientists to interpret satellite images and aerial photographs taken during the eruption. Volcanologists assisting in the fight against the volcano combined these images with past geodetic surveys to produce accurate topographic maps. From these they could assess the lava's different flow rates and show the crew where to bulldoze lava barriers in order to divert the flow elsewhere. By the end of April the surface of the lava had changed color from red to black and black to gray as it cooled. The crew had to tread carefully on the jagged surface rocks; the fluid lava deep below still oozed out between cracks. At this time the explosions from the fissure and the production of lava began to abate. The newly formed Eldfell volcano had risen to a height of 722 feet (220 m) matching the height of Helgafell. The worst of the disaster was behind them.

The volcano-fighting crew succeeded in saving Vestmannaeyjar from total destruction without any loss of lives. The cooling operation, in place until July 10, 1973, ultimately used 8 million cubic yards of seawater to turn 5 million cubic yards of molten lava into solid rock at a rate 50 to 100 times faster than it would have cooled otherwise. The cost for the operation came to $1.5 million. By the summer of 1974, half of the displaced community had returned to their homes. To their joy, they discovered the new addition of lava to the harbor wound up protecting it from storms and sea surges. They also discovered that they could harness the geothermal energy from the cooling lava on the island to heat homes and buildings. By 1979 engineers were building an extensive heating system to take advantage of the natural benefits from the new volcanic birth.

Soufrière Eruption Crisis in Guadeloupe

Volcanic earthquakes have become one of the most important indicators that a volcanic eruption is about to take place. Just how much time will elapse between the earthquakes and the eruption is difficult to determine. In the case of Eldfell on the island of Heimaey the eruption came 30 hours after the start of the earthquake swarm. The slight magnitude of the earthquakes gave little indication of the amount of magma preparing to surface. Sometimes the eruption does not come. Earthquake swarms are common on the islands of the Lesser Antilles in the Caribbean: striking St. Vincent in 1947, St. Kitts in 1950 and 1961, and Montserrat in 1966—all without eruptions.

Beginning in 1962, earthquake swarms became a yearly occurrence on Guadeloupe. When 25 microseismic earthquakes struck in November 1975, only the local French volcanologists on the Caribbean island took note. When the swarms escalated in March to 680 earthquakes, some big enough to be felt, Jacques Dorel of the Institute of Physics of the Globe (IPG)—which had built the seismic observatory to monitor La Soufrière, the island's stratovolcano—contacted the Smithsonian's Seismic Event Alert Network. Dorel did not anticipate an eruption but considered the activity worth the volcanological community's attention. "There is no important risk of an eruption of this volcano," the bulletin reported Dorel as saying. The temperature of the volcano had not changed, no *fumaroles* were emitting any gasses, and a flight over the volcano revealed no new surface changes. Despite these indicators that the earthquakes were benign, Dorel equivocally and prudently indicated that change could happen at any time. The bulletin reported that Dorel believed "it was impossible to make a long-term (several months or years) prognostication on the evolution of such volcanoes." Such was the case for any volcano at the time, not just the stratovolcanoes of the Caribbean.

In the early 1970s Robert Dietz and G. Freeland used plate tectonic theory to interpret the formation of the Caribbean Islands. Long after the mid-Atlantic spreading ridge had separated the Americas from Africa and Eurasia, the North and South American plates began moving in separate directions, with North America rotating anticlockwise relative to South America. This, they argued, resulted in a spreading center that opened the Caribbean. As the older and denser Atlantic Ocean crust continued to move westward away from the mid-Atlantic ridge, it encountered the newly formed Caribbean seafloor. The collision resulted in the subduction of the Atlantic below the Caribbean plate and the rise of the volcanoes along the Lesser Antilles. The Caribbean volcanoes—many of them named *soufrière*, French for source of sulfur—formed from partial melting of the subducting Atlantic oceanic crust. They had become infamous for their pyroclastic proclivity after Mount Pelée in 1902 demonstrated the typecast pelean eruption just hours after Soufrière on St. Vincent killed 1,600 with sulfuric gasses and hot ash.

When La Soufrière on Guadeloupe began burping ash, sand, and steam in July 1976, scientists presented officials with different opinions as to the extent of the danger. Two French geologists, a petrographer and a geochemist, expressed concern that phreatic eruptions could lead to mudflows or worse: a *nuée ardente*, the French term for a pyroclastic flow. The six French volcanologists in charge of the observatory requested the public remain calm and continued to consider the volcano a low threat.

The volcanologists compared the eruptive material to previous tephra falls and assured local authorities that the worst of the activity was over. When two weeks later the volcano released another burst of steam mixed with loosened old bits of rock and dust, the volcanologists again maintained that the threat was the same as ever. After the volcano cleared its throat for the third time on August 9, those stationed at the observatory compared the ratio of CO to CO_2 and H_2S to SO_2 and saw no change. The earthquake depths were the same; no magmatic activity was detectable; everything coming out of the throat of the volcano was old, hard, and crusty. They advised the officials to keep the public calm, an increasingly difficult strategy for the civil authorities to take—especially considering that half the volcanology team, including its director, had, by this time, left the island.

The messages coming from the two geologists combined with the appearance that some of the volcanologists did not find the situation remarkable enough to stay and observe, effectively diminished the public's confidence in the volcanologists. When the authorities made the announcement to evacuate the capital city of Basse-Terre, some 72,000 people left within three days. Against the volcanologists' advice, the civil authorities then kept the population out of the city for several months. The volcanic-seismic-events-turned-outbursts-crisis quickly spun into an economic and societal disaster without one red rock of lava erupting.

Haroun Tazieff (1914–98), the director of volcanology at IPG, received much of the blame. During the Soufrière crisis he left with two colleagues to search for three lost Britons in the Ecuadorian Andes. Despite Tazieff's insistence that Basse-Terre was safe, the press and his boss saw the decision to leave the volatile volcano as an abandonment of the French Caribbean people. Tazieff had a commanding presence in the media, having worked as a director and cinematographer since the late 1950s. In the early 1970s, he filmed a National Geographic television special titled "The Violent Earth," as well as provided the footage for "Pink Floyd: Live at Pompeii." When he learned of the evacuation, he reportedly disparaged the French geologists for providing alarmist advice, saying, "They are all perfectly competent in their own fields, but they should not try to interfere in vulcanology. If you have trouble with your liver you do not consult an ophthalmologist." According to a December 1976 news article in the journal *Nature*, Tazieff's decision to leave Guadeloupe for the expedition in the Andes coupled with his sound

Hydrothermal Vents

Marine geologists were prepared to find hot springs emanating from the ocean floor when they went searching for the source of temperature anomalies using the Woods Hole Oceanographic Institution's deep-sea submersible vehicle *Alvin* in 1977. The geologists with the project FAMOUS (French-American Mid-Ocean Undersea Study) however were not prepared to discover marine organisms thriving in the deep, dark waters off the Galápagos Islands. Not a single biologist was on board for the expedition. The team named the site of the strange life-forms Rose Garden. The red and white tubeworms, giant clams, and large white crabs relied on chemosynthesis rather than photosynthesis for energy, consuming the bacteria that survived on the minerals percolating from the undersea hot springs. Two years later, during the Scripps Institution of Oceanography

Woods Hole Oceanographic Institution completed construction of the Alvin submersible in 1965. The untethered three-manned submersible is seen here preparing for a dive into Oceanographer Canyon on the southern edge of Georges Bank off Cape Cod. (NOAA/Department of Commerce)

Life without photosynthesis; tubeworms feed off microbes in their guts using chemosynthesis. The ecosystem derives energy from minerals at a black smoker. (NOAA/Department of Commerce)

bites in the press cost him his job as director of volcanology at IPG. The journal later published Tazieff's testimony of events, in which he again criticized the two geologists for their lack of experience with eruptive

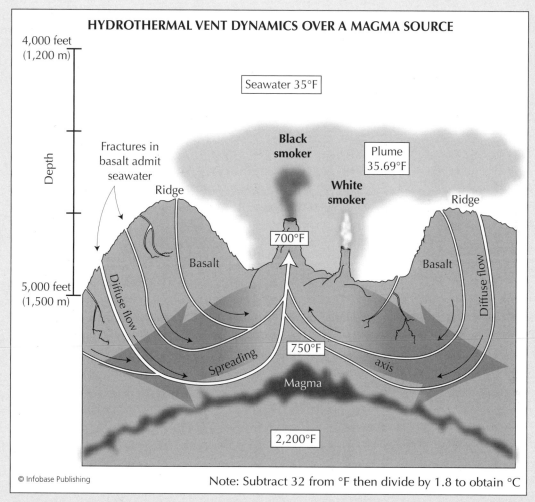

HYDROTHERMAL VENT DYNAMICS OVER A MAGMA SOURCE

4,000 feet
(1,200 m)

Depth

Seawater 35°F

Black smoker

Fractures in basalt admit seawater

Plume 35.69°F

Ridge

White smoker

Ridge

700°F

Basalt

Basalt

Diffuse flow

Diffuse flow

5,000 feet
(1,500 m)

Spreading

750°F

axis

Magma

2,200°F

© Infobase Publishing

Note: Subtract 32 from °F then divide by 1.8 to obtain °C

Cool seawater percolates through the cracks in the seafloor. As the ocean water sinks deeper into the crust, magma along spreading ridges heats the water, which dissolves minerals from the crust into the hydrothermal solution. The hot water rises by convection back to the seafloor surface where the minerals in the hydrothermal solution now in contact with cold seawater precipitate out of solution and form mineral deposits that build chimneys on the seafloor. The chimneys can range from as tall as buildings to as short as tree stumps.

Rise Expedition to the East Pacific, oceanographer Fred Spiess and others discovered black smokers: hydrothermal vent chimneys on the seafloor that emit dark, sulfur-rich plumes. They photographed the site using *Alvin*'s viewport and a camera attached to the unmanned vehicle *Deep Tow*.

phenomena. (In the testimony Tazieff also chastised Icelandic authorities. He disagreed with the decision to use fireboats to spray water against the lava flows closing in on the harbor entrance during the last few days of the Eldfell eruption on Heimaey—as well as a few other recent, "errone-ous volcanological diagnoses" around the world.)

In November 1976, a committee of international volcanologists was convened in Paris to assess the status of affairs in Guadeloupe. American volcanologist Frank Press chaired the committee, which also included Shigeo Aramaki from Japan; Franco Barberi from Italy; Jean Coulomb from France; Richard S. Fiske from the United States; Paolo Gasparini from Italy; Claude Guillemin from France; and Gudmundur Sigvaldason from Iceland. The committee gave a report that echoed with the familiar equivocal sentiments Dorel had made back in April when he alerted the volcanological community to the growing number of earthquakes on the island. The committee had found that by mid-November the probability of a dangerous eruption from Soufrière was low, but they cautioned that the situation could change. In a bold public relations move however, the committee presented a model to the French government about what they thought was happening below the surface. The seismic reports had indicated to them that the volcano was experiencing tectonic fractur-ing. They hypothesized that the fracturing allowed for groundwater and seawater to seep close enough to the volcano's magma source to create occasional explosions of steam. These phreatic outbursts, they proposed, were violent enough to rip out parts of the volcano's throat during their ejection—producing the clouds of ash and rain of cold rock that accom-panied the explosions. After the committee presented their report, those residents who had not yet already returned to Basse-Terre were given permission to come home on December 1. The occasional phreatic out-bursts from Soufrière continued until March 1977, and then the cough-ing fissures turned to steamy, stinky sulfuric fumaroles.

Cascade Concerns

In early February 1975, a warning went out to the scientific community to keep an eye on one of the Cascade Mountains on the west coast of the United States: "Mount St. Helens volcano in southern Washington has erupted many times during the last 4,000 years, usually after brief dormant periods. This behavior pattern suggests that the volcano, last active in 1857, will erupt again—perhaps within the next few decades," wrote Dwight Crandell and two colleagues with the U.S. Geological Survey in a report published in *Science*. The Cascade Range along the Pacific Northwest includes more than a dozen major volcanic peaks that rise snowcapped above the rest of the landscape stretching from British Columbia to northern California. Forecasting the next eruption for any one of the peaks seemed highly speculative, like looking at an intersection in the street and trying to predict the timing of the next accident. For eruptions the driver is always magma, and as with drivers of cars, history is only a guide for estimating future behavior. The reality of a situation could be very different than the prediction.

How much silica is in the magma determines whether the magma is fluid basalt or sticky andesite. Silica slows down the fluidity of magma like cornstarch in water. Higher concentrations of silica in basalt can slow an already fluid flow. Too much silica and the magma stops oozing out as lava and begins to plug up the volcano's interior, starting a dome building operation that can result in a catastrophic release. Coupled with the extent to which the magma is laced with gas or gas free, wet or dry, moving or still—and every magmatic eruption and noneruptive display of activity becomes a unique event with its own signature.

Mount St. Helens had demonstrated a variety of different eruptions since 400 B.C.E. The USGS scientists—Crandell and Donal R. Mullineaux based in Denver, Colorado, and Meyer Rubin of Reston, Virginia—discovered layers of basalt and andesite lava rocks interspersed with tephra deposits and signs of pyroclastic flows. Evidence of periods of dome building and collapse caked the flanks of the mountain. Precedent for cataclysmic power from Mount St. Helens was set on what would later be called a "junk pile" of debris and dusted with a history of activity every hundred or so years. Crandell and his co-workers found buried in the strata an eruption from 1900 B.C.E. that they compared to the historic eruption of Vesuvius in 79 A.C.E. that destroyed Pompeii, Italy. The USGS volcanologists suggested those in charge of policy decisions should keep this in mind: "Potential volcanic hazards of several kinds should be considered in planning for land use near the volcano." Anything could happen and soon something did.

A month after the *Science* report, Cascade volcanologists rushed to deal with a steam explosion that shot 2,493 feet (760 m) into the air, forming a dark cloud—but not over Mount St. Helens. Instead, the activity came from Mount Baker, a volcano in northern Washington. It was the first burst of activity in the Cascade Range since 1921, when Lassen Peak in northern California finally quieted down after an intense eruptive period between 1914 and 1917. That eruption scoured the region around Lassen Peak. Pyroclastic flows burned through 4 miles (6 km) of forest. Lahars formed from the melted snow and traveled 12 miles (20 km), converting creeks into muddy torrents. Ash explosions reached 6 miles (9 km) above the lava-filled crater and were then carried by the wind another 300 miles (500 km) east to fall in Nevada. When jets of steam and ash shot out from Mount Baker's Sherman Crater, people on both sides of the American-Canadian border wondered about the possibility of an eruption.

USGS scientists immediately began conducting geophysical surveys of the volcano and installed additional monitoring equipment to try and detect any movement of the magma. The seismic silence was both encouraging and confusing. The volcano was increasing its release of heat by a factor of 10. During this time, the energy company in charge of the recreational area around Baker Lake and the Upper Baker Dam temporarily closed the area to the public and lowered the level of the lake. If an eruption did strike, there was a risk that it would lead to an avalanche or debris

TABLE OF DATES, LOCATIONS, AND MAGNITUDE OF SELECTED VOLCANIC ERUPTIONS

Year	Volcano name	Country	Estimated volume in cubic miles (km³)
73,000 B.C.E.	Toba	Indonesia	600–720 (2,500–3,000) tephra
c. 1640 B.C.E.	Santorini	Greece	24 (100) tephra
79 C.E.	Vesuvius	Italy	0.8 (3.3) tephra
1783	Laki	Iceland	3.6 (15) lava/0.2 (1) tephra
1815	Tambora	Indonesia	36 (150) tephra
1883	Krakatau	Indonesia	5 (20) tephra
1902	Pelée	France	0.03 (.14) lava/0.05 (0.2) tephra
1902	Santa Maria	Guatemala	5 (20) tephra
1902	Novarupta	United States	6.7 (28) tephra
1980	Mount St. Helens	United States	0.02 (.07) lava/0.3 (1.2) tephra
1991	Pinatubo	Philippines	2.6 (11) tephra

© Infobase Publishing

Source: Smithsonian Global Volcanism Program

Because the predominant rock in tephra eruptions is pumice—a porous, gas-enriched rock—volumes are typically reported in dense rock equivalents. The world's two largest eruptions in the 20th century both occurred in 1902.

flow pouring into the lake and causing a seiche wave that could overtop or even destroy the dam. When the feared eruption did not materialize the region relaxed. The magma remained stationary. Curiously, the geothermal temperature spike lasted a year and then returned to normal.

Mount St. Helens

The volcano is heating up; magma is rising—that was the warning David Johnston gave reporters on March 27, 1980, while standing in the parking lot of Timberline Viewpoint on the north slope of Mount St. Helens. From that vantage point only clouds could block the view, and they frequently did. On that day it was difficult to tell from the ground where the clouds stopped and the steam began, but many had heard thunderous explosions indicating the start of an eruption. A radio reporter flying in the air was the first to describe the dark plume of ash that had blasted into the atmosphere punching out a crater through the summit. Johnston (1949–80) had hitched a ride on a helicopter from Seattle with a news crew to see and discuss the volcano's change in status. After a week of suddenly stronger earthquakes, the falling ash finally prompted an evacuation of loggers from the forested slopes and the lowering of lake levels behind dams. Johnston put a hand on his knit cap and squinted as he looked up at the summit. An earthquake of magnitude 4.2 had struck the region on March 20, alerting seismologists at the University of Washington that the volcano's dormancy had ended. There was something unsettling about that earthquake. A swarm of magnitude 3s and seven 4s followed the first tectonic strike, which also triggered an avalanche that swept down the mountain all the way to the parking lot Johnston and the news team were standing in now. Considering the volcano's potential power, Johnston nervously assessed the danger of their current situation. He had seen explosive eruptions while flying around volcanoes in Alaska. "It looks like there's a very good chance there will be an eruption. If there is an explosion, it is possible that very, very hot incandescent debris could come down on all sides. But right now, there's a very great hazard that on this side, the north side, that the glacier is breaking up. That could produce a very large avalanche." The cameras continued to roll. "This is not a good site to be in," he said. The volcano at this point was like a keg of dynamite. "The fuse is lit, but we don't know how long it is."

The unabating earthquake swarm had worried seismologist Steve Malone at the University of Washington who ran a small seismic network set up around the Cascades. When the magnitude 4.2 quake came in over the seismographs, USGS geophysicist Craig Weaver was monitoring the recordings and, as Dick Thompson describes the scene in his book *Volcano Cowboys*, Weaver ran out of the lab to Malone's office and excitedly announced an earthquake had struck Mount Hood. The network of seismometers did not cover the whole region extensively, and from Weaver's perspective in Seattle, Mount Hood in Oregon was just as likely as St. Helens to shake a bit more than usual.

An avalanche watcher stationed at Spirit Lake on St. Helens felt differently. She swayed like a drunken sailor toward the radio and, as the ground steadied, contacted Forest Service headquarters in Vancouver, Washington. The small office building was located across the Columbia River from the Portland International Airport in Oregon and an hour-and-a-half drive to Mount St. Helens National Park. The Forest Service contacted USGS headquarters in Denver where Donal Mullineaux and Dwight "Rocky" Crandell worked. The two had been coming out to St. Helens every summer since 1969 to camp on the flanks of the volcano and dig through layer upon layer of eruptive history. Theirs were the reports in 1975 and again in 1978 that predicted the volcano's reactivation. Mullineaux checked with the National Earthquake Information Service in Golden, Colorado. They put the earthquake at 15 miles north of St. Helens, closer to Mount Rainier.

Meanwhile the seismologists at the University of Washington crunched the information coming in from their network. As the earthquake propagated across the Cascades, a pendulum in each seismometer stayed still while the box containing it moved with the ground. The shift set off a series of electric sparks across the network, and the seismometers radioed the signals across the state to a wall of recorders in the basement of the university's seismic lab. The stylus needles scratched black ink across the rolling drum of paper: first the P wave and seconds later the wider S wave. Doing the math by hand and checking also with the lab's new computers, Malone, and those in his lab the commotion had attracted, triangulated the epicenter of the quake to directly below Mount St. Helens.

When the swarm showed no sign of stopping on Monday March 24, four days after the first large quake, Malone called for help. He talked to Crandell in Denver who was still under the same impression as Mullineaux that the original magnitude-4.2 earthquake had been further north. Given the intensity of the swarm and its epicenter under Mount St. Helens, Crandell had Mullineaux fly across the Rockies to Portland the next day. The U.S. Forest Service asked the Girl Scout and Boy Scout troops and other visitors camped around Spirit Lake as well as homeowners to leave. Harry Truman, an 84-year-old resident on the mountain, famously refused. Thousands of tourists relocated their campgrounds just shy of the 15-mile (24 km) evacuation radius around the volcano. After a press conference at the Forest Service headquarters in Vancouver on the 26th explaining the reason for the evacuation, Mullineaux called for more help from home.

Rick Hoblitt flew out that afternoon. Like many summer residents on the mountain, he and his wife had a trailer they camped in near the shores of Spirit Lake. Hoblitt had been combing the rock history of St. Helens for five years. He joined Mullineaux the morning of the 27th just as the USGS was upgrading the volcanic warning for St. Helens from normal to "hazard watch." Dan Miller flew out that day. Miller was also a seasoned expert of the mountain's history and with Hoblitt had helped Mullineaux and Crandell study the volcano in greater detail.

When the volcano coughed open a new crater the afternoon of the 27th, the Seattle press contacted Malone who was too busy and sent Johnston instead. The Federal Aviation Administration responded to the ash plumes by prohibiting commercial and private pilots from flying within 5 miles (8 km) of the volcano. Only officials should be flying in the air. Still more than 100 pilots took to the skies, flying dangerous aerobatics to avoid the plumes and each other. Many also flew in radio silence to avoid the $1,000 fine for ignoring the FAA warning. Mullineaux again called Crandell. This was not a drill. Time to pack.

Mullineaux, Crandell, Hoblitt, and Miller set up a base of operations at the U.S. Forest headquarters in Vancouver. They became the hazard mitigation team for the volcano working on four hours of sleep a night for weeks at a time. Crandell's first job was to provide the Forest Service with a hazard map of the most dangerous locations. Given the smooth conical shape of the volcano at the time and its history, he assumed the eruption would shoot straight into the air and the resulting pyroclastic flows, avalanches, and lahars would travel down the valleys and the forks of the Toutle River and be buffeted by the ridges. The wind would carry the ash perhaps as far as Montana. It was a map in progress.

Volcanologists from across the country started converging on the ignited powder keg as Johnston had referred to it on the 27th. If they could not determine how much time they had, perhaps they could help Crandell determine the size of the explosion before it hit.

Many of the Survey volcanologists had trained on the hot rocks and lava fountains in Hawaii. Three of these Hawaiian Volcano Observatory (HVO) graduates in particular were soon dominating the monitoring activities on St. Helens. Don Swanson and Jim Moore flew in from California on the afternoon of the 27th. Pete Lipman arrived a few days later. When Swanson and Moore arrived they unintentionally walked into the middle of a press conference. The national media had turned its eye west. A newspaper report alerted Lipman of the volcanic activity during a ski vacation in the Colorado Rockies. He immediately swapped out the old cratons for the young Cascades. The three set up operations 40 minutes to the north in a motel in Kelso. The logging town located on Interstate 5 sits halfway between two highway routes up the mountain. Highway 503 breaks away from the interstate and switchbacks up the southwest side of the mountain while highway 504, 10 minutes north of Kelso, follows a northwesterly route. Prior to the eruption, highway 504 followed the North Fork of the Toutle River, passed over Coldwater Creek along the Coldwater ridge, and then looped around the southern arm of Spirit Lake, ending at Timberline Viewpoint, about 4,500 vertical feet (1,400 m) from the peak. Hoblitt quickly established an observation camp about 10 miles (16 km) from the summit nicknamed Coldwater. This would later be called Coldwater I when on May 1 the USGS scientists established a new campground site they dubbed Coldwater II, which was about halfway between Coldwater I and Spirit Lake and, like Spirit Lake, was also about 5 miles (9 km) from the summit. The HVO volcanologists or "Three Musketeers," as Thompson reports they were called, commandeered the Survey's only helicopter and began making frequent trips to the even closer Timberline Viewpoint and to the crater itself.

The HVO crew brought a sizable amount of instruments and ordered a laser-equipped device for measuring surface deformation shipped from the Smithsonian in Washington, D.C. Meanwhile, they checked for surface deformation the old-fashioned way using the large, flat Spirit Lake. They hiked through snow to plant wooden stakes around the shore. When the water level of the 1,300-acre (5 km²) lake remained consistent through a few days of observations, the HVO team realized any magma that was moving underground was already in the volcano's throat and closer to the summit.

Over the course of two months more than 20 volcanologists and dozens more Earth scientists specializing in other fields came to St. Helens out of curiosity and stayed to help as long as they could. Sue Kieffer, a USGS planetary geologist in Flagstaff, Arizona, had worked in Wyoming studying the hydrothermal activity at Yellowstone. When she saw the steam plumes rising from St. Helens, they reminded her of Old Faithful. She could picture the magma in the throat of the volcano superheating the melted snow and ice that was leaking through the crater into underground channels and chambers. The immense pressure from the weight of the water prevents the water from boiling at the typical 212°F (100°C). Instead, vaporized gas bubbles collect along the sides and surfaces of the chambers. When enough bubbles accumulate they physically lift the water column, decreasing the pressure enough to allow for boiling and immediately the water column explodes into an erupting plume widening the crater and its channel and sending ancient tephra, ash, and steam into the atmosphere. The volcano grew two-toned as the steady wind from the Pacific blew the ash to the east leaving the snow on the west still white. The volcano looks as though a great shadow is cast over the summit and down the eastern flank, regardless of the angle of the sun. As the steam eruptions continued more glacial ice and snow pooled within the widening crater. While Sue Kieffer snowshoed around the volcano, her husband, planetary scientist Hugh Kieffer, looked at infrared satellite images and saw the geothermal temperature had risen significantly. Years later, Hugh would monitor infrared images of Mars, and Sue would apply her geyser analogy to eruptions on the outer planetary moons: Io, Triton, and Enceladus.

On the summit of St. Helens, another crater soon appeared and then the craters joined to form one gaping maw. At times, ash plumes reached 10,000 feet (3,048 m) above the 9,677-foot (2,950-m) summit. This was where the magmatic eruption everyone was waiting for was expected to happen. Only thus far not a rock of fresh lava had erupted. Thompson reports that Swanson, soon after arriving, had even bought a ladle and a yardstick, duct taped the two together and talked the helicopter pilot into hovering above the crater between eruptions so he could ladle up some ash, just to check. As with the ash everywhere on the eastern flank the ash around the mouth of the crater was solid, not molten. Where was the magma? Would this be another Soufrière, Guadeloupe? Was the evacuation necessary? Many people were climbing and flying over the mountain; the public was not convinced of imminent danger. T-shirt stands cropped up to commemorate the event. The National Guard was called in to help maintain roadblocks and set up safe viewing locations, but the extensive logging roads through the forest gave anyone who wanted access to the mountain unguarded back entrances.

The increasing number of earthquakes soon added a new feature specifically indicative of magma on the move. On April 1, the first *harmonic tremor* snaked like a sidewinder across the seismographs with no clear tectonic seismic waves initiating the motion. No lightning clap of a P wave; no thunderous echo and eventual decline of S waves: just small and steady tremors shook the mountain starting as suddenly as they stopped.

In early and mid April, clear views revealed a bizarre swelling on the northwest side of the summit. The surface deformation was so extensive it terrified Don Mullineaux to see it. Yet scientists continued to visit the summit. The helicopter pilot, a Vietnam War veteran, would keep the engine running. The HVO team flew out to Sugar Bowl, Goat Rocks, Dog Head, and other areas around the summit to hammer survey targets into the ice-covered, rocky dacite and andesite outcrops. The large highway reflectors bolted on top of the long steel pipes could be sited from miles away using the Smithsonian's *geodimeter*. From Timberline and other observations posts, the HVO monitoring team would repeatedly bounce a laser beam from the geodimeter off the reflectors on the summit and back to their instrument. Comparing the actual speed of the laser light beam to a calculated ideal wavelength of light given that day's temperature and atmospheric moisture, the team could measure the precise distance and, over time, the summit's rate of distortion. The process took hours. Typically the geodimeter was used to measure centimeters of surface change. "The Bulge," as it was soon called, was pushing out Goat Rocks dome and the surrounding flank at a rate of 5 feet (1.5 m) a day—directly in line with the soon to be established Coldwater II observation post. The swelling tore deep crevices into the glacier ice above the dome, the way a balloon covered heavily with fresh papier-mâché will crack the paste if inflated more. None of the volcanologists had ever seen a volcano behave in such a manner. They wondered how much further the Bulge could extend before collapsing and starting an avalanche or mudflow. When it collapsed they anticipated the awaiting magmatic eruption would follow.

By mid-April the phreatic explosions became quieter plume eruptions, some only 500 feet (152 m) high. These turned to steamy fumaroles by the end of the month. Johnston even dared a visit to the crater to collect water samples on April 30. Based on the reduction in plume ferocity, the volcano seemed to be calming down. The public increased pressure to return, but tiltmeters measuring the inclination of the domes continued to record changes to the slopes. A *correlation spectrometer* set up at Timberline also measured continuing emissions of sulfur dioxide coming from the crater. Forsythe Glacier in view of Timberline had risen 300 feet (91 m) higher than where it was when the avalanche that sprayed the parking lot hit on March 20. A staff writer at headquarters in Vancouver logging in the day's activities and notes on April 25, wrote that Crandell warned officials not to open Spirit Lake. The large earthquake or steam blast could send the 150-foot (46-m) thick mass of ice rushing down the mountain at speeds of 180 miles per hour (290 km/hr). The avalanche would reach Spirit Lake in two minutes, the log notes. Avalanche debris would scour highway 504. Crandell is reported as saying, "There will be no way to warn people. If they are in the path, they won't be able to get out of the way."

A compromise was made on April 30 that allowed some access to the mountain during daylight hours for loggers and property owners granted special permits. This was designated the Blue Zone. Anywhere within 3 miles (5 km) of the peak and ranging out as far as 7 miles (11 km) was designated the Red Zone—only officials such as law enforcement and scientists were still allowed access to this area. To better monitor the Bulge, the volcanologists decided on May 1 to move equipment and time-lapse cameras from the original Coldwater site to a new observation post closer to the summit they called Coldwater II. Perhaps to provide extra sleep time, or conserve fuel and costs (the helicopter made for an expensive mountain taxi), the USGS parked a camping trailer on the lookout so observers could spend the night rather than drive back down the mountain in the dark and return again before dawn.

Starting May 4, graduate student Harry Glicken (1958–91), working as a field assistant for Dave Johnston, volunteered to fill the post full-time. Given the new Red and Blue hazard zones and the acknowledgment that even the Blue zone was not a safe place to stay overnight, it is difficult to imagine today why the senior USGS volcanologists promoted taking such risk. The impromptu field station sat on a 1,200-foot (366-m) ridge, which theoretically should have contained any avalanche or mudflow. Geologically, it had done so in the past. Thirty-year-old David Johnston was not so certain history would play in their favor this time. He did not trust the Bulge and expressed concern about the possibility of a lateral blast. Though rare, lateral blasts were not without precedent at the time. Starting in late April, the team of volcanologists headquartered in Vancouver began combing through reports of such events in the past: Lassen Peak (Day and Allen, 1925), Bandai-san (Kuno, 1962), Bezymianny volcano (Gorshkov, 1959), Shiveluch volcano (Gorshkov and Dubik, 1970), and Mount Lamington (Taylor, 1958). Pictures of Bezymianny taken after its eruption look eerily like Mount St. Helens today.

By mid-May, Dan Miller and Rick Hoblitt had begun to worry about Glicken's safety. Hoblitt suggested that a video monitoring system would work as a 24-hour observer and even found a company that came out and set up a test of a system using a microwave signal to communicate to Vancouver. The only drawback was it would cost $40,000 to permanently install. With the monitoring operations already costing the USGS $2,000 a day plus $300 an hour for the helicopter, Robert Tilling, account supervisor for volcano monitoring, had to draw his purse string taut. Miller ordered an armored personnel carrier that would provide Glicken and any other visiting observers a place to batten down the hatches and maybe ride out the pumice and bomb falls Miller envisioned might accompany an eruption. The armored vehicle—likely an M113, the type used in Vietnam and later in Iraq, as well as on the NASA launch pad at the Kennedy Space Center in case of an emergency evacuation—was scheduled to arrive on Sunday May 18. Miller was the only one of the original Denver team in Washington that weekend. Crandell and Hoblitt had returned to Denver and Mullineaux was visiting his daughter in Southern California.

On May 17th, Glicken, who photojournalist James Balog described as a "hyper 22-year old budding volcanologist," had to leave his post for a few days to meet with his prospective adviser Richard Fisher (1928–2002) at the University of California in Santa Barbara. Despite the seeming benign steam eruptions that had dominated most of the month, the fear that the Bulge on the volcano had become unstable was palpable in Vancouver; even more reason to continue measuring its growth, some maintained.

Miller was convinced that if the volcano were going to release a magmatic eruption, their instruments would give them a couple hours of notice. So far, all the signals seemed to be marching along with no discernible change. Frequent earthquakes still rattled the ground, the sulfur dioxide continued to increase, the tiltmeters reported more tilt, but no change in the rate. No change in the status quo of a volcano that was already close to bursting. They would have to wait until the morning of the 18th for the Oregon National Guard to fly an infrared reconnaissance mission over the summit to check for any rise in magma closer to the surface. Until then, it seemed best to continue operations as planned. During the morning meeting at headquarters on the 17th, Swanson promised to take over for Glicken for the next few days. Then Swanson remembered that the graduate student who had been visiting him was heading back home to Germany on the morning of the 18th. Could Johnston spot the site for tonight? Swanson said he would take over with the geodimeter on the afternoon of the 18th. In the meantime, Johnston could use Caltech graduate student Mindy Brugman's newer Laser Ranger, which was slightly less precise than the old geodimeter, but at the rate the Bulge was growing a centimeter made no difference in a reading. The Laser Ranger also had the advantage of being less complicated and faster to point and shoot for long distance measurements of the Bulge. Johnston agreed—reluctantly. "Johnston would risk his neck when he thought he could get good data," wrote Thompson. "But just sitting on a ridge, with the bulge practically pushing directly at you, no, that wasn't anything he really wanted to do." Brugman had already showed Johnston how to use the instrument the previous week, and although he was impressed he was far more interested in the gas emissions from the fumaroles. Johnston was in charge of expanding the USGS monitoring system of volcanic gasses throughout the west coast. Before driving up to camp at the ridge he took one more flight out to the Bulge to check the temperature of a fumarole. Within 12 minutes the ground began to swell and crack open. Johnston having taken a temperature of a relatively cool vent at 190°F (88°C) ran back to the waiting helicopter pilot, who had kept the blades still spinning.

Brugman and USGS hydrologist Carolyn Driedger had spent much of the day driving within the mountain's Red Zone and arrived at Coldwater II expecting to stay overnight. The women had their camping gear in Brugman's truck. That same day a moving van accompanied a caravan of 50 homeowners escorted by officials into the restricted regions of the Red Zone to remove belongings. They were out before dark. By 7 P.M., Johnston convinced Brugman and Driedger to return to a safer venue as well. Glicken left an hour later. The sun set that night at around 8:40 P.M., three days after a new moon. The clear night would have made an impressive stargazing opportunity with the silhouette of St. Helens looming in the southern horizon.

The next morning, Johnston was not alone on the mountain. Two miles north of him, 65-year-old Gerry Martin, a retired Navy radio-operator helping with observations, had a view of Johnston's trailer and the Bulge. A small crew of loggers led by James Scymanky, 36, and father of four, continued to work over the weekend in the Blue Zone. In another part of the forest, Valerie Pierson, 23, a tree-planting inspector for the U.S. Forest Service, was leaping from one log to the next to catch up with her crew. After a visit to a school in Oregon on May 14, Harry Truman was back at his lodge near Spirit Lake with his 16 wild cats. From Portland, a mother and her 19-year-old daughter had driven up highway 504 to see the 5:30 A.M. sunrise from Elk Rock viewpoint, a ridge about 11 miles (18 km) northwest of the summit. Down in the valley, 21-year-old Venus Dergan and her friend Roald Reitan, 20, from Tacoma, Washington, were salmon fishing along the Toutle River about 35 miles (56 km) downstream of the summit.

Back at Coldwater II, Johnston fixed Brugman's Laser Ranger on the Bulge looming toward him. The Bulge was growing in spurts, as though someone was trying to blow up a giant air mattress inside the mountain without pinching the air tube shut between breaths. He marked the position of the highway reflectors starting at 5:53 A.M. and then monitored the distance every half hour for an hour. Johnston was sitting 4.80771 miles (7.73725 km) from the Bulge and it was getting closer. He radioed the readings to Vancouver and briefly joked with the radio dispatcher before ending the call.

At Bear Meadow, northeast of Spirit Lake and 11 miles (18 km) from the summit, photographer Gary Rosenquist set up his tripod and 35-mm camera while his friend William Dilley watched the mountain. Above them all, 23-year-old pilot Bruce Judson was flying geologists Dorothy and Keith Stoffel around the summit in a Cessna 182 plane. Dorothy would turn 31 on May 23; the flight was an early birthday gift for the volcano lover.

At 8:32 A.M. a shallow earthquake of magnitude 5.1 and a depth of 1 mile (1.6 km) struck beneath St. Helens. Swanson radioed Johnston, but the repeater that relays the signal did not pick up. Rosenquist snapped a photograph and advanced his film. The volcano looked fuzzy and out of focus, but it was not his eyes or the camera. Dorothy Stoffel sitting in the front passenger seat of the Cessna saw rocks and ice crumple into the crater. Less than 20 seconds later the Bulge on the northwest side of the volcano began to "ripple and churn" and then slide down the mountain in a single slice. The debris avalanche began racing down the flank at speeds of 110 to 155 miles per hour (177 to 250 km/hr). As the Bulge fell away, a hidden underground plug of cooled dark black magma, a cryptodome, exploded out laterally from the summit. The release of pressure sent high-temperature steam and gases previously trapped in channels and deep within fissures erupting through the surface. Seconds later half of the summit itself collapsed behind the falling Bulge. With the cryptodome exposed to two openings, both the top and northwest flank, the pressure of the hot magma behind the champagne cork of the cryptodome erupted with full fury. Johnston unsuccessfully radioed his last transmission to headquarters. Ham operators across the state listening in heard: "Vancouver, Vancouver! This is it!" A pause. "Vancouver, this is Johnston, over!"

Gerry Martin from the next ridge over from Johnston calls out over his ham radio: ". . . the northwest section and north section is blowing up, coming over the ridge towards me. I'm gonna back outta here. Gentlemen, the, uh, camper and car sitting over to the south of me is covered. It's gonna get me, too. We can't get out of here."

Judson dips the wing toward the summit to give the Stoffels a better view and seeing the erupting plume turns the plane and points the nose to the ground to build speed. Seeing the plume

Mount Saint Helens erupting May 18, 1980. (U.S. Geological Survey)

roiling to the northwest, Keith directs Judson to turn south. Lightning fills the sky but the only sound they hear is the props of the engine. On the ground the massive eruption was also seen but not heard for a radius of about 20 miles around the summit. The only sound of danger that James Scymanky heard in this "quiet zone" was the voice of one of his three crewmen, Jose Dias, 33, yelling in Spanish that the volcano was exploding, followed by the sound of trees being shredded as the blast passed close to where they stood. Of the four, three were found alive and rescued by National Guard helicopters nine hours later, but only Scymanky survived.

Valerie Pierson and her crew of tree planters also survived thanks to the Forest Service supervisor Kathy Anderson who coordinated their evacuation. Anderson had three teams on the south flank, and she drove closer to the erupting mountain to meet them when one of her inspectors radioed that he did not know the predetermined evacuation route. Anderson's was the first radio call from the field that Vancouver headquarters received. She had all three teams in an open field ready for a helicopter evacuation, but none was available. With hard hats on for safety, the three teams drove out in their trucks following Anderson's lead.

The magmatic blast emerged from the volcano, traveling 220 miles per hour up and out, quickly overtook the debris avalanche along the

Scientists of the Decade: U.S. Geological Survey Scientists

In 1979 the U.S. Geological Survey celebrated its 100th anniversary. Congress and then President Rutherford Hayes established the Survey in 1879 as part of the Department of Interior for the "classification of the public lands, and examination of the geological structure, mineral resources, and products of the national domain." Geologists surveyed and mapped the country and found that in some regions water was a scarcer resource than gold, silver, iron, coal, copper, lead, zinc, or petroleum. The Survey has continued to monitor these resources as part of its mission helping the government determine land use policies. The USGS led the 1970 census-based publication of *"The National Atlas of the United States of America,"* which went beyond combining population maps with natural resources, topography, and agriculture as was done with previous atlases. The maps in the 1970 atlas added historical comparisons of land use and descriptive details about how human activities change the environment. In its centennial decade, the Survey marked one of the longest standing scientific exploratory bodies established by the United States since President Abraham Lincoln ushered in the National Academies of Sciences.

In the second half of the 20th century, the development of nuclear weapons and the race to the Moon provided the Survey with new geological challenges. In 1956 USGS scientists were put in charge of evaluating the geologic and hydrologic contamination from underground tests at the Atomic Energy Commission's Nevada Test Site. Further investigations into nuclear power as an alternative energy source lead to debates about the safe disposal of radioactive wastes. Nuclear power plants generate safe electrical power, but what is left of the reactor fuel after the process remains a dangerous by-product. In 1957 the National Academies of Sciences recommended putting radioactive wastes deep underground. As a temporary solution until a permanent structure could be built, nuclear facilities responded by burying their waste in nearby locations. The

practice had been a standard means of disposal for toxic chemical wastes long before radioactive wastes became an issue. In the 1970s, the health hazard from the chemical landfill at Love Canal in Niagara Falls, New York, brought the issue of land use for toxic sites of all types to Congressional attention. In 1978, under the Carter administration, the U.S. Department of Energy began studying Nevada's Yucca Mountain as one of many possible storage areas for spent nuclear reactor fuel and other high-level nuclear waste. In the 21st century, the issue of geologic and hydrologic contamination is still a major part of the discussion regarding the construction of a repository for America's hazardous nuclear waste.

Also in the 21st century, as NASA begins again to plan lunar missions, the USGS will once more play an important role. Starting in 1959, USGS geologists began compiling photographs of the Moon to examine locations of craters. Multiple hypotheses about the origin of the Moon, its dusty surface, and its frequency for experiencing collisions with rogue asteroids, comets, or other bolides abounded. When President John F. Kennedy declared in 1961 a manned mission to the Moon by the end of the decade, USGS geologist and lunar enthusiast Eugene Shoemaker responded by establishing a new field in science called astrogeology. Also recognized as planetary science, the field draws on what is known in the Earth sciences to compare and understand geologic features on the Moon, as well as other planets and their satellites. Shoemaker (1928–97) used the desert in Flagstaff, Arizona, as an analogue for training astronauts how to examine geologic features they could expect to find on the Moon. At the time one of the questions regarding the craters on the Moon was whether they were impact events or volcanic in origin. Shoemaker had seen similar craters while evaluating the test site for atomic bombs in Nevada. He had also identified coesite, or *shocked quartz,* along the ring of the craters both at the test site and at the Barringer Meteor Crater in Winslow, Arizona,

NASA astronauts training in the Nevada desert in 1964. (NASA)

where he had done his Ph.D. dissertation. His work provided conclusive evidence for determining the origins of a crater, especially helpful when volcanic evidence was missing.

Shoemaker dreamed of surveying the Moon's surface as an astronaut, but a health issue hindered his ambitions. When the Apollo astronauts joined him in the desert in Arizona he prepared them in his stead to become lunar geologists. When the time came to share their adventures with the world, Shoemaker sat next to news reporter Walter Cronkite on the night of July 20, 1969, and provided a play-by-play of the evening's events. In 1972 the first geologist turned astronaut, Jack Schmitt, stepped on the Moon. His were also the last steps on the Moon during the 20th century. Although in a fitting tribute, Shoemaker posthumously crash-landed on the moon in 1999. Shoemaker died in a car accident in 1997 and his ashes were sent onboard *Lunar Prospector,* a spacecraft designed to end its mission as a man-made impact event on the moon to evaluate the crater-induced ejecta.

After completing detailed analyses of the Moon, the USGS and NASA turned their sights on Mars and other planets in the 1970s. In preparation for spacecraft reconnaissance, astrogeologists at the Flagstaff Science Center made 100 maps of Mars, Mercury, and Venus. When the Viking spacecrafts landed on the surface of Mars in 1976, astrogeologists had selected the landing sites. Before any human astrogeologists step foot on Mars in the 21st century, attempts at robotic missions to return with samples in tow will likely precede. The Apollo missions, primarily 15, 16, and 17, the last one, collectively brought back to Earth 841.5 pounds (381.7 kg) of dust and rock samples. The Soviet lunar sample return missions during the 1970s demonstrated the ability as well as the difficulties faced in robotic missions. After multiple attempts, the Luna missions 16, 20, and 24 collectively returned 0.66 pounds (326 g) of moon rocks, sand, and dust. In the 1970s it was unknown whether the meteorites might have originated from the Moon or Mars. Such a hypothesis would have to wait until the 1980s.

northwest flank, gained speed traveling down the flank, and flew over the distant ridges accelerating to 670 miles per hour. The cresting front wave of the lateral blast traveled even faster, at times breaking the 735 miles per hour sound barrier. People in the path of the eruption died of flash burns and asphyxiation. Others hit by the passing edge of the blast walked out of 300°C temperatures with only their hair singed.

The turbulent air sent the sound waves scattering to various temperature layers in the atmosphere. The sonic booms from the eruption could be heard as far away as Canada and echoed in some regions off the flanks of other Cascade volcanoes. Only 50 miles away in Portland, Oregon, the ash fell as silently as snow. The eruption obliterated everything in its path within 8 miles, felled the rest of the forest of 25-foot-high trees out to 19 miles, and left a periphery of standing trees torched dead. The North Fork of the Toutle River channeled the blast and debris down the valley where it overwhelmed Venus Dergan and Roald Reitan's camping site. Caught in the middle of the lahar as they scrambled to the roof of their car, Reitan escaped by jumping from one felled log sheared of its branches to another. He quickly learned to sit on them with his feet up to protect his legs from being crushed. When Dergan submerged into the milky white flow of ashy water Reitan tried three times to bring her up, finally lifting her above the surface by her hair. Dergan, Reitan, Pierson, Scymanky, Judson, and the Stoffels all shared their stories of survival with news teams in the Pacific Northwest years later in commemoration of the eruption's anniversary. Rosenquist spent 30 frantic seconds snapping pictures, and then he and Dilley dodged the blast driving as fast as they could down the mountain. Rosenquist would sell his photos to *National Geographic.*

The National Guard helicopter pilots would ultimately rescue 130 survivors by the end of the day. When Glicken heard of the eruption he spent the day jumping in one helicopter after another searching for Johnston. The region had changed so dramatically it was impossible to follow their maps with any accuracy. Shards from part of the camper and its propane tank were reportedly found in 1997, three miles from the newly established Johnston Ridge Observatory that sits on the former site of Coldwater II. The observatory is now the principal viewing site for the ongoing activity of the new dome growing within the horseshoe-shaped crater.

Further Reading

Balog, James. "Back to the Blast." *National Geographic Adventure* (December 2004/January 2005): 74–80, 92–95. Balog revisits the site of the eruption he witnessed in 1980.

Bentley, Charles. "Response of the West Antarctic Ice Sheet to CO_2 Induced Climatic Warming." In *Environmental and Societal Consequences* *of a Possible CO$_2$-Induced Climate Change* Vol. 2. Washington, D.C.: Dept. of Energy, 1980. Antarctic explorer and geophysicist Charles Bentley of the University of Wisconsin-Madison presents evidence of increased melting given an increased carbon dioxide environment.

Carson, Rob. *Mount St. Helens: The Eruption and Recovery of a Volcano.* Seattle, Washington: Sasquatch Books, 2002 (20th anniversary edition). This book details the history of the eruption and the amazing ecological comeback that followed within three years.

Cloud, Preston. *Cosmos, Earth, and Man: A Short History of the Universe.* New Haven: Yale University Press, 1978. This book summarizes the history of the planet and the evolution of life on its surface.

Crandell, Dwight R., Donal R. Mullineaux, and Meyer Rubin. "Mount St. Helens Volcano: Recent and Future Behavior." *Science* 187 (1975): 438–441. U.S. Geological Survey scientists warn of potential for disaster.

Crandell, Dwight R., and Donal R. Mullineaux. *Potential Hazards from Future Eruptions of Mount St. Helens Volcano, Washington: U.S. Geological Survey Bulletin 1383-C.* U.S. Geological Survey, 1978. Crandell and Mullineaux predict St. Helens will be the next Cascade volcano to erupt.

Eddy, Jack A. "The Maunder Minimum." *Science* 192 (1976): 1,189–1,202. The Maunder Minimum is the name of the period from about 1645 to 1715 C.E. when sunspots rarely occurred.

———. "The Maunder Minimum: A Reappraisal." *Solar Physics* 87 (1980). Further research on sunspot history.

Ehrlich, Paul R., and J. P. Holdren. "Impact of Population Growth." *Science* 171 (1971): 1,212–1,214. A look at the environmental risks from human overpopulation.

Eldredge, Niles, and Stephen J. Gould. "Punctuated equilibria: an alternative to phyletic gradualism." In *Models in Paleobiology*, edited by T. J. M. Schopf, 82–115. San Francisco: Freeman, Cooper, and Co., 1972. Eldredge and Gould criticize the hypothesis that evolution occurs through gradual phyletic changes and argue instead that evolution proceeds in a pattern of punctuated equilibrium.

Fisher, Richard V. *Out of the Crater: Chronicles of a Volcanologist.* Princeton: Princeton University Press, 1999. Fisher describes his early work in the military watching nuclear detonations at Bikini Atoll and his later work identifying volcanic base surges and pyroclastic flows.

Flohn, Hermann. "On Time Scales and Causes of Abrupt Paleoclimatic Events." *Quaternary Research* 12 (1979): 135–149. A look at what climate has done in geologic times.

Freeland, G. L., and Dietz, R. S. "Plate Tectonics in the Caribbean: a Reply." *Nature* 235 (21 January 1972): 156–157. In response to criticism the authors are given space to elaborate on their 1971 paper on the subject.

Freeman, Kenneth P., and Kuo-Nan Liou. "Climatic Effects of Cirrus Clouds." *Advances in Geophysics* 21 (1979): 231–287. Good? Bad? The debate is set.

Fritts, H. C. *Tree Rings and Climate.* London: Academic Press, 1976. What dendrochronology says about climate change.

GARP (National Academy of Sciences, United States Committee for the Global Atmospheric Research Program), *Understanding Climatic Change: A Program for Action.* Washington, D.C.; Detroit, Mich.: National Academy of Sciences; Grand River Books, 1975. People might not change the weather, but they might change the climate.

Gould, Stephen J. "Evolution's erratic pace." *Natural History* 86 (May 1977): 12–16. Gould discusses punctuated equilibrium.

Hammer, Claus U., et al. "Greenland Ice Sheet Evidence of Post-Glacial Volcanism and Its Climatic Impact." *Nature* 288 (1980): 230–235. Volcanism after the ice age.

Hansen, James E., et al. "Mount Agung Eruption Provides Test of a Global Climatic Perturbation." Science 199 (1978): 1,065–1,068. When aerosols reach the stratosphere they can circulate the heavens for years.

———, et al. "Climatic Effects of Atmospheric Aerosols." *Annals of the New York Academy of Sciences* 338 (1980): 575–587. The cooling effects of aerosols.

Hays, James D. et al. "Variations in the Earth's Orbit: Pacemaker of the Ice Ages." *Science* 194 (1976): 1,121–1,132. A renewed interest in Milankovitch cycles.

Holden, Constance. "Smithsonian Center: A Phenomenon in Its Own Right." *Science* 183, no. 4120 (Jan. 11, 1974): 55–57. A review of the Smithsonian Institution's Center for Short-Lived Phenomena.

Imbrie, John, and Katherine Palmer Imbrie. *Ice Ages: Solving the Mystery.* Cambridge, Mass.: Harvard University Press, 1979. A renewed look at Milankovitch cycles, this was followed by a revised 1986 edition.

——— and John Z. Imbrie. "Modelling the Climatic Response to Orbital Variations." *Science* 207 (1980): 943–953. The importance of Earth's orbit in driving climate change.

Keeling, Charles D. "The Influence of Mauna Loa Observatory on the Development of Atmospheric CO_2 Research." In *Mauna Loa Observatory. A 20th Anniversary Report. (National Oceanic and Atmospheric Administration Special Report, September 1978),* edited by John Miller, pp. 36–54. Boulder, Colo.: NOAA Environmental Research Laboratories, 1978. Available online. URL: http://www.mlo.noaa.gov/HISTORY/PUBLISH/20th%20anniv/co2.htm and http://www.mlo.noaa.gov/HISTORY/Fhistory.htm. Accessed February 5, 2007.

Leopold, Luna B. *Water: A Primer.* San Francisco: W. H Freeman Co., 1974. A classic in hydrology and the start of a movement in stream gauges.

Molina, Mario J., and F. S. Rowland. "Stratospheric Sink for Chlorofluoromethanes: Chlorine Atom-Catalysed Destruction of Ozone." *Nature* 249 (1974): 810–812. This paper provides evidence of human induced atmospheric change through the use of CFCs.

NASA "*Landsat* Then and Now." A history of how *Landsat* satellites will save the world. Available online. URL: http://landsat.gsfc.nasa.gov/about/ Accessed February 5, 2007.

National Academy of Sciences, Committee to Study the Long-Term Worldwide Effect of Multiple Nuclear-Weapons Detonations. *Long-Term Worldwide Effect of Multiple Nuclear-Weapons Detonations.* Washington, D.C.: National Academy of Sciences, 1975. A study on what might happen to the Earth's environment if all the bombs blew up at once.

Nature. "France: La Soufrière's first victim." *Nature* 264 (December 9, 1976): 500. A news report from La Recherche, France, discusses the "fierce disagreement" that characterized the debate among French scientists about La Soufrière, the volcano in Guadeloupe in the French Antilles of the Caribbean.

Ralph, Elizabeth K., and Henry N. Michael. "Twenty-Five Years of Radiocarbon Dating." *American Scientist* 62, no. 5 (1974): 553–560. A history of radiocarbon dating methods.

Sagan, Carl, et al., "Anthropogenic Albedo Changes and the Earth's Climate." *Science* 206 (1979): 1,363–1,368. How human induced changes to the landscape reflect heat differently than nature intended.

Tazieff, Haroun. "La Soufrière, volcanology and forecasting." *Nature* 269 (September 8, 1977): 96–97. A rebuttal to the 1976 news article in *Nature.* Tazieff gives his point of view about the events leading up to his dismissal as director of volcanology at the Institute of Physics of the Globe.

Thompson, Dick. *Volcano Cowboys: The Rocky Evolution of a Dangerous Science.* New York: St. Martin's Press, 2000. This *Time* reporter tells the story of the events leading up to the eruption of Mount St. Helens and the lessons volcanologists learned and applied to other volcanoes.

Urey, Harold C. "Cometary collisions and geological periods." *Nature* 242 (1973): 32–33. Urey strengthens his earlier cometary hypothesis that impact events punctuate the terminations of geologic periods in light of the recent lunar investigations.

Wang, Steve C., and Peter Dodso. "Estimating the Diversity of Dinosaurs." *Proceedings of the National Academy of Sciences* 103 (2006): 13,601–13,605. A statistical analysis of the fossil record.

Weertman, Johannes. "Milankovitch Solar Radiation Variations and Ice Age Ice Sheet Sizes." *Nature* 261 (1976): 17–20. Further investigation on Milankovitch cycles.

Williams, Richard S. Jr., and James G. Moore. *Man Against Volcano: The Eruption on Heimaey, Vestmannaeyjar, Iceland.* USGS, (second edition) 1983. When water worked to slow a lava flow. A pdf of the booklet is available online. URL: http://pubs.usgs.gov/gip/heimaey/ Accessed February 5, 2007.

9

1981–1990:
A Watchful Planet

Introduction

The 1980s provided much debate and focus on hazard mitigation. Further investigations into the 19th-century New Madrid earthquakes lent insight into inter-plate tectonics. Seismic studies along the Mississippi River showed the region under stress proportional to the rest of the continent, but responding differently due to ancient reactivated faults. The risk of strong earthquakes as these faults continue to respond to the stresses puts new attention on building codes in the region. Action to change remains a function of the economic costs to do so, in addition to the perception of risk.

One of the most astronomical risk hazards is an impact event from space. At the start of the 1980s few considered space debris a threat to life on Earth. By the end of the decade that view would change. Astronomers have taken the threat to the future seriously enough to catalog every large asteroid they find.

When it comes to perceiving risk, one of the most astounding aspects of humanity is a shared complacency to live on the flanks of a volcano. Mount St. Helens proved that even under high alert and evacuation orders people can be lulled into a sense of normalcy in regards to an eruption after only a few weeks. On St. Helens, the public and scientists alike sought the spectacular views out of curiosity and a desire to better understand what was happening. Mount St. Helens tested the skills of volcanologists and the mettle of authorities to enforce an evacuation and resist a naive public's desire to return to status quo despite the fact that the environment was no longer the same. At Nevado del Ruiz in Colombia, the situation could not have been more different.

Local Colombian authorities and scientists unfamiliar with volcanology sought help and received some international assistance in interpreting and monitoring the newly awakened volcano. Colombian geologists, hydroelectric engineers, and civil defense teams succeeded in producing a hazard map, but failed to adequately communicate the importance of a speedy evacuation or enforce the evacuation once the decision was

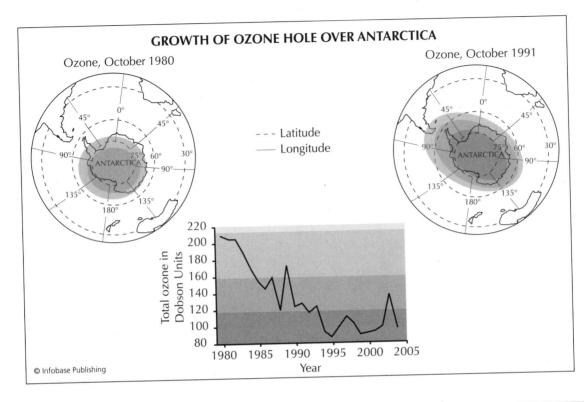

GROWTH OF OZONE HOLE OVER ANTARCTICA

Ozone, October 1980

Ozone, October 1991

- - - Latitude
— Longitude

© Infobase Publishing

Pagan Island in the Mariana Islands erupts explosively on May 15 prompting an evacuation. Volcanic activity continues for four years producing 0.06 cubic miles (0.25 km³) of tephra and 0.01 cubic miles (0.052 km³) of lava

U.S. Geological Survey under the Volcano Hazards Program began an intensive effort to monitor and study geologic unrest in Long Valley caldera in California

A severe El Niño develops in an unexpected manner; its evolution is recorded in detail with newly developed ocean buoys

Studies from the *Lageos* satellite indicate that the Earth's gravitational field is changing

MILESTONES

1981

1982

1983

Cambridge University amalgamates its departments of geology, mineralogy and petrology, and geophysics into a new department of Earth sciences. As a result of this change, the Sedgwick Geological Museum is renamed the Sedgwick Museum of Earth Sciences

El Chichón in Mexico erupts explosively on March 28 and April 3. Volcanic activity continues until September 11, producing 0.6 cubic miles (2.5 km³) of tephra, and causing pyroclastic flows, and lahars that kill 2,000 people

After years of intermittent eruptions, Kilauea in Hawaii begins a basaltic lava eruption in January that will continue well into the 21st century. On November 16, an earthquake of magnitude 6.7 causes a section of the road around Kilauea to fall into the crater

(Opposite page) NOAA atmospheric chemist Susan Solomon (b. 1956) led expeditions to observe the growth of the ozone hole.

made. The townsfolk, mayor, and religious leaders of Armero who were most at risk from volcanic mudflows after an eruption, had no previous experience to help them judge the risks or communicate the appropriate response to others. Many falsely equated a mudflow with something slow, like the lava flows on Hawaii. The promise prior to the eruption that they would have two hours to evacuate once the warning was made only reinforced the erroneous concept. Earth scientists studying natural hazards continue to learn from disasters the importance of educating the public about what to expect.

The Deadly Snow of Ruiz

After 140 years of providing a silent majesty of fertile soil for rice farms and coffee tree plantations, Colombia's Nevado del Ruiz volcano in the northern South American Andes shook to life. Locals in the city of Manizales, in the state of Caldas, searched for experts in the country who could help monitor the mountain and advise them about the significance of the earthquakes and the sulfuric gas clouds erupting from the summit. The Colombian Institute of Geology and Mining "INGEOMINAS,"

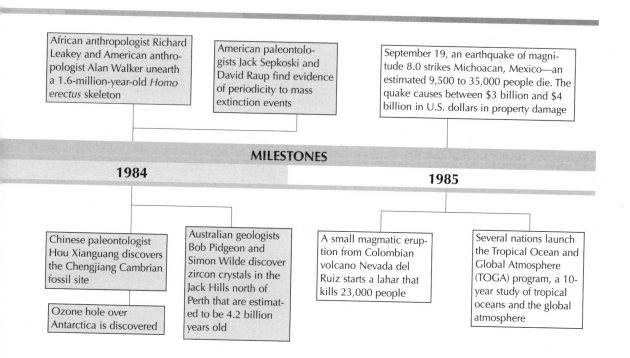

African anthropologist Richard Leakey and American anthropologist Alan Walker unearth a 1.6-million-year-old *Homo erectus* skeleton

American paleontologists Jack Sepkoski and David Raup find evidence of periodicity to mass extinction events

September 19, an earthquake of magnitude 8.0 strikes Michoacan, Mexico—an estimated 9,500 to 35,000 people die. The quake causes between $3 billion and $4 billion in U.S. dollars in property damage

MILESTONES

1984

1985

Chinese paleontologist Hou Xianguang discovers the Chengjiang Cambrian fossil site

Australian geologists Bob Pidgeon and Simon Wilde discover zircon crystals in the Jack Hills north of Perth that are estimated to be 4.2 billion years old

A small magmatic eruption from Colombian volcano Nevada del Ruiz starts a lahar that kills 23,000 people

Several nations launch the Tropical Ocean and Global Atmosphere (TOGA) program, a 10-year study of tropical oceans and the global atmosphere

Ozone hole over Antarctica is discovered

a government-run organization, agreed to help with monitoring even though they did not have any volcanologists on staff. A decision was made to send any seismic recordings to the National University in Bogotá, even though the geologists there were not familiar with an active volcano either. In November 1984, nobody in Colombia knew the difference between interpreting terrestrial earthquakes and volcanic tremors.

Borrowed seismometers were placed in various locations around the summit, and the state hydroelectric company gave the job of monitoring the volcano to a small team of employees in Manizales: a civil engineer, a chemical engineer, and a geologist trained in finding fossil fuel deposits and geothermal springs. Technicians helped them with setting up the seismometers and tried their best to keep them working. Unlike the telemetered seismometers on Mount St. Helens, these did not have radio transmitters to send their seismic signals to a university lab. The seismometers on Nevado del Ruiz recorded seismic tremors on a drum containing a roll of paper that had to be replaced every day with a fresh drum. Unfortunately, the civil engineer replacing the drums had no understanding of the significance of the seismograms. He and the technicians stayed in a house only a few miles from the summit and after a week or more of collecting the old drums, Bernardo Salazar would make

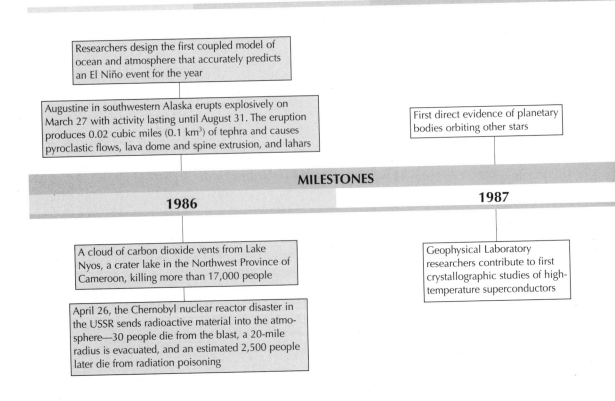

Researchers design the first coupled model of ocean and atmosphere that accurately predicts an El Niño event for the year

Augustine in southwestern Alaska erupts explosively on March 27 with activity lasting until August 31. The eruption produces 0.02 cubic miles (0.1 km^3) of tephra and causes pyroclastic flows, lava dome and spine extrusion, and lahars

First direct evidence of planetary bodies orbiting other stars

MILESTONES

1986

1987

A cloud of carbon dioxide vents from Lake Nyos, a crater lake in the Northwest Province of Cameroon, killing more than 17,000 people

Geophysical Laboratory researchers contribute to first crystallographic studies of high-temperature superconductors

April 26, the Chernobyl nuclear reactor disaster in the USSR sends radioactive material into the atmosphere—30 people die from the blast, a 20-mile radius is evacuated, and an estimated 2,500 people later die from radiation poisoning

the two-hour drive down the mountain 19 miles (30 km) to Manizales to meet the rest of the volcano monitoring team, Nestor García and Marta Calvache, and discuss the earthquake recordings on the seismograms. They could not differentiate between significant events and malfunctions in the instruments, and frequently attributed the strong winds on the summit as a source of the recordings. Still, they would send the seismograms on to the nation's capital, Bogotá, roughly 100 miles (161 km) east around the mountain and over the river valleys. Sometimes more than a month would pass before they received a report in return, one frequently accompanied with a complaint that an instrument was likely not working properly. The reports were deprived of practical significance. The fact that the volcano was active was something the new team of volcanologists-in-training could see for themselves.

In February 1985, the team scrambled over glaciers with a guide to the volcano's summit where they saw gray *pyroclastic debris*, ash, tephra, and a gaping crater with a steaming green lake in the middle. Next to the lake, mud gurgled to the surface forming a mud volcano. A year earlier 328 feet (100 m) of ice and snow had hidden all but the crater's brim. The 17,457 feet (5,321 m) high peaks of Colombia's Nevada del Ruiz are capped with 10 square miles (25 km²) of snow and ice. The lush valleys

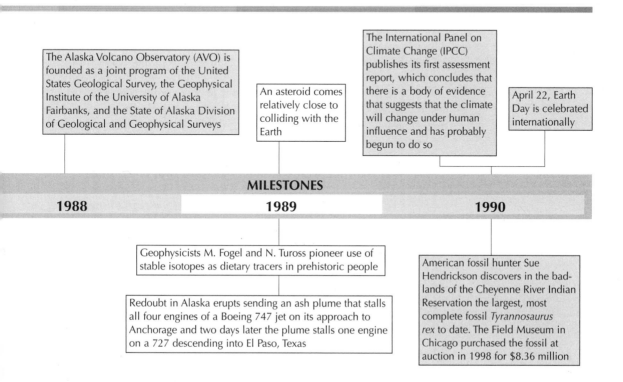

The Alaska Volcano Observatory (AVO) is founded as a joint program of the United States Geological Survey, the Geophysical Institute of the University of Alaska Fairbanks, and the State of Alaska Division of Geological and Geophysical Surveys

An asteroid comes relatively close to colliding with the Earth

The International Panel on Climate Change (IPCC) publishes its first assessment report, which concludes that there is a body of evidence that suggests that the climate will change under human influence and has probably begun to do so

April 22, Earth Day is celebrated internationally

MILESTONES

1988   **1989**   **1990**

Geophysicists M. Fogel and N. Tuross pioneer use of stable isotopes as dietary tracers in prehistoric people

Redoubt in Alaska erupts sending an ash plume that stalls all four engines of a Boeing 747 jet on its approach to Anchorage and two days later the plume stalls one engine on a 727 descending into El Paso, Texas

American fossil hunter Sue Hendrickson discovers in the badlands of the Cheyenne River Indian Reservation the largest, most complete fossil *Tyrannosaurus rex* to date. The Field Museum in Chicago purchased the fossil at auction in 1998 for $8.36 million

flanking the mountain are irrigated with meltwater and fertilized with mineral-rich mudflows. In her book on Colombia's volcanic disasters, *No Apparent Danger*, science journalist Victoria Bruce reports that Calvache drove out to the National Library in Bogotá to look up past eruptions. The geologist discovered that mudflows from Nevado del Ruiz had flowed down two rivers that meet to form the Langunillas River valley in 1595 and again in 1845, even topping over a ridge. She read descriptions of how most of the victims became immobilized in the mud. Many who survived the immediate tumult died days later when help could not reach them. Groups of people who had sought safety on hilltops in the middle of the valley found themselves on small islands without rescue. The ones who survived had run to the sides of the valley and scrambled up over the ridges when they heard the roar of the flow upstream. Faced with such devastating history and the town of Armero, with a population of 29,000, built unknowingly on century-old graves, Calvache realized they were going to need a lot more help.

Two volcanologists affiliated with the United Nations came to check on the volcano. Minard L. "Pete" Hall, of the Geophysical Institute in Quito, Ecuador, and John Tomblin of the UN Disaster Relief Office worked with the civil defense coordinator in Manizales. In May of 1985, the Smithsonian's Scientific Event Alert Network sent out its first report card about Nevado del Ruiz listing Hall, Tomblin, and civil defense coordinator O. Gómez of Manizales as contacts. The report stated that there were "no operating seismographs in the region," but that "Colombian officials have begun the necessary studies." From accounts of earthquakes that lasted a half hour in December, Hall and Tomblin recognized the earthquakes as harmonic tremors—magma in the volcano was on the move. They recommended setting up a proper monitoring system and establishing evacuation procedures. Hall told the government official he was visiting in Manizales that the monthlong delay in communications to Bogotá was a waste of everyone's time and they should keep the base of operations and seismic assessments in Manizales. What they really needed was someone with volcanic experience who could monitor the volcano permanently.

Swiss volcanologist Bruno Martinelli visited as well and brought three more seismographs, all of which still needed their records handchecked on site. He helped the team carry one of the instruments to the crater where it would be checked roughly once a week and positioned the rest around the summit in areas where they could obtain optimal recordings on a daily basis. The Smithsonian alert network reported that the hydroelectric employees made their second visit to the crater on July 8 and saw that the lake had grown larger and deeper, covering the mud volcano. Yellow sulfur grains lined the crater walls. "On 22 February, there had been only a thin film of sulfur covering the surface near the fumaroles, but by July sand-sized material on the inner slopes of the crater was impregnated with sulfur deposits, creating a crust 10 cm thick."

This time the report listed Salazar, Calvache, and García as the primary contacts. On September 11, an eruption that lasted seven hours released enough ash to dust the streets of Manizales. The city of 350,000 on the western flank of Nevado del Ruiz suddenly became the focus of attention. For 12 miles a lahar of mud with chunks of ice chased the rivers on the western flank.

The eruption stepped up concern and public awareness that Nevado del Ruiz was an active volcano. The U.S. Geological Survey sent Darrel Herd, who years earlier had studied the volcano as part of his Ph.D. thesis. Unfortunately, he did not bring any telemetered seismometers to set up remote monitoring of the volcano. Instead, he spent a week digging around the riverbanks and came to the conclusion that Manizales had nothing to fear; it was far from any river a lahar would likely hit. INGEOMINAS, Civil Defense, the Manizales-based monitoring team, as well as university geology professors and students used Herd's analysis and maps of the area to determine the regions of greatest risk. Geology students took colored pencils to the map and highlighted the rivers flowing from the summit. Two rivers met up to form a path directly through the city of Armero. INGEOMINAS issued the preliminary hazard map on October 7 along with the promise that Armero could be evacuated in two hours. Many found the warning that geologists were 100 percent certain of an impending catastrophe in Armero, given specific volcanic conditions, difficult to understand and harder to accept. The press splashed across the front page of newspapers quotes from congressional officials in Bogotá calling the warning an overly alarmist act that was frightening the public. The knee-jerk reaction from the government representatives was uninformed considering that Colombian Civil Defense had spent 5.3 million pesos since April on emergency equipment preparing for just such a disaster. The expenditure covered "emergency communication equipment, uniforms and boots, ambulance tires, gas masks, emergency food and rations, and other items, including body bags," according to a National Academies Report. "This effort to support preparedness and disaster response was spread throughout the entire area, in all the communities at risk." The hazard map was posted in every low-lying village around Ruiz.

Those in Armero did not know what to believe. Their mayor denied the hazard map's credibility. Their questions went unanswered. How would they know when it was time to evacuate? Who would alert them—their mayor who thought the geologists were overreacting, in which case the call might come too late, or the jittery geologists who might send them packing during a false alarm? Where would they go? If the scientists and engineers were so certain that a mudflow would hit Armero following an eruption should they really wait for the eruption to happen before sounding the alarm? How dangerous was a mudflow anyway? Most of Armero trusted the promise that they could react quickly enough to evacuate on two hours notice. Some were skeptical of the whole situation but stayed for lack of a better alternative. The geologists and engineers knew the mudflow was a certainty if a large enough eruption happened. They did not know if the eruption was a certainty and did not understand the warning signs. A few homeowners on the volcano who paid close attention to their neighboring rivers had noticed that the water had become murkier; when they read the hazard reports they left immediately, no questions asked.

The U.S. Geological Survey heads recognized they had to take further action. Since Mount St. Helens's eruption, volcanologist Norm Banks started campaigning for an international volcano assistance team that could set up monitoring stations on active volcanoes around the world. Now the Survey turned for funding from the State Department's Office of Foreign Disaster Assistance. Come the first week of November, the USGS had approval to send six telemetered or sound-ranging seismometers that could be placed on the summit and crater of Nevado del Ruiz where they would send seismic readings directly to a computer in Manizales. Seismologist David Harlow, a former Vietnam Marine and a seasoned volcanologist on active volcanoes in Central America, was asked to accompany the shipment on November 7. Finally Salazar and the monitoring team would learn how to interpret the readings for volcanic tremors and have a real-time monitoring station up and operating. Then came November 6.

On that morning, Colombia woke up to leftist rebels attacking and occupying the country's Supreme Court: the Palace of Justice in Bogotá. The M-19 guerrillas took lawyers and judges hostage. President Belisario Betancur ordered the army to surround the courthouse. A tank rolled up the front steps. Negotiations did not lead to the guerrillas' surrender and the army forcefully took control. More than 100 people died, including 11 Supreme Court justices who the guerrillas may have executed prior to their own deaths. The siege effectively delayed the delivery of the seismometers to Nevado del Ruiz.

Then came November 13. On that morning, everything was peaceful. The volcano looked serene. When the needle on one of the seismometers began to wildly scratch the surface of its paper drum just after 3 P.M. no one noticed. At 4:30 P.M. Salazar and a new recruit to the team, Fernando Gil, who started assisting Salazar after the September ash fall, changed the drum and pondered over the recent seismic event. They had not felt any tremors and heard only the wind screaming over the ridge where the seismometer was stationed. Clouds covered the summit. Gil later told science writer Victoria Bruce that he dismissed the needle marking as an error, perhaps the wind, he said.

By 5 P.M. ash was falling on the streets of Armero. Upon hearing the news from the Red Cross, the Regional Emergency Committee put local police and civil leaders across the region on high alert, the public was advised to cover their noses and mouths with wet handkerchiefs and remove the ash from their roofs. The Civil Defense and other agencies began to prepare for evacuations as they convened a regularly scheduled meeting. Speaking over the church's loudspeaker, the local priest in Armero told the townsfolk to remain in their homes and remain calm; the radio played music. Rain mixed with the ash and turned the streets a slick, glistening gray. Around 7 P.M. the ash fall reportedly lightened up as the rainstorm became heavier, marked with flashes of lightning that intermittently knocked out power and thunder that masked the sound of the distant roar.

The magmatic eruption came at 9:08 P.M. This time Salazar and Gil as well as the two technicians asleep in the house near the summit both felt and heard the volcano explode—a minor cough in comparison to the May 18th eruption of St. Helens, but even more deadly. The team ran outside and saw lightning illuminate the clouds over the summit. Rocks, not just ash, started to fall from the sky. Salazar sounded the alarm. Yelling into the radio, he told a night guard on duty at the hydroelectric company's headquarters to call Civil Defense and start the evacuations. They could hear the rush of the mudflow starting its descent. The men and a neighboring family of six, carrying pots over their heads, jumped in the team's truck and safely escaped to Manizales. The lahar followed down the low-lying Chinchina River valley on the western flank where an estimated 1,800 people were washed away in the volcanic mudflow.

Ash and fresh lava rocks 1,650°F (900°C) in temperature erupted into the sky. The pyroclastic debris burned into the snow-capped Ruiz. The lower edge of four glaciers flanking 2 miles (3 km) of the summit retreated 650 feet (200 m). On the north and eastern flanks, icy waterfalls poured into three rivers: Azufrado, Lagunillas, and Gualm. The Azufrado and Lagunillas rivers converged midway down the mountainside, channeling deep into a narrow canyon along the Lagunillas River valley. The waters mixed with hot debris turned to warm mud. The lahar reached speeds of nearly 100 miles per hour (160 km/hr) picking up trees and boulders along the way. The river water surged forward in front of the mudflow.

In Armero the mayor and the priest continued to call for calm. Some ignored the civil leaders when they heard from friends and relatives 12 miles upstream that they had heard the roar of the mudflow on its way. Then the electricity in Armero blinked out and the only lights came from cars in the streets. Ham radio operators from neighboring villages on higher ground near the Azufrado River continued to transmit evacuation warnings to the lower-lying villages. Firemen finally received the message to evacuate at 10:45 P.M. and began yelling, blowing whistles, and knocking on homes demanding that people leave. Their panic was confusing to many they addressed who had equated the threat of a mudflow with something slow moving and thought they would have plenty of time. The mayor was one of these people. He was reportedly talking over the ham radio when the first of the lahar surges hit the town at 10 minutes before 11 P.M. "For most families the first effective message came from either seeing the advancing mud or hearing or seeing others fleeing from it," assessed National Academies in a later report.

The first surge that washed across the town was clear and cold water displaced from a nearby lake. A wave of mud followed. As the U-shaped valley opened, the lahar stretched out to meet the canyon walls. Even with a slower velocity of 28 miles per hour (45 km/hr), the lahar, reaching 6 to 17 feet (2 to 5 m) deep, acted as a battering ram of debris as it plowed through Armero picking up cars and smashing through concrete houses. As in the past, the people who ran the mile it took to get to safety up the sides of the valley survived. Those in the middle of the valley became trapped and then inundated by another surge of mud as lahars caught upstream behind natural dams built up pressure to break through them. For two hours the lahars continued to pulse in smaller waves.

The National Academies report stated that Red Cross paramedics from the city of Ibague left for Armero after losing radio contact during a conversation with the Armero Red Cross office. "They had no other information about what was happening at this time. They were among the first responders on the scene, arriving at Armero around 1:00 A.M. Nonetheless, rescue and medical efforts were somewhat limited until daylight."

Military helicopters came in the morning to begin rescue. At first the pilots did not know if anyone had survived. Mud-caked skin and hair camouflaged the survivors and victims alike. Then they saw people moving. Thousands of survivors were airlifted to distant hospitals. Many more walked for hours through the forests to reach help. The Colombian Red Cross and Civil Defense teams set up makeshift shelters, but many of these were only places where survivors could seek transportation elsewhere. The emergency teams had precious little drinking water to give out, let alone use to wash away the mud from injured bodies. Not since Montserrat had the death toll from an eruption been so high: 23,000 died from Nevado del Ruiz. When Calvache drove out to Armero to help, she did not understand what she was seeing, "You don't realize it the first time, well, those are bodies," she told reporters later. "And then you see one and you start to distinguish, but many, many, many, many, many bodies there." News of the devastation traveled around the world. Besides the usual medical supplies and financial support, international aid also came in the form of volcanological monitoring equipment and training.

Finding the Faults of New Madrid

In the dark morning hours of December 16, 1811, an earthquake with the seismic strength of San Francisco's 1906 temblor shook the east coast of the United States. Accounts of the event described shaking in Kentucky that lasted 15 minutes. Aftershocks continued throughout the morning. A week later another earthquake struck, and then another a week after that. The rocking and rolling motion of the Earth jarred much of the new year in 1812, striking in January and frequently in February to the point that "hardly a day passes but the trembling of the Earth is more or less

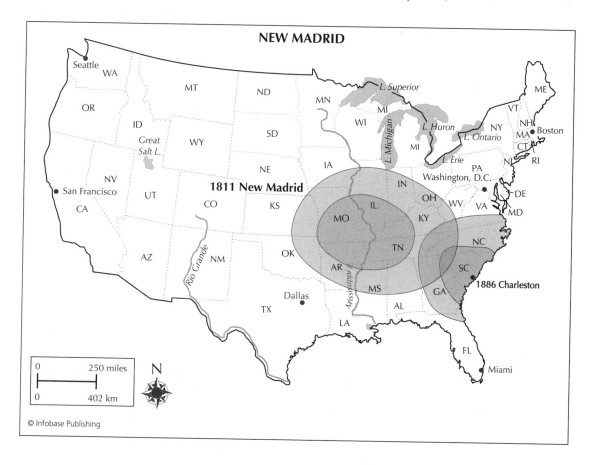

NEW MADRID

1811 New Madrid

1886 Charleston

0   250 miles

0   402 km

N

© Infobase Publishing

felt," wrote one Kentucky observer. Horses reportedly stopped mid-ride to stand with all four legs extended wider than their shoulders and their heads lowered, like giraffes at a watering hole. The changing topography resulted in lake levels dropping or draining altogether in some areas only to flood farmland and form new lakes in areas where the ground had fallen into depressions. Geysers of sand mysteriously shot into the air. Islands along the Mississippi River sank beneath the waves sending the river's first steamboat, *New Orleans*, adrift in the night. Along some stretches of the river the water became a confusing turbid chop that many of the Mighty Mississippi boatmen died trying to navigate.

In the 1970s, geophysicist Otto Nuttli (1926?/27?–88) of St. Louis University relied on newspaper reports from the time to backtrack where the greatest earthquake shaking was felt. He then convinced the university to install a network of seismometers across the region and was soon obtaining evidence of continued activity: microearthquakes with magnitudes of 1 and 2 were sending subterranean shivers through St. Louis.

Nuttli identified thousands of the 19th century earthquakes as aftershocks to three severe earthquakes striking closest to the town of New

Nineteenth-century earthquakes had a broad effect. The map shows the area that shook with an intensity that could be felt by people walking outside and could move heavy furniture inside, crack plaster, and damage chimneys. The New Madrid earthquakes of 1811–12 reached magnitudes of 8.0 or greater. In Charleston, the earthquake of 1886 had a magnitude of about 7.7.

Madrid, Missouri. The town sits on the north spit of a Kentucky oxbow in the Mississippi River, north of Tennessee. The 1811–12 earthquakes damaged houses as far as 250 miles away and rang church bells in Boston. For more than 150 years, the seismic explanation for the earthquakes remained a mystery buried deep under sediment and floodplains. As the understanding of plate tectonics developed, the east coast earthquakes seemed out of place.

In the early 1980s seismologists Mark Zoback with the USGS in Menlo Park, California, and Robert Hamilton of the Reston, Virginia, office, announced that they had found the hidden faults. To conduct their search, the two tapped 3-D technology newly invented for oil exploration. While one person drove a vibrator truck that pounded the surface sending shock waves or seismic waves through the ground, the other person sat in a recording truck, which towed a line of geophones across the surface recording the reflections of the seismic waves as they bounced off different rock and sediment layers. They found parallel fault lines running across New Madrid Valley.

USGS geologist David Russ in Denver examined the tectonic history of the region and found that 500 million years ago, even before Pangaea, the area was undergoing tensile stresses and tearing apart. The small rift along the New Madrid region failed to permanently cut the continent in any significant way but created a fault in the crust that, like a boat tied to a dock, alternates between being compressed and pulled apart. Zoback and his wife, Mary Lou Zoback, also with the USGS in Menlo Park, showed that the stresses on the fault were the same as the stresses elsewhere on the North American plate.

Scientists of the Decade: Luis (1911–1988) and Walter Alvarez (b. 1940)

For 165 million years, reptiles ruled the Mesozoic. Evolving on the southern continent of Gondwanaland from ancestors of archosaurs during the upper Triassic 230 million years ago, dinosaurs stomped across the breaking continents of Pangaea. Other prehistoric reptiles found new niches in the air and the seas.

The first known vertebrate to take flight, pterosaurs or pterodactyls, with their membrane wings stretched from their forefingers to their sides, likely preyed wetlands or the open oceans for fish. The smaller of these bird-like reptiles shared morphological analogies to today's storm petrels,

the larger ones shared the soaring and maneuverability mannerisms of pelicans, albatross, and condors, but were even larger still. *Quetzalcoatlus northrupi* had a wingspan of 40 feet (12 m).

The fast-swimming, dorsal-finned, live-birth-giving ichthyosaurs ate the ancestors of squid. The slower-swimming, long-necked, cold-blooded plesiosaurs competed for much of the same food source, paddling into position and snapping up unwary cephalopods and fish. Fossils of the aquatic air-breathers are often found in the same geologic strata, although no eggs and no embryos of plesiosaurs have yet been discovered. Whether

The west coast geophysicists continue to find east coast seismology full of tectonic surprises. In California, the strike-slip of the San Andreas is a visible tear running parallel with the coast. Satellite images of the state show geologic structures on the west side of the fault far north of the same features on the east side of the fault. The current slip rate for the San Andreas fault is about 2 inches a year (5 cm/yr). Over the last 20 millions years, the slip has moved western California about 600 miles (1,000 km) northwest with respect to North America. Given the paleo-seismic evidence that the faults in New Madrid were active millions of years ago, Mark Zoback, now at Stanford University, was stumped that the faults did not show kilometers of slip. It was as if the boat tied to the dock had long since settled down and only recently started pulling on its lines again. Why now, he wondered.

In 2001, with former graduate student Balz Grollimund, Zoback presented a model that provides one explanation as to why the fault line has reactivated. They blamed the Laurentide Ice Sheet, a culprit with an alibi: mostly Canada. The ice sheet did not make it to Memphis 20,000 years ago. The advancing 2 mile (4,000 m)-high tongue of ice may have just been visible on the northern horizon from St. Louis before it started retreating back north. Still, that was far enough, Zoback says. The effect of the enormous pressure from the ice stressed the continental crust and when the ice retreated the regional rebound reverberated in the New Madrid faults. Zoback estimates that the faults may again settle down, but he hesitates to say that this will happen any sooner than thousands of years from now. In the meantime, the focus on structural stability of buildings not designed in the 20th century for a "Big One" is a critical issue in the 21st century.

they gave live birth or laid eggs like sea turtles remains unknown. Another air-breathing marine reptile intruded into the shark-infested seas of the Cretaceous. The snake-like, legged-bodies of the mosasaurs could reach 56 feet (17 m) long and deftly take on plesiosaurs sneaking up on the creatures from below as they hunted the seafloor. Ichthyosaurs munched on the long-necked plesiosaurs as well, while sharks went tooth to tooth with the mosasaurs. Giant crocodiles, a different branch of the archosaur evolutionary line from dinosaurs, and sea turtles, armored reptiles of an even older more mysterious lineage of Triassic testudines, divided their time between the sea and the shore.

The land, the air, and the seas reverberated with the snapping of jaws, the cries of prey, and the whip of a furless tail. The predators of the Paleozoic oceans had crawled onto land only to return again as evolved enemy combatants. Then with the efficiency of a shark-bite, the Mesozoic megafauna were wiped off the face of the Earth. Only a layer of clay less than half an inch (1 cm) thick remained behind as a grave marker. The rise and fall of animals throughout the fossil record has been one of the most exciting mysteries for paleontologists to investigate. The mass extinction at the end of the Cretaceous and beginning of the

(continues)

(continued)

Tertiary period was not the biggest. Even more species were lost at the end of the Permian prior to the Triassic period. If that had been the geologic record readily visible on the valleys of Gubbio, Italy, then the mysterious death of the dinosaurs might still be one of speculations.

Walter Alvarez of the University of California at Berkeley found the pink and white limestone layers in the cliffs of central Italy as alluring as the people and cafés. The medieval town of Gubbio sits in the foothills of the Northern Apennine Mountains. After Qaddafi kicked out Americans from the oil fields of Libya, Alvarez, a petroleum geologist with a penchant curiosity for geologic history's impact on life, began charting the relationship between Italy's volcanoes and the Roman Empire. When he joined Columbia University's Lamont-Doherty Geological Observatory in New York in 1971, the search for understanding plate tectonic movements around the world sent him back to the Mediterranean mountains to date paleomagnetic reversals. In 1977 he joined the geology department at U.C. Berkeley. His father, Nobel Prize-winning physicist Luis Alvarez, worked at the Radiation Laboratory (now the Lawrence Berkeley National Laboratory) and the two shared long discussions about their different fields. Walter continued to spend summers in Italy, now focusing on the layer of clay in the geologic record that clearly distinguished the mass extinction event at the K-T boundary. (The Alvarez team originally used the abbreviation C-T, but geologists preferred using "K" for the Cretaceous and keeping "C" for the Cambrian. The "T" stands for Tertiary; the Triassic is abbreviated "Tr.")

Alvarez returned home one summer and handed his father a polished rock: pink limestone, above reddish clay, above white limestone.

He explained how the pink limestone from the Tertiary period contains a small percentage of clay along with microscopic shells of marine organisms called foraminifera, nicknamed forams for short. With the naked eye most forams look like nothing more than bits of white sand grains. Under a microscope the shells look like popcorn. Foraminifera species are identified by shape; their bulbous shell nodules, if they have more than one, are often arranged in a pattern around a cave-like opening. In the pink limestone the tiny foram with the long name of *Parvularugoglobigerina eugubina* salts the Tertiary ocean sediment with a light touch.

Like frosting between two layers of cake, the reddish clay between the upper and lower limestone units stands out as having a very different consistency. Close examination reveals nothing but clay.

Below the clay layer, the calcium carbonate fossils return. The white limestone of the Cretaceous marine sediments had a heavy dosing of the larger foram of the genus *Globotuncana*. The species *G. linneiana* from the upper Cretaceous has shelly nodules that spiral around the shell's opening—each bulbous bit getting progressively bigger and overlapping onto each other when seen from the bottom.

Luis Alvarez immediately wanted to know how many years had passed during that time when only the minerals that make up clay had rained on the ocean seafloor leaving a fossil-free matrix with no chalk to make limestone.

Walter could only speculate. The Earth's magnetic field was reversed during the time the clay layer occurred. He had 750,000 years of a reversal that lasted for 20 feet (6 m) of rock. That gave an average sedimentation rate of about four-tenths of an inch (1 cm) over 1,250 years for the limestone, but the clay could have been deposited at a very different rate; the geologist had no way to tell. Radiometric dating methods for rocks that old had error rates upward of 300,000 years. The physicist had an idea. Luis had worked with cosmic rays and had a tendency to think in cosmic terms. Walter went back to Italy to obtain more samples.

The father and son team handed the samples over to nuclear chemists Frank Asaro and Helen Michel in the Berkeley lab. Using the lab's nuclear reactor, they searched for the rare Earth element,

Berkeley nuclear chemists Helen Michel and Frank Asaro (left to right) teamed up with geologist Walter Alvarez and physicist Luis Alvarez to form the Asteroid Impact Research Team. (Ernest Orlando Lawrence Berkeley National Laboratory; AIP Emilio Segrè Visual Archive)

but common cosmic dust element: iridium. They bombarded the sample with neutrons that would force any iridium present to release gamma rays. Using a modified Geiger counter they could then count the radiation emitted per second. Because cosmic dust falls at a steady and known rate, Luis thought iridium would make an excellent geologic clock for measuring the rate of sedimentation in such a thin sedimentary layer. He had not read the literature that claimed otherwise and neither had Walter.

The team found the clay layer spiked with iridium. The surprising results were further con-

founded. The small percentage of clay found in both limestone units had a different mineral composition than the clay-only layer—like a strange book, between matching clay bookends. The clay layer was not only missing the chalky fossils it needed to make limestone, it was missing everything that Walter thought might have explained the clay's presence.

They looked at other clay-only layers in older and younger geologic strata in the Apennines and did not find an iridium spike. They needed

(continues)

(continued)

another K-T boundary example to test if this was a unique feature of the K-T boundary in Italy. The sea cliffs south of Copenhagen, Denmark, held the answer. Part of the "Terrain Cretace" that Belgian D'Omalius d'Halloy first named in 1822 for chalk deposits in the Paris Basin, the Cretaceous chalk was well surveyed from England eastward into Sweden and Poland. The Copenhagen K-T boundary also had a thin clay-only layer spiked with more than a hundred times the amount of iridium that was in the bordering limestone.

A spike in iridium from two separate parts of the world, from the same time interval that coincided with the demise of the dinosaurs, started to look suspicious. Hypotheses of extraterrestrial-induced mass extinction events were not new. Evidence for them was. The Alvarez team first considered the suggestion that a supernova had caused the spike. They looked for an isotope of plutonium: Pu 244. Asaro and Michel had to check their results twice. The marker ultimately proved to be missing. Walter published two reports on their iridium findings and their lack of evidence pointing to a super nova.

Luis followed Berkeley astrophysicist Chris McKee's advice that a 6-mile (10-km) asteroid hitting Earth would produce enough iridium to spike their clay layers. "But neither he nor I could invent a believable killing scenario," wrote Luis in his autobiography. The odds were in favor of the asteroid hitting the ocean. Luis imagined a giant tsunami but could not picture how the wave would annihilate species far inland from the shores. He moved on to other scenarios and shot down a different one each week for six weeks. "It wasn't at all obvious what brought in this pulse of iridium and killed most of the creatures on Earth," he wrote.

Then he remembered the story of Krakatau, the island volcano in the Sundra Strait between Java and Sumatra that erupted in 1883 with cataclysmic force. The explosion sent dust circling around the Earth for two years, turning the sky in Norway red and causing diffraction halos around a blue-colored moon. Luis was intrigued by Sir George Stokes (1819–1903) who estimated the time the dust would remain aloft before falling back to Earth. Dust particles hang in the air as though suspended in liquid. Stokes law calculates the observed viscosity of the medium from the particle's perspective. Stokes was wrong however about the dust being the culprit for the red sunsets. Aerosols from the volcano had reached the stratosphere and remained in circulation around the world for years. The dust had fallen to Earth within months, but the event was a "killing mechanism" Luis could use. Based on the average amount of iridium found in the clay boundary layer, he concluded that a 6-mile (10-km) "piece of solar system debris hit the Earth 65 million years ago and threw dust into the stratosphere that made the sky dark as midnight for several years, thereby stopping photosynthesis and so starving the animals to death."

Luis, Asaro, and Michel phoned Walter in Italy that summer of 1979 with the new idea. They wanted to join him at the paleontological meeting in Copenhagen he would be attending, but Walter urged them to stay home. With an idea this revolutionary, Walter knew the best procedure would be to present the theory to the geologic community after vetting it through peer-review for publication in a journal. By November they began circulating a preprint of their report to geologists and paleontologists.

In January Luis gave a presentation of the idea at the annual meeting of the American Association for the Advancement of Science, which publishes the journal *Science*. Thomas O'Toole reported the story for the *Washington Post* on January 6, 1980. The report on page A5 had the headline: "Dinosaur Extinction Linked to Collision With Asteroid." The story began: "The extinction of the dinosaurs some 65 million years ago, one of the major mysteries of geology, was probably caused by a collision between the Earth and a giant asteroid, according to a team of scientists led by Nobel Laureate Luis Alvarez." The Associated Press also reported the story for the newswires. The Alvarez team continued to refine and edit their paper as other scientists provided feedback and launched their own investigations.

The various hypotheses suggested for the mass extinction of the dinosaurs have included: climate change, floods of brackish water, disease, inbreeding, overgrazing of plant and food resources, sea-level variations, impacts from asteroids, radiation from supernova explosions, magnetic reversals, and volcanic eruptions from both Earth and even the Moon. When the editor of *Science*, Phil Abelson, read the Berkeley team's impact hypothesis his first response was *No*. When it came to dinosaur extinction theories, "At least n-1 of them must be wrong," he told Luis. The team shortened their lengthy paper, and Abelson eventually reconsidered it for publication. Before their formal report on the implications of their evidence was published in *Science*, it was already being discussed in the competing British journal *Nature*. In that same issue, Dutch geologist Jan Smit reported iridium spikes at the K-T boundary in Spain. By the time the Berkeley team's report came out in June the team had obtained another K-T clay-layer spiked with iridium in marine sedimentary deposits from New Zealand.

The first criticism of the Alvarez report was that all of their samples were marine deposits. Then in 1981, researchers with the Los Alamos National Laboratory and the U.S. Geologic Survey reported finding an iridium abundance anomaly in New Mexico with concentrations up to 5,000 parts per trillion over a background level of 4 to 20 parts per trillion. The sedimentary rock layers had been formed in a freshwater swamp during K-T times. Thus the impact theory passed the first test of many null hypotheses to come to try and prove the new theory wrong. Like all good scientific theories, it would have to hold up under fierce scrutiny to be accepted. During the process, the theory would either advance and become stronger or fall apart and be dismissed. Because of the respected work of Harold Urey and Eugene Shoemaker, the emerging evidence from other researchers such as Smit and others, and the evidence for craters on the Moon and Earth, the geologic community was

ready to embrace the theory of an impact event for causing a mass extinction as a valid one worthy of the process of peer review, null hypotheses, and testing. (If a theory cannot be tested with a null hypothesis that would prove the theory is false, then it is not considered scientific.) The debate that proceeded throughout the 1980s was thus one of active research into the subject.

The theory had a number of expectations that it consistently passed, further helping the theory's credibility. Many of these were observations that were used to develop the theory. Other ideas were drawn from discoveries made by other teams as they tested the theory:

- The iridium spike would be seen in K-T boundary clays worldwide
- The boundary clay was different from the clay in the adjacent limestones above and below. The clay in the limestones would be identical
- The boundary clay would have proportional abundances of elements found in stony meteorites and disproportional abundances of elements found in crustal rocks
- Plants as well as animals would have suffered or gone extinct after the impact
- The iridium spike would appear above the last known dinosaur fossils
- The boundary clay should show signs of exceedingly high temperatures and pressures from the impact (shocked quartz)
- Impact craters will show high levels of iridium
- In the geologic record iridium will be rare, allowing for the exception that other boundaries where mass extinctions have occurred might also contain high levels of iridium

(continues)

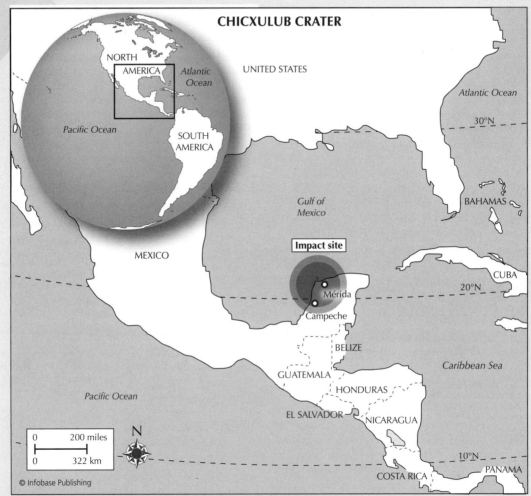

CHICXULUB CRATER

NORTH
AMERICA   *Atlantic Ocean*

UNITED STATES

Pacific Ocean

SOUTH
AMERICA

Atlantic Ocean

30°N

Gulf of Mexico

BAHAMAS

Impact site

MEXICO

Mérida

CUBA

20°N

Campeche

BELIZE

Caribbean Sea

GUATEMALA

Pacific Ocean

HONDURAS

EL SALVADOR

NICARAGUA

| 0 | 200 miles |
| 0 | 322 km |

N

10°N

COSTA RICA   PANAMA

© Infobase Publishing

An impact crater in Mexico's Yucatán Peninsula that dates back 65 million years correlates with the mass extinction event at the end of the Late Cretaceous.

(continued)

- A crater dating back to the K-T boundary will be found
- Unanticipated discoveries will be made

The theory that the impact event happened withstood all possible tests. The theory that the impact event killed the dinosaurs and caused a sudden mass extinction underwent significant revisions. The time of global darkness shortened to months. Devoid of sunlight as an energy source, photosynthesis came to a stop, starting a cascade of troubles through the marine environment. On the ground the lack of light for multiple months in a row might not have been so devastating, considering much of the Arctic and Antarctic are devoid of sunlight during the winters. Only a sudden dark winter was not the flora and fauna's only problem. Computer models showed that unlike a volcanic eruption, the cataclysm from an impact event that large would send ballistic projectiles of ejecta into orbit, raining back down as fireballs. Forests burned. The species that survived were small enough to find shelter, or adaptable enough to weather the trouble. Like the hibernating ground moles on Mount St. Helens, after the devastation the burrowing rodents, along with insects, fire-resistant plants, and wind-borne seeds quickly reestablished life's foothold. The discovery of shocked quartz at the boundary layer solidified the evidence for an impact event. Then, in 1992, the discovery that the Chicxulub crater in the Yucatán Peninsula of Mexico matched all the requirements for the K-T impact event, shifted the debate permanently from whether an impact event could cause a sudden mass extinction to whether it was the only one that did. This naturally led to the next question: what were the odds of it happening again?

Further Reading

Alvarez, Luis W. *Alvarez: Adventures of a Physicist.* New York: Basic Books, Inc., 1987. In this autobiography, Luis Alvarez discusses his research on the Manhattan Project, his aerial observations of the first two atomic bombs, the second being the one on Hiroshima, his work proving with physics that only one shooter was involved in the assassination of John F. Kennedy, his work searching for a chamber in the pyramids in Egypt using cosmic rays, his Nobel Prize and the impact theory for the mass extinctions at the K-T boundary with his son and fellow Berkeley nuclear chemists Frank Asaro and Helen Michel.

Alvarez, Luis W., Walter Alvarez, Frank Asaro, Helen V. Michel. "Extraterrestrial Cause for the Cretaceous-Tertiary Extinction: Experimental results and theoretical interpretation." *Science* 208 (1980): 1,095–1,108. The Berkeley team interprets their evidence as indication that an impact event caused a mass extinction event at the end of the Cretaceous.

Alvarez, Walter, Luis W. Alvarez, Frank Asaro, Helen V. Michel. "The End of the Cretaceous: Sharp Boundary or Gradual Transition?" *Science* 223 (1984): 1,183–1,186.

Bruce, Victoria. *No Apparent Danger: The True Story of Volcanic Disaster at Galeras and Nevado Del Ruiz.* New York: HarperCollins, 2001. Bruce reports on the Colombian volcano disasters of 1985 and 1993.

Comte, D., A. Eisenberg, E. Lorca, M. Pardo, L. Ponce, R. Saragoni, S. K. Singh, G. Suairez. "The 1985 Central Chile Earthquake: A Repeat of Previous Great Earthquakes in the Region?" *Science* 233 (1986): 449–453. "The great shocks of central Chile demonstrate that our understanding of the earthquake generation process is still very rudimentary and that there may not be a single universal model valid for all seismic regions of the world."

Farman, Joe C., B. G. Gardiner, and J. D. Shanklin. "Large losses of total ozone in Antarctica reveal seasonal ClO_x/NO_x interaction." *Nature* 315 (May 16, 1985): 207–210. Counter to computer models that predicted a small global loss of ozone from human activities the loss of ozone over Antarctica is large.

Ganapathy, R. "A Major Meteorite Impact on the Earth 65 Million Years Ago: Evidence from the Cretaceous-Tertiary Boundary Clay." *Science* 209 (August 22, 1980): 921–923. Research scientist with the J. T. Baker Chemical Company in New Jersey identifies meteoritic metal spikes in K-T boundary clay from Denmark.

Hsü, Kenneth J. "Terrestrial catastrophe caused by cometary impact at the end of Cretaceous." *Nature* 285 (22 May 1980): 201–203. A geologist at the Swiss Federal Institute of Technology in Zurich presents evidence that atmospheric heating during a cometary impact at the end of the Cretaceous caused the extinction of large terrestrial animals. He provides further evidence that cyanide poisoning released by the fallen comet caused the extinction of calcareous marine plankton.

National Academies of Science. *The Eruption of Nevado Del Ruiz Volcano Colombia, South America, November 13, 1985, Commission on Engineering and Technical Systems.* Washington, D.C.: National Academy Press, 1991. A report on the eruption. Available online. URL: http://books.nap.edu/books/0309044774/html. Accessed February 4, 2007.

———. *The March 5, 1987, Ecuador Earthquakes: Mass Wasting and Socioeconomic Effects Commission on Engineering and Technical Systems.* Washington, D.C.: National Academy Press, 1991. A report on the earthquakes. Available online. URL: http://books.nap.edu/books/0309044448/html. Accessed February 4, 2007.

NOVA. "Volcano's Deadly Warning." PBS Airdate: November 12, 2002. A transcript of interviews with volcanologists, including Marta Calvache of the Colombian Institute of Geoscience. Available online. URL: http://www.pbs.org/wgbh/nova/transcripts/2913_volcano.html. Accessed February 4, 2007.

Nuttli, Otto W. "The Mississippi Valley Earthquakes of 1811 and 1812: Intensities, Ground Motion and Magnitudes." *Bulletin of the Seismological Society of America* 63, no. 1 (February 1973): 227–248. This essay reviews the history of the earthquakes and identifies their epicenters. Available online. URL: http://www.eas.slu.edu/Earthquake_Center/SEISMICITY/Nuttli.1973/bssa.html. Accessed April 24, 2006.

Orth, Charles J., James S. Gilmore, Jere D. Knight, Charles L. Pillmore, Robert H. Tschudy, and James E. Fassett. "Disruption of the Terrestrial Plant Ecosystem at the Cretaceous-Tertiary Boundary, Western

Interior." *Science* 225 (1981): 1,030–1,032. USGS and Los Alamos National Laboratory researchers find iridium spikes and depletion of pollen from freshwater Cretaceous-Tertiary swamps in New Mexico.

O'Toole, Thomas. "Dinosaur Extinction Linked to Collision With Asteroid." *The Washington Post* (January 6, 1980): A5. A news report covering the recent evidence indicating a K-T impact event caused mass extinctions.

Powell, James Lawrence. *Night Comes to the Cretaceous: Dinosaur Extinction and the Transformation of Modern Geology.* New York: W. H. Freeman and Company, 1998. Director of the Los Angeles County Museum of Natural History, Powell reports on how the impact theory for the mass extinctions at the K-T boundary developed and its implications for other mass extinction events in geologic history. He also details how the Chicxulub Crater was found long before it was identified as *the* K-T Crater and its "rediscovery" in 1990.

San Diego State University. "How volcanoes work." An award-winning Web site on volcanoes and different volcanic eruptions. Available online. URL: http://www.geology.sdsu.edu/how_volcanoes_work/ Accessed April 24, 2006.

Sato, Tamaki, and Kazushige Tanabe. "Cretaceous plesiosaurs ate ammonites." *Nature* 394 (13 August 1998): 629–630. This report describes the discovery of ammonites found in fossil plesiosaur stomachs.

Smit, Jan, and J. Hertogen. "An Extraterrestrial Event at the Cretaceous-Tertiary Boundary." *Nature* 285 (May 22, 1980): 198–200. Smit reveals iridium spikes in clay boundary layers from Spain.

———. "Terminal Cretaceous Extinctions in the Hell Creek Area, Montana: Compatible with Catastrophic Extinction." *Science* 223 (1984): 1,177–1,179. The report provides evidence that disproves earlier indications of a gradual extinction of megafauna leading up to the end of the Cretaceous.

Surlyk, Finn. "The Cretaceous-Tertiary Boundary Event." *Nature* 285 (May 22, 1980): 187–188. This news and views article discusses the revival of the impact theory since the Alvarez discovery of an iridium spike in 1979.

———. "End-Cretaceous Brachiopod Extinctions in the Chalk of Denmark." *Science* 223 (March 16, 1984): 1,174–1,177. The discovery of Cretaceous extinctions of a benthic fauna.

Swisher, Carl C. III, Jose M. Grajales-Nishimura, Alessandro Montanari, Stanley V. Margolis, Philippe Claeys, Walter Alvarez, Paul Renne, Esteban Cedillo-Pardo, Florentin J-M. R. Maurrasse, Garniss H. Curtis, Jan Smit, Michael O. McWilliams. "Coeval 40Ar/39Ar Ages of 65.0 Million Years Ago from Chicxulub Crater Melt Rock and Cretaceous-Tertiary Boundary Tektites." *Science* 257 (1992): 954–958. The report announces the discovery that radioactive dating evidence puts the formation of the Chicxulub Crater at the K-T boundary.

Thompson, Dick. *Volcano Cowboys.* New York: St. Martin's Press, 2000. Thompson reports on multiple eruptions in the 1980s and 1990s and their impact on the history of the formation of USGS International Volcano Disaster Assistance Program.

Tilling, Robert I., Meyer Rubin, Haraldur Sigurdsson, Steven Carey, Wendell A. Duffield, and William I. Rose. "Holocene Eruptive Activity of El Chichón Volcano, Chiapas, Mexico." *Science*, New Series, 224, no. 4650 (May 18, 1984): 747–749. This report describes geologic evidence for historical eruptions that would have provided clues as to the eruptive potential of El Chichsón had they been investigated sooner.

Tschudy, Robert H., Charles L. Pillmore, Charles "Carl" J. Orth, James S. Gilmore, and Jere D. Knight. "Disruption of the Terrestrial Plant Ecosystem at the Cretaceous-Tertiary Boundary, Western Interior." *Science* 225 (1984): 1,030–1,032. USGS and Los Alamos National Laboratory researchers find further evidence for plant disruptions at freshwater Cretaceous-Tertiary swamps in Raton Basin in New Mexico and Colorado, and two more continental sites in the Hell Creek, Montana, area.

U.S. Geological Survey. *Ruiz-Tolima Volcanic Massif (Cordillera Central)*. Provides a map of the glaciers before and after the eruption of Nevado del Ruiz. Available online. URL: http://pubs.usgs.gov/pp/p1386i/colombia/ruiz.html. Accessed February 4, 2007.

———. Hazard-Zone maps and Volcanic Risk. A hazard zone map of Nevado del Ruiz. Available online. URL: http://vulcan.wr.usgs.gov/Vhp/C1073/hazard_maps_risk.html. Accessed February 4, 2007.

———. Deadly Lahars from Nevado del Ruiz, Colombia. Volcano Hazards Program. A geological description of the eruption and lahars that occurred on November 13, 1985. Available online. URL: http://volcanoes.usgs.gov/Hazards/What/Lahars/RuizLahars.html. Accessed February 4, 2007.

Ward, Peter D. "Impact from the Deep." September 18, 2006. Ward, a paleontologist at the University of Washington, describes the search for other causes of mass extinctions and focuses on climate change. Available online. URL: http://sciam.com/print_version.cfm?articleID=00037A5D-A938-150E-A93883414B7F0000. Accessed February 4, 2007.

10

1991–2000:
The Information Age

Introduction

The last decade of the 20th century started with a volcanic plinian-type eruption that cooled the Earth a degree, colored sunsets around the world, and threatened the lives of a million people, including American Air Force personnel and their families stationed on the largest U.S. military base outside of the United States. Mount Pinatubo on Luzon Islands in the Philippines was one of the most dangerous kinds of volcanoes—one awoken after hundreds of years asleep. Even on an island known for volcanoes that erupt on a regular basis, few regarded the threat of Mount Pinatubo seriously. The country's lead volcanologist, Raymundo "Ray" Punongbayan, worked diligently with his team to convince the authorities to evacuate surrounding danger zones as the activity progressed. Punongbayan called across the Pacific for assistance from volcanologists with the U.S. Geological Survey, who soon set up operations to evaluate, monitor, and advise. After a decade of volcano hopping around the world since Mount St. Helens, the Survey team had enough experience among them to guess correctly when luck would be on their side and when caution was preferable to scientific results. During this crisis, the volcanologists were sobered by the deaths of friends in Japan who despite precautions still underestimated the power of Mount Unzen. The Pinatubo team showed explanatory videos of volcanic events at every opportunity they could to inform the public on what to expect. Punongbayan's work on Philippine volcanoes earned him tremendous respect among geologists around the world. In 2003 the European Geophysical Society awarded him the Sergey Soloviev Medal for having shown "exceptional contributions to natural hazards by increasing our knowledge of their basic principles as well as their proper assessment with a view of protecting the environment and saving lives and properties."

The seismic monitoring done to evaluate earthquakes in the 1990s had taken on an evolutionary adaptation since the days of Charles Richter. From work done in the same laboratory at Caltech, Hiroo Kanamori in the 1970s introduced Moment Magnitude: a measurement of earthquake energy that could be calculated with or without a seismometer. For the first time, this allowed seismologists to accurately measure the energy of earthquakes larger than magnitude of 7.

While earthquakes and volcanoes shook the planet, two debates in the Earth sciences were climaxing—both in regards to carbon dioxide and climate change. Both were also studies that had roots in the early century investigations of ice ages. One looked at an Earth heating up, and the other examined evidence of an Earth trapped in a cold freeze. To understand the complexities of such large-scale phenomena as atmosphere-biosphere-geosphere interactions, an amazing number of scientists must delve into minutia—from the pebbles found encased in ancient sediments dropped into soft ocean seafloor from meandering icebergs, to the exhalations of microbes in soil of an Amazon rain forest. The scientist chosen to represent this decade, ecologist Pamela Matson, is one who like volcanologist Ray Punongbayan understands the importance of science education and public policy and epitomizes the importance of examining the details in order to gain an accurate understanding of the larger consequences.

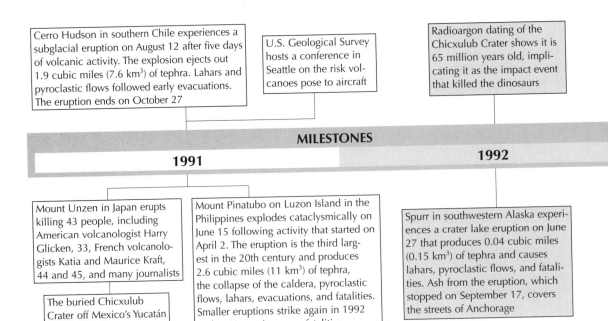

Cerro Hudson in southern Chile experiences a subglacial eruption on August 12 after five days of volcanic activity. The explosion ejects out 1.9 cubic miles (7.6 km³) of tephra. Lahars and pyroclastic flows followed early evacuations. The eruption ends on October 27

U.S. Geological Survey hosts a conference in Seattle on the risk volcanoes pose to aircraft

Radioargon dating of the Chicxulub Crater shows it is 65 million years old, implicating it as the impact event that killed the dinosaurs

MILESTONES

1991

1992

Mount Unzen in Japan erupts killing 43 people, including American volcanologist Harry Glicken, 33, French volcanologists Katia and Maurice Kraft, 44 and 45, and many journalists

The buried Chicxulub Crater off Mexico's Yucatán Peninsula is rediscovered

Mount Pinatubo on Luzon Island in the Philippines explodes cataclysmically on June 15 following activity that started on April 2. The eruption is the third largest in the 20th century and produces 2.6 cubic miles (11 km³) of tephra, the collapse of the caldera, pyroclastic flows, lahars, evacuations, and fatalities. Smaller eruptions strike again in 1992 and 1993 causing more fatalities

Spurr in southwestern Alaska experiences a crater lake eruption on June 27 that produces 0.04 cubic miles (0.15 km³) of tephra and causes lahars, pyroclastic flows, and fatalities. Ash from the eruption, which stopped on September 17, covers the streets of Anchorage

Mount Pinatubo: A Volcano Hiding in Plain Sight

Twenty-three volcanoes stand like dominoes across Luzon Island in the Philippines, an island that is about the size of Arizona. The average height of these jungle-covered mountain peaks is 4,556 feet (1,389 m). The tallest, Mayon, rises 8,077 feet (2,462 m) in perfect stratovolcano form reminiscent of a tropical miniature Mount Fuji. The shortest, Amorong, is a mere hill in comparison at 1,234 feet (376 m) and emits bursts of sulfurous gases and steam. The Philippines are made up of a number of islands and the second largest after Luzon is Mindanao, with 14 volcanoes. The country is awash with geothermal activity, small ash eruptions and earthquake swarms. When typhoons hit, the higher peaks release dangerous mudflows. Despite the natural hazards, the tropical islands, rich in fertile volcanic soil, today sustain a population of nearly 90 million people.

On April 2, 1991, Mount Pinatubo, a geologic conundrum, released a puff of ash that fell on a nearby village. Steamy plumes vented from newly formed fumaroles and for the second time in less than a year, rumblings

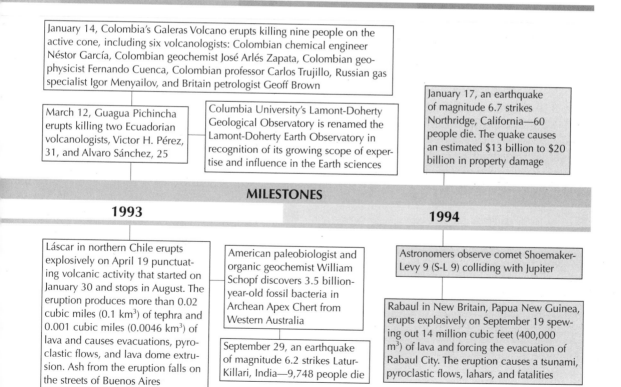

January 14, Colombia's Galeras Volcano erupts killing nine people on the active cone, including six volcanologists: Colombian chemical engineer Néstor García, Colombian geochemist José Arlés Zapata, Colombian geophysicist Fernando Cuenca, Colombian professor Carlos Trujillo, Russian gas specialist Igor Menyailov, and Britain petrologist Geoff Brown

March 12, Guagua Pichincha erupts killing two Ecuadorian volcanologists, Victor H. Pérez, 31, and Alvaro Sánchez, 25

Columbia University's Lamont-Doherty Geological Observatory is renamed the Lamont-Doherty Earth Observatory in recognition of its growing scope of expertise and influence in the Earth sciences

January 17, an earthquake of magnitude 6.7 strikes Northridge, California—60 people die. The quake causes an estimated $13 billion to $20 billion in property damage

MILESTONES

1993

1994

Láscar in northern Chile erupts explosively on April 19 punctuating volcanic activity that started on January 30 and stops in August. The eruption produces more than 0.02 cubic miles (0.1 km³) of tephra and 0.001 cubic miles (0.0046 km³) of lava and causes evacuations, pyroclastic flows, and lava dome extrusion. Ash from the eruption falls on the streets of Buenos Aires

American paleobiologist and organic geochemist William Schopf discovers 3.5 billion-year-old fossil bacteria in Archean Apex Chert from Western Australia

September 29, an earthquake of magnitude 6.2 strikes Latur-Killari, India—9,748 people die

Astronomers observe comet Shoemaker-Levy 9 (S-L 9) colliding with Jupiter

Rabaul in New Britain, Papua New Guinea, erupts explosively on September 19 spewing out 14 million cubic feet (400,000 m³) of lava and forcing the evacuation of Rabaul City. The eruption causes a tsunami, pyroclastic flows, lahars, and fatalities

and cracks in the ground sent a Catholic nun calling for help. Sister Emma Fondevilla contacted geologists with the Philippine Institute of Volcanology and Seismology (PHIVOLCS). They drove through the jungle roads to deploy seismometers on the volcano's western flank. As with Nevado del Ruiz, the instruments had to be checked daily by hand. The seismometers recorded a swarm of 500 earthquakes in the region. The Philippine Air Force sent a plane over the mountain to conduct an aerial survey. A geologic exclamation point, a steaming fissure punctuated with new craters, greeted the pilot. As the smell and eye-tearing haze from the venting volcano continued, five thousand people sought shelter in evacuation camps. On April 7, Raymundo Punongbayan (1937–2005), director of PHIVOLCS from 1983 to 2002, called his friend Chris Newhall at the U.S. Geological Survey in Reston, Virginia, and gave him the update.

Mount Pinatubo was a mystery. No one remembered the last time it erupted. No stories had passed down through the generations of its threatening violence. Some 20,000 Aetas, the indigenous people to the island, "knew Mount Pinatubo as their home, their hunting ground, and their haven from an ever-encroaching lowland population," wrote Newhall and colleagues in a later report. "For the Aeta, Mount Pinatubo was (and is) the home of Apo Namalyari, the Great Protector and Provider." For many of the lowlanders, including Americans at the U.S.

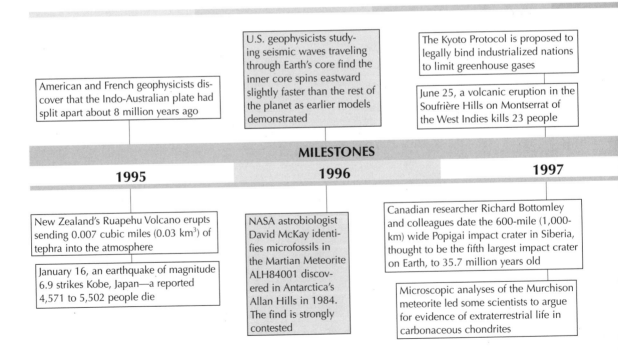

U.S. geophysicists studying seismic waves traveling through Earth's core find the inner core spins eastward slightly faster than the rest of the planet as earlier models demonstrated

The Kyoto Protocol is proposed to legally bind industrialized nations to limit greenhouse gases

American and French geophysicists discover that the Indo-Australian plate had split apart about 8 million years ago

June 25, a volcanic eruption in the Soufrière Hills on Montserrat of the West Indies kills 23 people

MILESTONES

1995

1996

1997

New Zealand's Ruapehu Volcano erupts sending 0.007 cubic miles (0.03 km³) of tephra into the atmosphere

January 16, an earthquake of magnitude 6.9 strikes Kobe, Japan—a reported 4,571 to 5,502 people die

NASA astrobiologist David McKay identifies microfossils in the Martian Meteorite ALH84001 discovered in Antarctica's Allan Hills in 1984. The find is strongly contested

Canadian researcher Richard Bottomley and colleagues date the 600-mile (1,000-km) wide Popigai impact crater in Siberia, thought to be the fifth largest impact crater on Earth, to 35.7 million years old

Microscopic analyses of the Murchison meteorite led some scientists to argue for evidence of extraterrestrial life in carbonaceous chondrites

Air Force bases, the ash explosion on April 2 was their first introduction to Mount Pinatubo, "save for a few who climbed for a respite from the heat and hassles of lowland life, and for military personnel who received survival training from the Aetas," the U.S. and Philippine volcanologists reported. Mount Pinatubo was fairly average in size for a Luzon volcano. It rose 5,725 feet (1,745 m), a slightly higher peak amid several of the western mountains. Even the smaller Mount Arayat seemed visually more volcanic looking, isolated as it was from the others and rising from the flat plains 25 miles (34 km) to the east.

After Punongbayan's call, Newhall searched for what little information he could find. What he learned was not good. Geologists who had surveyed Pinatubo in the 1980s for its geothermal energy identified the volcano as having erupted in the last millennium. Their maps of the mountain showed a dendritic drainage system, where many streams and rivers finger their way down the mountain branching off from each other in every which way. Rather than a few deeply cut river channels directing the waterworks, the pattern indicated the rains fell on soft ash and pyroclastic debris flows, hundreds of feet thick, and meandered as spindly veins cutting multiple paths that crisscrossed and braided before forming a major arterial river.

Mount Pinatubo presented Punongbayan and his team with an overwhelming abundance of additional complications. About a million people

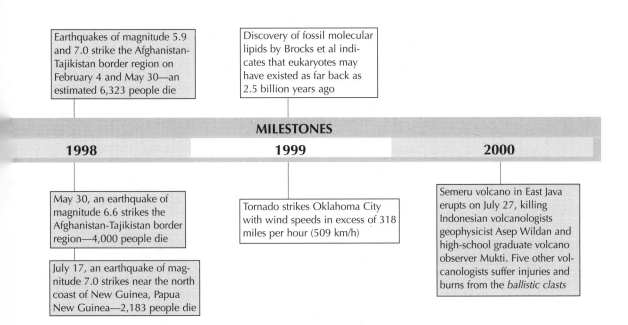

Earthquakes of magnitude 5.9 and 7.0 strike the Afghanistan-Tajikistan border region on February 4 and May 30—an estimated 6,323 people die

Discovery of fossil molecular lipids by Brocks et al indicates that eukaryotes may have existed as far back as 2.5 billion years ago

MILESTONES

1998   **1999**   **2000**

May 30, an earthquake of magnitude 6.6 strikes the Afghanistan-Tajikistan border region—4,000 people die

July 17, an earthquake of magnitude 7.0 strikes near the north coast of New Guinea, Papua New Guinea—2,183 people die

Tornado strikes Oklahoma City with wind speeds in excess of 318 miles per hour (509 km/h)

Semeru volcano in East Java erupts on July 27, killing Indonesian volcanologists geophysicist Asep Wildan and high-school graduate volcano observer Mukti. Five other volcanologists suffer injuries and burns from the *ballistic clasts*

Acceptable Risk: Living with a Known Hazard

Chris Newhall was working with the Peace Corps in the Philippines when the Luzon's tallest volcano, Mayon, erupted in 1978. He was back again with the U.S. Geological Survey advising his friend Ray Punongbayan, director of the Philippine Institute of Volcanology and Seismology (PHIVOLCS), when Mayon erupted again in September 1984. Punongbayan ordered a series of evacuations starting with everyone living within 3.7 miles (6 km) of the crater and expanding in circumference outward as the eruption progressed. By the end of September, the evacuated regions extended 6.2 miles (10 km) from the summit on the southwest side where the lava was actively flowing and about 5 miles (8 km) from the summit around the rest of the volcano. Punongbayan then stood firm in keeping the 73,000 evacuees from returning to their homes at the first sign of quiescence.

He and Newhall wanted to wait until after a fortnightly tide had passed. They did not want to bet so many lives against an emerging theory that magma can respond to the gravitational pull of the moon. The theory held that if a volcano were already at the point of bursting, a high tide could tip the balance. True to the prediction, the eruption ended with a final outburst of activity on October 6. Punongbayan's implemented evacuation plan worked. Although the evacuation caused economic hardship, it saved lives.

The Civil Defense authorities designated the area within 3.7 miles (6 km) of the summit as off-limits for settlement. Landowners still wanted access to the area. The authorities compromised and acknowledged farming as an acceptable use of the land given the risk. The volcano's habitual eruptions had sent lava flows following the same general southwest route for three decades running: 1968, 1978, and 1984. Farmers planted crops elsewhere on the summit and allowed their animals to graze the volcano's wild grasses. The vegetation on the summit had roots growing into the weathered layers of previous pyroclastic flows. Mayon had erupted in 1928, 1938, and 1947 as well. The volcano had a record of erupting equally as often if not more during the 19th century. The Filipinos respected Mayon, but not from a distance. They depended on the fertile soil and lived with the danger. Most of the evacuees

lived on the pyroclastic flows surrounding the peak. The volcanologists faced the daunting task of monitoring new volcanic activity, learning Pinatubo's particular eruptive habits, judging the risk and communicating the level of danger to the Philippine authorities and the American generals at Clark Air Base, the largest U.S. military air base outside of the United States at the time and one that sat 15 miles (24 km) east of Pinatubo. "Unlike Mayon, Bulusan, or Taal Volcanoes, where we had worked with one governor and one provincial staff, Mount Pinatubo was at the apex of three provinces," reported Punongbayan. "We had to work with three governors and three provincial staffs. In addition, we had to warn three large cities (Angeles, San Fernando, and Olongapo), several tens of smaller towns, U.S. and Philippine military bases, and hundreds of barangay (village) captains, minor officials, and nongovernmental organizations. Each of the three provinces speaks its own dialect, and the indigenous mountain people, Aetas, speak yet a fourth dialect."

As with Nevado del Ruiz in Colombia, the responsibilities of dealing with a potential natural disaster fell on a population already struggling

returned to their homes in the lowlands, picked up where they left off, and counted the years as they passed since the last evacuation.

On February 2, 1993, a pyroclastic flow exploded out of the crater and rolled down the southeast flank, killing 75 people, most of them farmers tending crops. As the eruption continued, 60,000 people evacuated the 6.2-mile (10-km) zone around the summit. A 3.7-mile (6-km) perimeter around Mayon was designated a permanent danger zone. After an eruption in 2000, an additional buffer on the southeast flank was designated an extended danger zone (between 3.7 miles and 4.3 miles [6 km and 7 km]). An evacuation of the danger zones in June 2001 sent about 25,000 people to temporary shelters. A Mayon task force made up of military and civilian members was given responsibility for spreading the news of an evacuation warning from PHIVOLCS to those in the danger and buffer zones. The evacuations happen when the volcano alert level reaches four on a scale between zero and five, with five indicating an eruption in progress. When a rapid evacuation warning of a level four alert went out at 4 in morning on July 26, 2001, only a week after PHIVOLCS had reduced the volcanic warning level back down to

three, the urgency of the evacuation was ignored. Farmers wanted to collect livestock from the danger zone before evacuating again. The eruption, a 1,640-foot (500-m) high plume of ash, struck an hour-and-a-half after the evacuation warning went out and none were injured. The mayor of Legaspi City was reported as saying, "We were surprised by its sudden explosion. We were told to evacuate last night but we did not know it would explode so fast."

In August 2006, authorities set up roadblocks and police checkpoints along the danger zone when tourists began seeking closer views of a Mayon eruption. In the lowlands 40,000 people sought shelter in evacuation centers. The drop in the number of evacuees during the years between 1984 and 2006 does not represent fewer people choosing to live near Mayon, but rather less explosive eruptions. "I wish the population near the volcano was decreasing but it isn't," Newhall says. The hazardous regions evacuated in recent years have been localized to the areas downslope from the lava flows. Newhall warns that the "next time there's an explosive eruption, the number [of evacuees] will jump up even higher than 73,000."

with social and economic conflict. The Filipinos were facing attempted guerrilla-led coups to remove President Corazon Aquino. After 40 years of American military presence on the island, the American and Filipino government had come to a $40 million disagreement on renegotiating a 10-year extension of use of the island for military bases. The government instability combined with the discrepancies between life on the American military bases and the poor neighborhoods outside their fences had given rise to anti-American sentiments. At least two separate murders of Americans had struck recently, including a geothermal surveyor on Pinatubo. The military bases, Clark and Subic Bay Naval Air Station, 24 miles (about 40 km) south of Pinatubo, were American-made oases complete with Baskin-Robbins and Pizza Hut. As Dick Thompson wrote in his book *Volcano Cowboys*, "The main gate at Clark was a portal between cultures." Beyond its walls was Angeles City, with a population of 300,000 people living in "a teeming, dirty, vibrant Third World urban center." The impression to outside visitors he reported, was that the military's presence did little to improve living conditions for the people in Angeles City and made it even worse in the zone closest to the base.

To maintain credibility, the volcanologists needed to make certain that they did not overstate the risks. They were very worried that repetitive warnings, if not followed by obvious volcanic activity, would lead to public apathy and ultimately undermine the volcanologists' primary goal of saving lives. As of mid-April, however, the PHIVOLCS team was still uncertain if the volcano was warming up for a big eruption or responding to a magnitude-7.8 earthquake that struck Luzon in July 1990. Building collapse from that shake had killed 1,600 people and opened steam vents on Pinatubo. Sister Emma Fondevilla had alerted PHIVOLCS of the situation, but at the time the activity was deemed part of the natural hydrothermal response to the tectonic shift. Small earthquakes continued to strike the mountain. Now Mount Pinatubo was quivering with as many as 500 quakes a day, many large enough to make the nuns and even the Aetas nervous.

Punongbayan needed help. The known hazardous volcano Taal, with its populated Volcano Island in the middle of its caldera lake, had recently become active again. The volcano was known for changing the landscape on Luzon and causing fatalities. He reported that President Aquino on April 1 had ordered the evacuation of the roughly 4,000 people living on Volcano Island in Lake Taal. His small staff was stretched thin with monitoring duties. Newhall suggested the U.S. Geological Survey's newly established Volcano Disaster Assistance Program (VDAP). After Nevado del Ruiz, the U.S. State Department had given its Office of Foreign Disaster Assistance the green light for funding a team of volunteer volcanologists to assist foreign countries that asked for help. The U.S. Agency for International Development had purchased $100,000 in equipment for VDAP to use in Central and South America. Volcanologists from the United States had since helped monitor volcanoes in Guatemala, Mexico, Bolivia, Ecuador, Argentina, Peru, and Chile.

Still in Reston, Virginia, Newhall started working the phones. He called the volcanologists in charge of the VDAP equipment at the Cascade Volcano Observatory in Vancouver, Washington. They had the instruments earmarked for Central and South America and would need funding to replace the cache if they sent it instead to the Philippines. The stock of tiltmeters, portable telemetered seismometers, and a gas-monitoring instrument used on planes to detect sulfur dioxide was otherwise ready to go, as soon as Newhall obtained a formal request from the host country and agency securing the funding for the trip.

With the Kurds struggling in northern Iraq after the Gulf War and Bangladesh underwater from spring floods, money from the U.S. Foreign Disaster Assistance was already allocated. Newhall called the U.S. AID office in Manila, the capital of the Philippines. They initially rejected Newhall's request to fund a volcano monitoring team of Americans in the region. Financially they could not afford it and logistically they did not see how more Americans running around the volcano would be a wise decision. At that point, Newhall turned to the U.S. Air Force, but rather than ask for funds directly he casually called the weatherman at Clark Air Base to discuss the volcanic activity at Pinatubo. Days later a colonel on the base wanted to know when Newhall would be arriving. As soon as funding was secured, he replied, only so far none was forthcoming. A few days after that call, Newhall received a fax from U.S. AID in Manila formally offering a maximum of $20,000 in return for help with Mount Pinatubo. The fax, as Thompson reported, also included the terse suggestion that Newhall not feel obligated to spend all the money. They had no idea what they were up against. Then again, no one did.

On April 23, 1991, Newhall arrived in Manila with geophysicist Andy Lockhart from Vancouver, Washington, and seismologist John Power from Anchorage, Alaska, to 92°F (33°C) heat at 4:00 A.M. A U.S. embassy caravan of bulletproof Chevy Suburbans met them and their 35 trunks filled with VDAP equipment. After a few days of searching for a suitable place to establish an observatory with a view of the volcano, the USGS team working with Punongbayan, Gemme Ambubuyog, and Sergio Marcial of the PHIVOLCS team finally set up a new Pinatubo Volcano Observatory headquarters in an apartment in the middle of Clark Base.

While waiting for helicopter time to establish a telemetered seismic network around the volcano, the seismologists on the PVO team set up one of the seismometers on a hill inside Clark Base. Newhall and others took to digging for clues on the volcano's hazard history. They looked for cliff faces and followed river channels for areas where the stratigraphic history was exposed. They confirmed Clark and much of Angeles City were built on eruptive debris. Indeed, the pumice, ash, and lahar flows were so thick it was difficult to tell one eruption from the next. They needed to do just that though to determine how frequently eruptions on Pinatubo occurred. They needed a historical frame of reference in order to put the current activity into context.

Pressed for time, they relied on their best estimates from radiocarbon dating done on charcoal and wood buried in the deposits. Whenever possible they looked for rooted trees buried by the debris and collected the bark, the youngest part of the tree. More often than not the carbon came from an unknown part of a tree, a less desirable sample. The burnt charcoal bits from unknown parts of a tree could be several hundred years older than the eruption layer now containing the charcoal. The carbon may have formed in the older heartwood of the tree or a fresh pyroclastic flow might have picked up the charcoal from an older eruption. With little else to distinguish the eruptive histories, the carbon story would have to do.

After sending the wood and charcoal samples back to the USGS labs in the states, the team received a fax a few days later with the results. The largest eruption in Pinatubo's modern history had left 330-feet (100-m) thick deposits of pumice and pyroclastic debris on all sides of the volcano about 35,000 years ago. Since then large eruptions had struck 17,000 years ago, 9,000 years ago, 5,500 years ago, and 3,000 years ago. Prior to 1991 the last major eruption occurred less than 500 years ago and may have happened as recently as 300 years ago. With deposits of incinerating pyroclastic flows piling up with increasing frequency, Mount Pinatubo had laid out a map of its typical and worst-case scenarios. Odds were Mount Pinatubo would erupt with tremendous force, releasing as much pyroclastic material as was typically deposited during its previous eruptions, but likely not as much as had been deposited 35,000 years ago.

The team set up a plan to increase the volcanic alert levels as the seismic activity and unrest intensified. USGS volcanologists had become adept at predicting the dome building eruptions on Mount St. Helens between 1980 and 1986 by monitoring seismicity, sulfur gas emissions, and the dome's habit of inflating slightly before erupting. The American and Philippine team now incorporated the importance of providing a timely notice of an eruption into their alert system for Pinatubo. At level one, the activity was not predictive of an eruption, meaning the seismicity and fumaroles were normal to the tectonics of the volcano. At level two, harmonic tremors or long period earthquakes indicated magma was on the move and might eventually lead to an eruption. Level three was considered the two-week notice that the volcano would erupt; the increasing intensity of harmonic tremors might be accompanied by sulfuric gases, but not necessarily. Level four meant an eruption was likely within the next 24 hours, and level five meant an eruption was happening. At level four the U.S. military agreed it would evacuate Clark Air Base. Punongbayan in the meantime planned to call for evacuations in concentrically larger distances away from the summit every time the alert level increased—similar to the actions he took with Mayon in 1984.

By the second week of May, the Pinatubo observation team finished installing six telemetered seismometers in areas around the volcano that were only reachable by helicopter. The volcanologists scythed down the tropical grasses with bush knives bought in a tourist shop, dug through the topsoil into the packed stony pumice, and poured quick-setting cement foundations for their instruments and radio antennas. Even at the higher elevation, it was sweaty work. Just as they completed setting up the network, the seismic activity on the volcano calmed down.

Thousand-foot-high steam plumes (200 to 500 m) shot into the sky throughout April and into May. Military and commercial pilots diverted flights to avoid the hazy hiccups. Newhall jury-rigged the sulfur gas detector for use in a helicopter. Sulfur dioxide absorbs light that is emitted in the ultraviolet wavelength. Usually the instrument, a spectrometer, points out a window in a plane to correlate the amount of incoming ultraviolet light against a standard. In the helicopter, Newhall had to point the spectrometer in such a way that the propellers did not block the instrument's view of the Sun. The amount of sulfur dioxide ejected out of the vents increased tenfold between May 13 and May 28. Combined with telemeters, which detected any signs of the summit bulging, the seismic network and sulfur readings gave the team a quick lesson in Pinatubo's ongoing eruptive status.

Toward the end of May, the volcanologists had learned how to read the volcano's changing complex. They began preparations for long-term monitoring. The USGS team brought in new volunteer observers to take over for those who had to return to work in the states. Dave Harlow, John Ewert, and Rick Hoblitt arrived as part of this second wave of VDAP volunteers with $40,000 worth of equipment from the Survey. Hoblitt took a look at the hazard maps, studied the pyroclastic debris fields around Clark Base, and suggested the team look for another spot for their observatory, just in case.

On June 4, the Pinatubo monitoring team received word that Mount Unzen in Japan had exploded, killing Cascade volcanologist Harry Glicken and French filmmakers and volcanologists Maurice and Katia Kraft as well as 40 journalists covering the recent dome-building eruptions. The group had been standing on a ridge above a valley they thought was a safe distance from the volcano when a lung-scorching pyroclastic flow raced down the summit at hurricane speeds into the valley then up and over the ridge as if hitting a ski jump. The rising heat and eruptive debris engulfed those on the ground in a matter of minutes.

To aid their education efforts, the Pinatubo monitoring team had been relying heavily on a video the Krafts had made about volcanic danger entitled *Understanding Volcanic Hazards.* "This video, made in response to the tragic misunderstanding and disaster at Nevado del Ruiz, shows graphic examples of hot ash flows, ash fall, volcanic mudflows, large volcanic landslides, volcanogenic tsunami, lava flows, and volcanic gases," Punongbayan reported. "Superb, sometimes shocking, footage and a simple text illustrate the nature of each phenomenon, how fast and far it travels, and its impact on people and houses. Knowing the principal hazards of Pinatubo, we showed sections of the video on hot ash flows, ash fall, and mudflows to as many audiences as we could reach—ranging from then-President Aquino, then-Secretary of Defense Fidel Ramos and other Department Secretaries, to Governors, the chief of the RDCC, military base commanders, local officials, students, teachers, religious leaders, and barangay residents. We made perhaps 50 copies of the tape and left a copy with each group that we briefed; an untold number of second-generation copies was made. Initial response to the tape was typically shock and disbelief or denial. However, slowly but surely, the tape did convert some skeptics, and people did start to plan for a possible eruption."

On June 5, Punongbayan raised the alert level for Pinatubo to level three and ordered the evacuation of 10,000 Aetas from off the mountain. For many of them it would be their second evacuation since April. PHIVOLCS staff living in a village 4 miles (7 km) west of the summit moved to a safer location 14 miles (22 km) from the summit. The raised alert level was based on two days of increasing activity in long period seismic events, an ominous decrease of sulfur dioxide to below May 13 levels, combined with an increase of ash in the steam plumes, and an aerial survey of the summit on the morning of the 5th that revealed hard rocky lava had emerged in the form of a spine, like a giant gravestone rising above the ground.

When a following survey found that the spine was in fact the remnants of a ridge between two widening fissures, the alert level remained the same. The team had made it a rule that once they declared a higher alert level they would not lower it back down for two weeks. This was done to prevent public confusion; volcanic activity prior to a major eruption was typically full of ups and downs, volcanic and human induced. Having committed to a level three alert however, the volcanologists had effectively given the military and the public their two-week notice to prepare for a major eruption. After two days of increasing seismicity and indications that the summit was inflating, Harlow alerted Clark base commander Colonel Jeffrey Grime that the volcanologists would be moving to their designated fallback location, just as soon as Colonel John Murphy installed the phone lines in the building. The previously abandoned and isolated structure was as far to the east away from the volcano that the team could find and still be on the base. That afternoon Harlow tentatively raised the alert level to four. Punongbayan ordered another round of evacuations off the mountain.

Despite more than a month of interactions with the Volcano Disaster Assistance Team, Grime authorized dissemination of evacuation procedures to the personnel on the base only after the volcano alert level went to three. Colonel John Murphy had previously gone ahead with planning the evacuation procedures weeks earlier, reportedly without authorization to do so. Most everyone on the base would evacuate to Subic Bay Naval Air Station more than 20 miles (32 km) to the southwest. Murphy identified a closer emergency fallback location at a college 10 miles east of Clark Base behind the afternoon shadow of Mount Arayat. In exchange for construction upgrades to its buildings, the Pampanga Agricultural College agreed to store extra Air Force supplies, food, and water. After the volcanologists declared a level four alert, Major General William A. Studer started evacuating hospital patients from Clark Air Base to Subic Bay Naval Air Station, but he did not yet make the call for a complete evacuation.

On the morning of June 8, an aerial survey spotted a lava dome extruding from the summit. "At this point, we began to question the wisdom of the five-level alert scheme, because dome growth was, technically, an eruption in progress," Punongbayan wrote in a later report. The solid mound of lava pushing up through the crust of the volcano was invisible to the public. Failing to see a Mount St. Helens-like explosion within 24 hours after the level four alert was raised, news reporters claimed the volcanologists had made the wrong call. Then on June 9, PHIVOLCS team members monitoring the western flank of the volcano mistook an ash plume blown westward along the ground for a pyroclastic flow; the alert level went to five. Hoblitt had been flying over the ash-venting summit in a helicopter with Colonel Grime and Major General Studer when the alert level was raised. The next morning at 6:00 A.M., Clark Base began evacuations.

In five days, 25,000 villagers had fled Pinatubo for evacuation camps set up in the lowlands. Now on June 10, with military efficiency, 14,500 people, many of them dependents—sons, daughters, husbands, and wives—of enlisted personnel, drove in a long slow caravan of buses and cars to Subic Bay Naval Air Station. F-15 fighter pilots took off, banked, and landed on safer ground minutes later. Of the military aircraft on the base only three helicopters remained. The evacuees packed enough clothes, food, and water for three days away from home. Within six hours, Clark Base was left with a skeleton staff of about 1,500 U.S. military personnel. Philippine military guards joined them to help protect the base from looters. At Subic Bay the evacuees found shelter wherever they could, including in classrooms, auditoriums, chapels, empty offices, and hallways in between. Those with pets camped near their cars in the heat. Subic families adopted hundreds of American ones. Thompson wrote that Hoblitt and Lockhart learned from their helicopter pilot the next day that some men at the Subic Bay base had "dug holes in the sandy soil under their cars and crawled into the shade."

With no explosive eruption in sight, the volcanologists again received strong criticism in the local papers; this time Maj. General Studer also took his share of the flack. Back in the states, the *Washington Post* and the *New York Times* carried stories quoting the mayor of Angeles City as calling the evacuation of Clark Base an overreaction that was "causing a panic." The volcanologists worried and waited.

Then starting on June 12, "the volcano spoke mainly for itself," the Pinatubo team reported. A burst of seismic intensity roused the volcanologists to full alert at 3:00 A.M. Andy Lockhart and others still living in the first Pinatubo observatory quickly drove the 3 miles (5 km) east to the fallback location to join the rest of the team. In the dark early hours lightning flashed above the summit. Daylight brought bright blue sky, a scattering of low cumulus clouds, and nonstop ash plumes rising about 10,000 feet (3,050 m) high. Aerial observations confirmed the pyroclastic flows had begun. Riding with Maj. General Studer and Lockhart, an hour after sunrise, Hoblitt could smell burning vegetation in the winds whipping through the helicopter. The pyroclastic flows had set fires to the forest and the helicopter crew saw the remnants of the debris flow still smoking and steaming along the river channel on the northwest slope, now choked with boulders.

Back at the base at 8:51 A.M., Hoblitt, again in the first observatory building, saw harmonic tremors, long period earthquakes, with high-amplitude signals saturate the seismic network. Hoblitt rushed outside with Lockhart in time to see a dark gray column of ash shoot through the clouds to an altitude of about 62,000 feet (19,000 m). As the thick stalky plume reached its maximum height the ash at the top started to churn and broil in the sky forming a cauliflower cloud of ash standing over the summit. Lockhart was terrified. For the second time that morning he drove to the fallback location with his heart racing. This time Hoblitt stopped to alert others on the base and take pictures. When they finally arrived at the fallback observatory building, they found Harlow also snapping photos and dancing an "eruption jig," to welcome them, wrote Thompson. The Pinatubo monitoring team had made the right call. The ash continued to pour into the sky for nearly an hour. It settled over the evacuated areas. President Corazon Aquino flew out from Manila to assess the damage. After her briefing with the PHIVOLCS team, she spoke to the press. Maj. General Studer evacuated another 600 military personnel from Clark Base.

An hour before midnight a second explosive eruption lasted for 14 minutes. Weather-radar observers at Clark saw the plume rise more than 78,800 feet (24,000 m) in 15 seconds. For two to four hours before the eruption the seismic activity had swarmed, giving the volcanologists advanced warning, which they passed on to the civil and military authorities. Over the next few days the seismic network would whittle down to the single seismometer in the middle of Clark Base as the eruption progressed. At 8:41 A.M. on June 13, a five-minute explosion was seen reaching a height of more than 15 miles (24 km) in altitude. Long-period earthquakes swarmed again that afternoon and the volcanologists sent out another ash advisory alert. Only instead of releasing its magmatic energy the volcano held back and continued to shiver. The seismic swarm continued through the night and into the next afternoon. The Pinatubo monitoring team saw the situation as exceedingly dangerous. "The big one is yet to come," they warned.

Then the bad news turned worse. The windless tropical depression that had allowed most of the ash from the first four explosive eruptions to fall within the evacuation zone had brewed a tropical storm off the country's southeast shore. Over the ocean the warm moist air condensed into clouds and started spinning in a counterclockwise circle. Typhoon Yunya was now traveling northwest and approaching Luzon. PHIVOLCS extended the evacuation radius to nearly 19 miles (30 km), and the number of evacuees increased to 58,000. At 1:00 P.M. on Friday June 14, a two-minute eruption exploded reaching a height of about 13 miles (21 km). At 2:00 P.M. General Studer flew with Hoblitt, Harlow, Murray, and the helicopter pilots to the summit to give the volcanologists a chance to try and fix the antenna on one of the seismometers. Thunder and lightning echoed and flashed around them as cumulonimbus clouds encroached around the vent containing the crater-plugging lava dome. They gave up after a half hour and left just before another explosion of ash surged out of the vent. The rains started thickening the ash to mud.

The eruptions continued throughout the evening in three energetic clusters with shorter plumes culminating in a spike of explosive material. The eruptions paused for an hour or two and then began again, ramping up to a peak explosion. Just as the typhoon was hitting land, the volcano was changing its strategy. Instead of vertical shots more than 12 miles (20 km) into the air, the ash billowed out in a squat mushrooming cloud that spread horizontally, blanketing the summit in a pyroclastic surge. The eruptions continued through the night as seen through an infrared telescope.

At 5:55 A.M. on June 15, the volcanologists witnessed with their own eyes a pyroclastic surge flowing off the summit and heading toward Clark Base. The cloud of hot ash and stone hugged the mountain slopes and expanded in the cooler air around the hot material. Then like a hot air balloon, the surge tumbled into a convection current formed under the eruption's own power and rose vertically with the rising warm air. Knowing when and if a vertical uplift will come is a volcanologist's life-saver. They wanted to stay on the base. Maj. General Studer evacuated all but 88 Air Force security guards and about a dozen officers. The next eruption came at 8:10 A.M. The fallout of ash sent the camp into a smothering blackout a half hour later. Pumice stones pinged on the roofs and walls. The typhoon hit land with close to 100 mph winds (161 km/h). Passing over Pinatubo the wind hurled lava bombs the size of lemons at the base. Starting at 10:28 A.M., the eruptions and ash-induced blackouts continued with increasing frequency.

The remaining seismic stations still in communications with the observatory were saturated with activity. Then at 1:42 P.M. the second largest eruption of the century tore out the lava dome permanently and flooded the sky with ejecta for hours. The seismic signals, one-by-one, stopped transmitting. When the seismic signal on the eastern flank of the volcano blinked out, the officers and volcanologists at the fallback location moved away from the windows to the far eastern wall and waited to see if the pyroclastic flow that had just destroyed their seismometer would hit their building. "And they wait," Thompson wrote. "Standing there, amid pallets of supplies, Andy Lockhart grabs a bag of popcorn and starts eating. Amazed, one of the PHIVOLCS geologists asks, 'How can you eat popcorn at a time like this?' 'I always eat popcorn at this part of the movie,' he says." The scare passed. With the typhoon whipping muddy rain over the base and all but the seismometer in the middle of the base left for seismic monitoring, the team agreed it was time to abandon their fallback location and head for the college behind Mount Arayat. At 3:00 P.M. they join the caravan of evacuees from Angeles City driving slowly away from the volcano.

Analysis of satellite images published two years later showed that the June 15 eruption that started at 1:42 P.M. formed the shape of an umbrella over the island. At 3:40 P.M. the eruption cloud had spread about 250 miles (400 km) in diameter. The eastern edge of the ash umbrella hung

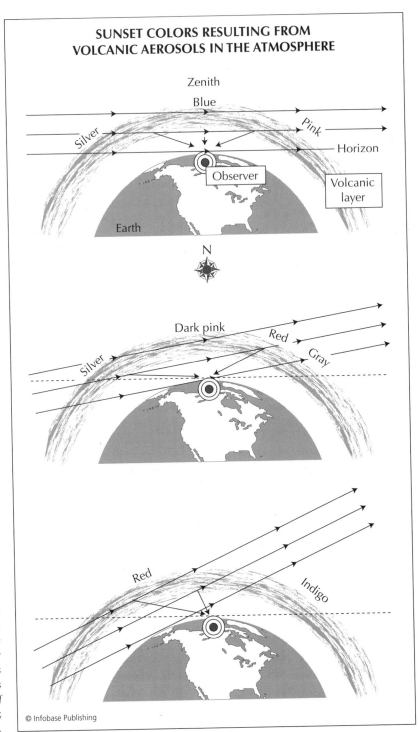

SUNSET COLORS RESULTING FROM
VOLCANIC AEROSOLS IN THE ATMOSPHERE

Sunset colors resulting from volcanic aerosols in the atmosphere. When the Sun sets after an explosive eruption has polluted the stratosphere with dust and gas, as was the case with Krakatau and Pinatubo, an observer on the ground can see the volcanic layer glow pink or red at twilight. Satellite images of the horizon after Pinatubo's eruption caught a spectrum of atmospheric colors: blue, silver, pink, yellow, and red.

© Infobase Publishing

about 16 miles (25 km) in altitude, and the handle of the plume reached directly from the summit to the stratosphere culminating in an elevation of 21 miles (34 km). The 1991 eruption of Mount Pinatubo lowered the height of the volcano from 5,725 feet (1,745 m) to 4,875 feet (1,486 m), leaving a 1.5-mile (2.5-km) wide caldera in place of the summit. The aerosols from the eruption lowered global temperature a degree. As with Krakatau in 1883, sunsets around the world glowed red. The damage to Clark Base was estimated at $300 million. The Air Force closed the base and evacuated the Clark personnel from Subic Bay Naval Air Station back to the United States and to other military bases in the South Pacific. In December the United States closed its base at Subic Bay as well.

In hindsight, the team of volcanologists recognized that the rains from Typhoon Yunya turned the ash fall into a deadly hazard they had not anticipated. "We did not give adequate warning that the accumulated ash would be much heavier than expected because of rain from the typhoon and did not anticipate that roofs which were already burdened by ash would be strained even more by earthquakes during the latter stages of the eruption. About 180 people were killed by roofs that collapsed under the weight of wet ash; another 50 to 100 people died from various other causes, including several tens from pyroclastic flows and another several tens from lahars." Given a similar situation in the future, the volcanologists vowed to give stronger warnings about the threat of ash mixing with heavy rains, and modify the alert levels to focus more on the different types of eruptions rather than the windows of time expected for an eruption to occur. As much as they worked to understand the eruption, luck also played a factor. "Pinatubo almost overtook us," wrote the team.

Moment Magnitude

Intensity scales, dependent as they are on how destructive an earthquake was to nearby buildings, are useless in comparing earthquakes that strike in regions where buildings are constructed differently. Bamboo homes in Japan can ride out the same energy waves that topple brick buildings in India, hence, the use of different intensity scales for different regions of the world. Even in the same region, new buildings are built differently from old, and, depending on the soil, the ground may deform differently than it does a mile away. Whether the buildings are on cliffs, landfills, karsts, swamps, or deserts are all factors that determine how much damage an earthquake might cause that are all unrelated to the earthquake itself. When seismologists Charles Richter and Beno Gutenberg of Caltech turned to magnitude rather than intensity to compare earthquakes they constrained such subjective analysis but did not eliminate it completely.

In 1935 Richter measured magnitude based on local seismic profiles from Caltech's Wood-Anderson seismometers. He measured the height of the seismic waves recorded on the seismograms and the time between the clearly defined P and S waves striking California. The Richter scale or local magnitude started a mathematical trend to assess earthquakes and seismic measurements of magnitude. Richter and Gutenberg developed a number of different magnitude scales depending on the earthquake's depth, distance from the seismometer, and what kind of waves the seismograms were recording and how these scales worked on different seismometers.

Seismologists around the world began comparing and assigning earthquake magnitudes. There were measurements of surface-wave magnitude (Ms), teleseismic body-wave magnitude (Mb), and duration magnitude (Md), in addition to the local magnitude (Ml) or the Richter magnitude that journalists reported to the public after any particularly devastating earthquake struck a region. Each type of magnitude tells one part of the earthquake story. All of these magnitudes were dependent on the type of seismometer used and its distance from the earthquake as well as the strength of the earthquake being recorded. The best estimate of a magnitude was the average from multiple seismometers. Surface wave magnitudes work best on shallow earthquakes with depths of less than 30 miles (50 km). To make the measurement of magnitude more meaningful, in 1956 Gutenberg and Richter introduced an equation to convert a measurement of surface-wave magnitude (Ms) to energy ($\log E = 1.5\,Ms + 11.8$). Energy was the true determinant of an earthquake's strength and a number that could be used for comparing non-tectonic seismic events, such as nuclear explosions. Most of the energy in a nuclear blast is converted to heat; relatively little finds its way through the Earth as a seismic wave, but the equation did not yield the comparisons seismologists were hoping to find for large earthquakes. Large earthquakes, with ruptures that exceed the wavelength of the seismic waves used to determine magnitude, overwhelm or saturate seismometers—making it exceptionally difficult to interpret their seismograms.

In 1977 seismologist Hiroo Kanamori (b. 1936), a professor at the Seismological Laboratory at Caltech, introduced a new method for determining the energy output of large earthquakes that did not rely on seismometers. For his solution, Kanamori turned to the geophysical roots of the problem. He estimated the earthquake's energy from the earthquake's *seismic moment* (Mo), which was defined as the rigidity of the rock type (μ) multiplied by the offset or distance the fault moved (D), and the area of the fault (A) as defined by the location of the aftershocks (such that $Mo = \mu DA$). Seismologists had previously searched for ways to estimate the seismic moment using long-period waves recorded on seismograms. Their success in finding the seismic moment for exceedingly large earthquakes inspired Kanamori. He calculated the relationship between seismic wave energy released during an earthquake and the earthquake's seismic moment by assuming certain theories in physics applied equally to the friction and stress in earthquakes as they do for other applications.

Kanomori found that the minimum amount of strain an earthquake released was equivalent to the seismic energy (Wo) and equal to a fraction of the seismic moment (Mo).

Where Gutenberg and Richter were searching for a way to convert magnitude to energy, Kanamori identified seismic energy first (Wo) and used the equation (log Wo = 1.5 (Mw) + 11.8) to convert seismic energy to a new moment magnitude scale (Mw). By the 1970s, seismologists and the public were accustomed to comparing and measuring the size of an earthquake by a magnitude scale. The moment magnitude (Mw) Kanamori identified gave the 1960 Chilean earthquake a magnitude of 9.5, the largest earthquake to strike during the 20th century. The surface-wave magnitude had reported the quake as an 8.3. Kanamori upgraded other previously designated magnitude 8's using his new moment magnitude scale. The 1964 Alaska earthquake equaled a magnitude of 9.2, the 1957 Aleutian Islands quake hit with a magnitude of 9.1, and the 1952 Kamchatka temblor had a magnitude of 9.0. He found that earthquakes with fault ruptures of about 62 miles (100 km) or less remained the same as the previous surface-wave magnitude scale had indicated. Kanamori suggested moment magnitude be used as a continuation of surface-wave magnitude for large earthquakes that would otherwise saturate the seismometers. He presented his work again in a 1978 report entitled "Quantification of Earthquakes" in the journal *Nature*, this time solving the Gutenberg Richter equation for moment magnitude based solely on seismic moment (such that Mw = [(log Mo)/1.5]-10.7).

The method was vetted throughout the 1980s and caught on quickly in the 1990s after Kanamori became director of the Seismological Laboratory at Caltech. He worked with Thomas Hanks of the USGS Earthquakes Hazard team in Menlo Park, California, in 1979 and others during the following decades to compute moment magnitudes. USGS seismologists began reporting earthquake magnitudes to the public as moment magnitude and were vexed when newspapers continued to refer to the earthquakes in terms of Richter magnitude or magnitudes on the Richter scale. The scientists still associated Richter magnitude with local magnitude.

In 2002 the National Earthquake Information Center in Golden, Colorado, established a formal earthquake magnitude policy that helped ease the tensions between the confused press and the scientists who by now found news reports of Richter magnitudes on Richter scales the new pet peeve. (For seismologists, this was equivalent to the physicists' top pet peeve of hearing journalists and politicians pronounce nuclear as nuk-u-lar rather than new-cle-ar.) The mission of the NEIC, part of the USGS since 1972, is to "determine rapidly the location and size of all destructive earthquakes worldwide and to immediately disseminate this information to concerned national and international agencies, scientists, and the general public." Seismologist Stuart Sipkin, cochair of the magnitude committee, says that moment magnitude became standard during the 1990s.

The policy in 2002 formalized the equation Kanamori presented in 1978 as the preferred method for determining moment magnitude over later equations that were presented. The policy also helped clarify that whenever magnitude is used it should be moment magnitude and it should be denoted as a single capital M. The other magnitudes would still have to keep their secondary clarifying letters—Ms, Ml, Mb, Md—but Mw could lose the archaic seismic wave energy (Wo) reference Kanamori had shyly given it in 1977 with its small w and proudly boast official magnitude "M" status. As for the tendency for the press to continue to report magnitudes on the Richter scale, the USGS policy stressed separating the method from the scale. "Richter's original methodology is no longer used," the committee wrote, because local magnitude does not give reliable results when applied to earthquakes of magnitudes greater than or equal to 7. Neither were Richter's original methods designed for seismometers located further than about 373 miles (600 km) from an earthquake's epicenter, the committee concluded. Still, the newer methods for determining magnitude are consistent with the magnitude scale that Richter originally proposed. "In fact, most modern methods for measuring magnitude were designed to be consistent with the Richter scale," the committee informed the public and reminded its seismologists.

The history of seismic monitoring would not be the same without Richter's contributions to the science, and the recognition of the magnitude scale as his is important. His was the start of a revolution in seismology. Magnitude distinguished seismic scales from earthquake intensity scales. The methods for determining magnitude have since evolved, with Kanamori providing the golden standard.

Snowball Earth

Under the draw of gravity, glaciers carve their way across continents to lower elevations grinding the path they follow to a fine dust; picking up pebbles, rocks, and boulders indiscriminately and pocketing them away to be dropped later when the glacier melts. Miles upon miles of fog-whispered and wind-loving *rime*, frozen precipitation crystals, and dusted snowdrifts stacked and squeezed into a clear blue ice—glaciers start out white on the surface and grow mud-caked tongues streaked black, gray, and brown with the flavors of the terrestrial Earth. When glaciers hit the coastline they keep going, becoming floating extensions of the land, until they calve and become icebergs—taking their assorted collection of ground cover with them, a one-way ticket on a slow, leaky boat to the soft sediments on the ocean floor. The technical term for ice-carried geologic paraphernalia far from home is *dropstones*.

During the 1950s, geologist Brian Harland (1917–2003) of Cambridge University in England became very familiar with a specific layer of red-colored dropstones because he kept finding them in strange locations. Granted he was surveying Norway's glacial-covered northern islands of

Svalbard, but the land that formed the islands were tropical carbonate seafloor crusts from the Precambrian. What were icebergs doing in the tropics 700 million years ago? Alternatively, what were the tropics doing near glaciers? Harland found the same red icy layer in Greenland and continental Norway. He read geologic reports of the strange layer being found elsewhere around the world. He collected enough evidence to convince himself that the layer was part of a global glaciation process, which he called the "Great Infra-Cambrian Glaciation."

While Harland was busy reading and digging for icy clues in the 1950s, marine geologists were hot on the trail of turbidity currents, or underwater avalanches. Oceanographers Bruce C. Heezen and Maurice Ewing of the Lamont Doherty Geologic Observatory pointed to a submarine slump causing a turbidity current that broke transatlantic telephone cables in 1929 after an earthquake in the Grand Banks. Paleoclimatologist John Crowell at the University of California, Santa Barbara, pointed to underwater rivers of mud and rocks as an alternative explanation to the idea that glaciers carved the canyons off the coast of California when they were still on dry land. Suddenly ice was not the only way to distribute rocks across the seafloor. When Harland presented his work on the curious global layer of glacial-born rocks at a meeting for paleoclimatologists in January 1963, he was met with deprecation.

The previous year, Dutch marine geologist Arnold Bouma published a book describing sedimentation sequences from turbidity currents. His sequence described turbidity flows as depositing heavy cobbles first and the smaller lighter pebbles later, followed by fine sand grains and silt. By July 1963, Bouma's analysis had caught the attention of the paleontology community.

Crowell, who had met Harland at the meeting, searched elsewhere around the world for examples of turbidites and dropstones. On all seven continents, he found evidence that the strange red Precambrian layer was clearly ice driven. As Harland described it, the iceberg rafted stones fell indiscriminate of size. Large and small rocks were mixed together. Another clue was that in cross-sections of sedimentary layer ice-rafted rocks look like they were dropped from above, forming small craters of compacted sediment under the rocks with normal sedimentation rates filling in the areas around and on top of the rocks. These were not stones that were dragged through the sediment, in which case they would form deformation lines on the top and bottom, squishing the sediment around the rocks as they moved. As a final clue, ice-carried rocks are scratched in parallel lines from slow steady pressure. As the paleoclimate community began to swing to the Precambrian ice age hypothesis, two lines of evidence stood in the way of the ice age being a global phenomena: plate tectonics and computer climate modeling.

Harland had been a long supporter of continental drift, acting as a contrarian to his teachers even when he was just in grade school. As continents in motion became an acceptable notion, there was only one way to find out if the continents had picked up the ice layer on their journey north or south or if they had been hit by ice on the equator. Harland began examining the paleomagnetic stories of the icy rocks. Remember the Earth's magnetic field is a dipole formed in the core that today travels out through the Arctic seafloor, through the Arctic ocean, past any seasonal Arctic sea ice in its way at the magnetic North Pole, stationed off the coast of the Northern Canadian islands. The field wraps the Earth and extends high into space as it travels longitudinally halfway around the planet passing perpendicular to the equator. The field flows back into Earth at the magnetic South Pole, stationed off the coast of Antarctica due south of Australia, where the field travels through the glacial ice sheet extending off of the Antarctic coast, through the Antarctic ocean and back through the crust and mantle to the faster spinning core. From a rock's magnetic perspective today, north is up, south is down, and the equator is horizontal. When the magnetic field reverses, north is down, south is up, but the equator is still horizontal. If the paleomagnetic fields from the ice rocks were horizontal, Harland would have some solid evidence in hand supporting equatorial glaciation. They were, but he did not. He had struggled to identify the weak horizontal magnetic signatures in the Svalbard rocks. Making sure the magnetic signature was original to the rocks and not a later alteration of their signal was beyond his ability. And then, as science journalist Gabrielle Walker reports in her book *Snowball Earth*, the university authorities dealt Harland a devastating blow. They built a parking lot outside his lab. "The rock magnets were so weak, and the instruments to measure them still so crude, that any slight changes in the field around them would wreck the results," Walker wrote. Now the magnetic field in Harland's lab changed every time a car entered or left the parking lot, she wrote. The understanding of plate tectonics put into question the global extent of Harland's "Great Infra-Cambrian Glaciation."

In 1969 a Russian climate modeler would single-handedly end the debate for nearly 30 years. Mikhail Budyko (b. 1920) of the Main Geophysical Observatory in St. Petersburg was one of the first to use computer modeling to compare the possible scenarios of Earth's heat budget with historical observations of climate. His book on the subject, *Heat Balance of the Earth's Surface*, published in 1956, introduced global climate models to a burgeoning generation of computer hungry scientists. In the 1960s as questions about man-made nuclear winter and the global extent of ice ages abounded. Budyko set his computer model to tackle the problem. He learned that Earth had a tipping point for keeping ice in check. As ice grows, its white surface reflects more heat back out to space, cooling the planet and allowing the ice to gain a stronger foothold. Normally, the Earth is warm enough to keep the ice above 40° latitude. If the detonation of nuclear bombs around the world blocked the sunlight, his model showed that the ice could extend to the tropics. At that point, the Earth would be so reflective of its heat that the warmth from the Sun would be inconsequential. His model showed that the ice would cover the planet and never recede.

As with all models, the output depends on the input. In the 1970s, Budyko would go on to model the relationship between rising carbon dioxide levels and global warming, but he did not think to look back at how an ice-covered world would change the feedback mechanisms in moderating this important greenhouse gas. There was a natural way out of global glaciation. Volcanic emissions provide a small but constant influx of carbon dioxide and other greenhouse gases. The atmosphere loses its carbon dioxide gas through chemical reactions with water and weathering of continental silica rocks. Rainwater becomes slightly acidic. Hydrocarbons and calcium carbonates form through gas exchange with the oceans and in reactions to minerals on land. (The chemical weathering of silicates on land is: $CaSiO_3 + CO_2 \leftrightarrow CaCO_3 + SiO_2$. In water the chemical reaction forms a weak hydrocarbon $CO_2 + H_2O \leftrightarrow H_2CO_3$. The weak acidic hydrocarbon breaks down easily into hydrogen and insoluble carbonate: $H^+ + CO_3^{2-}$.) The sinks for carbon provide a natural balance for the CO_2 sources. With the oceans and land ice-covered, and precipitation, if it was falling at all, coming down as frozen water less amiable to gas exchange, the sinks for carbon were clogged. Eventually the atmosphere would trap enough heat to send the glaciers in full retreat.

In 1986 magnet specialist Joe Kirschvink of Caltech received a manuscript investigating the paleomagnetic history of Precambrian ice-rafted rocks in Australia. Kirschvink developed a niche studying the biological and geological correlations with magnets and magnetic fields. Not surprisingly, he was asked to peer-review articles about magnetics that were under consideration for publication. The authors of this manuscript, Australian researchers George Williams and Brian Embleton, concluded that the outcrop containing the rocks had originated near the equator when the ice dropped the dropstones. Once again: evidence of equatorial ice! Only in scientific terminology the excitement of their findings were muted to: "Low palaeolatitude of deposition for late Precambrian periglacial varvites in South Australia." Their paper was met with skepticism from the Earth science community. Kirschvink was not convinced. Like Harland, they had not tested their results to determine if the outcrop's magnetic field was original or formed later in the rock's history. Kirschvink had the methods and the means to have the tests done at Caltech using an extremely sensitive magnetometer. The results put him on the case of what he would call the "Snowball Earth."

Other mysterious geological formations occurred around the same time as the Precambrian ice rocks. One of these was the presence of iron-rich rocks in an already oxygen-enriched Ediacarian world. By the 1980s, the evidence for life in the Precambrian was unmistakable. The Proterozoic seas swarmed with plants and later invertebrates. At least a billion years earlier, the tiny cyanobacteria forming stromatolites had packed a big punch to the atmosphere. Breathing in carbon dioxide and respiring oxygen, they transformed the planet. In oxygenated seas, soluble iron (Fe^{2+}) either rusts, falling to the seafloor as a solid precipitate, or is consumed through biological processes. The early Earth's geologic history is banded with seafloor sediments dyed red with insoluble ferric iron oxides (Fe^{3+}) in minerals of magnetite (Fe_3O_4) and hematite (Fe_2O_3). Then 1.8 billion years ago, the ironstones stopped forming—with the exception of a small blip on the geologic record of banded iron formations during the time of Harland's global ice coverage.

Kirschvink had a compelling explanation. The paleomagnetic evidence from Australia pointed to equatorial ice. From Budyko's model, equatorial ice indicated global ice coverage. Kirschvink had seen red ironstones in the upper Precambrian layers in Canada. He hypothesized that during this time in Proterozoic history, the ice not only covered the land but also the sea. Applying plate tectonic theory, he proposed that most of the landmasses were positioned in low latitudes—a belt of land around the planet's equatorial hips with its icy poles land-free. He suggested that the land at the equator prevented the oceans from absorbing the Sun's strongest rays and worked almost as well as the ice at the poles in reflecting heat back out to space. As the Earth spun closer to its tipping point for a global ice age the stops to prevent the icy onslaught were not in place. He coined the phrase "Snowball Earth" and turned to volcanism to explain both the ironstones and a way out of the never-ending ice spell Budyko concluded had never happened.

Volcanoes like Hekla erupt through the glaciers adding a breath more carbon dioxide and other aerosols to the atmosphere with every outburst. Underwater volcanoes and hydrothermal vents continue to add gases and dissolved chemicals such as ferrous iron to the oceans. Under snowball ice conditions, cut off from air-sea interactions by the ice, the seas would become depleted of oxygen as the iron concentrations accumulated. Kirschvink suggested the seas would turn anoxic and once more supersaturated with enough iron to color the seafloor sediments as red as they had been in the Archean. He suggested that when the global warming from the excess carbon dioxide melted the ice, the pockets of surviving plant life in the Proterozoic oceans would burst into overdrive, consuming CO_2 and respiring oxygen, which would send the excess iron rusting again to the bottom of the sea. Kirschvink wrote the two-page paper on his Snowball Earth hypothesis in 1988 as part of a book on Proterozoic life, but the book was not published until 1992. Kirschvink's hypothesis went largely unnoticed.

In the meantime, oceanographers in the 1990s began testing John Martin's (1935–93) iron hypothesis. "Give me a half tanker of iron, and I will give you an ice age," he famously quipped. He had carefully measured iron concentrations in seawater and found them exceedingly low in some parts of the world. Iron is abundant in the Earth's crust and winds also contribute iron to the oceans by driving it off the continents. In the Southern Hemisphere, where the largest landmass is ice-covered, the

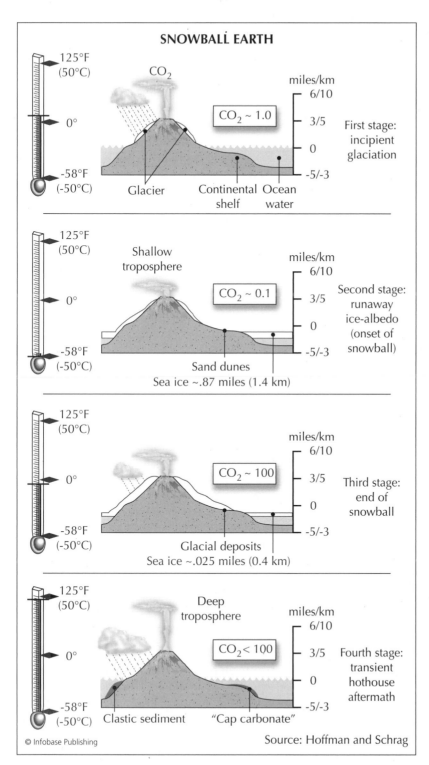

SNOWBALL EARTH

First stage: incipient glaciation

$CO_2 \sim 1.0$

Glacier   Continental shelf   Ocean water

Second stage: runaway ice-albedo (onset of snowball)

Shallow troposphere

$CO_2 \sim 0.1$

Sand dunes
Sea ice ~.87 miles (1.4 km)

Third stage: end of snowball

$CO_2 \sim 100$

Glacial deposits
Sea ice ~.025 miles (0.4 km)

Fourth stage: transient hothouse aftermath

Deep troposphere

$CO_2 < 100$

Clastic sediment   "Cap carbonate"

© Infobase Publishing

Source: Hoffman and Schrag

The Snowball Earth hypothesis outlines a period in Earth's history during the Proterozoic when ice covered the globe. The high reflectivity of heat from glaciers and sea ice further cooled the planet, allowing for greater ice coverage. The ice blocked the usual carbon sinks. The buildup of carbon dioxide in the atmosphere from volcanism melted the ice. When the carbon reacted with the ground-up glacial debris it formed carbonate structures. (Paul Hoffman, Harvard University)

oceans suffer from iron deficiency and low productivity despite being otherwise nutrient rich. In 1993 and 1995, experiments fertilizing the ocean with ferrous iron produced phytoplankton blooms. Having more plants in the ocean's surface waters, Martin hypothesized, would remove more dissolved CO_2 and allow the ocean to draw more carbon dioxide from the atmosphere, cooling the atmosphere.

In the mid to late 1990s, Harvard geologist Paul Hoffman remembered a conversation he had with Kirschvink about his Snowball Earth hypothesis years earlier. Hoffman and his students had been seeing some strange Precambrian geologic features in Namibia's Skeleton Coast. What if Kirschvink was right? He ran the idea and the findings from his geologic field trips past his best friend Dan Schrag. Every summer since 1993, Hoffman had been methodically collecting clues in the African desert without seeing how they fit together. Like Kirschvink and Harland, Hoffman had found the icy indications of dropstones, yes. These were curiously bounded on top and bottom with warm-water carbonate rocks, but where the carbonates were, apparently life was not. The carbon isotope of choice for carbon-consuming organisms is the light carbon-12 isotope, the green M&M's of the carbon world, leaving the heavy carbon-13 isotope as leftovers for the geologic record. In the Namibian carbonates, however, there was plenty of carbon-12 as well as carbon-13, as if the carbon bowl of chocolate candies had not been touched. In addition to the isotope enigma, the cap carbonates on one cliff above the dropstone layer had fans of red crystals embedded like a frozen fountain of fireworks. On the opposite valley wall, dark-brown, tubes shot vertically through the tan carbonate layers. The Snowball Earth hypothesis became one of many possible explanations, and one that was tough to disprove. After reading Hoffman's report, Schrag, a geochemist at Harvard and later the director of the Harvard laboratory for geochemical oceanography, was hooked.

Schrag helped Hoffman expand Kirschvink's Snowball Earth hypothesis to include what might have happened after the ice melted. Schrag considered the formation of the carbonates and the potential amount of heat the atmosphere would have had to produce in order to melt the glaciers back. The moisture released as the ice evaporated, mixed with the hot, dry, CO_2-choked air. The carbonates, Schrag reasoned, formed from the acidic rain that pounded the ground during torrential hurricanes. While on the carving course, the glaciers had left a fine silicate powder residue on the continents. What's the easiest way to dissolve rocks? Grind, heat, and add acid. A lump of sugar in iced tea will take longer to dissolve than granular sugar, and both will take longer than finely ground, powdered sugar. Heat the tea and even the lump of sugar will melt within seconds. Add lemon juice and the chemical reaction moves even faster. As Walker writes, "In the post-Snowball world, that combination of ground-up rock and torrential acid rain was a chemical factory waiting to happen. Rock dust and acid met, mated and were swept off into the sea. They set the waters fizzing and foaming, creating a Coca-Cola ocean."

The by-product of all this chemistry was insoluble carbonates: almost 200,000 cubic miles (800,000 km³) of it, enough to cover the present-day continental crust with a carbonate layer 16 feet (5 m) thick, Hoffman and Schrag concluded in their 1998 paper published in *Science* with coauthors Alan J. Kaufman and Galen P. Halverson. The tubes and crystal fans in the carbonates were harder to explain and they only briefly mentioned them in their report. Schrag suggested they were the product of rapid carbonate deposition: the tubes made from air bubbles that shot through the sediments and the red crystals from processes similar to those found in the acidic hot springs of Yellowstone. Hoffman interpreted the isotope ratio in the carbonates below the glacial deposits at least as suggestive of a collapse in biological productivity. Schrag added that during the snowball and afterward, the natural carbon sources likely overwhelmed the biological sinks and left an isotope ratio that matched what is normally emitted from hydrothermal vents and volcanoes. Where Kirschvink had provided a way into the snowball scenario (low-latitude landmasses with high albedos), Hoffman and Schrag now proposed at least three reasons why it had not happened since:

- older, warmer Sun
- evolution of worms and other seafloor creatures the burrow in the sediments reducing the amount of organic carbon that remains locked away
- limits on primary productivity from low levels of iron and phosphorus in a more oxygenated ocean

They speculated that the breakup of the continents around the equatorial belt would have helped draw down the amount of carbon dioxide in the atmosphere. Having continents in the upper latitudes would also likely prevent the ice from reaching the warm tropical seas. Many met the reemergence of the Snowball Earth hypothesis in 1998 with skepticism. In the 21st century, Hoffman and Schrag have continued to tackle every critique that comes their way.

Greenhouse Gases

In the last decade of the 19th century, Svante Arrhenius (1859–1927) quantified the importance of carbon dioxide as a greenhouse gas in the atmosphere. He hypothesized in his 1896 publication that variations in atmospheric carbon dioxide (carbonic acid as it was then called) had a 7.2 to 16.2°F (5 to 10°C) influence on Earth's temperature. The result, he said, might provide an explanation for glaciation trends and ice ages.

Since 1827, the idea that water vapor, carbon dioxide, methane, and other gases in the atmosphere acted like the glass in a winter garden hothouse—allowing the Sun's heat to penetrate while retaining Earth's heat—had fascinated physicists. They measured the reflected light from

Svante August Arrhenius, one of the founders of physical chemistry (E. F. Smith Collection, Rare Book & Manuscript Library, University of Pennsylvania)

the Sun off the Moon and came to the conclusion that Earth's atmosphere prevented the planet from becoming the cold wasteland they saw on the satellite. They later identified the Sun's light rays as shortwave radiation and the Earth's "dark" rays as long-wave radiation. Arrhenius in the first decade of the 20th century went on to predict that burning of fossil fuels would increase carbon dioxide in the atmosphere and prevent the return of an ice age. He was not worried about an ice age striking in the 20th century. His concern was for a far distant future. He estimated atmospheric carbon levels would have to double before significant warming would be seen.

Given the amount of CO_2 that fossil fuel combustion was producing at the turn of the 20th century, it would take 1,000 years to double the total atmospheric carbon dioxide concentration if 100 percent of emissions remained in the atmosphere. With Earth's land and seas locking away about 60 percent of the anthropogenic carbon dioxide emissions for decades to centuries, it would take 2,500 years to double the total amount of atmospheric carbon if emissions stayed at 1903 levels. Arrhenius did not anticipate the more than tenfold increase in emissions that occurred in the 20th century. If he started with 2003 levels, reaching a doubling of total atmospheric CO_2 concentrations would take only 210 years, even with the large percent of that extra carbon being taken up and stored by the world's oceans and forests.

Although ice ages continued to fascinate scientists, few continued Arrhenius's work on Earth's greenhouse gases. That changed after Charles Keeling of Scripps Institution of Oceanography started monitoring the amount of carbon dioxide in the atmosphere in 1958 from the mountaintop of Mauna Loa in Hawaii. The steady rise in the amount of carbon dioxide in the atmosphere alarmed scientists and boosted international efforts in the 1970s and 1980s to understand how different parts of the planet contribute to the global system. Atmospheric scientists,

In the 1980s, Wally Broecker of Columbia University's Lamont-Doherty Earth Observatory identified the global ocean circulation as a climate regulator. The Sun warms surface waters at the equator where rains dilute salinity levels. As water cools in the Northern Hemisphere, sea ice forms leaving the salts behind to sink in the cold dense currents. Upwelling brings the cold waters back to the surface.

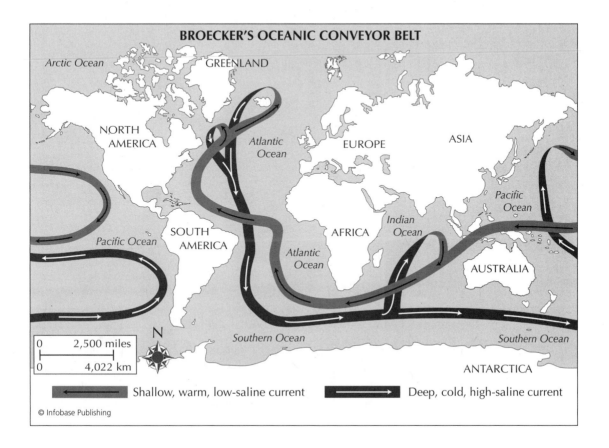

© Infobase Publishing

meteorologists, paleoclimatologists, astronomers, geophysicists, oceanographers, paleobotanists, dendrochronologists, and marine geologists for example examined their fields to understand the land-ocean-atmospheric and astronomical interactions that influence climate. Earth's own position in relationship to the Sun—the Milankovitch cycles in Earth's orbit, obliquity, and *axial tilt*—emerged as the dominant force driving climate change, with carbon dioxide as an important feedback mechanism. Other significant drivers of climate change include the ocean's thermalhaline circulation, its conveyor belt of salt and heat around the world, and the location of Earth's continental plates in routing the ocean currents. Recognizing that natural variations in climate will happen with or without

Wallace Broecker at the Moreno Glacier, an outlet glacier of the South Patagonian Ice Cap in the southern Argentine Andes (Steve Porter)

human contributions to the carbon cycle, many scientists wondered how much of an influence changes in carbon dioxide played in the past and could potentially play in the future.

By the end of the last decade of the 20th century, Keeling's record of the rapidly increasing carbon dioxide concentrations in the atmosphere had

This figure shows simplified averages of common sources and sinks for carbon. The dynamics of the cycle and contributions vary seasonally as well as year to year.

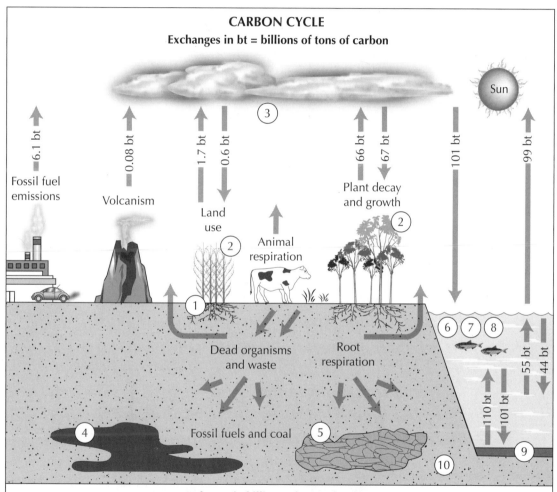

CARBON CYCLE
Exchanges in bt = billions of tons of carbon

Sun

6.1 bt

Fossil fuel emissions

0.08 bt

Volcanism

1.7 bt   0.6 bt

Land use

3

Animal respiration

2

66 bt   67 bt

Plant decay and growth

2

101 bt

99 bt

1

Dead organisms and waste

Root respiration

6 7 8

55 bt   44 bt

4

Fossil fuels and coal

5

110 bt   101 bt

10

9

Volumes in billions of tons of carbon

1. Soils and organic matter, 1,764
2. Vegetation, 595–672
3. Atmosphere, 827
4. Oil and gas deposits, 331
5. Coal deposits, 3,307
6. Dissolved organic carbon, 772

7. Marine organisms, 3.3
8. Surface water, 1,124
9. Surface sediment, 165
10. Sedimentary rock and marine sediment, 73,000,000–110,000,000
11. Intermediate and deep water, 42,000–44,000

© Infobase Publishing

Note: Multiply tons by 0.9072 to obtain metric tonnes

become the icon of global change in the Earth system. His measurements at the Mauna Loa Observatory traced the rise in carbon dioxide directly from the atmosphere. The short-term record since 1958 left scientists wondering if the current increase in carbon dioxide was part of the natural variation in the gas or the fault of human activity. That question was answered thanks to the analysis of gases in air bubbles that were trapped in ice as the major ice sheets were laid down in Antarctica and Greenland. The ice core data created a record of long-term changes in atmospheric concentrations that told the story of the rise and fall of carbon dioxide levels in the past hundreds of thousands of years. Concentrations were high in the interglacial eras, low during the full glaciers, but never as high as Keeling was measuring in the atmosphere. In 1850 the air contained a concentration of 288 parts per million by volume (ppmv) of carbon dioxide, a concentration that had remained steady for 850 years. In 2000 the air contained 369.5 ppmv of CO_2. The global atmospheric concentration of carbon dioxide in 2005 was 379 ppmv, exceeding the natural range of atmospheric carbon dioxide for the last 650,000 years (180 to 300 ppm), the Intergovernmental Panel on Climate Change reported in 2007.

Scientists also began to understand clearly why carbon dioxide was increasing. Since the start of the 20th century, emissions of carbon dioxide from human activities have increased dramatically, almost doubling in the last 40 years alone. Fossil-fuel burning emissions have gone from 680,126,079 tons (617 million metric tons) of carbon in 1903 to 8.0501795×10^9 tons (7,303 million metric tons) of carbon in 2003, reported Gregg Marland and colleagues of the U.S. Department of Energy's Carbon Dioxide Information Analysis Center in 2006. Fossil-fuel combustion is the primary driving force in the rise in atmospheric carbon since preindustrial time and makes up 64 percent of the carbon dioxide that humans contribute to the atmosphere. Of the total carbon

Paleoclimatologist Nicholas Shackleton (1937–2006) in his office in the Godwin Laboratory in autumn 2004. Shackleton examined climate cycles going back 400,000 years using glacial ice and marine sediment cores. (University of Cambridge Newsletter, December 2004)

dioxide in the atmosphere in 2000, 14 percent is from fossil-fuel combustion. Other significant sources of the increase in atmospheric carbon come from land use changes, such as deforestation, and production of cement. (Human respiration is not a significant source because humans breathe out as much carbon as they consume.) During the last 150 years, 40 percent of the significant anthropogenic sources of carbon dioxide have remained in the atmosphere with the Earth storing and sequestering the remaining 60 percent in the land and oceans.

The results on change in carbon and sources of carbon did not bode well. Humans were conducting a global experiment of rising atmospheric carbon dioxide beyond levels seen in the interglacial periods of the past. As scientists investigated the relationship between increased greenhouse gases and climate they began accumulating evidence that modern global warming had begun. Few thought like Arrhenius that global warming might still be good for humanity, or inconsequential, but the scientific debate over the relationship between the unmistakable rise in carbon dioxide to the potential effects of global warming was reframed in the political arena as a debate on whether or not global warming was really happening. Atmospheric and oceanic models of increased greenhouse gases showed that the trapped long-wave radiation and added CO_2 had many undesired consequences: rise in sea level, ocean acidification, loss of polar ice, loss of current agricultural farmlands, desertification, increased coastal erosion, and increased strength of hurricanes. The anticipated problems with global warming set a serious tone against the previously perceived advantages Arrhenius considered: new temperate regions closer to the poles, possibly larger crop yields, lower heating bills in the winter, possible prevention of a future ice age.

The environmental movement launched in the 1960s after Rachel Carson's investigation into the effect of pesticide use, specifically DDT, has for decades now derided companies for the pollution of lead, arsenic, asbestos, benzene, mercury, and soot into the environment. Industrially produced gases known for their contributions to air pollution include CFC's, sulfur dioxide, hydrocarbons, nitrogen oxides, and carbon monoxide. Government laws regulate the extent of industrial pollutants. When carbon dioxide, a nonpolluting natural gas, came under attack from scientists as a significant contributor along with methane to the greenhouse effect, there were no laws in place to force industry to curb these greenhouse gases. In the 1990s as the Intergovernmental Panel on Climate Change (IPCC) began reporting on the scientific consensus, international conventions on climate change convinced most politicians outside of the United States to begin working on ways to stabilize industrial emissions of greenhouse gases.

Society in the 21st century has much work to do to stabilize greenhouse gases. In 2007 the IPCC reported that the global atmospheric concentration of methane has increased from a pre-industrial value of about 715 parts per billion (ppb) to 1732 ppb in the early 1990s, and was 1774 ppb in 2005. "The atmospheric concentration of methane in 2005 exceeds by far the natural range of the last 650,000 years (320 to 790 ppb) as determined from ice cores," the authors concluded. The first step in trying to stabilize greenhouse gases is obtaining a linear growth rate—having the concentration of the gas increase the same amount in the atmosphere every year. Carbon dioxide is a concern because its growth rate is increasing more each year. The 2007 IPCC report indicates that perhaps the first

Ice cave, Erebus Glacier tongue, Antarctica, November 1978 (Commander John Bortniak, NOAA Corps; NOAA/ Department of Commerce)

goal toward stabilization has been reached for at least one greenhouse gas. Nitrous oxide (N_2O) also absorbs long-wave radiation and reduces the amount of Earth's heat that can escape to space. Nitrous oxide molecules are stable for more than 100 years in the atmosphere. "The global atmospheric nitrous oxide concentration increased from a preindustrial value of about 270 ppb to 319 ppb in 2005," the authors report. "The growth rate has been approximately constant since 1980," they add. While a constant growth rate is an achievement to be applauded, the rate is at about 0.25 percent each year. When considering that since the Industrial Revolution nitrous oxide has increased on the whole by about 8 percent, the last 25 years of steady state growth have contributed to more than half of the added nitrous oxide to the atmosphere.

Stabilization of greenhouse gases is a multipronged challenge, one that will require changes in energy production and use as well as changes to agricultural practices. People can take action to help reduce greenhouse gas emissions by increasing the efficiency of energy use in their homes and cars. Currently in America, each state government is setting its own precedent for regulating greenhouse gas emissions based on demand from their constituents. Developing alternative non-fossil fuel energy sources, removing the carbon from fossil fuels, and managing the emissions of methane and carbon dioxide from agricultural and industrial activities will reduce the amount of greenhouse gases humans produce. Many businesses, not-for-profit groups, and universities are focusing their attention on these opportunities.

Scientist of the Decade: Pamela Anne Matson (b. 1953)

While carbon dioxide is the most abundant greenhouse gas in the atmosphere after water vapor, less common greenhouse gases are not off the hook for their contribution to global warming. Like other scientists, American biogeochemist Pamela Anne Matson had her suspicions about the trace gas nitrous oxide (N_2O). She had become familiar with carbon and nitrogen cycles as a graduate student in the early 1980s. In the 1990s Matson led studies that would alert environmental scientists to the impacts that deforestation and agriculture have on nitrous oxide in the atmosphere. When she started her work, tropical deforestation was primarily under investigation as a potential source of CO_2 to the atmosphere. The effects of forest clearing on the movement of nitrogen in soils and the emission of nitrogen gases from soils to the atmosphere were of little concern. Matson and colleagues showed that converting tropical forests to other land uses could have important effects on nitrogen cycling in forests and increase the emissions of nitrous oxide and other nitrogen gases to the atmosphere.

Atmospheric scientist Arthur Adel of Arizona State College in Flagstaff, in 1939, was the first to identify nitrous oxide as a trace gas in the atmosphere. In the late 1940s, high-flying aircraft equipped with early spectrometers identified the gas as absorbing solar radiation. Nitrous oxide was also detected in trace amounts in the lower atmosphere. Adel relied on these studies and the discovery of nitrous oxide as an abundant gas found in the air within soil when he proposed in 1951 that nitrous oxide had a significant role in the nitrogen cycle. He explained that decomposition in soil of nitrogen compounds (such

as ammonium or nitrate) produce nitrous oxide (N_2O) as a byproduct; the gas escapes to the atmosphere where sunlight ultimately breaks the molecule down to its atomic level forming various combinations of nitrogen (N_2), oxygen (O_2) and nitrogen oxides (NO_x). "Presumably, the nitrous oxide accumulates above the Earth's surface until the rates of accumulation and decomposition are equal," he wrote. Careful measurements in later decades showed that nitrous oxide was accumulating more than it was decomposing.

Matson's research on nitrous oxide emissions from soils began as an offshoot of many years of study on how nitrogen, an important nutrient needed by all living things, moves or "cycles" between atmosphere, soil, water, and trees in forests. While still in high school, Matson loved forests and knew that she wanted to work with plants and animals. She followed those interests in college, and graduated *magna cum laude* in biology from the University of Wisconsin in 1975. After a short diversion to run a music store and grow orchids for a private greenhouse, she returned to her interests in forests and environment, attending Indiana University for a master's degree in environmental science, graduating in 1980. She then attended Oregon State University, earning a doctorate in forest ecology in 1983. In her graduate research, she studied the effects of human-caused disturbances (such as clear-cutting) and natural disturbances (such as insect and pathogen attacks) on nitrogen cycling in forests.

In the years immediately following her graduate education, Matson teamed with a number of

(continues)

(continued)

colleagues to continue these studies. Chief among her colleagues was ecologist Peter Vitousek, then a professor at the University of North Carolina at Chapel Hill and soon to become her spouse. Vitousek, Matson, and their collaborators studied the ways in which forest management practices affected the amount of nitrogen that was stored in soils and how that compared to the amount lost to water or the atmosphere after clear-cutting. Their work in loblolly pine plantations would lead to an article entitled "Mechanisms of Nitrogen Retention in Forest Ecosystems: A Field Experiment" in *Science* in 1984. Vitousek and Matson reported that the removal of whole trees, stumps and branches included, as opposed to collecting only the trunks was detrimental to the forest's ability to retain nitrogen. Removing the debris after harvesting the trees allowed nitrogen from the soils to leach into rivers and streams and also be emitted into the atmosphere. In contrast, leaving organic matter on the site provided soil microbes the food they needed to grow, increasing their uptake of nitrogen and thereby keeping nitrogen in the soils.

By the time the *Science* article was published, Matson and Vitousek had moved to California. In early 1984, Matson began working as a research scientist for NASA-Ames Research Center in Moffett Field and at the same time, Stanford University's Department of Biological Sciences hired Vitousek as a faculty member. The two continued to collaborate, shifting their focus to tropical forests in Brazil, Costa Rica, Panama, and in Vitousek's home state of Hawaii. Working for NASA, Matson and Vitousek teamed their skills in studying forests and soils on the ground with those of scientists who use satellite and aircraft remote sensing to study forests, as well as those of scientists who study the atmosphere above for-

ests with towers, aircraft, balloons, and satellites. In reflecting on those early years of research at NASA, Matson says "I was very lucky to work in interdisciplinary teams since the very beginning of my career, and I've continued to do so. Those interactions have led me in areas of research and places around the world that I never could have predicted as a graduate student."

In 1987—as nations around the world committed to the Montreal Protocol to reduce use of CFCs, the principal cause for the thin ozone hole over Antarctica—Matson worked as part of a large team of NASA and Brazilian scientists investigating the ways that the Amazon rain forests interacted with the atmosphere. Her team's research included a focus on the effects of land use changes in the Amazon rain forests on nitrous oxide emissions from forests to the atmosphere. With her were Gerald Livingston from Ames, Flavio and Regina Luizao of the Brazilian Institute of the Amazon, and Peter Vitousek of Stanford. They found that those tropical forests that were converted to cattle pastures had three times the level of annual nitrous oxide emissions as the undisturbed rain forests, an effect that lasted at least until the pastures were 10 years old. "This is the first study showing the potential importance of tropical land use changes on greenhouse gases other than carbon dioxide," Matson reported in 1990. "Given that tropical deforestation is occurring so rapidly, this effect could have global significance."

Deforestation and the agricultural land use that followed proved a twofold strike on the environment. The elimination of the terrestrial carbon sink left more carbon emissions in the atmosphere and agriculture brought required inputs of nitrogen fertilizer. A handful of researchers from around the world had begun to measure high nitrous oxide emissions from fertilized soils in the temperate zone. In the mid 1990s, Matson

Further Reading

Arrhenius, Svante. "On the Influence of Carbonic Acid in the Air Upon the Temperature of the Ground." *Philosophical Magazine* 41 (1896): 237–276. The first report to identify carbon dioxide as a greenhouse gas. Available

and her collaborators showed that fertilization of tropical soils could lead to very high fluxes of nitrous oxide, but that it mattered how the nitrogen was applied. In field sites in the Hawaiian Islands and in Mexico, their work illustrated that applying nitrogen fertilizer when the plants were actively growing and using it, resulted in very low emissions to the atmosphere. The typical application of large doses of fertilizer done in most places around the world led to large emissions of nitrous oxide into the atmosphere.

With these results in hand, Matson soon shifted her research focus from simply measuring how much nitrogen was lost from agricultural soils, to evaluating ways to reduce losses. "How we manage fertilization in agricultural soils influences how much is emitted," she says. When she left NASA in the early 1990s to take on teaching positions at the University of California at Berkeley and later Stanford University, she began to work with economists and agronomists as well as other Earth scientists to develop sustainable agricultural practices for rapidly developing countries in tropical areas. "This is where fertilizer use is increasing, and where there is a dramatic need for increasing food production as well. We want to find ways to maintain and increase food production while at the same time reducing the environmental consequences of fertilization and other agricultural management." One method that they use involves low-tech remote sensing approaches that identify areas that need fertilization, allowing farmers to target their use of fertilization rather than evenly distributing it across the whole field. Targeted applications reduce the farmer's costs and reduce the loss of fertilizer to the environment, a win-win situation.

In 1995 Matson was honored with a MacArthur Fellowship from the John D. and Catherine T. MacArthur Foundation for her interdisciplinary work on land-use effects on the atmosphere.

Matson and Vitousek are both elected members of the National Academy of Sciences and the American Academy of Arts and Sciences. They are married and have two children, Mat (b. 1988) and Liana (b. 1995). Matson began teaching as a professor of environmental science at UC Berkeley in 1993. She continued teaching and studying land-use issues when she took on the Richard and Rhoda Goldman professorship at Stanford in the Institute for International Studies and the Department of Geological and Environmental Sciences in 1997. At Stanford she directed the Earth Systems interdisciplinary undergraduate program and codirected the Center for Environmental Science and Policy, along with Walter Falcon, former director of the Freeman Spogli Institute for International Studies. Other colleagues in the center included Donald Kennedy, editor-in-chief of *Science* magazine; Stephen Schneider, Stanford's Melvin and Joan Lane Professor for Interdisciplinary Environmental Studies; and Roz Naylor, the Julie Wrigley Senior Fellow in Environmental Studies. The Ecological Society of America appointed Matson president for 2001–02. In October 2002, Stanford President John Hennessy appointed Matson the dean of the School of Earth Sciences.

"These are exciting times at Stanford University and other universities around the world," Matson says. "We're trying to harness the strengths of great universities like Stanford across many different disciplines, to help solve the enormous challenges facing the planet in the 21st Century. The most critical challenge, I think, is the sustainability challenge: finding ways to meet the needs of people today and in the future—for food, water, energy, employment, and so on—while still protecting the planet's environment and life support systems. We're making progress, but we're going to have to work even harder and in interdisciplinary ways in the decade to come."

online. URL: http://www.globalwarmingart.com/wiki/Image:Arrhenius_ pdf. Accessed February 28, 2007.

Bouma, Arnold H. *Sedimentology of some Flysch deposits: A graphic approach to facies interpretation.* Amsterdam, New York, Elsevier Pub. Co., 1962. With a foreword by Ph. H. Kuenen, and a preface by Francis P. Shepard, this book becomes a classic for its description of a turbidite sequence, later known as a Bouma sequence.

Broecker, Wallace S. "The Great Ocean Conveyor." *Oceanography* 4 (1991): 79–89. This paper lays out the atmospheric and oceanic interactions that have a hand in global climate change.

Budyko, Mikhail. *Heat Balance of the Earth's Surface.* Washington, U.S. Dept. of Commerce, Weather Bureau, 1958. Translated by Nina A. Stepanova from the Russian 1956 original edition and providing an introduction to computer climate modeling.

Caillon, Nicolas, Jeffrey P. Severinghaus, Jean Jouzel, Jean-Marc Barnola, Jiancheng Kang, and Volodya Y. Lipenkov. "Timing of Atmospheric CO_2 and Antarctic Temperature Changes Across Termination III." *Science* 299 (14 March 2003): 1,728–1,731. A report on carbon dioxide in ice cores.

Crowell, John C. "Climate Significance of Sedimentary Deposits Containing Dispersed Megaclasts," in *Problems in Palaeoclimatology: Proceedings of the NATO Palaeoclimates Conference held at the University of Newcastle-upon-Tyne, January 7–12, 1963*, edited by A. E. M. Nairn. London: Interscience Publishers, 1964, p. 86. A case against ice as the primary explanation for distributing rocks to the sedimentary seafloor.

Fritts, H. C. *Reconstructing Large-Scale Climatic Patterns from Tree Ring Data.* Tucson: University of Arizona Press, 1991. Using tree rings, scientists can explore climate change on various continents.

Hanks, Thomas C., and Hiroo Kanamori. "A moment magnitude scale." *Journal of Geophysical Research* 84, no. B5, (May 1979): 2,348–2,350. Further research into the moment magnitude of earthquakes.

Harland, W. Brian. "Evidence of Late Precambrian Glaciation and Its Significance," in *Problems in Palaeoclimatology: Proceedings of the NATO Palaeoclimates Conference held at the University of Newcastle-upon-Tyne, January 7–12, 1963*, edited by A. E. M. Nairn. London: Interscience Publishers, 1964, p. 119. A case for the Great Infra-Cambrian Glaciation.

Heezen, Bruce C., and Maurice Ewing. "Turbidity Currents and Submarine Slumps, and the 1929 Grand Banks Earthquake," *American Journal of Science* 250 (December 1952): 849–873. A breakthrough in understanding the effects of underwater avalanches.

Hoffman, Paul F., Alan J. Kaufman, Galen P. Halverson, and Daniel P. Schrag. "A Neoproterozoic Snowball Earth." *Science* 281 (1998): 1,342–1,346. The report discusses evidence indicating global glaciation 700 million years ago.

Kanamori, Hiroo. "The energy release in great earthquakes." *Journal of Geophysical Research* 82 (1977): 2,981–2,876. This report introduces moment magnitude as a means for measuring the energy of great earthquakes, determined by an earthquake's seismic moment.

———. "Quantification of Earthquakes." *Nature* 271, no. 5644 (1978): 411–414. This report provides the explicit equation for finding moment magnitude of earthquakes.

Kennedy, Martin J., Nicholas Christie-Blick, and Linda E. Sohl. "Are Proterozoic cap carbonates and isotopic excursions a record of gas hydrate destabilization following Earth's coldest intervals?" *Geology* 29, no. 5 (May 2001): 443–446. A report questioning aspects of the Snowball Earth hypothesis.

Koyaguchi, T., and Tokuno, M. "Origin of the giant eruption cloud of Pinatubo, June 15, 1991." *Journal of Volcanology and Geothermal Research* 55, nos. 1 and 2 (1993): 85–96. This report discusses the satellite images of the eruption.

Luizao, Flavio, Pamela Matson, Gerald Livingston, Regina Luizao, and Peter Vitousek. "Nitrous oxide flux following tropical land clearing." *Global Biogeochemical Cycles* 3 (1989): 281–285. Preliminary evidence indicating a slight increase in emissions of nitrous oxide after deforestation.

Marland, G., T. A. Boden, and R. J. Andres. Global, Regional, and National CO_2 Emissions. In Trends: A Compendium of Data on Global Change. Carbon Dioxide Information Analysis Center, Oak Ridge National Laboratory, U.S. Department of Energy, Oak Ridge, Tenn., 2006. This report discusses the global trends in carbon dioxide emissions. Available online. URL: http://cdiac.ornl.gov/trends/emis/em_cont.htm. Accessed February 28, 2007.

Matson, Pamela A., and Peter M. Vitousek. "Nitrogen mineralization and nitrification potentials following clearcutting in the Hoosier National Forest, Indiana." *Forest Science* 27 (1981): 781–791. Matson and Vitousek's early work examining land use changes on nitrogen cycles.

——— and Peter M. Vitousek. "Cross-system comparisons of soil nitrogen transformations and nitrous oxide flux in tropical forest ecosystems." *Global Biogeochemical Cycles* 1 (1987): 163–170. This report examines nitrous oxide emissions from tropical forests.

———, Peter M. Vitousek, Gerald P. Livingston, and N. A. Swanberg. "Sources of variation in nitrous oxide flux from Amazonian ecosystems." *Journal of Geophysical Research* 95 no. D10, (1990): 16,789–16,798. Evidence that nitrous oxide emissions are greatest from clear-cut forests that are converted to cattle pastures as opposed to undisturbed or recently burned or clear-cut forests.

———, C. Billow, S. Hall, and J. Zachariesson. "Nitrogen trace gas responses to fertilization in sugar cane ecosystems." *Journal of Geophysical Research* 101 no. D13 (1996): 18,533–18,546. Examination of fertilization contributions to the nitrogen cycle.

———, W. J. Parton, A. G. Power, and M. J. Swift. "Agricultural intensification and ecosystem properties." *Science* 277 (1997): 504–509. Ecologically based management strategies can increase the sustainability of agricultural production.

———, Rosamond Naylor, and Ivan Ortiz-Monasterio. "Integration of Environmental, Agronomic, and Economic Aspects of Fertilizer Management." *Science* 280 (1998): 112–115. "In the intensive wheat systems of Mexico, typical fertilization practices lead to extremely high fluxes of nitrous oxide (N_2O) and nitric oxide (NO). In experiments, lower rates of nitrogen fertilizer, applied later in the crop cycle, reduced the loss of nitrogen without affecting yield and grain quality."

Mount Pinatubo, Philippines. The Cascade Volcano Observatory provides a list of relevant publications and photographs regarding the 1991 and 1992 eruptions. Available online. URL: http://vulcan.wr.usgs.gov/Volcanoes/Philippines/Pinatubo/framework.html. Accessed February 28, 2007.

Newhall, Christopher G., and Raymundo S. Punongbayan, editors. *Fire and mud: eruptions and lahars of Mount Pinatubo, Philippines.* Quezon City: Philippine Institute of Volcanology and Seismology; Seattle: University of Washington Press, 1996. This book details the events surrounding the 1991 eruption of Mount Pinatubo. Available online. URL: http://pubs.usgs.gov/pinatubo/index.html. Accessed February 28, 2007.

Punongbayan, Raymundo S., Christopher G. Newhall, Ma. Leonila P. Bautista, Delfin Garcia, David H. Harlow, Richard P. Hoblitt, Julio P. Sabit, and Renato U. Solidum. "Eruption Hazard Assessments and Warnings." In *Fire and mud: eruptions and lahars of Mount Pinatubo, Philippines*, edited by Christopher G. Newhall and Raymundo S. Punongbayan. Quezon City: Philippine Institute of Volcanology and Seismology; Seattle: University of Washington Press, 1996. Punongbayan and colleagues discuss their role in communicating the risk of the eruption. Available online. URL: http://pubs.usgs.gov/pinatubo/punong2/index.html. Accessed February 28, 2007.

Schopf, J. William. "Microfossils of the Early Archean Apex Chert: New Evidence of the Antiquity of Life," *Science* 260 (1993): 640–646. Schopf reports on the discovery of fossil microbes in Australia that are 3.465 billion years old.

———. *Cradle of Life: The Discovery of Earth's Earliest Fossils.* Princeton: Princeton University Press, 1999. This book describes the story of the search for Earth's earliest evidence of life.

Thompson, Dick. *Volcano Cowboys.* New York: St. Martin's Press, 2000. Thompson reports on multiple eruptions in the 1980s and 1990s and their impact.

Tilman, David, Kenneth G. Cassman, Pamela A. Matson, Rosamond Naylor, and Stephen Polasky. "Agricultural sustainability and intensive production practices." Nature 418 (August 8, 2002): 671–677. "A doubling in global food demand projected for the next 50 years poses huge challenges for the sustainability both of food production and of terrestrial and aquatic ecosystems and the services they provide to society."

Vitousek, Peter M., James R. Gosz, Charles C. Grier, Jerry M. Melillo, William A. Reiners, and Robert L. Todd. "Nitrate Losses from Disturbed Ecosystems" *Science* 4 May 1979, 204: 469–474. "A systematic examination of nitrogen cycling in disturbed forest ecosystems demonstrates that eight processes, operating at three stages in the nitrogen cycle, could delay or prevent solution losses of nitrate from disturbed forests."

————— and Pamela A. Matson. "Mechanisms of Nitrogen Retention in Forest Ecosystems: A Field Experiment." *Science* 225, no. 4657 (July 6, 1984): 51–52. A report demonstrating that the removal of residual organic matter after deforestation reduces the environment's ability to retain nitrogen.

Walker, Gabrielle. *Snowball Earth*. New York: Three Rivers Press, 2003. Walker reports on the personalities and the science that brought about the idea of a Snowball Earth.

Wallace, Paul J., and Terrence M. Gerlach. "Magmatic Vapor Source for Sulfur Dioxide Released During Volcanic Eruptions: Evidence from Mount Pinatubo." *Science* 265 (July 22, 1994): 497–499. Sulfur dioxide (SO_2) released by the explosive eruption of Mount Pinatubo on June 15, 1991, had an impact on climate and stratospheric ozone.

Williams, George, and Brian Embleton. "Low palaeolatitude of deposition for late Precambrian periglacial varvites in South Australia." *Earth and Planetary Science Letters* 79 (1986): 419–430. The paper put forth preliminary evidence of equatorial glaciation during the Precambrian.

Wolfe, Edward W. *The 1991 Eruptions of Mount Pinatubo, Philippines: Earthquakes and Volcanoes*. U.S. Geological Survey, 1992. This report was one of the first to examine the events of the eruption and list the Philippine and American team members involved in monitoring the eruption. Available online. URL: http://vulcan.wr.usgs.gov/Volcanoes/Philippines/Pinatubo/Publications/Wolfe/wolfe_report.html. Accessed February 28, 2007.

————— and Richard P. Hoblitt. "Overview of the Eruptions." In *Fire and Mud*, edited by Christopher G. Newhall and Raymundo S. Punongbayan. Quezon City: Philippine Institute of Volcanology and Seismology; Seattle: University of Washington Press, 1996. This article summarizes the 1991 eruptions of Mount Pinatubo. Available online. URL: http://pubs.usgs.gov/pinatubo/wolfe/index.html. Accessed February 28, 2007.

—————. Map of Mount Pinatubo and the surrounding areas. Available online. URL: http://pubs.usgs.gov/pinatubo/wolfe/fig4.jpg. Accessed February 28, 2007.

—————. Graphic of Mount Pinatubo's 1991 explosive eruptions, their height and time of occurrence. Available online. URL: http://pubs.usgs.gov/pinatubo/wolfe/fig10.gif. Accessed February 28, 2007.

Conclusion: Into the Twenty-First Century

Earth science is a broad field encompassing a number of specialties. This book has touched on some of the major and minor contributions to the field in the last hundred years, and how the science has changed, but the history discussed in this book is in no way exhaustive. Developments in marine geology, oceanography, and atmospheric science—all Earth sciences in their own right—are presented in more detail in other books in this series. Many Earth scientists, in their search for understanding the origins of life and the evolution of life on our planet, have become involved in the advancements in planetary science, astrobiology, and archaeology. The Apollo astronauts relied on Earth as an analogue for their mission to the Moon. Those who will walk on the Moon again in the future must first understand Earth's biogeochemical cycles to appreciate the history and complexity of the lunar landscape, or any other planetary object humans dare to explore, such as Mars, Europa, or the asteroid 2002 AA29 discovered in 2002 that shares Earth's orbit around the Sun and in 600 years will again orbit Earth as a second natural satellite with the Moon.

Like the monarch butterflies that take many generations to complete their species' migration across North America, humans must also consider their long-term goals for future generations when burning fossil fuels, consuming energy, applying fertilizers, establishing and adhering to regulations on atmospheric chemicals, and populating areas with known natural hazards. An understanding of the Earth sciences can help in these decisions. Many earthquake-prone regions have yet to develop building codes, properly enforce them, or update older structures to the newer codes. Even in California, where the hazard is common knowledge, U.S. Geological Survey seismologists Susan Hough and Lucy Jones warned that some schools built before 1970 have yet to modernize to 1990 standards. "In 1990, the provisions of the Field Act were extended to strengthen requirements for new (although not existing) private schools, although charter schools and day-care centers remain exempt," they wrote in the *San Francisco Chronicle* in 2002. Earth scientists have taken on the responsibility in modern society of moving beyond educating, informing, and advising on what *can* be done to advocating what *should* be done to prepare for natural disasters before they strike. Some are more comfortable with this responsibility than others. USGS volcanologists who assist other countries typically advise civil authorities on the importance of an evacuation plan and the inherent dangers involved with the specific volcano they are helping to monitor—rather than call for an evacuation themselves, for fear of being wrong and not being taken seriously the next time an evacuation is needed; for fear of being right and not having the public's immediate trust to convince them of their need to leave their homes and property. People educated and knowledgeable about the risks and dangers of a potential natural disaster in their area are more likely to make the right decisions and take appropriate and immediate action. In Papua New Guinea when Rabaul volcano's Tavurvur crater began erupting in 1994, the people in the city of Rabaul left before any evacuation order was made. In October 2006 volcanologists again reported the city had "self-evacuated" when the volcano started coughing up ash and lapilli.

Unfortunately in many situations people do not understand the risks, tend to underestimate the consequences of inaction, make wrong decisions, and, if they survive, become dependent on others for help. Evacuations can be economically costly, put personal and commercial property at risk to looters, and cause a great deal of stress to the evacuating population and the areas receiving them. Authorities recognize this and do not make evacuation orders lightly. In cases where an evacuation order is not made in time, or at all, the public is left to act on their own. Without the preparation and education to recognize the signs of danger, it is impossible to expect anything other than disastrous consequences. Such was the case during the 2004 Sumatra tsunami. The Pacific Ocean is a region renowned for tsunamis; a warning system is in place, signs are posted on beaches, drills are conducted, and the public is for the most part aware of the risk. Few people in the countries with coastlines in the Indian Ocean studied the risk of tsunamis in their own backyard. When on December 26, 2004, an earthquake of magnitude 9.3 struck off the coast of Sumatra, few people in Indonesia at the time were aware that a tsunami might follow. Few people who saw the waves at the beach suddenly pull back into the sea, as if the area was experiencing an exceptionally fast onset of a low tide, knew to run to higher ground for safety, to shout out to those around them to do the same, to warn the laborers in the low-lying fields of the approaching wave. Three hundred thousand people died.

Training and education of tsunami risk would have helped, but it is not enough. Sometimes the signs of impeding disaster are too subtle to notice. The Australian plate, which on average creeps 2.3 inches (59 mm) a year in route under Indonesia, staggered on July 17, 2006. The earthquake struck northeast of Christmas Island, and 124 miles (200 km) south

The Sri Lanka coastline before the 2004 tsunami (NASA)

The Sri Lanka coastline on December 26, 2004, during tsunami flooding (NASA)

of Pangandaran, Java, Indonesia. The distance and physical characteristics of the seafloor dampened the land-shaking effects of the magnitude 7.7 quake, but not the amount of water it displaced. Those inside buildings and homes in Jakarta felt the earthquake, but few walking outside noticed anything more than a slight tremor. If they looked to the beach the already low tide revealed no obvious change. Those near the shore did not know a tsunami was racing toward them until after the first wave began flooding the coast. Seismometers on the other side of the globe in Hawaii recorded the earthquake, but there is only so much seismologists an ocean away can do. The Pacific Tsunami Warning Center in Hawaii issued an alert, 17 minutes after the earthquake. The warning was not communicated to people on the coast of Indonesia in time. A wave at least 6 feet (1.8 m) in height carried away boats, buildings, and people. The tsunami left 730 people dead. A similar earthquake in 1994 in the region had produced a tsunami with a wave 43 feet (13 m) high and killed more than 200 people.

The risk of a tsunami is not a new phenomenon in the Indian Ocean; but it is still one the countries are ill prepared to handle, even two years after the 2004 disaster. On January 24, 2007, 21 countries participated in the first test of satellite phones planned for use in a future Indian Ocean tsunami warning system. When the call went out at 6 A.M. six countries reported receiving the alert within two minutes: India, Madagascar, Maldives, Mozambique, France's Réunion Island, and Thailand. Sri Lanka reported receiving the call within 10 minutes, East Timor after 18 minutes, and others hours later. Bangladesh, Kenya, and Mauritius did not respond at all. It will be years before the Indian Ocean tsunami warning system is complete; in the meantime education and low-tech warnings such as signs are critical to keep people safe. Understanding the dynamics of plate tectonics, the workings of the Earth's interior and how that impacts the crust are vital in the 21st century.

Volcanoes

January 3, 2007, marked 24 years of lava flowing from Kilauea's vent Pu`u `O`o on Hawaii. The eruption that started in 1983 will likely continue pouring lava through underground lava tubes into the sea for many years to come. The area is dangerous to tourists because most of the fresh hot lava is under a thin black crust; roofs on inland lava tubes and lava-formed cliffs over the sea can collapse. Cracks in the crust expose areas where the lava can be seen glowing red at night. Volcanologists with the Hawaiian Volcano Observatory don heat-resistant clothing and tread carefully on older Pahoehoe lava flows that they determine are thick enough to be safe in order to conduct their studies on the basalt flows. Currently, an extension of new volcanic land 55 acres across is poised to crumble into the ocean.

Mount Etna on Sicily, Italy, has erupted every year since the 21st century began. In fact, only four or five years since 1877 has Etna not had an eruption explode from one of its craters. In 2006, seismologist Domenico Patanè of Italy's National Institute of Geophysics and Volcanology in Catania and colleagues reported mapping the movement of magma through the interior of the volcano using time-lapse seismic profiles: "Time-Resolved Seismic Tomography Detects Magma Intrusions at Mount Etna." The Sicilian volcano is also attracting those interested in sound patterns. Geophysicists are also experimenting with converting Mount Etna's seismic patterns into volcanic melodies using Domenico Vicinanza's music pattern recognition (data sonification) software at the Italian National Institute for Nuclear Physics. Perhaps with further study, evacuation sirens in the future will be accompanied by the musical sounds of the volcano itself. Nicolas Houlié of the University of California at Berkeley uses satellite images of Mount Etna and other volcanoes to examine tree growth. He and colleagues are finding that the taller, greener vegetation tends to grow in areas where the volcano is most likely to fissure. They hypothesize that added carbon dioxide and water vapor to the soil from cracks in the volcano's structure may be a reason for the forest's boost in greenness.

Like a litmus test, the color of Lake Voui in the crater of Aoba volcano, Vanuatu, in the South Pacific changed from blue to red in late May of 2006. The change in color followed a series of explosions since November 2005. Strangely, the volcano's other crater lake, Lake Manaro Ngoru, remained turquoise blue. The volcanologists observing the Aoba explained the red coloring as the result of iron oxidation in Lake Loui.

Currently non-erupting volcanoes under close surveillance include Vesuvius in Italy and in the United States: the Three Sisters in Oregon and Mount Rainier in Washington. Since 2000, the following volcanoes have erupted cataclysmically with ejecta reaching 6 miles (10 km) or more above sea level:

- Rabaul, Manam, and Ulawun volcanoes in Papua New Guinea
- Reventador volcano in Ecuador
- Ruang volcano in the Sangihe Island arc of Indonesia
- Shiveluch volcano on Russia's Kamchatka Peninsula

Other volcanoes active in the 21st century include:

- Akan, Suwanose-jima and Miyake-jima, Japan
- Karymsky and Bezymianny, Russia
- Pagan (Mariana Islands), Anatahan (Mariana Islands), Atka (Alaska), Cleveland (Alaska), Veniaminof (Alaska), Fourpeaked (Alaska), Augustine (Alaska), and St. Helens (Washington), United States
- Soufrière Hills (Montserrat), United Kingdom
- Popocatépetl, México
- Fuego and Pacaya, Guatemala
- Santa Ana, El Salvador
- San Cristóbal, Nicaragua
- Poás, Costa Rica
- Galeras, Colombia
- Ubinas, Perú
- Láscar and Villarrica, Chile

- Montagu Island, South Sandwich Islands
- Grímsvötn, Iceland
- Etna, Italy
- The Lokbatan mud volcano, Azerbaijan
- Nyiragongo and Nyamuragira, Democratic Republic of the Congo
- Ol Doinyo Lengai, Tanzania
- Karthala, Comoros
- Piton de la Fournaise (Réunion Island) France
- Barren Island, India
- Canlaon, Bulusan and Mayon, Philippines
- Merapi, Soputan, Talang, Karangetang (Api Siau), and the Lusi mud volcano, Indonesia
- Bagana, Ulawun, Sulu Range, Ritter Island, and Langila, Papua New Guinea
- Heard, Australia
- Tinakula, Soloman Islands
- Lopevi and Aoba, Vanuatu
- Home Reef, Tonga
- Raoul Island and Ruapehu, New Zealand

Twentieth Century eruptions ongoing in 2007 include:

- Yasur, Vanuatu (since or before 1774)
- Santa María, Guatemala (since June 22, 1922)
- Dukono, Indonesia (since August 13, 1933)
- Stromboli, Italy (since February 2, 1934)
- Sangay, Ecuador (since August 8, 1934)
- Sakura-jima, Japan (since October 13, 1955)
- Erta Ale, Ethiopia (since in or before 1967)
- Semeru, Indonesia (since August 31, 1967)
- Arenal, Costa Rica (since July 29, 1968)
- Erebus, Antarctica (since in or before December 1972)
- Kilauea, United States (since January 3, 1984)
- Colima, México (since November 22, 1997)
- Shiveluch, Russia (since August 15, 1999)
- Tungurahua, Ecuador (since October 5, 1999)

Volcanoes present a variety of dangers, not always from eruptions. Experts working to safeguard the public are the ones who put themselves at most risk. Mammoth Mountain, famous for its Southern California ski slopes, actively vents carbon dioxide from fumaroles. The gas collects around the base of trees and in snow-covered fissures, usually marked by ski patrol as an off-limits area. In April 2006, a ski patrol team was fixing a fence around a fissure when two of them fell about 15 feet (5 m) into a hole 6 feet (2 m) in diameter. A third man on the ski patrol team died trying to bring the fallen men oxygen. Four others were hospitalized.

Dangerous areas are not always fenced off, and visitors to a volcano should always stick to the trails and watch their step. In April 2005, a British tourist died after falling into a boiling hot spring on the volcanic islands of the Azores, Portugal. She had been taking pictures when a steam cloud engulfed her and her husband. The wife fell backward and was able to cling to the edge of the pool where she was quickly rescued. Although burned, she was still coherent as she was airlifted to the hospital but soon died from a bacteria infection in her bloodstream.

Volcanoes are not immune to human intervention. People can change the landscape for better or for worse. On May 29, 2006, a gas pipeline explosion ignited an eruption of flames and hot mud from the middle of a rice paddy in Sidoarjo, East Java, Indonesia. In February 2007, the company blamed for the mudflow, PT Lapindo Brantas, which was drilling for hydrocarbons, started dropping concrete balls linked with chains into the mud volcano in an effort to plug the flow. Nicknamed Lusi, as a cross between Sidoarjo and *lumpur*, meaning mud, the geyser-like eruption has destroyed farmland, schools, highways, and factories in the region and displaced 11,000 people.

In 2001 Raymundo Punongbayan in the Philippines led an engineering expedition to drain 25 percent of the 7,416 million cubic feet (210 million m^3) of lake water that had collected in the crater of Mount Pinatubo since the 1991 eruption and threatened to flood villages. With picks and shovels, the team dug a ditch 17 feet (5.1 m) deep into the side of the crater to the lake and lined the flank of the volcano with sandbags to direct the draining water. The labor-intensive low-tech solution worked flawlessly.

The Twenty-First Century's Largest and Deadliest Earthquakes:

2001

- January 26, an earthquake of magnitude 7.7 strikes India—20,023 people die
- June 23, an earthquake of magnitude 8.4 strikes near the coast of Peru—138 people die

2002

- March 25, an earthquake of magnitude 6.1 strikes the Hindu Kush Region of Afghanistan—1,000 people die
- November 3, an earthquake of magnitude 7.9 strikes Central Alaska—no fatalities reported

2003

- September 25, an earthquake of magnitude 8.3 strikes Hokkaido, Japan Region—no fatalities reported
- December 26, an earthquake of magnitude 6.6 strikes Southeastern Iran—31,000 people die

2004

- December 26, an earthquake of magnitude 9.3 strikes off the coast of Northern Sumatra, Indonesia—283,106 people die

2005

- March 28, an earthquake of magnitude 8.6 strikes Northern Sumatra, Indonesia—1,313 people die
- October 8, an earthquake of magnitude 7.6 strikes Pakistan—80,361 people die

2006

- May 26, an earthquake of magnitude 6.3 strikes Java, Indonesia—5,749 people die
- November 15, an earthquake of magnitude 8.3 strikes the Kuril Islands—no fatalities reported

2007

- January 13, an earthquake of magnitude 8.1 strikes East of the Kuril Islands—no fatalities reported
- April 1, an earthquake of magnitude 8.1 strikes the Solomon Islands—54 people die
- August 15, an earthquake of magnitude 8.0 strikes the Solomon Islands—337 people die

Earth's Freshwater and Deserts

Around the world freshwater or the lack of it drives political, economical, and environmental debates and changes to the landscape. Once consid-

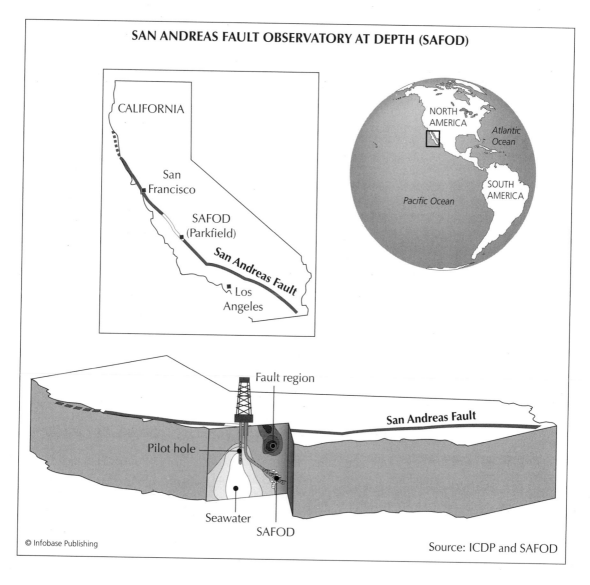

SAN ANDREAS FAULT OBSERVATORY AT DEPTH (SAFOD)

CALIFORNIA

San Francisco

SAFOD (Parkfield)

San Andreas Fault

Los Angeles

NORTH AMERICA

Atlantic Ocean

SOUTH AMERICA

Pacific Ocean

Fault region

San Andreas Fault

Pilot hole

Seawater

SAFOD

© Infobase Publishing

Source: ICDP and SAFOD

ered a local or regional issue, the impacts of desertification in the 21st century are now recognized to have a global impact. Satellite imagery is tracking dust clouds traveling across the United States from China's Gobi desert as winds over Saharan Africa send dust to the Caribbean. In the Middle East, Iraq's once lush wetlands have turned to deserts. Lake levels are dropping across tropical Africa, and ancient aquifers around the world are being pumped to compensate for low surface water supply. Israeli hydrologists continue to debate the environmental and societal costs and benefits of resurrecting the Dead Sea with water from the Red Sea. In the Water Wars of California, farmers in the valleys east of the

San Andreas Fault Observatory at Depth (SAFOD): Completed in 2005, the borehole drilled through the San Andreas Fault in Parkfield, California, reaches a depth of about 2 miles (3.2 km) (From Earthscope and the International Continental Scientific Drilling Program)

Sierra Nevada Mountain Range are waiting to see the literal fruits of their first victory. In 2006 Los Angeles began returning a small percentage of water back to the Owens River, a source of drinking water and irrigation water for the desert valleys west of the Sierra Nevada Mountains since the 1920s. As a result of the diverted waterway, the valleys east of the mountain range saw extensive desertification and landowners started suing the city. In China construction on the Three Gorges Dam began in 2001 with the last of the concrete for the structure poured in 2006. When all of the generators for the dam begin operation in 2009, the dam will provide China with the world's largest supply of hydroelectric power.

Medical Geology

Epidemiologists, health scientists, and medical doctors are teaming up with Earth science Ph.D.'s to analyze how the planet impacts human health. Henry Spiller Poison Center at Kosair Children's Hospital in Louisville, Kentucky, teamed up with geologist J. Z. de Boer of Wesleyan University in Connecticut to examine gas from nonvolcanic fissures and springs emanating near Greece's ancient temple of the Oracle of Delphi. The gas, mainly ethylene, is a narcotic—evidence supporting the ancient legend behind the source of the prophetic women's power as emanating from the temple's springs. Atmospheric oceanic changes in the Pacific initiate periods of El Niño and La Niña that have human health impacts around the world, bringing drought to some regions and floods to others. Mapping wetlands helped in tracking mosquitoes carrying the West Nile virus as it moved across the United States. Dust from the collapse of the World Trade Center has led to lung infections and deaths many years after the 2001 terrorist attack. Analyzing mineral content from the dust in the air for asbestos and other known carcinogens did not at first sound any human health alarms. Revaluations of those data and the legal ramifications for family members are current issues. In Bangladesh, wells built to help provide a fresh source of drinking water are contaminated with natural arsenic from groundwater and poisoning the population with a slow and painful death. Thirty percent of the world's population suffers from dental fluorosis caused by drinking from wells that provide more than 1.5 milligrams of fluoride per liter of water. In Hawaii, the winds carry sulfur dioxide from Kilauea south to the Kau district polluting the air with almost three times as much as the U.S. Agency for Toxic Substances and Disease Registry has deemed the minimal risk level. To the north the air above Honolulu registers only one-tenth of the risk. In comparison the air above Los Angeles has seven-tenths the amount considered a minimal risk for sulfur dioxide levels. Natural radiation in the bedrock can leak dangerous amounts of radon in homes, equivalent to smoking 16 packs of cigarettes a day in some cases. Atmospheric pollution, whether it is dust from coal mines in China or volcanoes in Hawaii and mineral toxicity levels in drinking water, whether chemically contaminated or from natural sources in the groundwater, the field of medical geology is playing an ever increasing role in monitoring human health.

Earth's Interior

From the inner core to the outer core; lower mantle to upper mantle; asthenosphere, lithosphere, and crust, the Earth is a flux of spinning contradictions and quagmires. Unraveling all of its secrets is still part of the fun.

One of the benefits of having established a significant seismological network across the planet during the 20th century is the ability to track when an earthquake strikes twice. Curiously, the second time an earthquake hits the same exact fault, the speed of its waves traveling through the inner core are faster than they were the first time the earthquake struck. Not so for earthquake waves that pass only through the mantle or outer core. These have stayed exactly the same. Seismologists first took notice of this variation in earthquake wave propagation in the 1980s. They reported an increase in speed in waves traveling north–south through the inner core and hypothesized that the phenomena was the result of the way the iron in the inner core likely lined up north–south, parallel with Earth's axis of rotation. In the 1990s, seismologists reconsidered this model. They shifted the north–south axis of the inner core away from the Earth's axis of rotation and hypothesized that the inner core was spinning faster on its own axis of rotation than the rest of the planet. The observational data of seismic histories fit neatly with this new model. Careful observations of seismic waves into the 21st century confirmed a faster inner core.

Another curious aspect of the inner core is its role in reversing the Earth's magnetic field. The last time Earth's magnetic North Pole was located near the geographic South Pole was 780,000 years ago. As the planet and inner core spin, the outer core responds with turbulent eddies in the molten iron. Recently the magnetic field has been fading, becoming weaker in certain regions. This is dangerous for satellites traveling through these weak zones as the magnetic field protects the machinery from damaging high-energy particles. Geophysicists interpret the recent decline in the field as knots in the chaotic eddies of the liquid outer core. In the next 2,000 years, Earth may see its north–south dipole dissolve to a multi-pole with other magnetic "north" poles of 90° inclination spouting momentarily in strange places like the equator before the planet switches to a south–north dipole for thousands or millions of years. Whether such multi-poles precede reversals remains a mystery. Currently the Earth is awash with small variations of such poles in the upper Northern and Southern Hemispheres, but the main magnetic "north" and "south" poles dominate the magnetic field. It is conceivable that the field may weaken and enter a transition period only to bounce back to normal.

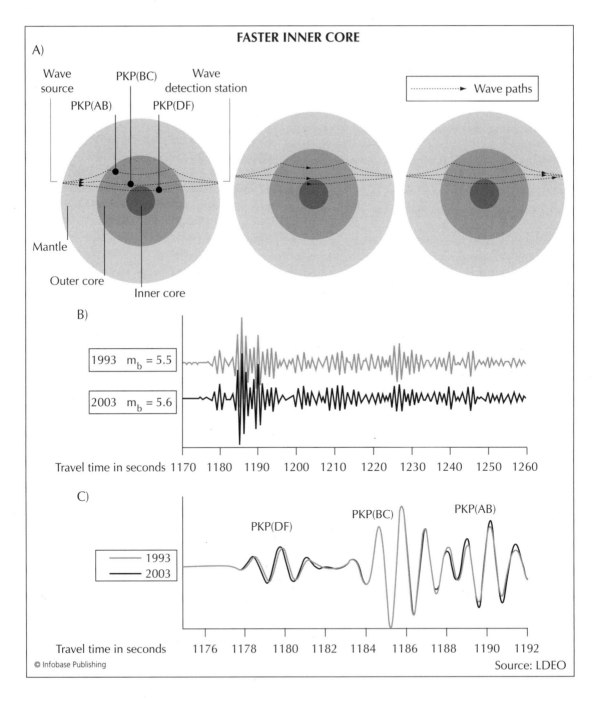

FASTER INNER CORE

A)

Wave source

PKP(AB)   PKP(BC)   PKP(DF)   Wave detection station

············► Wave paths

Mantle

Outer core

Inner core

B)

1993 $m_b = 5.5$

2003 $m_b = 5.6$

Travel time in seconds 1170 1180 1190 1200 1210 1220 1230 1240 1250 1260

C)

PKP(DF)   PKP(BC)   PKP(AB)

——— 1993
——— 2003

Travel time in seconds   1176 1178 1180 1182 1184 1186 1188 1190 1192

© Infobase Publishing   Source: LDEO

The transition zones are exceedingly more difficult to study than the rocks within time periods of normal or reversed magnetic fields. Paleomagneticist Brad Clement of Florida International University care-

(Opposite page) *When an earthquake strikes (A), seismic waves follow different directions as they pass through different parts of the Earth's interior. When another earthquake strikes the same fault again 10 years later (B), the seismic waves appear the same. When the P and S waves from the two earthquakes are overlaid slight variations between the two earthquakes are seen (C), showing that the wave PKP(DF) traveled faster through the inner core in 2003 than it did in 1993.*

fully analyzed minute ocean sediment samples from transition zones and found the time period for the change took as little as 1,800 years to as long as 7,000 years. His report, "Dependence on the duration of geomagnetic polarity reversals on site latitude," appeared in *Nature* in April 2004. Paleontological evidence shows that life on Earth ignores such magnetic reversals, although migration patterns may change. The time the Earth takes to switch from a north-south to a south-north magnetic field happens quickly in geologic timescales, but it takes more than 40 to 140 generations in human timescales. Generations from now humans may have to build a compass that can operate with multipoles.

Hot spots—those mantle plumes that form island archipelagos such as Hawaii in the middle of tectonic plates, and keep Iceland growing in the same spot in the middle of the Mid-Atlantic spreading ridge—are still hot topics for Earth scientists. Do they sometimes move? Do they change size? Where do the plumes start, deep in the mantle near the core or higher up in the convection process? In July 2006, Japanese geophysicists introduced the term *petit spots* to explain tiny, young volcanoes on the old Pacific crust dipping into the trenches off Japan and Kuril islands. The team identified a small percentage of mantle melt mixed in with the asthenosphere in the baby volcanoes. They hypothesize the volcanoes formed when the higher lithosphere began to crack during subduction, allowing the asthenosphere and parts of the upper mantle to bleed through the crust. The hunt is now on for petit spots elsewhere subduction takes place. "I'd bet we will recognize 'petit spots' in the Mediterranean, where microplates are being stressed and subducted in strange geometries," says Richard Cowen of the University of California at Davis.

Michael Wysession of Washington University in St. Louis, Missouri, found what he calls "wet spots." Beneath eastern Asia the lower mantle is acting like a wet sponge, locking moisture in the rocks. Jesse Lawrence of Scripps Institute of Oceanography in La Jolla, California, worked with Wysession to analyze the seismic signals through the mantle in the area beneath Asia's subduction zone. Just how far a subducting plate travels with all of its descending waterlogged makeup is a mystery. The scientific consensus has subducting plates reaching the lower mantle. "Whether slabs penetrate to the core-mantle boundary or founder within the lower mantle, subduction clearly transports large volumes of material down into the lower mantle," Lawrence and Wysession write in their report "Seismic Evidence for Subduction-Transported Water in the Lower Mantle." Finessing the plate tectonic paradigm continues. One of the most divisive of the debates remains whether the older, thicker subducting slaps do more of the work in pulling the thin young spreading ridges apart or whether the convecting mantle pushes the spreading ridges open. Plate tectonics experts on both sides of that debate are absolutely convinced of their having the correct interpretation, providing graduate students a potential minefield of opportunity.

Paleoclimate from Caves and Lightning Bolts

In the 20th century, Earth scientists turned to tree rings, pollen, corals, seashells, and ice cores to understand Earth's past climate history. In the 21st century, a new generation of Earth scientists are also exploring the secrets of stalagmites in caves and finding unusual glassy shards in deserts that reveal shifts in climate as well. Geologist Jessica Oster began her work on stalagmite mounds in 2001 as an undergraduate conducting research at Oberlin College in Ohio. After studying Sweden's Quaternary landscape on a Fulbright scholarship, she turned her headlamp to the caves in California's Sierra Nevada Mountain Range. Around the world speleothems—icicle-shaped stalactites, stalagmite mounds, and flat flowstones that look like paint splatters on the ground—protected from erosion in caves, record in their drop-by-drop growth of mineral deposits how much moisture is in the soil and the air. In 2007 paleoclimatologists in Austria and Germany presented in their report "Speleothems and paleoglaciers" evidence that ice does not preclude the formation of these water-borne structures. Geochemist Kathleen Johnson at the University of Oxford, United Kingdom, is investigating with colleagues the annual variations of trace gases in speleothems from Chinese caves. Having the advantage of annual or seasonal variation in mineral deposition, without erosion or bioturbation from worms, makes caves an ideal paleoclimate laboratory and new caves are being discovered every year. In 2006 amateur cavers found a million-year-old labyrinth in Sequoia National Park. The newly discovered cave section stretched more than 1,000 feet into the mountain.

Whether they are searching cool wet caves or hot dry deserts, 21st-century paleoclimatologists are finding fascinating new ways to examine ancient structures. Geochemist Rafael Navarro-González of the National Autonomous University of México in México City, collects lightning bolts. Lightning strikes the ground at temperatures exceeding 2000 Kelvin or 3,140°F (1,727°C). The heat immediately melts and fuses sand in soils to form glass replicas of the strike, called fulgurites from the Latin word for lightning: *fulgur*. The 15,000-year-old glass shards Navarro-González found in the Libyan Desert did not form in the same sands that surrounded them in 1999. Navarro-González worked with colleagues from France, India, Niger, and the U.S. Geological Survey and NASA in the United States, to examine the gas bubbles trapped in the wrist-thick spindly black glass. The team presented their report, "Paleoecology reconstruction from trapped gases in a fulgurite from the late Pleistocene of the Libyan Desert" in the February 2007 issue of *Geology*. Fulgurites have fascinated scientists for centuries. One of the earliest known studies dates back, appropriately, to Alexander von Humboldt's report in 1822 about findings from his expeditions. Most scientists in the field seek fulgurites after a lightning storm and study the atmospheric signals the glass reveals. By analyzing the gas bubbles in the ancient fulgurites, Navarro-González and his team discovered that the sand dune region today had desert plants in the past and something else that has been missing recently: lightning.

Summary

Earth scientists have resolved a number of mysteries during the 20th century. They established the fundamental periods of the geologic timescale; dated meteorites, the oldest known rocks in the solar system, to 4.56 billion years of age; and discovered the earliest signs of continental crust formation in 4.4 billion-year-old zircon crystals. Theories on the formation of the Moon were tested with direct evidence from lunar rocks recovered during the space race. Lunar rocks and lunar impact craters show that the Moon formed after a massive collision with Earth 4.53 billion years ago. During the 20th century, Earth scientists proved that continents are not permanent but part of Earth's ongoing plate tectonic processes. Twentieth-century Earth scientists revealed much of the planet's internal and external complexity, as well as how humans contribute globally to the environment. Earth is a dynamic mix of spinning pressurized fluids, minerals, and magma that collide and impact neighboring materials, break through the surface, drag and pull ridges apart, explode and sink, erode, recycle, and start again. Humans are caught on the surface of this planet and contribute to the biogeochemical cycles and interactions between the Earth's landscapes, ocean, and atmosphere. Earth scientists delve into the hidden realms of the planet's interior, dive into the dark abyss of the oceans, and dare to expand their earthly horizons with human exploration into space. In the last hundred years the field has gone from colored pencil marked maps to 3-D computer models, from radioactive rocks to Martian meteorites, from single fossils to mass extinctions, and from greenhouse gasses as good to bad. Natural disasters although no longer enigmatic remain a threat that is difficult to address. From Messina, Italy, in 1908 to Sumatra in 2004, earthquakes and tsunamis strike with little to no warning. Volcanic and atmospheric hazards can be anticipated, but to minimize risk, evacuation orders must be made in time and followed—a task that can become quickly convoluted by local politics and attitudes toward authority as much as by the natural phenomena itself. With a global population that is projected to reach 8 billion by 2028, learning to live with and being prepared for natural disasters will be a formidable challenge in the 21st century. Understanding the history of the field provides modern Earth scientists with a map marked by successes and failures. The map of history provides perspective. The Earth explorer must choose the direction of travel. The field is limited only by imagination, for in the 21st century the boundaries of Earth science are expanding and accelerating—capturing the context of how this blue marble that humans call home fits into the cosmic picture of the universe.

Modified Mercalli Intensity Scale

Before the magnitude scale was used to measure the energy of an earthquake, intensity scales provided a means for comparing the severity of an earthquake's effect on buildings and people. Because countries use different building materials and building practices, the same magnitude earthquake can have very different effects in different locations. This has resulted in a variety of different intensity scales. The United States uses the Modified Mercalli Intensity Scale. The U.S. Geological Survey provides the following abbreviated description of the 12 levels of Modified Mercalli intensity:

    I. Not felt except by a very few under especially favorable conditions.

    II. Felt only by a few persons at rest, especially on upper floors of buildings.

    III. Felt quite noticeably by persons indoors, especially on upper floors of buildings. Many people do not recognize it as an earthquake. Standing motor cars may rock slightly. Vibrations similar to the passing of a truck. Duration estimated.

    IV. Felt indoors by many, outdoors by few during the day. At night, some awakened. Dishes, windows, doors disturbed; walls make cracking sound. Sensation like heavy truck striking building. Standing motor cars rocked noticeably.

    V. Felt by nearly everyone; many awakened. Some dishes, windows broken. Unstable objects overturned. Pendulum clocks may stop.

    VI. Felt by all, many frightened. Some heavy furniture moved; a few instances of fallen plaster. Damage slight.

    VII. Damage negligible in buildings of good design and construction; slight to moderate in well-built ordinary structures; considerable damage in poorly built or badly designed structures; some chimneys broken.

VIII. Damage slight in specially designed structures; considerable damage in ordinary substantial buildings with partial collapse. Damage great in poorly built structures. Fall of chimneys, factory stacks, columns, monuments, walls. Heavy furniture overturned.

IX. Damage considerable in specially designed structures; well-designed frame structures thrown out of plumb. Damage great in substantial buildings, with partial collapse. Buildings shifted off foundations.

X. Some well-built wooden structures destroyed; most masonry and frame structures destroyed with foundations. Rails bent.

XI. Few, if any (masonry) structures remain standing. Bridges destroyed. Rails bent greatly.

XII. Damage total. Lines of sight and level are distorted. Objects thrown into the air.

Awards of Merit
in Earth Science

Recipients of the Crafoord Prize in Geosciences

The Crafoord Prize is equivalent to winning the Nobel Prize for geo-scientists. The Royal Swedish Academy of Sciences began awarding the prize sum of U.S. $500,000 to scientists in the fields of astronomy and mathematics; geosciences; biosciences; and when warranted polyarthritis (rheumatoid arthritis) on a rotating yearly schedule in 1982. His Majesty the King of Sweden presents the prize to the laureates on "Crafoord Day" in April. The Royal Swedish Academy of Sciences hosts a symposium that day in connection with the year's honored discipline. Information about the prize is available online. URL: http://www.crafoordprize.se/ Accessed February 28, 2007.

1983

Edward N. Lorenz and Henry Stommel

1986

Claude Allègre and Gerald J. Wasserburg

1989

James A. Van Allen

1992

Adolf Seilacher

1995

Willi Dansgaard and Nicholas Shackleton

1998

Don L. Anderson and Adam M. Dziewonski

Notable John D. and Catherine T. MacArthur Foundation Fellows

The MacArthur Fellows Program awards unrestricted fellowships to talented individuals who have shown extraordinary originality and dedication in their creative pursuits and a marked capacity for self-direction. Each fellowship comes with a stipend of $500,000 to the recipient, paid out in equal quarterly installments over five years. Although nominees are reviewed for their achievements, the fellowship is not a reward for past accomplishment but rather an investment in a person's originality, insight, and potential. The purpose of the MacArthur Fellows Program is to enable recipients to exercise their own creative instincts for the benefit of human society. Further information about the Foundation and Fellows is available online. URL: http://www.macfound.org. Accessed February 28, 2007.

1981

Michael Ghiselin, Evolutionary Biologist

1981

Stephen Jay Gould, Paleontology

1981

John Imbrie, Climatologist

1981

Robert W. Kates, Geographer

1981

Paul G. Richards, Seismologist

1982

Richard A. Muller, Geologist and Astrophysicist

1984

Carl R. Woese, Molecular and Evolutionary Biologist

1984

Bret Wallach, Geographer

1986

John Robert Horner, Paleobiologist

1986

Richard P. Turco, Atmospheric Scientist

1987

Stuart Alan Kauffman, Evolutionary Biologist

1987

Michael C. Malin, Geologist and Planetary Scientist

1987

Jon Seger, Evolutionary Ecologist

1988

Charles Archambeau, Geophysicist

1988

John G. Fleagle, Primatologist and Paleontologist

1988

Raymond Jeanloz, Geophysicist

1988

Alan Walker, Paleontologist

1989

Leo William Buss, Evolutionary Biologist

1989

Daniel H. Janzen, Ecologist

1991

James A. Westphal, Engineer and Planetary Scientist

1992

Stephen H. Schneider, Climatologist

1992

Geerat J. Vermeij, Evolutionary Biologist and Paleontologist

1993

Maria Luisa Crawford, Geologist and Petrologist

1993

Margie Profet, Evolutionary Biologist

1995

Susan W. Kieffer, Geologist and Planetary Scientist

1995

Pamela A. Matson, Ecologist

1997

Eric L. Charnov, Evolutionary Biologist

1997

Nancy A. Moran, Evolutionary Biologist and Ecologist

1998

Benjamin David Santer, Atmospheric Scientist

1999

Jillian Banfield, Geologist

2000

Christopher Beard, Paleontologist

2000

Daniel P. Schrag, Geochemist

Presidents of AGU (American Geophysical Union)

AGU is a worldwide scientific community that advances the understanding of Earth and space for the benefit of humanity. Since its establishment in 1919, AGU has grown into a community of 45,000 scientists from 140 countries; 20 percent of its members are students. The organization stands as a leader in the increasingly interdisciplinary global endeavor that encompasses the Earth and space sciences. Presidents are elected for two-year terms. A Web site on the history of AGU leadership is available online. URL: http://www.agu.org/inside/insidaguls.html. Accessed February 28, 2007.

1920–22

William Bowie

1922–24

L. A. Bauer

1924–26

H. F. Reid

1926–29

H. S. Washington

1929–32

William Bowie

1932–35

W. J. Humphreys

1935–38

N. H. Heck

1938–41

R. M. Field

1941–44

W. C. Lowdermilk

1944–47

L. H. Adams

1947–48

O. E. Meinzer

1948–53

W. H. Bucher

1953–56

James B. Macelwane

1956–59

Maurice Ewing

1959–61

Lloyd V. Berkner

1961–64

Thomas F. Malone

1964–66

George P. Woollard

1966–68

William C. Ackerman

1968–70

Helmut E. Landsberg

1970–72

Homer E. Newell

1972–74

Philip H. Abelson

1974–76

Frank Press

1976–78

Arthur E. Maxwell

1978–80

Allan V. Cox

1980–82

J. Tuzo Wilson

1982–84

James A. Van Allen

1984–86

Charles L. Drake

1986–88

Peter S. Eagleson

1988–90

Don L. Anderson

1990–92

G. Brent Dalrymple

1992–94

Ralph J. Cicerone

1994–96

Marcia Neugebauer

1996–98

Sean C. Solomon

1998–2000

John A. Knauss

Recipients of the William Bowie Medal

The William Bowie Medal is the American Geophysical Union's highest honor. The medal was established in 1939 in honor of AGU's first president William Bowie for his "spirit of helpfulness and friendliness in unselfish cooperative research." As one of the founders of AGU and the International Union of Geodesy and Geophysics, Bowie worked as an architect of international cooperation in geophysical research. The Bowie medal is awarded annually and acknowledges an individual for outstanding contributions to fundamental geophysics and for unselfish cooperation in research, one of the guiding principles of AGU. The list of recipients of the Bowie Medal and other AGU awards is available online. URL: http://www.agu.org/inside/honors.html. Accessed February 28, 2007.

1939

William Bowie

1940

Arthur Louis Day

1941

John Adam Fleming

1942

Nicholas Hunter Heck

1943

Oscar Edward Meinzer

1944

Henry Bryant Bigelow

1945

Jacob Aall Bonnevie Bjerknes

1946

Reginald Aldworth Daly

1947

Felix Andries Vening Meinesz

1948

James Bernard Macelwane

1949

Walter Davis Lambert

1950

Leason Heberling Adams

1951

Harald Ulrik Sverdrup

1952

Harold Jeffreys

1953

Beno Gutenberg

1954

Richard Montgomery Field

1955

Walter Hermann Bucher

1956

Weikko Aleksanteri Heiskanen

1957

William Maurice Ewing

1958

Johannes Theodoor Thijsse

1959

Walter M. Elsasser

1960

Francis Birch

1961

Keith Edward Bullen

1962

Sydney Chapman

1963

Merle Antony Tuve

1964

Julius Bartels

1965

Hugo Benioff

1966

Louis B. Slichter

1967

Lloyd V. Berkner

1968

Roger Revelle

1969

Walter B. Langbein

1970

Bernhard Haurwitz

1971

Inge Lehmann

1972

Carl Eckart

1973

George P. Woollard

1974

A. E. Ringwood

1975

Edward Bullard

1976

Jule G. Charney

1977

James A. Van Allen

1978

Helmut E. Landsberg

1979

Frank Press

1980

Charles A. Whitten

1981

Herbert Friedman

1982

Henry M. Stommel

1983

Syun-iti Akimoto

1984

Marcel Nicolet

1985

H. William Menard

1986

James C. I. Dooge

1987

Robert N. Clayton

1988

Hannes Alfven

1989

Walter H. Munk

1990

Eugene N. Parker

1991

Don L. Anderson

1992

Alfred O. Nier

1993

Irwin I. Shapiro

1994

Peter S. Eagleson

1995

Claude Allégre

1996

Eugene Shoemaker

1997

Raymond Hide

1998

Richard M. Goody

1999

J. Freeman Gilbert

2000

John A. Simpson

Presidents of the Geological Society of London

Since 1807, the Geological Society of London has promoted the geosciences. Currently the society has more than 9,000 members, 2,000 of which are outside of the United Kingdom. Presidents are elected for two-year terms. A list of past presidents is available online. URL: http://www.geolsoc.org.uk/template.cfm?name=past_presidents. Accessed February 28, 2007.

1900–02

Jethro Justinian Harris Teall

1902–04

Charles Lapworth

1904–06

John Edward Marr

1906–08

Sir Archibald Geikie

1908–10

William Johnson Sollas

1910–12

William Whitehead Watts

1912–14

Aubrey Strahan

1914–16

Arthur Smith Woodward

1916–18

Alfred Harker

1918–20

George William Lamplugh

1920–22
Richard Dixon Oldham

1922–24
Albert Charles Seward

1924–26
John William Evans

1926–28
Francis Arthur Bather

1928–30
John Walter Gregory

1930–32
Edmund Johnston Garwood

1932–34
Thomas Henry Holland

1934–36
John Frederick Norman Green

1936–38
Owen Thomas Jones

1938–40
Henry Hurd Swinnerton

1940–41
Percy George Hamnall Boswell

1941–43
Herbert Leader Hawkins

1943–45

William George Fearnsides

1945–47

Arthur Elijah Trueman

1947–49

Herbert Harold Read

1949–50

Cecil Edgar Tilley

1950–51

Owen Thomas Jones

1951–53

George Martin Lees

1953–55

William Bernard Robinson King

1955–56

Walter Campbell Smith

1956–58

Leonard Hawkes

1958–60

Cyril James Stubblefield

1960–62

Sydney Ewart Hollingworth

1962–64

Oliver Meredith Boone Bulman

1964–66
Frederick William Shotton

1966–68
Kingsley Charles Dunham

1968–70
Thomas Neville George

1970–72
William Alexander Deer

1972–74
Thomas Stanley Westoll

1974–76
Percy Edward Kent

1976–78
Wallace Spencer Pitcher

1978–80
Percival Allen

1980–82
Edward Howel Francis

1982–84
Janet Vida Watson

1984–86
Charles Hepworth Holland

1986–88
Bernard Elgey Leake

1988–90

Derek John Blundell

1990–92

Anthony Leonard Harris

1992–94

Charles David Curtis

1994–96

(Robert) Stephen (John) Sparks

1996–98

Richard Frederick Paynter Hardman

1998–2000

Robin (Leonard Robert Morrison) Cocks

Recipients of the Wollaston Medal

The Wollaston Medal is the Geological Society of London's highest honor. The medal is given to geologists who have obtained the heights of international recognition through their outstanding work. In 1831 William Smith (1769–1839) was the first person awarded the medal for his geological map published in 1815 of England, Wales, and part of Scotland. A list of Wollaston recipients and other society award winners is available online. URL: http://www.geolsoc.org.uk/template.cfm?name =medallistsfrom1831_. Accessed February 28, 2007.

1900

Grove Karl Gilbert

1901

Charles Barrois

1902

Friedrich Schmidt

1903

Heinrich Rosenbusch

1904

Albert Heim

1905

Jethro Justinian Harris Teall

1906

Henry Woodward

1907

William Johnson Sollas

1908

Paul von Groth

1909

Horace Bolingbroke Woodward

1910

William Berryman Scott

1911

Waldemar Christopher Brogger

1912

Lazarus Fletcher

1913

Osmond Fisher

1914

John Edward Marr

1915

(Tannatt William) Edgeworth David

1916

Alexander Petrovich Karpinsky

1917

(Francois Antoine) Alfred Lacroix

1918

Charles Doolittle Walcott

1919

Aubrey Strahan

1920

Gerard Jacob De Geer

1921

Benjamin Neeve Peach

1921

John Horne

1922

Alfred Harker

1923

William Whitaker

1924

Arthur Smith Woodward

1925

George William Lamplugh

1926

Henry Fairfield Osborn

1927

William Whitehead Watts

1928

Dukinfield Henry Scott

1929

Friedrich Johann Karl Becke

1930

Albert Charles Seward

1931

Arthur William Rogers

1932

Johan Herman Lie Vogt

1933

Marcelin Boule

1934

Henry Alexander Miers

1935

John Smith Flett

1936

Gustaaf Adolf Frederik Molengraaff

1937

Waldemar Lindgren

1938

Maurice Lugeon

1939

Frank Dawson Adams

1940

Henry Woods

1941

Arthur Louis Day

1942

Reginald Aldworth Daly

1943

Aleksandr Evgenevich Fersmann

1944

Victor Moritz Goldschmidt

1945

Owen Thomas Jones

1946

Emanuel de Margerie

1947

Joseph Burr Tyrrell

1948

Edward Battersby Bailey

1949

Robert Broom

1950

Norman Levi Bowen

1951

Olaf Holtedahl

1952

Herbert Harold Read

1953

Erik Andersson Stensio

1954

Leonard Johnston Wills

1955

Arthur Elijah Trueman

1956

Arthur Holmes

1957

Paul Fourmarier

1958

Penti Eskola

1959

Pierre Pruvost

1960

Cecil Edgar Tilley

1961

Roman Kozlowski

1962

Leonard Hawkes

1963

Felix Alexander Vening Meinesz

1964

Harold Jeffreys

1965

David Meredith Seares Watson

1966

Francis Edward Shepard

1967

Edward Crisp Bullard

1968

Raymond Cecil Moore

1969

William Maurice Ewing

1970

Philip Henry Kuenen

1971

Ralph Alger Bagnold

1972

Hans Ramberg

1973

Alfred Sherwood Romer

1974

Francis John Pettijohn

1975

Hollis Dow Hedberg

1976

Kingsley Charles Dunham

1977

Reinout William van Bemmelen

1978

John Tuzo Wilson

1979

Hatton Schuyler Yoder

1980

Augusto Gansser

1981

Robert Minard Garrels

1982

Peter John Wyllie

1983

Dan Peter McKenzie

1984

Kenneth Jinghwa Hsu

1985

Gerald Joseph Wasserburg

1986

John Graham Ramsay

1987

Claude-Jean Allègre

1988

Alfred Ringwood

1989

Drummond Hoyle Matthews

1990

Wallace S. Broecker

1991

Xavier Le Pichon

1992

Martin Harold Phillips Bott

1993

Samuel Epstein

1994

William Jason Morgan

1995

George Patrick Leonard Walker

1996

Nicholas John Shackleton

1997

Douglas James Shearman

1998

Karl Karekin Turekian

1999

John Frederick Dewey

2000

William Sefton Fyfe

Recipients of the Penrose Medal

The Penrose Medal is the Geological Society of America's highest honor. Mining geologist and millionaire entrepreneur Richard A. F. Penrose, Jr., (1863–1931) established the medal in 1927 to recognize eminent geological research and award geologists for outstanding original contributions or achievements that mark a major advance in the science. Nominees, represented by the Society's Council, may or may not be members of the Society, and may be from any nation. A list of recipients of the medal and other society awards is available online. URL: http://www.geosociety.org/aboutus/awards/aboutAwards.htm. Accessed February 28, 2007.

1927

Thomas Chrowder Chamberlin

1928

Jakob Johannes Sederholm

1929

No award given

1930

François Alfred Antoine Lacroix

1931

William Morris Davis

1932

Edward Oscar Ulrich

1933
Waldemar Lindgren

1934
Charles Schuchert

1935
Reginald Aldworth Daly

1936
Arthur Philemon Coleman

1937
No award given

1938
Andrew Cowper Lawson

1939
William Berryman Scott

1940
Nelson Horatio Darton

1941
Norman Levi Bowen

1942
Charles Kenneth Leith

1943
No award given

1944
Bailey Willis

1945

Felix Andries Vening-Meinesz

1946

T. Wayland Vaughan

1947

Arthur Louis Day

1948

Hans Cloos

1949

Wendell P. Woodring

1950

Morley Evans Wilson

1951

Pentti Eskola

1952

George Gaylord Simpson

1953

Esper S. Larsen, Jr.

1954

Arthur Francis Buddington

1955

Maurice Gignoux

1956

Arthur Holmes

1957

Bruno Sander

1958

James Gilluly

1959

Adolph Knopf

1960

Walter Herman Bucher

1961

Philip Henry Kuenen

1962

Alfred Sherwood Romer

1963

William Walden Rubey

1964

Donnel Foster Hewett

1965

Philip Burke King

1966

Harry H. Hess

1967

Herbert Harold Read

1968

J. Tuzo Wilson

1969

Francis Birch

1970

Ralph Alger Bagnold

1971

Marshall Kay

1972

Wilmot H. Bradley

1973

M. King Hubbert

1974

William Maurice Ewing

1975

Francis J. Pettijohn

1976

Preston Cloud

1977

Robert P. Sharp

1978

Robert M. Garrels

1979

J. Harlen Bretz

1980

Hollis D. Hedberg

1981

John Rodgers

1982

Aaron C. Waters

1983

G. Arthur Cooper

1984

Donald E. White

1985

Rudolf Trümpy

1986

Laurence L. Sloss

1987

Marland P. Billings

1988

Robert S. Dietz

1989

Warren Bell Hamilton

1990

Norman D. Newell

1991

William R. Dickinson

1992

John Frederick Dewey

1993

Alfred G. Fischer

1994

Luna B. Leopold

1995

John C. Crowell

1996

John R. L. Allen

1997

John D. Bredehoeft

1998

Jack E. Oliver

1999

M. Gordon Wolman

2000

Robert L. Folk

Recipients of the Vetlesen Prize

In 1959 the Georg Unger Vetlesen Foundation established an award for scientific achievement that resulted in a clearer understanding of the Earth, its history, or its relations to the universe. About every two years Columbia University's Lamont-Doherty Earth Observatory administers the $100,000 prize and its accompanying medal, which is inscribed with the words "for achievement in the sciences of the Earth and the universe." Additional information regarding Georg Unger Vetlesen and the prize recipients is available online. URL: http://www.ldeo.columbia. edu/vetlesen/index.html. Accessed February 28, 2007.

1960

W. Maurice Ewing, Geophysics, Seismology, Study of the Ocean Bottom

1962

Sir Harold Jeffreys, Mathematical Methods Applied to the Study of the Interior of the Earth, Great Britain; Felix Andries Vening Meinesz, Gravity and the Interior of the Earth

1964

Pentti Eelis Eskola, Chemistry of Rocks, Finland; Arthur Holmes, Geology

1966

Jan Hendrik Oort, Astrophysics

1968

Francis Birch, Physical Properties of Rocks; Sir Edward Bullard, Interior of the Earth, Magnetism

1970

Allan V. Cox, Paleomagnetism; Richard R. Doell, Paleomagnetism; S. Keith Runcorn, Paleomagnetism

1973

William A. Fowler, Astrophysics

1974

Chaim Leib Pekeris, Mathematical Methods Applied to Earth's Interior

1978

J. Tuzo Wilson, Geology

1981

Marion King Hubbert, Geophysics and Geology

1987

Wallace S. Broecker, Geochemistry; Harmon Craig, Geochemistry and Oceanography

1993

Walter Munk, Geophysics

1996

Robert E. Dickinson, Atmospheric Sciences, Climate Modeling, Climate-Biosphere Interactions; John Imbrie, Sedimentary Records, Orbital Variations, Climate Change

2000

W. Jason Morgan, Seafloor Spreading, Plate Tectonics and Mantle Convection; Walter C. Pitman III, Plate Tectonic Theory, Theoretical Geomorphology and Tectonics; Lynn R. Sykes, Earthquake Forecasting and Prediction, Seismological Verification of Underground Nuclear Test-ban Treaties

 # Glossary

accelerograph a device made to respond to acceleration, such as a SEISMOMETER designed with a natural period smaller than that of ground motion. Accelerographs are also used during gravity surveys to measure the motion of the ship, helicopter, or aircraft. Also called an accelerometer

aerosol natural or man-made particles of solid or liquid material—such as dust, mist, smoke, haze, or fog—that are small (0.01 to 10 μm) enough to remain suspended in a gas, such as the atmosphere. Precipitation removes most aerosols from the TROPOSPHERE in days or weeks. In the STRATOSPHERE, aerosols such as sulfur particles from volcanic eruptions can remain aloft for years or more. Generally aerosols absorb, reflect, or scatter radiation

asthenosphere the weak layer in Earth's interior below the LITHO-SPHERE and in the upper MANTLE

axial tilt the difference between the Earth's axis of rotation and a right angle to the orbital plane. This tilt varies between 21.5° and 24.5° over a cycle of 40,000 years and at present is about 23.5°

ballistic clast an ejected rock fragment

calcareous of or containing calcium carbonate, for example shells, LIMESTONE, some soils, and chalk

CFCs an abbreviation for chlorofluorocarbon, any of several simple gaseous compounds that contain carbon, chlorine, fluorine, and sometimes hydrogen, that are used as refrigerants, cleaning solvents, and AEROSOL propellants and in the manufacture of plastic foams, and that are believed to be a major cause of stratospheric ozone depletion

clasts rock fragments

convection currents a vertical current formed when changes in temperature between layers cause differences in density

Coriolis effect the deviation away from a straight line that a moving object makes on a rotating body, as seen from the reference frame of that rotating body; a result of the CORIOLIS FORCE

Coriolis force an apparent force caused by the rotation of the Earth that results in moving objects such as air currents to deflect to the right in the Northern Hemisphere and to the left in the Southern Hemisphere

correlation spectrometer a SPECTROMETER used to measure the amount of sulfur dioxide or other gases emitted from a volcano based on wavelengths of light

cosmic ray ionizing radiation from particles entering the Earth's atmosphere from space at the speed of light

crystal a body that is formed by the solidification of a chemical element, a compound, or a mixture and has a regularly repeating internal arrangement of its atoms and often external plane faces

crystallography a science that deals with the forms and structures of CRYSTALS

Curie point the temperature above which thermal vibrations destroy FERROMAGNETISM or remnant magnetization of an element. Each element has its own specific Curie point, for iron it is 1,400°F (760°C)

daughter element an element that forms as a result of radioactive decay of another element

dipole magnetic poles of opposite sign

dipole field the best mathematical fit to Earth's geomagnetic field using a single DIPOLE (north and south). The geocentric dipole field is inclined 11° to the Earth's axis of rotation. Also called a geomagnetic dipole field

dropstones iceberg-rafted or glacier-carried rocks deposited away from where they originally formed

earthquake a term used to describe both a sudden slip on a fault and the resulting ground shaking, as well as the radiated seismic energy caused by the slip, or by volcanic or magmatic activity, or other sudden stress changes in the Earth

Earth science any of the sciences (as GEOLOGY, meteorology, or oceanography) that deal with the Earth or with one or more of its parts

eccentricity Earth's deviation from a circular to more elliptical orbit over time

endocranial cast a cast of the interior of the skull or cranial cavity, showing the approximate shape of the brain

electromagnetic radiation the form of energy that can travel at the speed of light in a vacuum and ranges in wavelengths from short gamma rays to long radio waves on the ELECTROMAGNETIC SPECTRUM

electromagnetic spectrum the range of frequencies or wavelengths of ELECTROMAGNETIC RADIATION

epicenter the point on the Earth's surface situated directly above the FOCUS of an EARTHQUAKE

evolution changes introduced through heredity that effect a population; the process of change

ferromagnetism   a type of magnetism occurring in substances such as cobalt, iron, nickel and other metal alloys—where all electron spin vectors are in the same direction; also remnant magnetism

ferruginous   an iron-bearing rock

focus   where the seismic waves of an EARTHQUAKE originate along a fault plane

fumaroles   a volcanic vent in the ground that emits steam or other gases

geocentric axial dipole (GAD) hypothesis   states that the geomagnetic field, when averaged over tens to hundreds of thousands of years, corresponds to that of a DIPOLE located at Earth's center and aligned with Earth's rotation axis

geochronology   the science of dating geologic formations on Earth using absolute or relative dating methods

geodesy   the science of determining the shape of the planet and changes in the gravitational field

geodimeter   a tool used on volcanoes to accurately measure growth from a distance using a laser light

geodynamo   the physical processes that take place within the Earth

geology   the science that deals with the history of the earth and its life especially as recorded in rocks; a study of the solid matter of a celestial body such as lunar or Martian geology

geoscience   the sciences (as GEOLOGY, geophysics, and geochemistry) dealing with the Earth

harmonic tremor   a continuous release of seismic energy typically associated with the underground movement of MAGMA. It contrasts distinctly with the sudden release and rapid decrease of seismic energy associated with the more common type of EARTHQUAKE caused by slippage along a fault

holotype   the physical example or illustration that is used in the first formal description of a biological name

hotspot   an area of high volcanic activity

hydrothermal vent   areas on the seafloor where heated water emerges. Typically when such vents form near spreading ridges they can include black smoker and/or white smoker chimneys formed when molten rock heats seawater as it circulates through the crust. Other vents are formed as olivine minerals in the crust react with seawater to form serpentine and the chemical reaction of serpentization produces the heat needed to warm the water

ice age   a period during which the Earth is substantially cooler than usual and glaciers cover a significant portion of the land surfaces

igneous   relating to, resulting from, or suggestive of the intrusion or extrusion of MAGMA or volcanic activity; formed by solidification of magma

ionosphere   the layer of Earth's atmosphere where ionization of atmospheric gases form charged particles that affect the propagation of radio waves around the planet

isoseismal   having equal seismicity. An isoseismal map is composed of isoseismal lines that depict areas of equal EARTHQUAKE intensities

isostasy   a crustal equilibrium model that holds differences in elevations are compensated with differences in density and subcrustal extension (roots under mountains). Processes such as erosion or deposition change the balance and result in vertical movement of the crust in order to compensate for the imbalance

isotope   a version of an element with the same atomic number and nearly identical chemical behavior, but a different number of neutrons giving it a different atomic mass or mass number and different physical properties

jökulhlaup   Icelandic term for a flood through an ice dam that typically occurs after a subglacial volcanic eruption

lahars   a torrent of volcanic debris mixed with water

lava   MAGMA that has reached the surface

limestone   a type of SEDIMENTARY rock composed primarily of calcium carbonate, either from shells of marine animals or inorganic carbonates

lithosphere   the layer of rock in Earth's interior that is above the asthenosphere and includes the crust and part of the upper MANTLE

Love wave   a seismic surface wave with horizontal motion across the surface that is perpendicular to the direction the wave is traveling

magma   hot silicate liquid beneath the Earth's surface that contains dissolved gases and suspended CRYSTALS and, when cooled, forms IGNEOUS rocks

magnitude   a number that characterizes the relative size of an EARTHQUAKE. The motion a SEISMOMETER records provides a measurement of magnitude, as does the SEISMIC MOMENT of an earthquake. All magnitude scales should yield approximately the same value for any given earthquake. Different magnitude scales include:

- M_L local magnitude (commonly referred to as "Richter magnitude")
- Ms   surface-wave magnitude
- Mb   body-wave magnitude
- Mm   macroseismic magnitude
- Md   duration magnitude
- Mw   moment magnitude, calculated from the seismic moment of an earthquake or the amplitude spectra of seismic waves, a graph showing how much of each type of shaking there is from an earthquake

mantle   the part of the Earth's interior between the core and the crust

mass spectrometry   an instrumental method for identifying the chemical constitution of a substance by means of the separation of gaseous ions according to their differing mass and charge. Also called mass spectroscopy

metamorphic   a description of rocks formed from pronounced change effected by pressure, heat, or water that result in a more compact and more highly crystalline condition

natural selection   a mechanism for EVOLUTION first advocated by Darwin. Natural selection is the theory that individual organisms are susceptible to natural or environmental pressures—such as drought, disease, and predation—and that those organisms with hereditable characteristics that allow them to survive and reproduce under such situations will produce offspring with similar characteristics for survival and reproductivity or "fitness." Hence the saying commonly associated with natural selection as being the "survival of the fittest"

nuée ardente   a French term for a highly heated mass of gas-enriched ash that is erupted with explosive force and moves at hurricane speeds down a volcano's slope. See PYROCLASTIC FLOW

obliquity of the ecliptic   see AXIAL TILT

oolite   small round grains of calcium carbonate cemented together to form a rock

osteology   a branch of anatomy dealing with bones; the bony structure of an organism

pelean eruption   named after the eruption of Mount Pelée in 1902. A pelean eruption displays ground-hugging lateral PYROCLASTIC FLOWS on volcanoes that are choked with hard, crusty silica-rich MAGMAS, which tend to form rocky volcanic domes that erupt catastrophically after a period of ash emissions

petrology   a science that deals with the origin, history, occurrence, structure, chemical composition, and classification of rocks

phosphorescence   a slow release of low-temperature light after absorption of radiation that then continues even after the source of radiation is removed

photon   a small increment of ELECTROMAGNETIC RADIATION

phreatic explosion   a MAGMA-free explosion of steam and pulverized rocks that occurs when water mixes with hot volcanic material. Magma heating the water remains in place, but can drive the hot water to vaporize and explode, clearing rocky material out of the volcanic vent

pillow lava   mounds of basaltic LAVA that erupted and cooled underwater

plinian eruption   named after the Vesuvius eruption in 79 C.E., which Pliny the Younger described. A plinian eruption shoots a vertical column of turbulent TEPHRA—ash, gas, and PYROCLASTIC DEBRIS—high into the atmosphere often reaching the STRATOSPHERE and can strike with or without ash warnings prior to the cataclysmic explosion

plumb line   a string with a lead weight used for determining a vertical reference to the ground

polymorphism   having different forms. In materials science this includes crystallizing into two or more distinct structures

precession   a slow gyration of the rotational axis of a spinning body that describes the shape of a cone

proton   an elementary particle that is identical with the nucleus of the hydrogen atom

pumice   gas-riddled volcanic glass formed from foamy, gassy magma that cools quickly during a volcanic eruption. Pumice stones are full of cavities, making them surprisingly light in weight and allowing them to float

P wave   the primary, and compression, seismic body wave that strikes during an EARTHQUAKE. The P wave strikes first because of high speed of travel

pyroclastic debris   volcanic fragments of rocks, CRYSTALS, ash, pumice, and glass shards

pyroclastic flow   ground-hugging, lateral flows of turbulent hot gases and unsorted PYROCLASTIC DEBRIS that can move at hurricane speeds. The term also can refer to the deposits that are formed from such flows

quartz   a mineral consisting of silicon dioxide that forms hexagonal crystals or crystalline masses that when placed in an electric field oscillate at a constant frequency. Used to control watches and other devices that require precise regulation

radioactivity   the process of atomic nuclear disintegration that some elements and ISOTOPES undergo resulting in emission of energetic particles and the conversion to a DAUGHTER ELEMENT

radiocarbon   radioactive carbon, namely carbon 14, which is the radioactive ISOTOPE of carbon with a mass number of 14. Radiocarbon is used especially in tracer studies and in dating organic materials

radioisotope   a radioactive ISOTOPE

radium   used chiefly in luminous materials and in the treatment of cancer, radium is an intensely radioactive, white metallic element that occurs in minute quantities in minerals and emits alpha particles and gamma rays; its daughter element is the radioactive gas radon

Rayleigh wave   a seismic surface wave that strikes during an EARTHQUAKE, causing the ground to shake in an elliptical motion, that feels like being on a boat at sea

Richter scale   a logarithmic scale that measures the amount of energy released during an EARTHQUAKE on the basis of the amplitude of the highest peak recorded on a SEISMOGRAM. Each unit increase in the Richter scale represents a 10-fold increase in the amplitude recorded on the seismogram and a 30-fold increase in energy released by the earthquake. Theoretically the Richter scale has no upper limit, but the YIELD POINT of the Earth's rocks imposes an effective limit between 9.0 and 9.5

rime   frozen precipitation CRYSTALS that grow into the wind

Rossby waves large-scale, meandering motions that arise as a result of the Coriolis effect

satellite a celestial body or object that orbits a planetary body. The Moon is a satellite of Earth, as was SPUTNIK

sediment the material that water, wind, or glaciers deposit

sedimentary relating to or containing SEDIMENT. Sedimentary rock is formed from hardening of sediments into stone, such as sandstone or LIMESTONE

seiche an oscillation of the water in a lake or other landlocked body of water, that like water sloshing in a bathtub, causes the surface water to rise at one end of the lake as it drops at the other end—usually wind driven

seismic moment a measure of the size of an EARTHQUAKE based on the area of fault rupture, the average amount of slip, and the force that was required to overcome the friction sticking the rocks together that were offset by faulting

seismogram the paper or computer record of the Earth's movements produced by a SEISMOMETER

seismometer an apparatus to measure and record vibrations within the earth and of the ground. Also called a seismograph

serpentinization the process by which the mineral olivine converts to the mineral serpentine in the presence of seawater. The reaction is exothermic and produces heat

shield formations old crustal material forming the interior of continents

shield volcano a volcano formed from basaltic eruptions that produce slopes that taper gradually (like the shape of a shield resting on the ground) rather than obliquely rising to a high peak. The Hawaiian Islands are shield volcanoes

shocked quartz deformations in the crystalline structure of quartz. First discovered after underground nuclear bomb testing, shocked quartz form naturally during impact events

sial another term for continental crust; low-density rocks rich in silica and aluminum

sima high-density rocks, such as basalt, rich in silicates and magnesium

special relativity mass (m) and energy (E) are related to the speed of light (c) through the equation $E=mc^2$

spectrometer an instrument used to measure the properties of light over a specific portion of the electromagnetic spectrum

spicules the skeletal structure found in most sponges

Sputnik Russian term for SATELLITE; also the first satellite launched in space

stratosphere the atmospheric layer above the TROPOSPHERE where temperatures are warmer at the top and cooler near the bottom of the air layer

stratovolcano   a steeply sloped volcano made from many layers of both LAVA flows and pyroclastic material. Also called a composite volcano. The MAGMA source driving the eruptions is typically rich in silica

stromatolite   cyanobacteria that grow in layers collecting calcium carbonate and trapped sediment to form mounds in shallow water; also the laminated sedimentary fossil formed from this biological process

S wave   the secondary, seismic body wave that is a shear wave moving the ground side-to-side, perpendicular to the direction the wave is moving

tephra   a collective term for fragmental volcanic materials of all types and sizes ejected into the air from a crater or volcanic vent

theropod   a carnivorous, bipedal dinosaur typically having small forelimbs, such as a tyrannosaur or velociraptor

thin section   a thinly sliced section of a rock ground smooth such that when viewed under a polarizing microscopic the minerals and CRYSTALS in the rock are identifiable based on their color, opaqueness, or translucence to light

troposphere   the atmospheric layer closest to the ground where temperatures cool with elevation

turbidity currents   a gravity-driven, fast moving, broiling torrent of water filled with SEDIMENTS that falls down a slope through air, water, or another fluid, because of its high density

uranium   a heavy, silvery radioactive metallic element that exists naturally in some in soil, rocks and water and is mined from the mineral uraninite. The most common uranium ISOTOPE on Earth is uranium-238, and less common is uranium-235.

varves   an annual layer of SEDIMENT

xenolith   an older rock fragment trapped inside a newer rock; typically inclusions of older rocks can get caught in magmatic eruptions and are embedded in the LAVA rocks when the MAGMA cools

X-ray   any of the ELECTROMAGNETIC RADIATIONS of the same nature as visible radiation but having an extremely short wavelength of less than 100 angstroms. X-rays are produced by bombarding a metallic target with fast electrons in a vacuum or by transition of atoms to lower energy states. X-rays have the following properties: they ionize gas, penetrate various solids, produce secondary radiations, act in a similar way as light does to photographic films and plates, and cause fluorescent screens to emit light

X-ray diffraction   the particular scattering pattern produced when X-RAYS are passed through a mineral sample

yield point   the maximum stress a rock can withstand before becoming permanently deformed

# Further Resources

Berry, William B. N. *Growth of the Prehistoric Timescale Based on Organic Evolution.* San Francisco: Freeman, 1968. This book examines how geologists organized geologic time prior to radiocarbon dating. Blackwell Science Inc. published a revised edition in 1987.

Bolt, Bruce. *Earthquakes: A Primer.* San Francisco: W. H. Freeman & Co., 1978. This book provides an introduction to the history of seismology.

Bowen, Mark. *Thin Ice. Unlocking the Secrets of Climate in the World's Highest Mountains.* New York: Henry Holt, 2005. This book examines climate studies of the upper atmosphere.

Bowie, William. *Isostasy.* New York: Dutton, 1927. In this review on the theory of isostasy, Bowie examines different models of the theory that the Earth's crust maintains equilibrium.

Broecker, Wallace S. "Future Global Warming Scenarios." *Science* 304 (2004): 388. In this letter to the editor, Broecker clarifies the miscommunication about the science on global warming coming from the Pentagon.

———. "Was the Younger Dryas Triggered by a Flood?" *Science* 312 (2006): 1,146–1,147. Broecker proposes that the draining of a huge lake caused a freshwater spike in the North Atlantic about 12,900 years ago that may have triggered a cold period in Earth's climate.

———. "CO_2 Arithmetic." *Science* 315, no. 5817 (March 9, 2007): 1,371. Broecker argues that strict emission limits are necessary to stem the rise of atmospheric carbon dioxide.

Bruce, Victoria. *No Apparent Danger: The True Story of Volcanic Disaster at Galeras and Nevado Del Ruiz.* New York: HarperCollins, 2001. Bruce reports on the Colombian volcano disasters of 1985 and 1993.

Change, Kenneth. "Magnetic Field Is Fading, but No Dire Effects Are Foreseen." *New York Times* (December 12, 2003). This news report discusses the consequences of a weakening magnetic field. Available online. URL: http://www.nytimes.com/2003/12/12/science/12MAGN.html?ex=1386565200&en=ef28481df905b6c5&ei=5007&partner=USERLAND. Accessed February 28, 2007.

Chiang, John C. H., and Athanasios Koutavas. "Tropical Flip-Flop Connections." *Nature* 432 (2004): 684–685. This report examines how devastating droughts in Brazil are tied to the ocean-atmosphere system in the Atlantic.

Clement, Brad. "Dependence on the duration of geomagnetic polarity reversals on site latitude." *Nature* 428 (April 2004): 637–640. A study on paleomagnetic transitions zones. Commentary on the report from Steven Earle of Malaspina University-College. Available online. URL: http://www.mala.bc.ca/~earles/turnaround-time-apr04.htm. Accessed February 28, 2007.

Cowen, Richard. Cowen is a geologist at the University of California at Davis who has collected on his Web site a plethora of Earthly news updates since 1999. Available online. URL: http://www.geology.ucdavis. edu/~cowen/ Accessed February 28, 2007.

Crutzen, Paul J., and Veerabhadran Ramanathan. "The Ascent of Atmospheric Sciences." *Science* 290, no. 5490 (2000): 299–304. This report provides a historical review of the atmospheric sciences.

Cyranoski, David. "Indonesian Eruption: Muddy Waters." *Nature* 445 (22 February 2007): 812–815. A man-made mud volcano destroys Indonesian village.

dal Sasso, Cristiano, S. Maganuco, E. Buffetaut, and M. A. Mendez. "New Information On The Skull Of The Enigmatic Theropod *Spinosaurus*, With Remarks On Its Sizes And Affinities." *Journal of Vertebrate Paleontology* 25 no. 4 (2006): 888–896. This scientific report officially dethroned *T. rex* as the largest carnivorous dinosaur.

De Angelis, Hernán, and Pedro Skvarca. "Glacier Surge after Ice Shelf Collapse." *Science* 299 (2003): 1,560–1,562. Concerned over the debate on the potential collapse of the West Antarctic Ice Sheet, these scientists examined the glaciers that fed the Larsen Ice Shelf prior to its collapse in 1995.

Dewey, James, and Perry Byerly. "The Early History of Seismometry (to 1900)." *Bulletin of the Seismological Society of America* 59, no. 1, (1969): 183–227. This report examines the development of seismometers and earthquake science prior to the 20th century. Available online. URL: http://wwwneic.cr.usgs.gov/neis/seismology/history_seis.html. Accessed April 24, 2006.

Doel, Ron. "Why Value History?" *Eos* 83, no. 47 (2002): 544–545. Doel presents an essay on the importance of understanding the theories scientists have embraced and rejected.

Earle, Steve. Geologist Steve Earle of Malaspina University-College lists new developments in Earth Science on his Web site. Available online. URL: http://www.mala.bc.ca/~earles/news.htm. Accessed February 28, 2007.

Earthguide. An interactive online educational resource about the Earth, oceans, and the environment, this Web site is part of the Geosciences

Research Division at Scripps Institution of Oceanography. Available online. URL: http://earthguide.ucsd.edu/ Accessed February 28, 2007.

———. "Global Change and Global Warming." This Web site provides an introduction to the problems of climate change and a review of the importance of the Keeling curve. Available online. URL: http://earthguide.ucsd.edu/globalchange/ Accessed February 28, 2007.

Earth Observatory. Nearly 1,000 people die in Philippine mudslide. Satellite imagery reveals the extent of the damage. Available online. URL: http://earthobservatory.nasa.gov/Newsroom/NewImages/images.php3?img_id=17203. Accessed February 28, 2007.

Earth References. Antarctica Expedition Studying the Geological History of Earth's Magnetic Field. Available online. URL: http://earthref.org/ERESE/projects/GOLF182/index.html. Accessed February 28, 2007.

Essene, E. J., and D. C. Fisher. "Lightning Strike Fusion: Extreme Reduction and Metal-Silicate Liquid Immiscibility." *Science* New Series, 234, no. 4773 (October 10, 1986): 189–193. A study on a recent fulgurite formation in southeast Michigan.

Glatzmaier, Gary A., and Paul H. Roberts. "A three-dimensional self-consistent computer simulation of a geomagnetic field reversal." *Nature* 377 (1995): 203–209. This report shows a 3-D model of the Earth's magnetic field as it undergoes a reversal.

———, and Paul Roberts. "3D Numerical Simulation of the Geodynamo and the Earth's Magnetic Field." This Web site provides comments and images from the model. Available online. URL: http://www.psc.edu/research/graphics/gallery/geodynamo.html. Accessed February 28, 2007.

Gohau, Gabriel. *A History of Geology.* Revised and translated from the French by Albert V. Carozzi and Marguerite Carozzi. New Brunswick: Rutgers University Press, 1990. This book reviews the history of geology.

Good, Gregory A., ed. *Sciences of the Earth: An Encyclopedia of Events, People, and Phenomena.* 2 vols. New York and London: Garland Publishing, Inc., 1998. This two-volume book examines the Earth sciences throughout history.

Gould, Stephen Jay. *The Structure of Evolutionary Theory.* Cambridge, Mass.: Harvard University Press, 2002. This book examines the paradigm leaps and minor mutations that lead to evolution.

Haag, Amanda. "Church Joins Crusade over Climate Change." *Nature* 440 (March 9, 2006): 136–137. Religious leaders are calling for governmental caps on carbon emissions.

Hansen, James E. "A Slippery Slope: How Much Global Warming Constitutes 'Dangerous Anthropogenic Interference'?" *Climactic Change* 68 (2005): 269–279. Hansen advises against a wait-and-see policy on global warming.

Hellman, Hal. *Great Feuds in Science.* New York: John Wiley & Sons, Inc., 1998. This book examines the debates that caused paradigm shifts in scientific thinking.

Hirano, Naoto, et al. "Volcanism in Response to Plate Flexure." *Science* 313, no. 5792 (September 8, 2006): 1,426–1,428. Originally published in *Science* Express on 27 July 2006, the report introduces the term *petit spots* to explain tiny volcanoes in the Pacific forming on the plate as it subducts into the Kuril and Japan trenches.

Hoffman, Paul. Snowball Earth publications. This Web site provides a list of Hoffman's publications on the Snowball Earth hypothesis. Available online. as URL: http://www-eps.harvard.edu/people/faculty/hoffman/recent_pub.php. Accessed February 28, 2007.

———. Snowball Earth publications. Additional information, including upcoming conferences and teaching slides, Available online. URL: http://www.snowballearth.org/ Accessed February 28, 2007.

———. A diagram on Earth's dipolar magnetic field. Available as a PDF online. URL: http://www-eps.harvard.edu/people/faculty/hoffman/Snowball-fig6.pdf. Accessed February 28, 2007.

Holmlund, Per, et al. "Assessing the Palaeoclimate Potential of Cave Glaciers: The Example of the ScĂRişoara Ice Cave (Romania)." *Geografiska Annaler, Series A: Physical Geography* 87 no.1 (March 2005): 193–201. Ice caves can also provide Paleoclimate records.

Holtz, Thomas R. Jr. "Spinosaurs as Crocodile Mimics." *Science* 282, no. 5392 (November 13, 1998): 1,276–1,277. Theropod dinosaurs—the bipedal, carnivorous ancestors of birds—were "one of the most successful radiations of terrestrial predators in Earth history."

Hough, Susan, and Lucy Jones. "Earthquakes don't kill people, buildings do." *San Francisco Chronicle* (Wednesday, December 4, 2002): An example of scientists speaking out from the ivory tower to advocate societal change. Available online. URL: http://sfgate.com/cgi-bin/article.cgi?f=/c/a/2002/12/04/ED79702.DTL. Accessed February 28, 2007.

Imbrie, John, and Katherine Palmer Imbrie. *Ice Ages: Solving the Mystery.* Cambridge, Massachusetts: Enslow Publishers, 1979. This book examines how scientists unlocked the secrets of glacial epochs.

Jardine, N., Secord, J. A., and Spary, E. C. (editors). *Cultures of Natural History.* Cambridge; New York: Cambridge University Press, 1996. This book examines the importance of natural history to civilizations.

Johnson, Kathleen R., Chaoyong Hu, Nick S. Belshaw, and Gideon M. Henderson. "Seasonal trace-element and stable-isotope variations in a Chinese speleothem: The potential for high-resolution paleomonsoon reconstruction." A study on the annual variation of trace gases in speleothems from caves in China. Available as a PDF online URL: http://www.earth.ox.ac.uk/~gideonh/pdffiles/Johnson%20et%20al.%202006.pdf. Accessed February 28, 2007.

Kerr, Richard. "Stealth Tsunami Surprises Indonesian Coastal Residents." *Science* 313, no. 5788 (11 August 2006): 742–743. The July 17, 2006, tsunami came without warning and little notice.

———. "Fathers and Children Profile: Inheriting the Family Science." *Science* 301, no. 5638, (5 September 2003): 1,312–1,316. Continuing the

Keeling curve with Dave Keeling's son Ralph and other adult children who are now standing on their father's impressive scientific shoulders.

Khalturin, Vitaly I., Tatyana G. Rautian, Paul G. Richards, and William S. Leith. "A Review of Nuclear Testing by the Soviet Union at Novaya Zemlya, 1955–1990." *Science and Global Security* 13 (2005): 1–42. A report on the world's largest detonated nuclear bomb and other Russian nuclear tests.

Kintisch, Eli. "Evangelicals, Scientists Reach Common Ground on Climate Change." *Science* 311 (February 24, 2006): 1,082–1,083. Religious leaders are calling for governmental caps on carbon emissions.

Kious, W. Jacquelyne, and Robert I. Tilling. "This Dynamic Earth: The Story of Plate Tectonics." This Web site provides an online edition to the book. Available online. URL: http://pubs.usgs.gov/gip/dynamic/dynamic.html. Accessed February 28, 2007.

Kozák, Jan. "100-Year Anniversary of the First International Seismological Conference." Studia Geophysica et Geodaetica 45, no. 2 (October 28, 2004): 200–209. This report provides a picture and list of participants at the first International Seismological Conference, which occurred in 1901.

Krajick, Kevin. "Ice Man: Lonnie Thompson Scales the Peaks for Science." *Science* 298 (2002): 518–522. Krajick follows the adventures of world-renowned glaciologist Lonnie Thompson as he races to collect climate records from retreating glaciers around the world.

Lawrence, David M., and Andrew G. Slater, "A Projection of Severe near-Surface Permafrost Degradation During the 21st Century." *Geophysical Research Letters* 32 (2005): L22401. Global warming thaws permafrost in the northern territories.

Lawrence, Jesse, and Michael Wysession. "Seismic Evidence for Subduction-Transported Water in the Lower Mantle." The authors find moisture-containing rocks in the lower mantle. Available as a pdf online. URL: http://titan.ucsd.edu/PUBS/Lawrence_and_Wysession_2006_AGU_MONOGRAPH.pdf. Accessed February 28, 2007.

Le Grand, H. E. *Drifting Continents and Shifting Theories.* Cambridge: Cambridge University Press, 1988. Written by a scientist who helped to transform the scientific understanding of the subject, this book examines the plate tectonic revolution.

Lehmann, Inge. "Seismology in the Days of Old." *Eos* 68, no. 3 (January 20, 1987): 33–35. Lehmann looks back at the contributions of her discovery. Available online. URL: http://www.geus.dk/departments/geophysics/seismology/seismo_lehmann_art-dk.htm. Accessed February 28, 2007.

Le Pichon, Xavier. "Sea-floor spreading and continental drift." *Journal of Geophysical Research* 73, no. 12 (1968): 3,661–3,697. With this report analyzing lithospheric plates of the world, Le Pichon mapped the boundaries of plate tectonic theory for the scientific community.

Lindsay, Ron W., and J. Zhang. "The Thinning of Arctic Sea Ice, 1988–2003: Have We Passed a Tipping Point?" *Journal of Climate* 18 (2005):

4,879–4,894. Once covered in ice, the Arctic Ocean has seen a reduction in sea ice that may not recover.

Lovett, Richard A. "Huge Underground 'Ocean' Found Beneath Asia." For National Geographic News, February 27, 2007. A news report on the collection of waterlogged rocks in the lower mantle. Available online. URL: http://news.nationalgeographic.com/news/2007/02/070227-ocean-asia.html. Accessed February 28, 2007.

———. "The Wave From Nowhere." *New Scientist* no. 2592 (February 24, 2007). This article discusses the events of November 18, 1929, when an offshore earthquake generated a tsunami that struck Newfoundland's Burin peninsula.

Lyell, Charles. *Principles of Geology, being an attempt to explain the former changes of the earth's surface, by reference to causes now in operation.* London: John Murray, 1830–33. This book is a classic in geology on the principles of uniformitarianism. Available online. URL: http://www.esp.org/books/lyell/principles/facsimile/title3.html. Accessed April 24, 2006.

Marland, G., T. A. Boden, and R. J. Andres. "Global, Regional, and National CO_2 Emissions." In *Trends: A Compendium of Data on Global Change.* Oak Ridge, Tennessee: Carbon Dioxide Information Analysis Center, Oak Ridge National Laboratory, U.S. Department of Energy, 2006. This government Web site examines the trends in datasets on carbon dioxide. Available online. URL: http://cdiac.ornl.gov/trends/emis/em_cont.htm. Accessed February 28, 2007.

Mathez, Edmond A. (editor). *Earth: Inside and Out.* New York: The New Press, 2001. An American Museum of Natural History book that examines the Earth from a 21st century perspective.

Metzger, Ellen. "A Model of Seafloor Spreading Teacher's Guide." A how-to on building a model of seafloor spreading. Available online. URL: http://www.ucmp.berkeley.edu/fosrec/Metzger3.html. Accessed February 28, 2007.

NASA. "Exploration of Earth's Atmosphere." This Web site explains the differences in the layers of Earth's atmosphere. Available online. URL: http://liftoff.msfc.nasa.gov/academy/space/atmosphere.html. Accessed February 28, 2007.

———. This Web site examines the state of the ozone hole as of May 2006. Available online URL: http://science.nasa.gov/headlines/y2006/26may_ozone.htm?list832167. Accessed February 28, 2007.

Natural Resources Canada. History of Geomagnetism: Early Concept of the North Magnetic Pole. This Web site examines the science history of magnetism. Available online. URL: http://gsc.nrcan.gc.ca/geomag/nmp/early_nmp_e.php. Accessed February 28, 2007.

Navarro-González, Rafael, Shannon A. Mahan, Ashok K. Singhvi, Rafael Navarro-Aceves, Jean-Louis Rajot, Christopher P. McKay, Patrice Coll, and François Raulin. "Paleoecology reconstruction from trapped gases in a fulgurite from the late Pleistocene of the Libyan Desert." *Geology*

35 (February 2007): 171–174. Abstract available online. URL: http://geology.geoscienceworld.org/cgi/content/abstract/35/2/171. Accessed February 28, 2007.

Oldroyd, David R. *Thinking about the Earth: A History of Ideas in Geology.* Cambridge, Massachusetts: Harvard University Press, 1996. This book studies the history and philosophy of the Earth sciences.

Oreskes, Naomi. *The Rejection of Continental Drift.* Oxford: Oxford University Press, 1999. Oreskes examines the history of Wegener's continental drift hypothesis and the varying reactions from Earth scientists at the time.

Patanè, Domenico, G. Barberi, O. Cocina, P. De Gori, and C. Chiarabba. "Time-Resolved Seismic Tomography Detects Magma Intrusions at Mount Etna." *Science* 313 (August 11, 2006): 821–823. A CT scan of Mount Etna done with seismic profiles. PBS. "Then and Now." This PBS Web site compares what we know now in earth science to what we knew 100 years ago. Available online. URL: http://www.pbs.org/wgbh/aso/thenandnow/earth.html/ Accessed April 24, 2006.

Perkins, Sid. "Stroke of Good Fortune: A wealth of data from petrified lightning." *Science News* 171, no. 7 (February 17, 2007): 101. A news report on Rafael Navarro-González's fulgurite research. Available online. URL: http://www.sciencenews.org/articles/20070217/fob5.asp. Accessed February 28, 2007.

Queen's University Belfast. "What is Radiocarbon Dating?" A Web site on the basics of radiocarbon dating. Available online. URL: http://www.qub.ac.uk/c14/whatc14.htm. Accessed February 28, 2007.

Rabbitt, Mary C. *Minerals, Lands, and Geology for the Common Defense and General Welfare.* 3 vols. Washington D.C.: Government Printing Office, 1979–86. Land use polices in the 1980s.

Richards, Paul. A lecture about the research revealing Earth's faster inner core. Available online. URL: http://www.ldeo.columbia.edu/~richards/Jefflec.html. Accessed February 28, 2007.

Schneider, Michael. "Understanding the Earth: When North Goes South." In *Projects in Scientific Computing.* Pittsburgh Supercomputing Center, 1996. This Web site provides a description of Glatzmaier and Roberts's 3-D model of the geomagnetic field. Available online. URL: http://www.psc.edu/science/Glatzmaier/glatzmaier.html. Accessed February 28, 2007.

Sigurdsson, Haraldur. *Melting the Earth: The History of Ideas on Volcanic Eruptions.* New York: Oxford University Press, 1999. This book examines the history of volcanology. Smithsonian Global Volcanism Program. For ongoing and past volcanic eruptions around the world, this Web site provides extensive information. Available online. URL: http://www.volcano.si.edu. Accessed February 28, 2007.

———. This Web site provides reports from Herman Patia and Steve Saunders from Rabaul Volcano Observatory in October 2006. Available online. URL: http://www.volcano.si.edu/world/volcano.cfm?vnum=0502-14=&volpage=weekly&VErupt=Y&VSources=Y&VRep=Y&VWeekly=Y #mar2004. Accessed February 28, 2007.

Soden, Brian J., Richard T. Wetherald, Georgiy L. Stenchikov, and Alan Robock. "Global Cooling after Eruption of Mount Pinatubo: A Test of Climate Feedback by Water Vapor." *Science* 296 (2002): 727–730. After the eruption of Pinatubo, the global atmosphere cooled and dried. Modeling of this response shows the importance of water vapor as a feedback mechanism.

Spötl, C., and A. Mangini. "Speleothems and paleoglaciers." *Earth and Planetary Science Letters* 254 (2007): 323–331. The presence of ice does not necessarily prevent the formation of stalactites, stalagmites, and flowstones. Available online. URL: http://www.uibk.ac.at/geologie/staff/pu_spoetl_en.html. Accessed February 28, 2007.

Thompson, Dick. *Volcano Cowboys*. New York: St. Martin's Press, 2000. Thompson reports on multiple eruptions in the 1980s and 1990s and their impact on the history of the formation of USGS International Volcano Disaster Assistance Program.

Underwood, James R., and Guth, Peter L. (editors). *Military Geology in War and Peace*. Boulder, Colorado: Geological Society of America, 1998. The writers show the strategic side of geology.

United Nations Environment Programme. "Vital Climate Graphics." This Web site provides a cartoon on the carbon cycle. Available online. URL: http://www.grida.no/climate/vital/13.htm. Accessed February 28, 2007.

U.S. Climate Change Science Program. "Strategic Plan for the Climate Change Science Program." This Web site on key contributions to the IPCC includes a cartoon of long-range transport of aerosols and gases. Available online. URL: http://www.climatescience.gov/Library/stratplan2003/final/graphics/images/SciStratFig3-1.jpg. Accessed February 28, 2007.

United States Congress. Senate (107:1) Committee on Governmental Affairs, *The Climate Change Strategy and Technology Innovation Act of 2001: Hearings*. Washington, D.C.: U.S. Government Printing Office, 2001. This committee report discussed the political response to climate change in the early 21st century. Available online. URL: http://www.access.gpo.gov/congress. Accessed February 28, 2007.

Walker, Gabrielle. *Snowball Earth*. New York: Three Rivers Press, 2003. Walker reports on the personalities and the science that brought about the idea of a Snowball Earth.

Webb, George Ernest. *Science in the American Southwest: A Topical History*. Tucson: University of Arizona Press, 2002. From astronomy to dendrochronology, this book examines the unique science found in the American southwest.

———. *Tree rings and telescopes: the scientific career of A. E. Douglass*. Tucson, Arizona: University of Arizona Press, 1983. When astronomer Andrew

Douglass looked to trees to help with his astronomical research he established a new method for examining climate change.

Woods Hole Oceanographic Institution. "Dive and Discover." This "Deeper Discovery," reviews the basic of hydrothermal vent structures. Available online. URL: http://www.divediscover.whoi.edu/vents/vent-infomod.html#. Accessed February 28, 2007.

Yochelson, Ellis L. *Charles Doolittle Walcott, Paleontologist.* Kent, Ohio: The Kent State University Press, 1998. This book provides a biography on the man who discovered the Burgess Shale in Canada.

Zhang, Jian, Xiaodong Song, Yingchun Li, Paul G. Richards, Xinlei Sun, and Felix Waldhauser. "Inner Core Differential Motion Confirmed by Earthquake Waveform Doublets." *Science* 309, no. 5739 (August 26, 2005): 1,357–1,360. "Differences in seismic waves generated by nearly identical earthquakes occurring years apart confirm that Earth's inner core is rotating more rapidly than the rest of the planet."

Zwally, H. Jay, Waleed Abdalati, Tom Herring, Kristine Larson, Jack Saba, and Konrad Steffen. "Surface Melt-Induced Acceleration of Greenland Ice-Sheet Flow." *Science* 297 (2002): 218–222. During the summer, the ice on the surface of Greenland's ice sheet melts and drains to the bedrock where it lubricates the bottom of the glacier and increases its flow rate.

Index